Daniel
Baratz

A Guide to the Complex
Contemporary Halakhic Debates

מגיד
MAGGID

Shlomo M. Brody

A GUIDE TO THE COMPLEX

CONTEMPORARY HALAKHIC DEBATES

Maggid Books

A Guide to the Complex
Contemporary Halakhic Debates

First Edition, 2014

Maggid Books
An imprint of Koren Publishers Jerusalem Ltd.

POB 8531, New Milford, CT 06776-8531, USA
& POB 4044, Jerusalem 91040, Israel
www.korenpub.com

The publication of this book was made possible through
the generous support of *Torah Education in Israel.*

ISBN 978 1 59264 351 6, *hardcover*

A CIP catalogue record for this title is
available from the British Library

Printed and bound in the United States

To Rocky, with love and affection

Contents

SECTION VI:
ISRAEL

SECTION VII: KASHRUT

SECTION VIII: JEWISH IDENTITY AND MARRIAGE

Preface

This book is the culmination of several years of study and writing on topics related to contemporary controversies in Jewish law. In many ways, it stems from a sense of frustration I had during my years as a student in college and yeshiva over the discourse within the Orthodox community. When it came to controversies in Jewish law, many people had strong opinions that were not fully grounded in the sources and particulars of halakhic discourse. As such, these opinions – though sometimes resonant within the halakhic literature – were impassioned but inarticulate. There was much heat but little light.

To my mind, this state of dialogue harms the community of those committed to Jewish law. First, it prevents people from appreciating the nuances of the debate. Without the requisite knowledge, it's impossible to understand the complexity of the subject. Second, it's very difficult to understand someone's perspective if one does not speak the same language. Halakha has been the traditional language of the Jewish world for many centuries, and the ability to converse about halakhic matters facilitates greater understanding while forcing one to sharpen his own perspective. Third, lack of knowledge leads to the (frequently unnecessary) delegitimization of others. Many times people speak passionately and dogmatically not only because they believe their opinion is correct, but because they don't even realize there's another legitimate option out there. Yet a perusal of any quality halakhic journal will show that on most contemporary controversies, there is a range of opinions, all grounded in Jewish sources and halakhic reasoning. This is especially true if one includes (as one should) scholars from the full range of the halakhic community, without excluding anyone for his ideological stances on, say, Zionism or secular studies. Admittedly, not all opinions expressed in popular dialogue are well-grounded in traditional sources. Yet one cannot coherently exclude a position if there is no shared language for the conversation. This, I believe, is the fourth problem with contemporary discourse. Many do not feel bound to shape their opinions around Jewish sources, whether theological, legal, or historical. Yet if you want people to recognize the importance of rooting their beliefs, you need to create access to those sources.

Thus I began an ongoing project to teach these topics in depth, with the goal of increasing the number of informed participants in halakhic dialogue. This book includes essays on more than 130 issues, covering most of today's controversies. The essays cite scholars across the ideological spectrum, with the conviction that true discourse is created only when one respects the scholarship of the entire community. I hope readers will use this work not only to become informed about specific topics, but also to get a general sense of contemporary halakhic discourse.

The breakthrough for this project was the offer to become the *Ask the Rabbi* columnist for *The Jerusalem Post*, the most widely read English-language newspaper and website in the Jewish world. On the one hand, this was an amazing opportunity to present contemporary issues to a broad audience. On the other hand, the limitations of an eight-hundred-word column presented a daunting challenge to articulating halakhic debates in a manner that would reflect the nuances – legal, historical, and sociological – of each. I don't trust the way halakha is sometimes presented in popular media, including five-word SMS responses or populistic declarations. That said, it remains critical for the religious community to utilize media, both new and old, to explicate matters of contemporary debate.

I have been buoyed by the responses I have received from a wide spectrum of readers, ranging from unaffiliated Jews to erudite rabbis. I hope these essays succeed in giving a good sense of the major texts, considerations, and players involved in these legal dilemmas. For the publication of this book, I have re-edited every essay, including significant elaborations on many topics, in order to give a more complete or accurate picture. Yet I've kept the basic format of my writing to preserve the accessibility of the essay. Many changes were made in response to reader feedback, and I encourage people to continue sending their comments or questions via my Facebook page, www.facebook.com/RabbiShlomo-Brody, where I also post new writings.

Nonetheless, nothing replaces in-depth study of primary sources. For that reason, I have included, as much as possible, citations of the original sources, so readers may pursue further study of a given topic. Many of these topics have also been covered at greater length in book series like Rabbi J. David Bleich's *Contemporary Halakhic Problems* (six volumes), Rabbi Chaim Jachter's *Gray Matter* (four volumes), and Rabbi Dr. Avraham Steinberg's *Encyclopedia of Jewish Medical Ethics* (three volumes), or journals such as *Tradition*, *Tchumin*, and *The Journal of Halakha and Contemporary Society*. I encourage readers to avail themselves of these resources.

When confronting particular questions, readers should consult a rabbinic scholar before taking a course of action. To take a couple of extreme examples, I would not, based on reading these essays, make a decision regarding aborting a Tay-Sachs fetus or determine how a community should address the problem of burying non-Jewish spouses within Jewish cemeteries. Ultimately, nothing can replace the expertise and wisdom culled from years of in-depth study and experience in issuing rulings of Jewish law. I do believe, however, that the more knowledgeable a person is on a given subject, the better his chances of asking appropriate questions and receiving suitable answers. In general, a well-informed laity can create a healthy conversation with legal decisors, advancing legal consensus in many positive ways.

Some readers of my columns have expressed disappointment that I do not give my personal opinion on a given topic. Sometimes I actually do, either explicitly or implicitly, particularly on issues close to my heart. Yet my primary goal is to facilitate understanding and dialogue, and I do not want readers to believe my own inclination has biased the presentation. I hope that in all the essays I have succeeded in being informative and impartial.

Each essay stands alone, yet many clearly intersect, directly or indirectly. To help readers connect the dots, I have organized the essays around several themes and, when possible, referred to other relevant pieces. Classifying each topic, however, is clearly not an exact science. For example, essays related to Shabbat observance can be found in the sections on "Shabbat and Holidays," "Technology," and "Medical Ethics." Similarly, the discussion of civil marriage in Israel or the recitation of Hallel on Israel Independence Day could have been included in the "Israel" section. I therefore recommend perusing the entire table of contents to find articles of interest.

Many thanks to the editor of the *Jerusalem Post Magazine*, Israel Kasnett, and his predecessor, Amanda Borschel-Dan, for giving me the opportunity to write the *Ask the Rabbi* column. Additional thanks to the paper's editor, Steve Linde, as well as his predecessor, David Horovitz. I also thank my old friend Miriam Abramowitz Shaviv, former literary editor at the *Post*, for recommending me for the column.

In the past few years, I have received great intellectual stimulation from various projects sponsored by the Tikvah Fund, especially the Tikvah Overseas Seminars for Yeshiva and Midrasha Students, which I direct. I thank Roger Hertog and Eric Cohen, the Tikvah Fund's chairman and executive director, respectively, for their continued leadership and support. Special thanks go to Rabbi Mark Gottlieb for his constant mentorship and guidance. Many thanks as well to Rabbi Nathan Laufer and Neal Kozodoy for their friendship and encouragement of my endeavors.

I owe a tremendous debt of gratitude to the faculty and students at Yeshivat Hakotel, led by Rabbi Baruch Vider, where I have taught for the last decade. Many of these essays originated as lectures in the yeshiva, where, along with classes in Talmud and Jewish philosophy, I taught a weekly, source-based *shiur* (class) on contemporary halakhic dilemmas (better known in the yeshiva as the "Spicy Topics *Shiur*"). I thank my thoughtful and dedicated students for asking probing questions and challenging me to present each dilemma in a coherent, exhaustive, and nuanced manner. Many thanks to my friend and teacher, Rabbi Reuven Taragin, for giving me my first opportunity to teach Torah at an advanced level and deliver *shiurim* on these topics. I am also thankful to the many synagogues and university groups that have invited me to serve as a scholar-in-residence and present these issues to lay audiences.

I would also like to acknowledge my debt of gratitude for my *semikha* (rabbinic) studies to the faculty at Yeshivat Har Etzion and especially to the senior *rosh yeshiva, mori verabbi* Rabbi Aharon Lichtenstein.

Thanks to Rabbi Ira Bedzow for skillfully reviewing most of these essays for literary clarity and precision. Many students helped check citations within the essays, and I thank them for their help. They include Adam Goldstein, Zack Fagan, Dani Forman, Adin Kanefsky, Barak Klammer, Avi Geller, Sammy Schwartz, Tamir Sugarman, Rafi Miller, Jake Wilner, Joseph Tuchman, and especially Mordy Dubin, whose help was extraordinary. Special thanks to Rabbi Michael Broyde for his support of my writing and willingness to discuss complexities related to the topics covered in this book.

Many thanks to the wonderful people at Maggid Books, including Matthew Miller, Gila Fine, and Rabbi Reuven Ziegler, for recognizing the value of this book and bringing it to fruition, and to the talented editors Tomi Mager and Tali Simon. Special thanks to Tani Bayer for the great cover design.

Heartfelt thanks go to my immediate family, including my in-laws, Irv and Lynn Shapiro; their parents, Bill and Sylvia Shapiro and Sandor, *a"h* (may he rest in peace), and Margit Kirsche; and my siblings, Todd and Ellen Brody, Jeremy and Rocky Brody, Mikey and Tova Perl, Sammy and Debbie Shapiro, and Aaron Shapiro, for their constant love and support, as well as the feedback they have given to me on these essays over the years.

This book represents the renewal of a long line of *sefarim* (Jewish works) written by my ancestors. I am privileged to be part of that tradition, and I thank my grandparents Rabbi Lester (Eliezer) and Gussie Brody, *a"h*, for passing the torch on to me. I deeply regret that my beloved grandfather Samuel (Shea) Grosser, *a"h*, did not live to see the publication of this book. His unflinching love remains with me every day, as does the backing of my grandmother Fredda Grosser, who undoubtedly remains the biggest fan of my writing.

My parents, Baruch and Dena Brody, were my first teachers, and constantly encouraged me to examine questions with sophistication and nuance. I cannot thank them enough for instilling in me an appreciation for intellectual study of both Jewish and secular wisdom as well as the importance of applying that knowledge to the real world.

This book is dedicated to my beloved wife, Rocky. Her support for my work – including many all-nighters writing these essays – has made this book possible. More importantly, she provides the warmth, care, and insight that makes our home so special. I hope and pray that our adorable children – Gila, Amichai, Maayan, and Amalia – will grow up to appreciate the wisdom of our tradition and use the Torah as their primary resource in developing their own views on contemporary dilemmas.

Upon entering and exiting the beit midrash (study hall), Jews recite a traditional prayer expressing their joy at the opportunity to study Torah and their concomitant fear of erring in its study (Berakhot 28b). I conclude this introduction in the spirit of those words, which encapsulate my feelings as I complete this book:

> *I give thanks to You, O Lord my God, for having set my portion among the scholars of the study hall. May it be Your will that no mishap in Jewish law transpire because of me: that I not err in any matter of halakha – permitting the forbidden, prohibiting the permissible, or mispresenting any positions of our great sages. May my colleagues rejoice in these words of Torah, and may my readers find direction and inspiration in them, that we may glorify the study of Torah and its implementation in the modern world.*

Shlomo Brody
Jerusalem, Israel
Autumn 5774/2014

List of Abbreviations

AH: *Arukh HaShulḥan*
BH: *Bei'ur Halakha*
BY: *Beit Yosef*
EH: *Even HaEzer*
EJME: *Encyclopedia of Jewish Medical Ethics* by Rabbi Dr. Avraham Steinberg
Guide: *Guide for the Perplexed* by Maimonides
ḤM: *Ḥoshen Mishpat*
IM: *Iggerot Moshe* by Rabbi Moshe Feinstein
JHCS: *Journal of Halacha and Contemporary Society* (RJJ School)
MB: *Mishna Berura*
MT: *Mishneh Torah*
OḤ: *Oraḥ Ḥayim*
SSK: *Shemirat Shabbat KeHilkhata* by Rabbi Yehoshua Neuwirth (2nd ed.)
YD: *Yoreh De'ah*

Section 1

Medical Ethics

Chapter 1

Doctors in Judaism

Should we always embrace modern medicine?

Someone recently told me that every Jewish family needs at least one doctor…and one rabbi. I think this person was simply trying to patronize me. Frankly, I myself have bemoaned the lack of a doctor in my immediate family, especially a pediatrician! Nonetheless, despite the sociological fixation on Jewish doctors, our tradition has at times expressed ambivalence toward medicine and its practitioners.

Judaism emphasizes the importance of saving lives, most explicitly in the biblical injunction, "You shall not stand idly by the blood of your fellow" (Lev. 19:16). This verse, however, applies more directly to ad hoc cases of saving a person from a precarious situation, such as drowning (Sanhedrin 73a). The Torah similarly exhorts, "Live by the commandments" (Lev. 18:5), enjoining us to violate almost any prohibition in order to preserve life (Sanhedrin 74a).

Perhaps the most explicit biblical commandment relating to medicine appears in connection with remunerations owed for battery assault. The Torah states, "he shall surely be healed," thereby obligating reimbursement for medical expenses (Ex. 21:19). The sages derive from this verse that a physician has permission to treat the wounded (Bava Kamma 85a). Though we might have thought that we dare not interfere with God's choice to strike the patient, the Torah indicates here that we may attempt to heal him (*Tosafot*).

A patient's right to seek treatment, however, remains subject to greater scrutiny, as his efforts might reflect a lack of trust in God and

His healing powers. King Asa was severely criticized for his reliance on medicine to the exclusion of prayer and self-reflection (II Chr. 16:12). The Talmud likewise relates that the sages praised King Hezekiah for concealing the "Book of Cures" because it was too effective, rendering supplications superfluous (Rashi, Pesaḥim 56a). The Torah, moreover, refers to God as the Great Healer who prevents those loyal to Him from falling ill, which might suggest that the righteous do not require medical intervention (Ex. 15:26).

Indeed, according to one Babylonian sage, R. Aḥa, the entire enterprise of medicine was initially undesirable; prayer was the preferred response. Once humans resorted to medical intervention, however, R. Aḥa composed a prayer to recite before treatment (such as bloodletting, the preferred remedy in his era!), so the patient would remember that healing ultimately depends on God (Berakhot 60a). This theme was later adopted by Nahmanides (thirteenth century, Spain), himself a doctor, who contended that in truly righteous eras, medicine was unnecessary, and further implied that even today the pious could rely solely on faith to heal them (Lev. 26:11). Rabbi Chaim Soloveitchik (d. 1918) was so shocked by this statement that he claimed Nahmanides never said it.

The dominant stream of Jewish thought, however, embraced medicine as a tool God grants humans to heal themselves. "One may not rely on miracles," the Talmud declares (Shabbat 32a); rather, one must use all available resources to keep himself alive (*Otzar HaMidrashim*, p. 580). The sage Abbaye rebutted the sentiment of R. Aḥa, stating that the requirement to compensate for rehabilitation constitutes an implicit endorsement of medical treatment (*Tzitz Eliezer* 5:20). Not surprisingly, Maimonides, the great scholar of both Torah and medicine, deemed medical care a mitzva (Commentary on the Mishna, Nedarim 4:4), a position later codified into law (YD 336:1). He further contended that King Hezekiah buried the Book of Cures because it was quackery that endangered lives. Maimonides derided those who abstained from medical treatment as hypocrites for consuming food, a natural resource that, like medicine, God provides for our well-being (Commentary on the Mishna, Pesaḥim 4:9).

Nonetheless, the sages remained concerned with the spiritual pitfalls of medicine, best encapsulated by their declaration that "the best doctors are destined for hell" (Kiddushin 82a). Some commentators explain that this scathing remark refers to physicians who suffer from a "God complex," becoming overconfident and arrogantly claiming healing powers. Others understand it as a censure of the over-commercialization of medicine, to the point where the poor might not be treated. Alternatively, this statement might criticize medical malpractice stemming from negligence, laziness, or a haughty refusal to consult other experts (Rashi).

These pitfalls notwithstanding, medicine remains both praiseworthy and a mitzva. To maintain the appropriate perspective on their vocation, many physicians recite a short daily prayer, erroneously attributed to Maimonides, which reads, in part:

> You have blessed Your earth … with healing substances …. You have chosen me to watch over the life and health of Your creatures …. Support me, Almighty God, in these great labors, that they may benefit mankind, for without Your help not even the least thing will succeed …. Do not allow thirst for profit, ambition for renown and admiration, to interfere with my profession, for these are the enemies of truth and of love for mankind, and they can lead astray in the great task of attending to the welfare of Your creatures.

Amen.

Chapter 2

Medical Fees

May physicians dispute their wages?

While work stoppages are a contentious topic within Jewish law, doctors' strikes remain particularly complex, because health care is essential. The extended labor dispute between physicians and the Israeli government in 2011, for example, delayed many elective surgeries and other important procedures. Those of us, including myself, who had loved ones in the hospital during the strike certainly understand the angst created by these slowdowns. Though most medical services remained intact, it behooves us to reflect on the morality of such methods.

Significantly, in the 2011 strike, doctors claimed they sought not only increased wages, but also better health care conditions, including more hospital staff and beds. Indeed, the state comptroller contended that shortages have caused neglect in certain circumstances, leading four eminent religious Zionist decisors – Rabbis Aharon Lichtenstein, Yaakov Ariel, Ḥayim Druckman, and Dov Lior – to support the strike. This essay will not take sides on any particular dispute, but instead elucidate general halakhic principles.

Saving a life fulfills the biblical injunction, "You shall not stand idly by the blood of your fellow" (Lev. 19:16), as well as the obligation to restore someone's property (Deut. 22:2), which includes his physical welfare (Sanhedrin 73a). While one need not become a doctor, these commandments dictate that all medical treatment fulfills a biblical imperative (YD 336:1). As a rule, one should not receive money for performing commandments, and therefore judges, teachers, and rabbis were classically forbidden to charge for their services (Bekhorot 29a).

Yet the Talmud is replete with discussions about responsibilities for medical fees. The Torah itself mandates that victims of violence are entitled to compensation for medical expenses (Ex. 21:19), with the ancient *Targum* translating the relevant phrase as "he shall pay the doctor's fee." As Rabbi Yisrael Meir Lau has noted (*Yaḥel Yisrael* 2:59), some medieval commentators understood this verse as permitting doctors to receive remuneration, even though medical care is a mitzva (*Tosefot HaRosh* Berakhot 60a). The Talmud goes so far as to say that the victim may refuse free health care provided by the assailant's friend, on the assumption that "a physician who heals for nothing is worth nothing," since he will be less attentive (Bava Kamma 85a).

However, Nahmanides (thirteenth century, Spain), himself a physician, asserted that health care providers, like judges, may receive remuneration only for their trouble (*tirḥa*) and lost time, but not for their knowledge, diagnoses, and treatment (YD 336:2). While commentators debate the parameters of these variables, they clearly limit medical fees. Doctors who charge more are reproached, though most decisors rule that a patient must pay in full, since one cannot compel a physician to treat someone in a non-emergency situation (YD 336:3). Nonetheless, if a medical practitioner has unique expertise in an illness (*Shu"t HaRadbaz* 3:556), or an indigent person cannot get health care elsewhere (*Teshuva MeAhava* 3:408), local authorities may force a doctor to offer his services, with some asserting that society must (minimally) establish health care systems for the underprivileged (*Tzitz Eliezer, Ramat Raḥel* 5:24).

Despite these historical sentiments, most decisors justify the contemporary reality in which doctors receive salaries well beyond their effort and loss of time. Rabbi Shaul Yisraeli asserted that the extensive time and money necessary for medical training permits greater compensation (*Ḥavvat Binyamin* 3:110), with others further noting all the hours physicians spend on call and in hospitals (*Nishmat Avraham* 336:9). Rabbi Moshe Feinstein (d. 1986) contended that unlike in earlier eras, doctors today have no other profession and therefore may receive full compensation (as do rabbis and teachers), especially since their fees are agreed upon by their patients (IM YD 4:52). Others have argued that physicians must be paid enough to make it worth their while to risk costly malpractice suits (*Teshuvot VeHanhagot* 1:897).

Despite these dispensations, health care providers may not endanger patients – thereby neglecting the commandment of saving lives – while disputing wages. As Rabbi Dr. Mordekhai Halperin has documented, this stance was highlighted in 1983, when Israel suffered from a four-month physicians' strike, which included mass walkouts from hospitals and hunger strikes (*Assia* 5). While acknowledging that his directive would impair the strike, Rabbi Shlomo Goren criticized any neglect of patient care, even as he permitted doctors to demand higher wages and collect private payment in the interim. Rabbis Shlomo Zalman Auerbach and Yitzḥak Weiss asserted that while physicians could implement slowdowns (such as working on Shabbat schedules, meaning fewer doctors on duty), they could not simply walk away from their treatment responsibilities. This was definitely true, asserted Chief Rabbis Avraham Shapira and Mordechai Eliyahu, once the government agreed to mediation.

Looking toward the future, one can only hope that all parties in the health care system will work together to ensure that the crucial mitzva of saving lives is performed to the highest possible standard.

Chapter 3

Family Planning

Are newlyweds allowed to use birth control to delay parenthood?

Contraception in Jewish law remains a very sensitive issue. Some have even argued that scholars should address it only orally and on an individual basis, without writing anything for public consumption (IM EH 1:64). Given the unhindered and uninhibited use of contraceptives in today's society, however, as well as the manner in which society discusses intimate matters, there is a growing consensus as to the necessity of engaging in public dialogue regarding these issues. Nonetheless, all agree that personal circumstances must be addressed individually. As such, this essay will only present general considerations in order to facilitate more informed conversations.

The Bible depicts procreation as both a blessing and a commandment (Gen. 1:28, 9:1–7). Some medieval scholars count it as the first mitzva, both in order and in importance, since it enables the settlement of the world and the performance of other mitzvot (*Ḥinukh* 1). Procreation is further deemed a central purpose of marriage, albeit not its exclusive goal (*Tur* EH 1), and one may even sell a Torah scroll to facilitate a marriage (Megilla 27a). Conversely, the Talmud declares, "He who has not engaged in procreation is as if he has committed murder," or alternatively, "it is as if he has diminished the divine image" (Yevamot 63b).

The sages debate the number of children one must have to fulfill the mitzva (61b), with normative law requiring one child of each gender, provided that these children themselves are physically capable of procreation (EH 1:5–6). Some decisors rule that infertile couples may fulfill this commandment through adoption, since the Talmud equates rearing an orphan with giving it life (*Ḥokhmat Shlomo* EH 1:1).

The sages enjoin us to go beyond the minimum, citing Isaiah's exhortation (45:18) to inhabit the world (*lashevet*). Moreover, Ecclesiastes (11:6) advises that one not stop sowing his seed as he ages, especially given the unpredictability of life and the potential mortality of progeny (Yevamot 62). While scholars debate the legal nature of these statements (AH EH 1:8), their sentiment has significant influence. Particularly after the Holocaust, scholars like Rabbis Aharon Lichtenstein and Yaakov Breisch (*Ḥelkat Yaakov* EH 61) have stressed the centrality of childbirth for the nation's revitalization. These considerations have, in part, motivated the Israeli health care system to generously finance fertility treatments and reproductive technologies.

Decisors generally agree that if a couple has not yet fulfilled this mitzva, they may not arbitrarily put it off (EH 76:6). (Such delays might also be imprudent for relatively older couples, since fertility rates drop and childbearing becomes more complicated as people age.) Often, however, the desire to use contraceptives stems from medical, emotional, and/or economic concerns, which vary in severity for each couple (another reason every case must be examined individually).

The permissibility of delaying pregnancy hinges in part on our understanding of the commandment to procreate. Unlike time-bound precepts, such as the daily recitations of *Shema*, mitzvot such as procreation have no set time for performance; a person simply must fulfill them before he dies. Scholars discuss whether economic or other considerations may delay the performance of these mitzvot (*Ḥazon Ish* YD 154:5). Rabbi Moshe Schick suggests that one not tarry in choosing a spouse, lest he die beforehand and leave no descendants (*Shu"t Maharam Schick* EH 1). Yet one might contend that this idea, along with the general principle of trying to perform commandments at the earliest moment (*zerizin makdimin lamitzvot*), may be pushed aside due to conflicting needs. A precedent for such reasoning might already exist in our case, as the rabbinic authorities have already postponed the mitzva of marriage – and consequently the ability to procreate – from the age of majority (until at least age eighteen) to allow for proper education (*Ḥelkat Meḥokek* EH 1:2).

Rabbi Getsel Ellinson and others have cited these factors to suggest that newlyweds may temporarily use permissible forms of birth control so as to firmly establish their relationship before becoming parents. Rabbi Yaakov Ariel, however, has retorted that these sources allow for the postponement only of marriage, not of childbearing (*BeOhola shel Torah* EH 1:66).

Rabbi Yehuda Henkin (*Bnei Banim* 4:15) and a growing number of rabbis have alternatively noted that in an age where some fear marriage and others seek illicit premarital relations, it definitely remains preferable for couples to wed and use contraceptives. However, at least in their published works, many decisors – including Rabbis Moshe Feinstein (IM EH 4:72), Hershel Schachter (JHCS 4), and Shlomo Aviner (*Assia* 4) – have argued that marriage entails raising a family. Therefore, newlyweds must try to procreate immediately, unless serious health problems dictate otherwise.

Chapter 4

Contraceptives

When birth control is permitted, which forms may be used?

In the previous essay, regarding birth control for newlyweds, we discussed whether couples must immediately attempt to fulfill the obligation to procreate. Inevitably, however, the risks and responsibilities of bearing and raising children lead to questions of what constitutes proper spacing between pregnancies. Scholars debate the appropriateness of such family planning as well as which mechanisms may be employed toward that goal.

In a complex talmudic passage, the sages discuss the propriety of using a *mokh* (usually translated as an absorbent tampon) to avoid pregnancy (Yevamot 12b). While most scholars understand the talmudic debate as revolving around whether this practice is obligatory or optional, they disagree as to whether the discussion pertains to a pre-coital insertion (*Yam shel Shlomo* Yevamot 1:8) or post-coital absorbent (*Ḥatam Sofer* YD 2:172). While primarily focused on health concerns for the mother or fetus, the sages also considered that an infant might be weaned prematurely if his mother became pregnant before completing two years of nursing, the standard in talmudic times (Yevamot 36b).

Many scholars, including Rabbi Moshe Feinstein, opine that barring health hazards, one should not use contraceptives, particularly if the precept of procreation has not yet been fulfilled (IM EH 1:64, 102; 3:24).

Legitimate concerns include the risk of disease, postpartum depression, and bearing unhealthy children (*Nishmat Avraham* EH 5:13).

Other decisors are more lenient, however, based on precedents from the sages. In the Talmud, mothers are granted certain dispensations (regularly given to the moderately sick) for the first two years following childbirth (Nidda 9a), which might result in a relaxation of the obligation to procreate. Equally significant, women nursing full-time are unlikely to become pregnant (this was particularly true in talmudic times, when nutrition was limited), yet the Talmud does not limit nursing (Ketubbot 60a). As such, Rabbi Yosef E. Henkin permitted a mother to take birth control in order to be more attentive to her children, although he questioned whether this dispensation applied to women seeking to return to work (*Bnei Banim* 1:30).

Rabbi Yaakov Ariel (*BeOhola shel Torah* EH 1:67), however, has contended that following the birth of her first child, a young mother may (temporarily) employ birth control for financial or educational reasons, since according to halakha, the onus of procreation falls upon men alone (Yevamot 65b). Some have explained that women have a stronger inclination to motherhood than men do to fatherhood, so they need no command. Others trace women's exemption to the fact that the Torah does not obligate acts of self-endangerment (*Meshekh Ḥokhma* Gen. 9:7). Scholars debate whether women have an ancillary obligation to partner with their husbands in fulfilling this commandment (*Shu"t HaRan* 32), or whether they are included in the general obligation of populating the world (AH EH 1:4). Be that as it may, Rabbi Ariel contends that this level of obligation does not preclude the spacing of children to allow for basic educational and economic advancement, especially given the considerations above. Similarly, in the context of permitting spacing, Rabbi Nachum Rabinovitch (*Siaḥ Naḥum* 94) cited the famed tenth-century philosopher Saadia Gaon (*Emunot VeDe'ot* 10:9) for noting the emotional, societal, and economic complexity of raising families.

Leaving aside the larger question of preventing procreation, various contraceptive methods might also lead to violations of a woman's conjugal rights (*ona*, EH 76) or the illicit emission of semen (*hotzaat zera levatala*, EH 23). To circumvent these problems, preferred contraceptives are those that minimally obstruct natural intercourse (EH 23:5).

Therefore, condoms and *coitus interruptus* should be avoided (*Otzar HaPoskim* EH 23). Abstinence is also an option (EH 76:6), though many scholars permit (when birth control is sanctioned) other contraceptive methods to preserve a healthy marital relationship (IM EH 1:63). Tubal ligation and vasectomies should not be regularly performed, since the Torah forbids permanent sterilization, except in cases of medical necessity (EH 5:11).

Many decisors favor diaphragms over the talmudic *mokh*, since they block the entrance of sperm into the cervix, as opposed to catching the semen (*Shu"t Maharsham* 1:58). This device remains an option when necessary, even if used with spermicide (*Ḥavatzelet HaSharon* 2, *Hashmatot*). Yet most scholars prefer hormone pills, which temporarily inhibit fertility by preventing ovulation, since they do not affect the natural manner of intercourse and are possibly similar to a potion permitted in talmudic times (EH 5:12). Medical interventions have many ramifications, however, so couples should consult their rabbi and their doctor to determine the appropriate contraceptive for them.

Chapter 5

Abortion

May one abort a Tay-Sachs fetus?

Judaism abhors the termination of any life, including that of a fetus. Procreation represents a definitive commandment, and the notion that abortion is simply a woman's prerogative, as advocated in "pro-choice" circles, is entirely absent from traditional Jewish sources. Nonetheless, the various stages of embryonic development may create room for dispensation in cases of great need, such as preventing the birth of Tay-Sachs babies destined to suffer and die.

Shortly after detailing the severe punishment for murder (Ex. 21:12), the Torah discusses a case in which a man accidentally strikes a pregnant woman and causes a miscarriage (21:22–23). If the woman dies, her assailant is punished as a killer, albeit with a lower-grade penalty, since his crime was accidental (Sanhedrin 79). Yet if she survives, the assailant must pay only the remuneration offered in cases of battery, though the fetus was killed.

Interestingly, some early Church fathers understood from the verse that the assailant is treated as a murderer even if the *fetus* is killed. This interpretation led to the "abortion = homicide" equation advanced by some contemporary Christian denominations. The rabbinic tradition says otherwise. When a woman is endangered during childbirth, the sages ruled that once the baby emerges from the womb, it cannot be sacrificed to save its mother (Ohalot 7:6). Beforehand, however, the fetus is not considered a full-fledged human (*nefesh*), and doctors may terminate it, though we would normally do everything to save its life, including violating Shabbat (Arakhin 7a–b). This latter dispensation, in turn, highlights the general value we attribute to saving lives, including ones not yet born (Nahmanides, Nidda 44a).

While one might conclude from these sources that there is no definitive prohibition of feticide (*Tosafot* Nidda 44a), such a proscription is included within the seven Noahide laws (Sanhedrin 57b), which also apply to Jews (*Tosafot* Sanhedrin 59a). As such, it is prohibited to request or perform abortions unjustified by Jewish law, regardless of the religion of the patient or doctor (IM ḤM 2:73, para. 8).

The nature of this prohibition remains debatable. Some scholars asserted that abortion falls under the general ban on assault (*Shu"t Maharit* 1:97). Others place it within the rabbinic proscription of preventing the creation of life (*Mishpetei Uziel* ḤM 4:46). These lenient assessments might allow for greater exceptions, including cases in which the pregnancy might aggravate pre-existing medical conditions that are not life-threatening.

In fact, the Talmud asserts that if a pregnant woman is on death row, we kill the fetus before the execution to prevent undue embarrassment to the mother (Arakhin 7b). Consequently, Rabbi Yaakov Emden allowed an abortion following an adulterous affair, since the child born would have been illegitimate (*mamzer*). Others strongly disagreed with this opinion, arguing that such dispensations would encourage promiscuity (*Ḥavvot Yair* 31) and that this case differs from the death row fetus, since it would die with its mother anyway (*Zera Emet* YD 2:116).

The majority of scholars, however, view feticide as a lower-level form of murder that is permitted only to save the mother's life. In that case alone, we treat the fetus as a *rodef*, a potential assailant (*Noda BiYehuda Tinyana* ḤM 59) and assert that "the mother's blood is redder than the fetus'" (*Melamed Leho'il* YD 2:69). Otherwise, abortion remains a grave offense. A few scholars even included it among the cardinal sins concerning which a person should die rather than transgress (*Shu"t Maharam Schick* YD 155).

Even according to the stringent school, one mitigating factor might be the stage of pregnancy. When a fetus is within the first forty days after conception, many sources indicate that halakha does not yet treat it as a life force (Yevamot 69b), with other sources indicating that we do not acknowledge the pregnancy for the first trimester (Nidda 8b). While a few scholars insist we recognize life from conception (*Shevet MiYehuda* 1, p. 24), many disagree and assert that there is room for leniency during the earlier period (*Seridei Esh* 1:162). On this basis, Rabbi Shlomo Zalman Auerbach allowed the termination of a Tay-Sachs fetus diagnosed within the first six weeks of pregnancy (*Nishmat Avraham* ḤM 425:18).

Prenatal diagnosis of Tay-Sachs, however, has historically been possible only after the first trimester, through amniocentesis. At this stage of development, Rabbi Auerbach and Rabbi Moshe Feinstein (IM ḤM 2:69) both prohibit aborting a Tay-Sachs fetus or even testing for the disease, lest it encourage the termination of the pregnancy. However, Rabbi Eliezer Waldenburg, citing sources from the lenient school, allowed aborting such a fetus until the seventh month of pregnancy, thereby sparing parents the mental anguish of watching their infant suffer (*Tzitz Eliezer* 13:102). (Advances in prenatal DNA testing, including the introduction of the MaterniT21 DNA test, which detects Down syndrome at ten weeks, might transform this debate, even as it remains unclear how the technology will develop.)

Fortunately, such dilemmas are largely preventable if couples undergo genetic testing before marriage or having children. Society must encourage such screening to prevent undue suffering.

Chapter 6

Stem Cell Research

Does halakha support the scientific use of embryonic stem cells?

The acrimonious debates during the Bush and Obama administrations over funding cell lines will undoubtedly continue in the coming years. To my mind, the media's portrayal of the "religious perspective" has regretfully ignored the Jewish position, and it behooves our community to publicize our nuanced support for this research.

Stem cell research focuses on the pluripotent stem cells that develop in the earliest stages of the embryonic process. Since these "precursor" cells later divide into cells with specific functions (e.g., nerve cells, liver cells, etc.), scientists believe that a greater understanding of them will generate treatments for abnormal or diseased cells that cause ailments ranging from Parkinson's and strokes to burns and arthritis. Scientists obtain stem cells from different sources, including surplus embryos from fertility treatments, embryos cloned for research purposes, and aborted fetuses. (While helpful for some functions, mature stem cells in umbilical-cord blood remain less efficacious for research and potential treatments.)

Judaism wholeheartedly endorses medicine, viewing the saving and nurturing of life as a mitzva. Disease research therefore represents an important communal responsibility, similar to a nation's obligation to prepare itself militarily. However, as Rabbi J. David Bleich has emphasized, not all means justify the desired end of medical breakthroughs

(*Tradition* 36:2). We must investigate and overcome the potential legal and moral problems of stem cell research before advocating its use.

Given the moral sensitivity of "beginning of life" issues, such as abortion and birth control, the different sources of embryonic stem cells raise various legal and ethical questions. As might be expected, the most controversial sources are aborted fetuses. The "pro-choice" camp sees less of a problem in utilizing these fetuses. Opponents of abortion, however, don't want to encourage unjustified feticide. Yet they must balance this concern with the recognition that these fetuses will otherwise be discarded.

One prominent Conservative bioethicist, Rabbi Elliot Dorff, contends that we should utilize aborted fetuses, particularly when the abortions were halakhically justifiable. In light of alternative sources, however, many Orthodox rabbis believe we should not benefit from – and thereby implicitly condone – immoral behavior. Given their accessibility, unused embryos generated by fertility treatments are the best source of stem cells. To protect the mother's health, doctors cannot implant all the embryos created through the union of sperm and eggs in petri dishes. Rather than dispose of these embryos, couples may donate them to research. The question is whether we consider in-vitro gametes or early-stage embryos human.

As noted in our previous essay, while feticide is forbidden in later stages of pregnancy, many decisors aver that within forty days of gestation, an embryo is "mere water" (*Aḥiezer* 3:65). They base this categorization, in part, on a mishnaic statement that unlike childbirth, the miscarriage of such an embryo does not render a woman ritually impure (Nidda 30a). Others contend that life begins at conception, and therefore any destruction of an embryo remains forbidden. Former Israeli Chief Rabbi Isser Unterman, for example, held this position, maintaining that our obligation to violate the Sabbath in order to save such a fetus indicates that it is human (*Shevet MiYehuda* 1, p. 24).

Many contemporary decisors counter that this debate regarding feticide within forty days of gestation is irrelevant, since we are dealing with destroying an embryo conceived and developed ex utero. Rabbi Moshe Sternbuch, for example, contends that since the embryo will die in the petri dish unless implanted in the woman's uterus, it can be destroyed at will (*BiShevilei HaRefua* 8). Combining the two factors of an ex-utero embryo within forty days of gestation, most rabbinic scholars today believe that “spare” embryos produced by fertility treatments may be used to study stem cells.

Oversight remains necessary to prevent the abuse of this powerful technology for nefarious eugenics. That said, attempts to severely limit federal funding of this potentially lifesaving research might have gone too far. We hope and pray that ethical stem cell research will lead to divine blessings in the form of medical advances and treatment.

Chapter 7

Conjoined Twins

Is it permissible to surgically separate them?

Newspapers periodically report ethical dilemmas and legal battles regarding the separation of conjoined twins. Estimates of the incidence of conjoined twins range from 1 in 50,000 to 1 in 100,000 births, and a significant majority of these infants are stillborn or die within twenty-four hours of birth.

Historically, the most famous twins were Chang and Eng Bunker of Siam (hence the colloquial term Siamese twins), participants in P. T. Barnum's exhibitions, who were connected at the sternum but had separate limbs and organs. They lived active lives until age sixty-three and fathered many children with their respective wives.

Medical advances today would allow doctors to separate similarly connected twins. Yet most have a more complex interdependency of organs and limbs, making them more difficult to separate, and frequently one sibling dies during the surgery. An additional moral complication occurs when one twin is weaker than the other and utterly dependent on him.

Perhaps the first question is whether conjoined twins should be treated as one person or as two. The Talmud relates that R. Yehuda HaNasi was asked on which head of conjoined twins one should place *tefillin* (Menaḥot 37a). He took the question more seriously after a second person asked whether the father of a two-headed firstborn should treat his offspring as one child or two for the purposes of *pidyon haben* (ritual redemption of the firstborn). Yet the Talmud notes that this question has its own unique considerations, leaving unanswered the larger dilemma of identity and its implications for other legal matters, such as inheritance.

The medieval Tosafist commentators, after confessing ignorance of this medical phenomenon, quote a midrash in which King Solomon poured boiling water on the head of a conjoined twin, and the other twin screamed, whereupon he ruled that the two heads shared one identity (*Shita Mekubbetzet*). Since contemporary conjoined twins do not have such reactions, but rather display distinct personalities and nervous systems, Jewish law treats conjoined twins as separate individuals. Rabbi Yaakov Reischer (eighteenth century) further noted that according to one talmudic account, Adam and Eve were created conjoined and only later separated (Eiruvin 18a). As separate individuals, conjoined twins cannot legally marry, since a sibling may not share a bed with his twin's spouse (*Shvut Yaakov* 1:4).

This legal determination of separate identities creates difficulties regarding surgical separation, as it frequently results in the death of one twin. Some unseparated twins survive, but in many cases, their conjoining leads to the death of both, especially when their shared organs cannot support them.

In 1977, an Orthodox couple from Lakewood, New Jersey, agonized over whether to separate conjoined twins who shared organs, including a six-chamber heart, thereby killing the weaker sibling but giving the stronger one a chance to survive. While their physician, C. Everett Koop (who later became US surgeon general), received legal permission to separate the siblings, the operation proceeded only following the oral directive of Rabbi Moshe Feinstein.

Rabbi Feinstein's reasoning, as recorded by his son-in-law Rabbi Dr. Moshe D. Tendler, was that we generally do not sacrifice one life to save another. Yet Jewish law permits the killing of a fetus when it endangers its mother, deeming it a *rodef* (attacking pursuer) (Sanhedrin 72). Rabbi Feinstein therefore contended that since there was no way to save the first baby, which would have died in utero without the support of its twin, it was permissible to kill the first twin based on the *rodef* principle. Rabbi Dr. Mordekhai Halperin contends that one may similarly operate in comparable circumstances of asymmetric conjoined twins, including the controversial 2000 case of British twins separated against their parents' wishes (*Assia* 4).

However, as Rabbi J. David Bleich notes, other scholars reject the *rodef* analogy (*Tradition* 31:1, 34:4). First, since both twins compete for the same contested resources, it would be a case of mutual pursuit, in which case Jewish law does not mandate third-party intervention. Moreover, since the weaker sibling is definitively alive and has no malevolent intentions, the case is more analogous to an innocent newborn who has already emerged from the womb of its endangered mother. In that case, the Talmud declares, the child is not a *rodef*, since the mother is being "pursued by Heaven," and as Maimonides tragically adds, "This is the natural course of the world" (MT *Hilkhot Rotze'aḥ* 1:9).

The debate continues, with scholars ultimately deliberating whether humans should choose between lives or leave such matters in God's hands.

Chapter 8

Smoking

Is this dangerous habit justifiable?

This question bothers many people who cannot understand how so many Jews, particularly those who display tremendous piety in other areas, can reconcile this dangerous addiction with the Torah's ordinances against harmful behavior. This phenomenon becomes particularly painful in cases of loved ones whose addiction ultimately kills them.

When tobacco was introduced in Europe in the late 1500s, doctors considered it healthful, especially in warding off digestive and (ironically) respiratory diseases. While a few, including King James of England, opposed smoking as sinister behavior, it became socially acceptable among non-Jews and Jews alike. Hasidic rabbis promoted the use of tobacco and snuff for spiritual purposes (*Taamei HaMinhagim*, p. 102), earning the scorn of the *mitnagdim*. The idling and sometimes decadent tobacco culture irked the famed Rabbi Yisrael Meir Kagan (Poland, 1839–1933), who denounced smoking in his lesser-known writings as physically deleterious and a waste of time and money (*Likkutei Amarim* 13). Yet the practice remained prevalent.

Before the contemporary era, smoking was discussed in the halakhic literature most frequently with regard to whether it is permissible on festivals. As opposed to Shabbat, when tampering with a flame is forbidden, the rules of Yom Tov allow for kindling a fire from a pre-existing one, although one may not extinguish it (OḤ 511). However, one must use the flame for an enjoyable purpose that is customary among the vast majority of people (*shaveh lekhol nefesh*).

Some rabbis claimed that smoking was not enjoyed by most people, especially first-time smokers, who frequently cough and become disoriented (*Ḥayei Adam* 2:95, para. 13). Yet smoking was historically permitted by most decisors, who cited its social acceptance as proof that it constituted permissible use of a flame on Yom Tov (BH 511:4, s.v. *ein*). Other common questions included whether one must recite a blessing over tobacco as one does with food (MB 210:17), and whether cigarettes contain *ḥametz* prohibited on Passover (*Yeḥaveh Daat* 2:61).

While a few physicians expressed concern over smoking in the eighteenth and nineteenth centuries, it was only in the 1950s that research definitively documented the harmful effects of tobacco on smokers and those around them, including a direct link to lung cancer. Since public health services began campaigns against tobacco, the number of new smokers has sharply declined, although the addictive nicotine in cigarettes makes it difficult for many to quit.

One immediate consequence of the reduction in smokers relates to the permissibility of smoking on Yom Tov. Since cigarettes are no longer enjoyed by most people, many contemporary decisors, including Rabbi Shlomo Zalman Auerbach, forbid smoking on Yom Tov (*Pe'er Taḥat Efer*). Most scholars have also ruled that a person bothered by smoke may demand that a smoker refrain from smoking or leave the area, even in public places or houses of study (IM ḤM 2:18).

The major issue, however, is the permissibility of smoking altogether. The Torah commands us to "greatly beware for your souls" (Deut. 4:15), admonishing us to avoid dangerous behavior. Maimonides contends that anyone who dismisses warnings of such dangers should receive lashes (MT *Hilkhot Rotze'aḥ* 11:5). Yet the sages determined that risks taken by the masses remain permissible, citing the verse that "God protects the foolish" (Shabbat 129b). As such, defining dangerous activity remains contingent on the knowledge and norms in a particular era.

In a landmark 1976 responsum, Rabbi Ḥayim David HaLevi (d. 1998), Sephardic chief rabbi of Tel Aviv, banned smoking, contending that previous generations would never have permitted it had they known of its dangers (*Aseh Lekha Rav* 2:1). His announcement received widespread attention in Israel and around the world (it was covered on page 2 of *The New York Times*). He forbade purchasing cigarettes for others, even when requested by one's parent (*Aseh Lekha Rav* 6:58), and further asserted that in light of anti-smoking campaigns around the world, continued smoking in Israel desecrated God's name (3:18).

While in 1982 Rabbi Eliezer Waldenburg similarly forbade smoking (*Tzitz Eliezer* 15:39), most decisors in the 1980s did not, since its deleterious effects were not immediate. Yet these authorities forcefully discouraged smoking as an unhealthy habit (IM ḤM 2:76). As the perils of smoking have become better understood, however, rabbis from across the spectrum have forbidden it. Most recently, Rabbi Ovadia Yosef and Rabbi Yosef Shalom Elyashiv joined these voices. Indeed, one can confidently say today that every Jew has an obligation to help smokers kick the habit and prevent others from starting.

Chapter 9

Blood and Bone Marrow Donation

Is one obligated to save a life?

Bone marrow and blood transfusions are miracles of modern medicine and gifts from God, but they also raise grave questions regarding the obligation to endanger oneself in order to save others. The sages compared saving a life to saving the entire world (Sanhedrin 37a). Yet how far must we go to perform this great act?

The Talmud cites two biblical passages obligating us to save lives (Sanhedrin 73a). The first (and less obvious) verse comes from the general commandment to restore another's property, including his body (Deut. 22:2). The second verse, "You shall not stand idly by the blood of your fellow" (Lev. 19:16), mandates going beyond general assistance and committing financial resources to saving the lives of others.

Rabbinic authorities have debated whether these commandments demand even risking one's own life. When the sage R. Ami was abducted and faced execution, his colleagues disagreed as to whether a daring rescue effort was appropriate (Y. Terumot 8:4). While R. Yonatan answered negatively, Resh Lakish insisted on attempting a rescue mission (which ultimately succeeded). Based on this story, some have determined that if someone will definitely die, one must make every effort to save him, since the threat to the rescuer remains uncertain (*Kesef Mishneh, Hilkhot Rotze'aḥ* 1:14).

The vast majority of scholars, however, have rejected this position. In one celebrated responsum, Rabbi David ibn Zimra (sixteenth century, Egypt) ruled that a person need not volunteer to have a limb amputated by a despotic ruler in order to prevent him from killing another Jew (*Shu"t HaRadbaz* 3:627). Alluding to the talmudic dictum that one's life takes precedence over another's, Radbaz further claimed that dictating such self-endangerment would be immoral and go against the notion that the Torah represents "ways of pleasantness and peace" (Prov. 3:17). With the exception of committing the three cardinal sins, the Torah commands us to preserve our lives, even by violating commandments such as "You shall not stand idly by the blood of your fellow." As such, one need not endanger himself to save someone from imminent death (*Shulḥan Arukh HaRav* OḤ 329:8).

In an extreme formulation, Rabbi Meir Simḥa of Dvinsk (Latvia, d. 1926) applied this principle even when many Jews or the entire nation faced an imminent fatal threat (*Or Same'aḥ* Laws of Murderers 7:8). This position was challenged by others, such as Rabbi Meir Plotzky (*Klei Ḥemda, Parashat Pinḥas* 1), and in a lengthy treatise, Rabbi Abraham Isaac Kook (d. 1935) contended that under those circumstances, self-sacrifice is mandatory (*Mishpat Kohen* 143).

In general, many scholars recognize a range of life-threatening actions, and somewhere along that continuum, certain conduct becomes meritorious or mandatory, given the circumstances (AH ḤM 426:4). Rabbi ibn Zimra himself ruled in a different responsum that one should act if the potential threat to the rescuer is unlikely to occur (*Shu"t HaRadbaz* 5:218). In cases of somewhat greater but nonetheless distant threats, many authorities deem it permissible and even meritorious to risk one's life in order to save another's, as long as the rescuer's actions are not suicidal (IM YD 2:174). Decisors also debate whether a person must endure pain to save others (*Nishmat Avraham* YD 157:4).

For most people operating in hygienic conditions, donating blood entails minimal pain. The risk is also negligible, since the lost blood easily regenerates. As such, scholars including Rabbis Shmuel HaLevi Wosner (*Shevet HaLevi* 5:219) and J. David Bleich (*Tradition* 27:3) contend that one must donate blood if a patient requires an immediate transfusion.

Donating to blood banks, especially amid shortages, also represents a definitive mitzva (*Nishmat Avraham* YD 349:3).

While bone marrow naturally regenerates, donors previously had to be placed under general anesthesia and hospitalized for a couple of days. Therefore Rabbi Moshe Sternbuch did not require one to donate, though he deemed it extremely meritorious (*Teshuvot VeHanhagot* 5:387). Rabbi Shlomo Zalman Auerbach believed a potential donor should be cajoled into donating, especially if he did not fear the surgery (*Nishmat Avraham* EH 80:1). Yet Rabbi Bleich and Rabbi Mordechai Willig obligate one to donate, since the dangers represent common and minimal risks regularly taken for less pressing needs. This is especially true today, when most bone marrow donations take place on an outpatient basis, without general anesthesia.

Gaining consent from minors to donate bone marrow for family members remains ethically complex. Rabbi Auerbach believes that an older, mentally competent child can consent, but remains conflicted regarding younger or mentally incompetent children. Rabbi Bleich, however, requires parental consent.

Since bone marrow matches are based on genetic similarities, the Jewish community must participate in bone marrow drives (such as those organized by the Gift of Life Bone Marrow Foundation) to ensure that enough potential donors are registered. God blessed us with these medical tools – it is our responsibility and obligation to use them to save lives.

Chapter 10

Kidney Donation and Compensation

May one donate a kidney and receive payment for it?

In the preceding essay, regarding blood and bone marrow donations, we concluded that most decisors believe halakha excuses (and sometimes prohibits) people from endangering themselves to save another's life. However, measures like donating blood or bone marrow entail minimal risk; therefore, it remains meritorious and possibly obligatory to perform such lifesaving actions.

Donating a kidney, on the other hand, clearly constitutes a greater endangerment. Unlike blood or bone marrow, the missing kidney does not regenerate. While a person can function normally with one kidney (as we hope the recipient will), the donor places himself at risk if his remaining kidney is damaged in an accident or through dehydration. (Regarding the latter danger, most kidney donors and recipients should therefore not fully fast on Yom Kippur.) Moreover, the procedure is much more invasive and entails at least a few weeks of outpatient recovery.

Rabbi Isser Unterman contended that the invasiveness of the surgery alone was sufficient to forbid live kidney donations, since he believed that self-injury (*ḥabbala*) represented a form of self-endangerment prohibited by halakha, even to save a life (*Shevet MiYehuda* 1, p. 53).

Others similarly prohibited renal transplantation in the early 1960s, deeming it too dangerous for the donor (*Minḥat Yitzḥak* 6:103).

However, most decisors, including Rabbi Moshe Feinstein, concluded that live kidney donations were permissible and meritorious, though the possible risks prevented halakha from compelling them (IM YD 2:174, para. 4). Today, transplants are no riskier than routine surgeries involving general anesthesia. Therefore, since halakha generally permits people to take common risks (*shomer peta'im*) (Shabbat 129b), donating a kidney would not constitute inappropriate self-endangerment.

While the pain remains significant, Rabbi Shlomo Zalman Auerbach ruled that temporary severe discomfort does not negate the requirement to save lives (*Nishmat Avraham* YD 157:2). Moreover, since the life expectancy and general health of successful transplant recipients greatly exceeds those of patients on dialysis, most believe that donating a kidney fulfills the mitzva of saving a life (*pikuaḥ nefesh*), which overrides any prohibitions of self-injury. Nonetheless, because of the risks entailed by the procedure, the vast majority of decisors deemed it meritorious but not compulsory, though Rabbi Ovadia Yosef intimates that donating might be obligatory (*Yeḥaveh Daat* 3:84). Similarly, many scholars prohibit children or the mentally incompetent from donating, since they cannot reasonably consent to these risks.

In countries where organ sale is illegal, all agree that Jews may not engage in such activity. The wisdom of such a ban, however, remains subject to a heated debate in Jewish and general ethics.

Jewish law requires, when economically possible, that a person compensate his savior for the financial losses incurred in the course of the rescue (*Kesef Mishneh, Hilkhot Rotze'aḥ* 1:14). While this requirement allows the donor to recoup medical and non-medical expenses incurred through the transplant, it does not cover recompense for agreeing to the procedure in the first place.

The Talmud allows for the sale of one's hair (Nedarim 65b), but this permission cannot serve as a precedent, because the loss entails no injury. Rabbis Feinstein (IM ḤM 1:103) and Auerbach (*Nishmat Avraham* YD 349:3) allowed people to receive money for donating blood, despite the physical intrusion, but this case is also not entirely analogous, since blood regenerates and the procedure is minimally invasive. Nonetheless, Rabbi Auerbach asserted that since one is permitted to donate an organ in order to save a life, he may also receive a financial incentive to perform this meritorious act (*Nishmat Avraham* ḤM 420:1). Rabbis Yaakov Ariel (*BeOhola shel Torah* ḤM 1:100) and Yisrael Meir Lau (*Tchumin* 18) similarly contend that humans retain sufficient autonomy over their bodies to sell these organs, while patients are entitled to pay to save their lives.

Opponents of organ sales, including Rabbis Shabtai Rappaport and Dr. Moshe D. Tendler, contend that serious self-injury remains prohibited when performed primarily for financial gain (*Nishmat Avraham* ḤM 420:31). They further argue that organ sales will lead to extortion and manipulation that will void the legitimacy of the sales, create further socioeconomic disparity of access to health care, and discourage "free" transplants from live donors or cadavers. Proponents retort that this paternalistic approach violates human autonomy, and that government regulation would prevent manipulation while facilitating lifesaving treatments.

Many of these deep ethical quandaries could be avoided by increasing the number of organs donated from cadavers. For those of us who follow the ruling of the Israeli Chief Rabbinate (discussed in the next essay) to permit posthumous organ transplants, it remains imperative to sign a donor card and save the lives of thousands waiting on organ transplant lists.

Chapter 11

Time of Death and Organ Donation

Does halakha permit the signing of an organ donor card?

From the outset, it is important to distinguish between different ethical dilemmas that are sometimes grouped together. For example, some mistakenly compare this question to donating one's body to science, though that dispute stems from very different issues. Everyone agrees that one may use a dead body to save a person's life (see chapter 14). In the case of willing a body to science, the decisors debate whether the potential long-term scientific benefit of dissecting the body qualifies as a lifesaving action. In the case of organ donation, however, the dispute surrounds whether the allegedly deceased donor is actually dead! Thus at stake in this case is the very definition of death.

While defining death might seem like a purely scientific issue, it involves a complex set of moral, religious, and legal factors. Scientists delineate the *process* of death by quantifying the increasing dysfunction of an organism. They can describe how the cerebellum, which controls muscle functions, ceases to operate; when a damaged cerebrum causes memory loss; how respiration desists when the nerves in the brain stem cease functioning; or when the heart irreversibly stops beating. Science, however, cannot decide which form of dysfunction defines an organism as "dead." This is ultimately a cultural decision that demands a legal criterion with an ethical justification.

Historically, how to define death was not a major issue, since the different signs of dysfunction – including cessation of respiratory and cardiac activity – largely coincided. Modern medical advances, however, prevent the domino effect that causes an entire body to shut down. In particular, respirators can provide oxygen to the heart even if the lungs have stopped functioning independently.

In 1968, a Harvard Medical School committee declared a person dead when the lungs no longer function spontaneously because of irreversible neurological damage, even if the heart continues beating through artificial respiration. Physiologically, this "brain-stem death" differs greatly from a coma or a persistent vegetative state, and there are no documented cases of a brain-dead patient recuperating. The Harvard criterion made way for transplants, since doctors could remove body parts from a brain-dead patient whose organs continued to receive blood from an artificially supported heart.

While this definition has received almost universal endorsement, Jewish legalists continue to debate whether halakha recognizes this criterion. The sages state that to determine if a person is living or dead, we must examine their nostrils for signs of breathing (*Yoma* 85a). Respiration is a sign of life, since God created Adam by "breathing into his nostrils the breath of life" (Gen. 2:7). Accordingly, the nineteenth-century Hungarian decisor Rabbi Moshe Sofer ruled that cessation of breathing constitutes death (*Ḥatam Sofer* YD 2:338). European doctors at that time were concerned that scientists could not accurately determine death, and many governments demanded the delay of burial for two to three days to ensure that the "corpse" was really deceased. Rabbi Sofer, however, saw no need for such precautions, since cessation of respiration clearly indicated death.

Based on this ruling, Rabbi Moshe Feinstein declared in 1976 that brain-stem death fulfills the halakhic criterion of death, even if the heart continues beating due to artificial respiration (IM YD 3:132). Rabbi Feinstein drew on a mishna that deems a decapitated animal dead though it continues to spasm (Oholot 1:6). Brain-stem death, he reasoned, equals physiological decapitation. While some have deemed this responsum ambiguous, Rabbi Feinstein's family has affirmed that such was indeed his opinion (*Assia* 7). In 1987, the Chief Rabbinate of Israel endorsed this position, pronouncing conventional, non-experimental organ transplants a great mitzva.

However, numerous decisors, including Rabbis Shmuel HaLevi Wosner (*Shevet HaLevi* 8:86) and Eliezer Waldenburg (*Tzitz Eliezer* 10:25), oppose brain-stem death. They contend that the Talmud used respiration as the criterion for death only when there were no other signs of life; if the heart continues beating, the person is halakhically alive, and removing his organs constitutes nothing less than murder. These scholars further cited a responsum of Rabbi Shalom Schwadron (Poland, 1835–1911), who asserted that any signs of life override the cessation of respiration (Maharsham 6:124).

One should settle matters regarding life and death decisions, including signing an organ donor card, in careful consultation with family members and competent rabbinic authorities. While I strongly advocate brain-stem death and organ donation, I encourage everyone to find out more about this sensitive and important topic. One good resource is the Halakhic Organ Donor Society, www.hods.org.

Chapter 12

Assisted Suicide and Euthanasia

What is the halakhic view?

Tragically, many terminal patients can be kept alive yet suffer greatly, or remain in a comatose or vegetative state for years. Expensive medications and cardiopulmonary resuscitation (CPR) machines extend life but cannot guarantee a dignified quality of life. The heated debates surrounding figures like Karen Ann Quinlan, Dr. Jack Kevorkian, Terri Schiavo, and Benjamin Ayal highlight the severity of the moral issues underlying such cases.

Classic Jewish discussion of these dilemmas begins with the premise that humans do not possess full autonomy over their bodies. Jewish law prohibits not only murder and battery, but also suicide and self-infliction (Bava Kamma 91b). As such, all Jewish denominations have traditionally opposed active euthanasia, or even the more moderate assisted-suicide model proposed in several countries, in which physicians facilitate but do not actually perform "mercy killings." As one 1994 Reform responsum declared, "Such an action is the ultimate arrogance, for it declares that we are masters over the one thing – life itself – that our faith has always taught must be protected against our all too human tendency to manipulate, to mutilate, and to destroy." While certain sources sympathize with (without necessarily condoning) a person who, like King Saul, hastens his own death under the duress of suffering (1 Sam. 31:4–5), this clemency is not extended to his accomplices.

There is an equally broad consensus that one may employ palliative measures to reduce suffering, such as those promoted at hospices. This license even includes gradually increasing morphine injections, as long as one intends to reduce pain, not to hasten death.

However, Jewish bioethicists significantly disagree regarding "passive euthanasia," meaning either the withholding or withdrawing of treatment from the terminally ill. In the sixteenth century, Rabbi Moshe Isserles codified three major principles regarding the treatment of a patient approaching death (*goses*): (1) One may not cause him to die more slowly, (2) one may not hasten death, and (3) one may remove something that is merely hindering the soul's departure (YD 339:1). Unfortunately, these principles remain subject to different interpretations, and the examples given in *Shulḥan Arukh* – including placing salt on the tongue and synagogue keys under the pillow – remain difficult to translate into modern technological terms.

Regarding the withholding of treatment, Rabbis Eliezer Waldenburg and J. David Bleich contend that the value of every moment of life remains infinite and absolute. One must therefore administer all life-extending treatments, even under the most miserable circumstances, and even over the patient's protest (*Tzitz Eliezer* 9:47). Others, like Rabbis Shlomo Zalman Auerbach (*Minḥat Shlomo* 1:91) and Moshe Feinstein (IM ḤM 2:74–75), assert that such treatment may be withheld in cases of intense anguish. Accordingly, one may fill out a halakhic living will to authorize, under certain conditions, the withholding of life-prolonging treatments, such as resuscitation (DNR) or intubation (DNI). Orthodox authorities almost universally contend that food, fluids, and oxygen constitute natural substances that should not be withheld. While many non-Orthodox bioethicists support this position, others view feeding tubes as medical treatments, which the patient (or caretakers) may decline.

Once doctors administer a life-prolonging mechanism, it is difficult to discontinue, even as one may cease futile therapies for the underlying disease. Rabbi Ḥayim David HaLevi classifies a respirator as a mere impediment to death, which doctors may therefore disable to prevent continued suffering (*Aseh Lekha Rav* 5:29). While this view has support in some non-Orthodox circles, the nearly universal Orthodox position – advocated by Rabbis Auerbach and Feinstein – is that one may not remove a respirator, as doing so will directly hasten death. One need not reconnect the machine, however, if it is disconnected for servicing or to suction the patient (IM YD 3:132). Rabbis Auerbach and Shmuel HaLevi Wosner also allow the oxygen rate to be lowered to the level found in the air we breathe, provided that the patient can breathe on his own (EJME, p. 1059).

In 2006, a fifty-nine-member committee representing the full Israeli ideological spectrum, led by the esteemed Rabbi Dr. Avraham Steinberg, attempted to formulate a halakhically defensible national policy regarding these issues. The Steinberg committee proposed that all respirators operate on timers and thus shut off automatically should the hospital deem this act of omission appropriate given the patient's condition. Unfortunately, the Israeli health system has not implemented this proposal. Instead, more radical laws have been drafted, meeting the standards of no Jewish denomination. While no agreement is perfect, one hopes that the committee's two years of work will help create greater national consensus on these sensitive matters.

Chapter 13

Prayers for the Terminally Ill

May I pray for the death of a relative who is suffering greatly?

Those of us who have experienced the agonizing extended death of a loved one certainly understand this concern. Modern medicine gives doctors the ability to heal – or at least to keep alive – many patients who in previous decades would have died quickly. The blessing of longer life, however, does not always improve quality of life, and in certain circumstances, patients are kept alive in excruciating conditions. While controversies over euthanasia and withholding treatment dominate public debate, the independent question of how we should direct our prayers deserves greater attention.

Judaism attributes great importance to preserving life, with the Mishna even stating, "Anyone who saves a life is as if he has saved the entire world" (Sanhedrin 37a). One does not even have the right to harm oneself, as Judaism prohibits suicide and all forms of self-mutilation. Nonetheless, even life is trumped at times by other values. Jewish law allows for the death penalty, sends soldiers out to battle, and demands that one be killed rather than commit idol worship, illicit relations, or murder. In our case, the question is whether Judaism attributes enough value to the quality of life to allow a person to pray for the suffering patient to die. (To reiterate: This inquiry remains independent of the question of "mercy killing" and less drastic interventions, which is discussed in previous essays.)

Classic sources attribute spiritual benefits to suffering. Pain is often understood not only as divine punishment, but also as atonement. "Suffering erases all of a person's sins," the sages declared (Berakhot 5a). Anguish should prompt repentance, the desire to come closer to God, as the Psalmist exclaims, "I found trouble and sorrow; then I called upon the name of the Lord" (Ps. 116). Consequently, other sources speak of suffering as a sign of God's love or as a purification process that makes one worthy of the World to Come. However, these benefits are merely a silver lining, with affliction seen as an undesirable curse. When asked whether they welcomed suffering, one group of sages hastily responded, "Neither it nor its reward!" (Berakhot 5b).

Noting that we violate the Sabbath to treat someone even on his deathbed, Rabbis Eliezer Waldenburg (*Tzitz Eliezer* 9:47) and Shmuel HaLevi Wosner (*Shevet HaLevi* 10:292) conclude that every breath is valuable and that one should never pray for death. They cite a remarkable talmudic statement deeming it meritorious for an otherwise righteous adulteress (*sota*) to endure a protracted, painful death (Sota 20a), proving that life always remains precious, especially given the spiritual implications of suffering. God will decide the fate of all, but we must do everything we can – prayer included – to extend life.

Several talmudic stories, however, seem to encourage the beseeching of God to put the dying out of their misery. The handmaiden of R. Yehuda HaNasi prayed for her ill master to decease, and her requests were ultimately answered over the fervent entreaties of his students, who declared a fast day for his recovery (Ketubbot 104a). R. Akiva, moreover, criticized his students for not visiting the sick enough, preventing themselves from "praying for their recovery or their death" (Nedarim 40a). As Rabbenu Nissim (fourteenth century, Spain) explained, the very least we can do for those who suffer with no chance of recovery is to pray for their death and an end to their suffering.

This position was adopted by such modern decisors as Rabbis Yeḥiel Michel Epstein (d. 1908) (AH YD 335:3), Moshe Feinstein (IM ḤM 2:74), and Shlomo Goren (*Torat HaRefua*, p. 58). The fact that we violate the Sabbath to save a life does not preclude our desiring a merciful death. One suggested prayer reads, "Please, God, in the power of Your great mercy, and in Your great benevolence, may it be Your will to remove so-and-so's soul from its prison in order to relieve him of his suffering, and may his soul return to the God who granted it to him" (EJME, p. 1062).

In a nuanced position, Tel Aviv Chief Rabbis Ḥayim David HaLevi (*Aseh Lekha Rav* 5:112) and Yisrael Meir Lau (*Torah SheBe'al Peh*, vol. 25) contend that caretaking relatives may not pray for death, as such entreaties might reflect a desire (conscious or otherwise) to relieve themselves of their burdensome responsibilities. Other decisors approve of seeking God's mercy in any form, but without explicitly praying for the patient's demise (*Be'er Moshe* 8:239, para. 4).

May God provide mercy and comfort to the terminally ill and their loved ones.

Chapter 14

Donating the Body to Science

Can one will his body to research or medical training?

The question of cadaver research balances different elements of Judaism's sanctification of human life. On the one hand, the Torah asserts that the human body represents the *tzelem Elokim* (the image of God) and therefore prohibits its physical desecration, even when willfully self-inflicted (Rashi, Deut. 21:23). Yet for the same reason, Judaism also deeply values medical research and all other attempts to preserve human life. This conflict goes so deep, in fact, that the opening of the Hebrew University medical school was delayed twenty-two years until the issue of anatomical dissection was resolved!

In antiquity, gentiles – and particularly Christians – eschewed anatomical research as immoral. While medieval doctors (as well as the artist Leonardo da Vinci) performed rare dissections, only in the seventeenth and eighteenth centuries did it become standard practice for medical training. The first decisor to address the issue, Rabbi Yaakov Emden (1697–1776, Germany), forbade this research because it violated the prohibition of benefiting from corpses (*She'elat Yaavetz* 1:41). Other rabbis ruled against it since it delayed burial (*halanat metim*) and desecrated the human body (*nivvul hamet*).

In theory, however, the obligation to save human life (*pikuaḥ nefesh*) overrides these (and almost all other) prohibitions. Rabbi Yeḥezkel Landau (eighteenth century, Prague) was asked about performing an autopsy on a patient who died after unsuccessful treatment, in order to learn for future cases (*Noda BiYehuda Tinyana* YD 210). He prohibited the dissection, contending that *pikuaḥ nefesh* trumps other commandments only when there are immediate lifesaving benefits; potential benefits are too remote or theoretical. He further worried that any leniency might lead to excessive and unjustified dissection of Jewish corpses by non-Jewish doctors. The majority of leading scholars – including Rabbis Moshe Sofer (*Ḥatam Sofer* YD 2:336), Abraham Isaac Kook (*Daat Kohen* 199), and Moshe Feinstein (IM YD 3:140) – adopted this position.

Rabbi Ben-Zion Uziel, the first Sephardic chief rabbi of Israel, contended that Rabbi Landau failed to recognize the immediate benefits of medical research (*Mishpetei Uziel* YD 1:28). There are always patients with illnesses similar to those of the deceased, and if doctors never pathologically examine corpses, these ailments will remain incurable. Rabbis Shlomo Goren (*Torat HaRefua*, p. 235) and Shaul Yisraeli (*Amud HaYemini* 1:17, 34) further argued that in a national context, *pikuaḥ nefesh* must be defined from a broader, long-term perspective. As such, they contended that Israel must establish medical schools with anatomical training to educate doctors in order to establish a functioning society. Nonetheless, they cautioned students to handle the corpses with utmost respect and meticulously bury all body parts following dissection.

A different basis for permitting the willing of one's body to medicine was advanced by Rabbi Yaakov Ettlinger. This nineteenth-century German authority affirmed the severity of desecrating a body, and forbade autopsies even when there was an immediate lifesaving benefit. He contended, however, that a person may waive (*moḥel*) all regulations aimed at preserving his dignity after death. One may choose how to forego this honor, as long as all body parts ultimately receive a proper burial (*Binyan Tziyon* 170).

Based on these sentiments, in 1947 Ashkenazic Chief Rabbi Isaac Herzog – backed by Rabbis Eliezer Waldenburg and Tzvi Pesaḥ Frank – allowed the Hebrew University medical school to perform anatomical studies, and further permitted a person to donate his body for medical training (EJME, p. 82). Like Rabbi Ettlinger, these decisors ruled that this right remained exclusively with the donor; the deceased's family or doctors could not donate the corpse on their own. Where the deceased did not will his body, however, but died from an illness with an unknown cure, they ruled that a special committee of rabbis should determine the propriety of performing an autopsy (*Tzitz Eliezer* 4:14).

Interestingly, these scholars buttressed their opinion with talmudic stories in which the sages examined the remains of death penalty victims to determine biological data with legal implications (Bekhorot 45a and Tosefta Nidda 4:17). Yet these cryptic stories do not present bona fide proof of this position.

Most Orthodox rabbis have forbidden people to will their bodies to science. Since earlier sages rejected many of the arguments for leniency, later decisors saw no reason to abandon these rulings. Throughout the twentieth century in Europe, America, and Israel, these scholars forcefully prohibited this practice, contending that particularly in our times, Jews must uphold the sanctity of the human body (EJME, p. 74). However, many decisors allow autopsies in cases of genetic diseases or violent crimes. One should consult a rabbinic authority in each case.

Chapter 15

Fertility Treatments

Is artificial insemination permitted?

Unlike their counterparts in some religions, most Jewish medical ethicists have generally favored assisted reproductive technologies, despite restricting their use. This essay will focus on artificial insemination (AI) with sperm from either the recipient's husband (AIH) or a donor (AID). As always, one should consult a doctor and rabbi to determine the proper approach in each case.

One immediate legal problem facing all reproductive treatments is the method of semen procurement necessary to test whether the infertility stems from the male contribution. Throughout the world, this semen is usually produced through some form of masturbation that induces ejaculation. However, the wasteful emission of seed (*hash'ḥatat zera*) is prohibited by Jewish law, as exemplified by the biblical episode of Er and Onan (Rashi, Gen. 38:7–10). (This is the origin of the term "onanism" for *coitus interruptus.*) Commentators dispute whether this prohibition falls within the general proscription of illicit sexual relations (MT *Hilkhot Issurei Biah* 21:18), represents an independent biblical interdiction (*Smak* 292), or was instituted by rabbinic decree (*Pnei Yehoshua* EH 2:42). In any case, kabbalistic sources emphasize the prohibition, leading a few decisors to ban fertility treatment entirely (*Divrei Malkiel* 4:107–108). Others permit testing for male infertility, although many contend that men shouldn't be tested until other possible sources of the problem have been examined (*Nishmat Avraham* EH 23:2).

In contrast, decisors such as Rabbis Chaim Ozer Grodzenski (*Aḥiezer* 3:24, para. 4) and Ovadia Yosef (*Yabia Omer* EH 2:1) asserted that seminal emission pursuant to procreation was not considered "wasteful." They based their position, in part, on rabbinic sources that allowed the spillage of seed for some overriding purpose, such as preventing a prohibited sexual relationship (*Sefer Ḥasidim* 176) or, significantly, testing for certain forms of sexual impotence that would impose severe marital restrictions (Yevamot 76a). Other scholars cited medieval precedents permitting the occasional, inevitable spilling of seed to prevent high-risk pregnancies (*Tosafot Rid* Yevamot 12b) or even for intimate pleasure (Rema, EH 25:2).

Following this approach, most decisors today permit AIH, either through the placement of the husband's sperm into his wife's reproductive tract or through in-vitro fertilization (IVF), in which the couple's sperm and egg are combined in an incubator, then transferred to the uterus. When possible, semen procurement with a medical condom is preferred (IM EH 3:14). Several decisors also strongly suggest supervision to prevent mix-ups in the laboratory, though most fertility labs are extremely cautious in handling specimens.

Frequently, however, the husband is infertile, giving rise to a heated debate over the propriety of using a donor's sperm (AID). Many decisors objected to AID for moral and legal reasons. Rabbi Immanuel Jakobovits, for example, decried the "mechanical" nature of artificial reproduction outside the marital framework, while Rabbi Yaakov Breisch deemed it an abominable act akin to the sexual depravities of ancient Canaan and Egypt (*Ḥelkat Yaakov* EH 12). Other authorities, like Rabbi Yoel Teitelbaum (*Divrei Yoel* EH 107–110), likened AID to adultery, with any children produced thereby being illegitimate (*mamzerim*). Furthermore, Jewish law recognizes only the natural paternity of the biological parent, thereby making the anonymous sperm donor the legal father. As such, some decisors prohibited AID lest the child stumble into an incestuous relationship (*Zekan Aharon* 2:97).

Other scholars, however, led by Rabbi Moshe Feinstein, forcefully rejected the equation of AID and adultery, contending that only sexual relations violate that severe prohibition (IM EH 1:71). As proof, these thinkers cited two rabbinic texts – one talmudic (Hagiga 15a) and the other medieval (*Taz* YD 195:7) – depicting how a woman accidentally became pregnant without sexual relations, yet the child was legitimate. In one case, the woman conceived by using bathwater in which a man had previously bathed, while in the other, she lay on soiled sheets. As Prof. Simcha Emanuel has documented, medieval Muslims and Christians also believed in this type of insemination, though many dismissed such tales as mythical.

While some decisors claimed that bizarre acts of unintentional insemination prove nothing, Rabbi Feinstein inferred from these passages that a child born of non-sexual insemination would not be illegitimate, because no illicit sexual relations occurred. Others added that there was nothing abominable about infertile couples bearing children in this manner, provided they were emotionally and psychologically prepared.

Nevertheless, Rabbi Feinstein shared concerns that the product of AID would unintentionally become involved in an incestuous relationship. He therefore argued that one should use only sperm from a non-Jewish donor, whose paternity is not recognized when his seed produces a Jewish child born to a Jewess. (Outside of Israel, Rabbi Feinstein argued, one can assume the donor is not Jewish, while in Israel, reproductive centers can ensure, upon request, that he is gentile.) Initially scorned by some scholars, Feinstein's position has become dominant within rabbinic circles, leading to the birth of countless Jewish babies.

Chapter 16

Egg Donations

What is the maternal status of donors?

As opposed to the male contribution to fertility treatments, which is clearly defined, there are several stages of reproductive activity for females – ovulation, conception, pregnancy, and birth – raising complex questions regarding maternity when two women contribute to the process. The legal and moral dilemmas regarding various fertility treatments and surrogacy arrangements have sparked an ongoing debate within both rabbinic circles and legislatures around the world.

Because of these complexities, Rabbi Eliezer Waldenburg opposed in-vitro fertilization (IVF) altogether, even when a husband donated the sperm and his wife contributed the egg and carried the baby. He objected to the "unnaturalness" of this process and further claimed that children born in this manner lack legal parents (*Tzitz Eliezer* 15:45). Most decisors disagreed with him, however. Rabbi Avigdor Nebenzahl, for one, argued against outright rejection of reproductive technology, especially when no outside donors are necessary and the couple faces physiological problems or concerns about genetic diseases (*Assia* 5). In such cases, Jewish law considers the genetic father and mother the legal parents.

Regarding more complex applications of reproductive technology, many suggested that we determine parentage using the paradigm of adoption, the classic context in which earlier generations theorized about paternity and maternity. While many Jewish sources praise adoption (Sanhedrin 19b), and the adoptive couple acquires certain rights and responsibilities, the biological mother and father remain the legal parents (EH 15:11).

This principle helps clarify the legal status of "natural surrogacy," a form of surrogate motherhood made famous by the 1986 "Baby M" case. In this arrangement, a husband's sperm is implanted in a host mother, who abdicates legal rights to the newborn and allows the wife to adopt him. As Rabbi Michael Broyde has noted, when the genetic mother not only provides the egg but also carries the baby, Jewish law recognizes her as the legal mother. (It also recognizes the paternal rights of the father, and his wife's right to become the adoptive mother.)

More complex scenarios involve one woman donating the egg that undergoes in-vitro fertilization, and another woman carrying the embryo. In "egg donation," the carrier is the sperm donor's wife, with the egg donor playing no continued role. In "gestational surrogacy," a third-party woman carries the embryo created from the sperm and egg of a couple (or possibly other donors). In these cases, one cannot simply determine the "natural mother," since two women play critical roles in biological development. Jewish law must establish whether such combinations are permissible and what factors determine maternity.

Several decisors, including Rabbi Shmuel HaLevi Wosner, prohibit both egg donation and gestational surrogacy, because they complicate lineage and lead to multiple health and moral concerns. Yet numerous scholars permit these methods when other fertility options have failed, though these authorities remain concerned with the social implications and demand strict regulation of the process.

Although many doctors prefer that the host mother have previously had successful pregnancies, most Jewish scholars insist that she be single, thereby avoiding additional questions regarding infidelity. Yet in a controversial case in 2006, Israeli Chief Rabbi Shlomo Amar allowed a married woman to volunteer to carry the child of a couple who had suffered several miscarriages and could not afford to hire an unmarried surrogate mother.

To determine the identity of the legal mother, numerous decisors have sought to delineate at what stage of development maternity is established. Based on a complex talmudic law affirming the fraternal relationship of twins born to a woman who converted to Judaism during pregnancy (Yevamot 97b), many authorities have concluded that maternity is established at parturition, i.e., the woman who gives birth to the child is his legal mother. Yet a growing number of decisors, including Rabbis Shlomo Goren and Ovadia Yosef, have contended that maternity is determined at the point of fertilization, i.e., the genetic mother is the legal mother. One consequence is whether the child in the talmudic case requires conversion, since his status as a Jew stems from the Jewishness of his legal mother. Some decisors maintain that the child has, for some purposes, two legal mothers, prohibiting him from marrying the children of either one.

This remains a complex area in which the law has not fully caught up with technology. Time will tell how our society ultimately resolves these dilemmas.

Chapter 17

Halakhic Infertility

What can I do if I ovulate before I'm allowed to immerse in the mikve?

This problem, colloquially known as "halakhic infertility," is so sensitive a topic that I hesitate to write about it. It represents conflicting religious values, with the emotional mitzva of procreation hindered by the observance of family purity laws. Moreover, each woman's body works differently, so to give an answer to any individual requires a lot of personal information that remains irrelevant when considering the situation of another woman. That said, friends convinced me that an overview of the topic would help clarify many issues and hopefully create greater awareness as to what is involved in considering these problems.

The Torah prohibits two types of women with uterine bleeding to be intimate with their husbands (Lev. 15). The first, a *nidda,* is one who menstruates during an expected period, and she must abstain from sexual contact for seven days starting from the *beginning* of the bleeding. The second type, a *zava,* is one who bleeds unexpectedly, and if she does so for three or more consecutive days, she must abstain from sexual activity for seven days *after* the bleeding ceases. Thus, according to biblical law, a menstruant would count only seven days from the beginning of her period, and if she has stopped bleeding, she could immerse in a *mikve* (ritual bath) and engage in sexual intercourse.

Yet already in talmudic times, this two-tiered system of *nidda* and *zava* created much confusion. Eventually Jewish women took it upon themselves to treat all bleeding – even a speck of blood – as a sign of becoming a *zava* (Nidda 61a). As such, *any* time a woman bleeds, she must count seven consecutive days in which she no longer sees blood, beginning with the night following the cessation of bleeding. This stringency, known as the *Ḥumra DeRebbi Zeira,* was subsequently deemed a "*halakha pesuka,*" a bona fide law (Berakhot 31a), with Nahmanides (thirteenth century, Spain) declaring that one may not waive it (*Hilkhot Nidda* 1:19).

Additional medieval rulings, based on talmudic sentiments, assert that a woman may not begin counting the "seven clean days" until several days have passed since the onset of bleeding. (Ashkenazic decisors require five days, while many Sephardic figures require only four.) While the initial concern related to the possibility of post-coital emissions, Rabbi Moshe Isserles and his predecessors mandated this waiting period for all women, even if they did not engage in sexual relations before seeing blood (YD 196:11). (While this issue is irrelevant for many menstruating women, for whom it takes at least four to five days to stop bleeding, there might be room for dispensation in cases where women unexpectedly stain briefly in the middle of their cycle and must then wait eleven to twelve days before immersing again.)

With this legal background, we can now understand "halakhic infertility." Ovulation occurs fourteen days before the onset of menstruation. For many couples, this timing works out particularly well, as the wife ovulates around the time she goes to the *mikve.* Yet if a woman has a particularly short cycle, her ovulation will occur while contact with her husband is still prohibited. Extra-long menstruation or frequent mid-cycle staining can also cause this problem. One should always consult a halakhic authority to ensure that the spotting or staining actually renders her a *nidda,* since self-imposed stringencies have led to much unnecessary suffering.

In cases of confirmed halakhic infertility, several solutions might alleviate the problem. As noted, under some circumstances one need not wait four to five days before beginning to count seven clean days, especially if the couple abstained from sexual relations before the bleeding began (*Minḥat Shlomo* 2:72). This waiver, however, is not helpful for women who menstruate for several days. Many decisors also permit artificial insemination (using the husband's sperm) while the woman is still a *nidda* (IM EH 2:18). The solution most frequently advised today is to use hormonal treatments to delay ovulation. Yet this method does not always work, especially for women who react poorly to the medication.

When these halakhic alternatives or medical interventions prove ineffective, some have suggested other legal solutions (*Galya Masekhta* 10:4). Since each case requires individual attention, I highly recommend consulting with the rabbis at Machon Puah (puahonline.org) or the *yoatzot halakha* of Nishmat (www.yoatzot.org).

Chapter 18

Pet Neutering

Is there a halakhically permissible way?

In recent years, both health officials and animal rights groups have urged pet owners to neuter their pets. They note that excessive reproduction and overpopulation can endanger the animal, the species, and the public. These campaigns, however, potentially conflict with the spirit, and possibly the letter, of Jewish law, which prohibits sterilizing any creature.

Judaism may be the only religion that has consistently prohibited castration. In ancient cultures, castrations were performed on royal servants (eunuchs), to preserve sweet young voices, to punish criminals, and for religious purposes, such as to prevent sexual perversion. Animals were also sterilized to improve agricultural productivity and to control the supply of prized species for export.

The Torah prohibits the sacrificial use of animals whose "testicles are bruised, crushed, torn, or cut," and forbids any such mutilation of a person's sexual organs (Lev. 22:24). The sages understood this verse to prohibit sterilization of all males, human and animal (Shabbat 110b). According to the medieval commentators, castration defies the divine blessing to "be fruitful and multiply" and ultimately destroys God's creation (*Ḥinukh* 291). As with almost all mitzvot, however, sterilization becomes permissible when done for urgent therapeutic needs.

A related commandment severely limits the kind of spouse a male may have if his genitals are damaged (Deut. 23:2). A person with this impairment may also not serve in the Temple (Lev. 21:20). One medieval writer speculates that the marital restrictions were intended to combat ancient social incentives to become a eunuch, which might explain why these limitations apply only to injured males rather than those born defective (*Ḥinukh* 559). Said restrictions are independent of the ban on sterilization, however, and therefore indispensable medical treatment that causes infertility (as do some prostate surgeries) does not impact the patient's ability to marry (*Tzitz Eliezer* 10:25:24).

Given the prohibition of sterilization, rabbis uniformly prohibit sex-change surgery, although they debate whether, ex post facto, halakha recognizes a change in sexual identity (*Tzitz Eliezer* 10:25, para. 26). What about male fertility treatments that include incisions, as do testicular biopsies, which were once harmful but today are part of the diagnostic process? Most scholars allow such procedures, since they help cure infertility (IM EH 2:3).

While the biblical commandment remains clear for men, scholars discuss whether it applies to women. Some rabbis say it does, but normative halakha deems the removal of female reproductive organs a lesser, rabbinic violation (EH 5:11). One significant decisor even states that the prohibition for women stems only from the larger proscription of causing a person pain (*Taz* EH 5:6). As such, many authorities permit hysterectomies and tubal ligation for therapeutic purposes as well as to prevent dangerous or unusually painful childbirth (*Baḥ* EH 5), although when possible, non-surgical forms of contraception are preferable (IM EH 4:34).

Another significant debate pertains to whether sterilization is prohibited by the Noahide laws (Sanhedrin 56b). While some scholars believe that gentiles are also prohibited, many decisors assert that non-Jews have the prerogative to perform these procedures (AH EH 5:26). (This question has great implications for the Jewish attitude toward world population control, advocated by many international bodies, even as it might contravene the spirit of the prohibition.) Nonetheless, Jewish urologists or veterinarians may not perform non-therapeutic sterilization for non-Jews and animals. Moreover, as with other prohibitions, a Jew may not ask a non-Jew to sterilize him (*amira le'akum*), even in a subtle or indirect manner (EH 5:14), although using non-Jewish doctors may be preferable when the procedure is medically required.

To prevent severe financial loss caused by the mating of animals used for commercial purposes, some nineteenth-century scholars allowed owners to sell their livestock to gentiles, who would in turn arrange for a second non-Jew to neuter the creatures (*HaElef Lekha Shlomo* EH 23). Several contemporary decisors, however, do not approve of this leniency for neutering individual pets, and recommend buying or adopting already neutered animals instead, or using hormonal treatments or contraceptives to limit fertility (*BeMareh HaBazak* 6:77).

Given the lighter strictures regarding females, as well as the claim of significant health benefits for pets, Rabbi Shlomo Aviner allows Jewish veterinarians to spay female animals (*She'elat Shlomo* vol. 6), while Rabbi Shmuel HaLevi Wosner (*Shevet HaLevi* 6:204) more hesitantly tolerates non-Jews performing the procedure. During his term in office, Sephardic Chief Rabbi Shlomo Amar proclaimed that due to the hazards posed by wild and stray animals, one may ask a non-Jewish veterinarian to neuter pets of both genders. I subsequently read that some Israeli animal-rights organizations are matching religious pet owners with non-Jewish veterinarians, although it remains to be seen whether this leniency will take root.

Chapter 19

Medical Care for Non-Jews on Shabbat

May Jews save the lives of gentiles on Shabbat?

From the outset, let me state very clearly: Jewish law obligates Jews to save the lives of all humans, Jews and gentiles alike, even if doing so entails violating the Sabbath. This is the conclusion of all contemporary decisors, despite occasional confusing reports of a few scholars contending otherwise. While this conclusion is undisputed, scholars disagree regarding the legal argumentation behind it.

While Judaism greatly promotes the value of life, it is not always the supreme value. God, the Bible tells us, took the Jews out of Egypt so they could serve Him. This service requires giving one's life rather than committing idolatry as well as other the unconscionable transgressions of murder and illicit relations. Given the importance of Sabbath observance, a biblical reader might think this value also trumps the saving of life. Indeed, in the time of the Hasmoneans, some Jews refused to go to battle on the Sabbath, leading to their quick decimation.

To negate this sentiment, the Talmud declares that the preservation of life supersedes Sabbath observance (*pikuaḥ nefesh doḥeh Shabbat*). God commands us to "Guard My laws and statutes ... and live by them" (Lev. 18:5), not to die by them. Consequently, even in cases of *possible* danger to life, one violates the Sabbath to avert this danger (Yoma 85a–b). The Sabbath remains sacrosanct, however, and if it does not compromise the speed or efficacy of lifesaving efforts, one should minimize its desecration.

A number of talmudic texts permit Shabbat desecration only to save Jews (Yoma 83a). Some have criticized this view as falling short of the ethical standards found in the Hippocratic oath. Others have notoriously accused Jews of believing gentile blood is less red than Jewish blood. One infamous incident occurred in 1965 when an anti-religious Israeli journalist, Yisrael Shaḥak, allegedly witnessed an Orthodox Jew refusing to use his phone on Shabbat to help save a non-Jew. Shaḥak had no proof of this incident, and many dismissed his tale as a modern-day blood libel. Be that as it may, Chief Rabbi Isser Unterman clarified that Shaḥak's claim utterly distorted Jewish law, which mandates saving the lives of all humans, even if one must desecrate the Sabbath to do so.

While the Talmud never provides a definitive rationale for its distinction between Jews and gentiles, one passage implies that Jews needed a dispensation to save their own, while non-Jews could supply their own lifesavers without resorting to Jews violating the Sabbath (Avoda Zara 26b). But what about emergencies in which a gentile can be saved only by a Jew? The Talmud, followed by medieval sages, contended that for the sake of preventing gentile enmity, Jews may violate certain prohibitions. This dispensation was used by many scholars to justify transgressing the Sabbath in order to save the lives of gentiles.

Rabbinic scholars dispute whether this concern justifies violating a biblical prohibition or only a rabbinic edict (MB 330:8). Be that as it may, Rabbi Moshe Sofer noted that failure to save non-Jews could lead not only to enmity, but to gentiles refusing to treat Jews, or even to pogroms (*Ḥatam Sofer* YD 2:131). As such, Jews must save the lives of all humans, even if doing so entails violating biblical prohibitions on the Sabbath, because a lack of reciprocity endangers the Jewish community. This obligation remains in force even when one might think no one will notice the shirking of lifesaving responsibilities (IM OḤ 4:79).

Some scholars, including Rabbi Yeḥiel Yaakov Weinberg, felt that this logic stemmed from overly particularistic and pragmatic considerations (*Torah U-Madda Journal* 7). During the Shaḥak affair, Rabbi Unterman contended that concerns for enmity reflected more fundamental beliefs in peaceful relations (*darkhei shalom*). While this position was shared by Rabbis Ḥayim David HaLevi and Immanuel Jakobovits (*Tradition* 8:2), others derided it as apologetics.

Rabbis Eliezer Melamed and Nachum Rabinovitch (*Melumdei Milḥama* 43) have noted that according to Nahmanides (*Hashmatot LeSefer HaMitzvot, Aseh* 16) and others, Jewish law mandates Sabbath desecration to save a *ger toshav*, a gentile who follows the seven Noahide laws. Other scholars, moreover, have pointed to the thirteenth-century commentary of Rabbi Menaḥem HaMeiri, who broadly contended that the talmudic failure to apply the dispensation to save the lives of gentiles applied only in ancient societies in which the non-Jewish majority regularly abused Jews (*Beit HaBeḥira* Avoda Zara 26a). Yet in ethical cultures, no lifesaving distinction is made between Jew and gentile. For all these reasons, contemporary Jewish law definitively mandates the treatment on Shabbat of Jew and gentile alike. In the words of Rabbi Rabinovitch, "Compassion and mercy for all men are the mark of the Jew, just as they are of God" (*Tradition* 8:3).

Chapter 20

Vaccinations

Does Jewish law mandate preventative vaccines?

Beginning in February 2013, health officials found strains of the polio virus in many parts of Israel and identified several dozen carriers. That August, to prevent an outbreak, Israel launched a nationwide campaign to vaccinate all children under age nine. The campaign raised the question of whether halakha mandates participation in this undertaking, even to the point of forcing parents to inoculate their children.

This question touches on the obligation to administer preventative medicine. The Torah promises that God will protect those who observe the commandments (Ex. 15:26). Yet Jewish sources have long recognized that no one can be sure he merits such divine providence, nor should one rely on miracles (*Ḥinukh* 546). The Torah commands, "Be careful and watch yourselves" (Deut. 4:9), which is understood as a directive to avoid danger (Berakhot 32b). Jewish law requires us to remove hazardous objects from our environs, ranging from shoddy ladders to dangerous dogs to unguarded weapons (ḤM 427:8). The spirit of these norms derives from the biblical obligation to place a guard railing around one's roof (Deut. 22:8). Both Maimonides (MT *Hilkhot Rotze'aḥ* 11:5–6) and Rabbi Joseph Karo (YD 116) prohibit various dangerous activities, with Rabbi Moshe Isserles adding that "one should avoid all things that endanger oneself, as we treat physical dangers more stringently than ritual prohibitions" (YD 116:5).

How proactively must a person protect himself? Generally, Jewish law asserts that one may undertake risks that most people accept with equanimity (Shabbat 129b). We ski, drive, and undergo elective surgery, for example, despite the risks. Yet vaccinations are intended to protect not only oneself but the entire community, nation, or even world. Anyone familiar with the history of smallpox or rubella knows the horrors they caused. The Torah commands us not to stand idly over someone else's blood (Lev. 19:16), thereby imposing a responsibility to care for others.

In the late eighteenth century, doctors attempted to prevent the continued onslaught of smallpox by inoculating healthy people with a low grade of fluid taken from stricken patients. The hope was that a mild, controlled dose would allow the body to protect itself from a wild, spontaneous outbreak, even as this preventive measure imposed a risky level of exposure. As David Ruderman has documented, Rabbi Avraham Nansich, himself mourning the death of two children, published a pamphlet in 1785 urging Jews to participate in this initiative. While one might not normally permit such precarious inoculations, he argued that all humans are threatened by a deadly outbreak, and therefore everyone must accept the risks of inoculation. Edward Jenner's invention of a safer smallpox vaccine at the turn of the nineteenth century was celebrated by scholars like Rabbis Israel Lifshitz (*Tiferet Yisrael – Boaz,* Yoma 8:3) and Mordekhai Benet, who strenuously advocated vaccination and noted that this option was far superior to the solution mentioned in earlier halakhic literature: leave town. When vaccinations were locally available only for a limited time, many decisors allowed Jews to desecrate Shabbat in order to be inoculated (*Teshuva MeAhava* 1:134–35).

Vaccinations are undoubtedly one of the outstanding innovations of the modern era and have saved countless lives. This blessing sometimes leads to complacency as people become insulated from mass outbreaks. Some fear the risks associated with vaccines. In effect if not in intent, they rely upon the "herd immunity" created when most people are immunized, thereby reducing the chance of contagion. Health officials have forcefully countered that vaccines present minimal risks (especially relative to other health care procedures) and that many of the sensationalistic claims linking vaccines to autism and other terrible side effects have been scientifically refuted. Furthermore, we must reserve herd immunity for those whose weak immune systems preclude vaccination. Nonetheless, people around the world continue to avoid vaccinations, including ultra-Orthodox elements in America, which recently suffered tragic outbreaks of mumps and measles.

As Rabbi Asher Bush has noted, Rabbi Yosef Shalom Elyashiv argued that given the contemporary medical consensus in support of universal vaccination, parents must vaccinate their children, and schools or camps may exclude those who have not been inoculated. Numerous Jewish decisors, including Rabbi Yehoshua Neuwirth, have asserted that in the absence of an outbreak or national legal mandate, schools cannot demand vaccination, though they should strongly encourage it (*Nishmat Avraham* ḤM 427:3). Likewise, many countries allow conscientious objectors to avoid vaccinations.

All scholars agree that preventing the return of polio is a national mission. We must support the call of Israel's chief rabbis, who have declared that Jewish law mandates that all children be vaccinated in accordance with Health Ministry regulations.

Section II

Technology

Chapter 21

Circumcision and *Metzitza BaPeh*

What is the controversy behind this practice?

Circumcision has suffered from many controversies over the centuries. Christianity abolished it, claiming that God desires only "circumcision of the heart," embodied by faith. Early Reform Judaism vilified it as unaesthetic and barbaric, ranking it among the primitive ceremonies of the ancient Near East. Nonetheless, the ritual has retained its hold on Jewish culture, enjoying nearly universal practice among observant and non-observant Jews alike.

The final element of the procedure, known as *metzitza* (lit. suctioning), remains disputed. Historically, the circumcision rite entails three stages: the primary excision (*ḥitukh*), which removes the foreskin; the *peria* (uncovering), in which the *mohel* (ritual surgeon) peels back a thin membrane to fully expose the corona; and *metzitza*, the act of drawing the blood from the wound. Following these stages, the *mohel* dresses the wound, allowing for full recovery.

Reflecting ancient medical concerns over inflammation and swelling, the sages demanded that the *mohel* draw blood to prevent the excesses from decaying into pus. Based on this medical assessment, the rabbis allowed *metzitza* to be performed on the Sabbath, and discredited any *mohel* who omitted the procedure (Shabbat 133b).

While the Talmud never specifies how to remove the blood, historical evidence indicates that *mohelim* orally suctioned the wound.

This practice is taken for granted in many early medieval sources (*Maḥzor Vitry* 505), with authorities demanding that the *mohel* rinse off any remnants of blood before reciting the post-ritual blessings (YD 265). Kabbalistic sources further emphasized the mystical significance of performing *metzitza* orally (*Tikkunei Zohar* 18).

While the first objection regarding the hygiene of oral *metziza* occurred in the beginning of the nineteenth century, the historically most significant medical objection was raised in Vienna in 1837, following a series of fatalities of newborn babies. At the behest of local doctors, Vienna's chief rabbi, Elazar Horowitz, received permission from the eminent Hungarian decisor Rabbi Moshe Sofer to soak up the blood with gauze sponges instead of suctioning (*Yad Eliezer* 55). While a few later authorities challenged the authenticity of this ruling, their skepticism seems to be unfounded. Sofer's permissive ruling was subsequently affirmed by Rabbi Tzvi Hirsch Chajes and other scholars (*Shu"t Maharatz Chajes* 60).

Sofer's and Chajes' argument was quite simple: Since the Talmud never specifies how to perform *metzitza*, there is no reason an alternative method cannot accomplish the same task, especially in the face of health hazards. Moreover, this alternative seems just as innocuous as another well-accepted "innovation" in the circumcision rite, in which the stages of excision and uncovering came to be performed simultaneously, as opposed to consecutively.

In the 1840s, the nascent Reform movement launched a blistering attack on circumcision, with *metzitza* serving as a particularly vulnerable target. One extreme and polemical response was issued by Rabbi Moshe Schick (*Shu"t Maharam Schick* YD 244). He contended that beyond its therapeutic purpose, *metzitza* represented an integral part of the circumcision ritual, which ultimately derived from ancient oral traditions originating at Sinai (*halakha leMoshe miSinai*). In addition, as the focus of Reform attacks, *metzitza* could not be waived under any circumstances (*Shu"t Maharam Schick* OḤ 152). Similarly vociferous declarations were made throughout the nineteenth and early twentieth centuries by many leading scholars. This conservative argumentation stymied the claim that either nature or scientific knowledge had changed since talmudic times, a historically well-trodden position (documented in the following essays) that obviates the need for preserving many procedures based on outdated medicine (*Tiferet Yisrael – Boaz,* Shabbat 19:1).

In 1885, the Frankfurt Jewish community, led by Rabbi Samson Raphael Hirsch, began using a glass pipette or tube to facilitate oral *metzitza,* preventing direct contact with the mouth. This technique was endorsed by such prominent Lithuanian sages as Rabbis Yitzḥak E. Spektor and Chaim Soloveitchik, and became the preferred method in many communities around the world (*Har Tzvi* YD 214), especially with increased understanding of the science of germs and the specter of AIDS and other diseases.

This debate flared up most recently in 2004, when a group of Orthodox doctors alleged in a *Pediatrics* article that a few babies had contracted herpes after oral *metzitza* was performed at their circumcisions. While some Orthodox writers fiercely defended the practice, with a few disputing the medical basis for these claims, I believe the safer alternatives (e.g., pipettes) are definitively warranted, an approach endorsed by the Rabbinical Council of America and many leading decisors.

Chapter 22

Paternity and DNA Testing

Does halakha recognize the results?

On a recent trip to America, I was greeted outside the airport by the following advertisement: "Who's the Father? Call 1-800-DNA-Test."

Leaving aside the moral and societal problems reflected by the ad, the propriety of employing blood or DNA tests to determine paternity raises complex legal issues. Jewish scholars maintain the legal system's integrity by balancing traditional sources, scientific advances, and ethical imperatives to help prevent *mamzerim* (illegitimate children, whose marital opportunities are severely limited) and *agunot* (abandoned spouses unable to marry because they cannot locate their missing partner).

When paternal blood testing originated in the early twentieth century, courts deemed ABO tests sufficient to disprove paternity (negative identification), but not to prove it. That is to say, the tests could prove that *x* is not the father of *y*, but not that *x* is the father of *y*. In trying to resolve custody, inheritance, and other disputes, jurists debated whether courts could order paternity tests, and whether failure to cooperate authorized legal bodies to infer appropriate conclusions.

The scientific premise of this test – that blood type is determined by both parents – might conflict with a talmudic statement that one's mother provides her child with blood: "There are three partners in creating a human: God, the father, and the mother.... The mother supplies the red substance from which his skin, flesh, hair, blood, and pupils are formed..." (Nidda 31a). While this passage appears, as Rabbi Shlomo Zalman Auerbach noted, to be a metaphysical statement, it was employed in medieval judicial literature regarding medical matters (YD 263). This literature also cites a case in which Saadia Gaon exhumed a man's corpse and tested it with various claimants' blood to determine his rightful heir (*Sefer Ḥasidim* 232).

In the earliest halakhic decision, Israeli Sephardic Chief Rabbi Ben-Zion Uziel (d. 1953) rejected the use of blood tests because their scientific assumptions conflicted with the talmudic passage above (*Shaarei Uziel* 2:40:18). This position was supported by Rabbis Yehoshua Ehrenberg (*Devar Yehoshua* 3 EH 5) and Eliezer Waldenburg (*Tzitz Eliezer* 13:104), who cited this as a case where halakhic principles should be upheld despite contrary (and sometimes transient) scientific claims.

This viewpoint was rejected by Rabbis Ḥayim Regensburg (*Mishmeret HaḤayim* 37) and Ovadia Hedaya (*Yaskil Avdi* EH 5:13), who cited a significant strain of classic Jewish thought that dismissed talmudic medicine as antiquated science. As Prof. Dov Frimer has documented, Ashkenazic Chief Rabbi Isaac Herzog (d. 1959) was particularly adamant on this matter, accusing fellow scholars of "burying their head in the sand like ostriches" while scientific knowledge advances.

Rabbi Chaim Jachter, however, has noted that many decisors objected to paternity tests because they can open up a Pandora's box of legal problems. For example, if a divorcing husband, trying to avoid paying child support, proves that the child in question was actually born of his wife's adultery, he also turns the child into a *mamzer*, causing a tragic legal situation that the sages attempted to avoid. Jewish law recognizes a strong legal assumption that women are faithful to their husbands, even to the point where a child born twelve months after a woman's husband travels overseas is still presumed to be his (EH 4:14). Some have further cited this factor as a reason jurists never adopted Saadia Gaon's bone/blood test (Rashash, Bava Batra 58a). On the other hand, particularly since paternity tests have become more accurate through the development of DNA testing, this assumption might be overridden by scientifically proven evidence.

One attempt to resolve this conundrum was offered by Rabbi Shlomo Dichovsky, who argued that DNA testing cannot prove a child a *mamzer*, but it can create enough doubt to prevent him from receiving an inheritance or child support (*Assia* 5). Rabbi Shmuel HaLevi Wosner has also distinguished between the admissibility of DNA evidence in different areas of law, stating that it remains insufficient to convict criminals or create *mamzerim*, but it can be used in inheritance cases when there are no competing claims, and in certain cases of *agunot* (*Tchumin* 21). While some decisors, including Rabbi Avraham Shapira, rejected all DNA evidence, Rabbi Auerbach allowed its use to identify babies mixed up in a hospital, and further asserted that it could be used for paternity testing if the science backing this procedure becomes universally accepted (*Nishmat Avraham* EH 4:35).

Following this assertion, Rabbi Zalman Neḥemia Goldberg and the Rabbinical Council of America employed DNA (and other) evidence to prevent spouses of 9/11 victims from becoming *agunot*. While some authorities still ignore DNA evidence in order to prevent *mamzerim*, others believe that when confronted with incontrovertible scientific data, Jewish law must recognize the truth, whichever way it cuts.

Chapter 23

Spontaneous Generation

May one kill lice on Shabbat?

Treating hair infested with lice is no fun, yet parents must promptly and thoroughly disinfect their children (even if this includes school absence!) and homes to prevent further infestation.

Matters become more complex on Shabbat, when it is biblically prohibited to kill any creature, unless it poses an acute health risk. Lice might be an exception to the rule, however, and presents a fascinating illustration of the tension between Jewish law and contemporary science.

The sages asserted that one may kill lice on Shabbat (Shabbat 107b), since they "do not reproduce" but instead generate spontaneously from sweat (MB 316:38). Such was the widespread ancient belief, articulated by Aristotle and others, that some forms of life do not emerge from seeds, eggs, or parents. Belief in spontaneous generation remained prevalent until Louis Pasteur debunked the theory in 1859 (though skeptics had questioned it for two centuries beforehand).

The sages maintained that the prohibition of killing on Shabbat applies only to creatures that reproduce sexually. The rabbis similarly exempted organisms that reproduce asexually from the biblical proscription of consuming insects (Lev. 11:10–11), and therefore permitted the consumption of worms found within the flesh of fish or fruit, which they believed were generated there (YD 84:16).

With regard to non-legal matters, many scholars, such as Maimonides' son, Rabbi Avraham (d. 1237), have written that despite our reverence for the talmudic sages, their statements regarding medicine, astronomy, and other sciences remain entirely non-authoritative (*Maamar al Aggadot Ḥazal*). What about when faulty scientific assumptions were the basis for legal declarations? No consensus has emerged with regard to the status of these laws, with acrimonious debates occasionally dividing the scholarly world.

This controversy exploded in 2010 over the discovery of the Anisakis worm in the flesh of many popular kosher fish, including wild salmon, flounder, sardines, and herring. These worms are parasites whose eggs travel through the aquatic food chain until they ultimately emerge in the organs and flesh of a large host fish.

Since the worms also appear in the cavity of the fish (not just in the flesh), and their origins are well-documented, contemporary decisors like Rabbis Yosef Shalom Elyashiv and Shmuel HaLevi Wosner (*Shevet HaLevi* 4:83) assumed that these worms are not identical with the permissible creatures mentioned in the Talmud. As such, followers of these decisors have produced lists of commonly contaminated fish to carefully inspect or avoid. This approach, in practice, accepts contemporary scientific analysis, while avoiding any claim that the sages held errant scientific beliefs. Rabbi Elyashiv reportedly took a similar stand on lice, prohibiting their killing on Shabbat (*Shevet HaKehati* 3:126).

Others, including Rabbi Yisrael Belsky of OU Kashrut, have defended the continued consumption of these fish, citing numerous historical sources (*Imrei Yosher* 2:11) indicating that decisors have been aware of such worms, yet upheld the talmudic rule that insects found within the flesh do not affect kashrut (*Shulḥan Gavoa* YD 84:51). Nothing has changed, asserts Rabbi Belsky, and there is no reason to depart from long-standing practice.

Of course, this approach does not address the fact that the entire dispensation for worms found in the flesh of fish was based on a now-debunked scientific theory. Historically, a few rabbinic figures denied the claims of contemporary science in order to defend talmudic law. This position was criticized by Rabbi Yitzḥak Lampronti (Italy, d. 1756), who asserted that the sages were limited by the knowledge of their times, and that failure to correct the law in accordance with current scientific knowledge would cause people to desecrate the Sabbath by killing lice (*Paḥad Yitzḥak,* s.v. *tzeida*). While Rabbi Yosef Kapaḥ adopted this approach, Rabbi Eliyahu Dessler countered that the unalterable talmudic law was based on ancient traditions and not solely on scientific assumptions. He and Rabbi J. David Bleich (*Tradition* 38:4) have further suggested that the sages based their assessment on the fact that the sexual reproduction of lice is unobservable, and that contemporary findings do not alter that legal criterion.

Rabbi Natan Slifkin (*Sacred Monsters*) recently advocated a different approach, found in the writings of Rabbis Moshe Glasner (*Dor Revi'i*, introduction) and Isaac Herzog (*Heikhal Yitzḥak* OḤ 29). These figures acknowledged that contemporary science was correct and that the sages erroneously believed in spontaneous generation, but they asserted that talmudic law had become canonized and therefore should not be altered. Thus the dispensation to kill lice remains authoritative, though its scientific basis no longer holds water.

Even if one adopts a lenient position regarding the killing of lice, other prohibitions – such as plucking or wringing out hair – might preclude the intensive treatment necessary to rid oneself of lice infestation on Shabbat, and one should consult his rabbi for further guidance.

Chapter 24

Microphones and Hearing Aids on Shabbat

Why is one prohibited while the other is permitted?

The permissibility of using microphones during synagogue Sabbath services generated major disputes within and between the Orthodox and Conservative movements. While this debate has partially abated, its larger implications, both for hearing aids and for the halakhic process as a whole, remain poignantly relevant.

A microphone operates by converting sound waves into electric signals. In earlier generations, some scholars raised concerns that microphones heat metal and cause sparks, thereby violating the prohibition of lighting a fire on Shabbat (*Minḥat Yitzḥak* 3:38). These concerns, at times based on misinformation, might have applied to old amplifiers like the radio tube, but have no bearing on contemporary systems. Another question involves panels that light up to indicate volume and create an entertaining sound-and-light effect. While rabbinic restrictions might forbid LCD or LED displays, one can easily purchase microphones without such panels. As such, the use of microphones relates directly to the permissibility of creating or increasing electric currents on Shabbat.

The status of electricity was one of the twentieth century's great halakhic quandaries. On the one hand, electric power, which revolutionized modern culture, clearly facilitates creative activity. Nonetheless, it remains difficult to define this action as any of the activities categorically prohibited on the Sabbath (*melakhot*). One prominent scholar,

Rabbi Yitzḥak Shmelkes (*Beit Yitzḥak* YD 2:31, addendum), contended that creating an electric current violates the talmudic prohibition of producing new entities (*molid*), such as a scent in one's clothing (Beitza 23a). Rabbi Avraham Karelitz alternatively asserted that the completion of a live circuit violates the Sabbath proscription of building (*boneh*), since it transforms something completely useless into a functioning wire, much like completing a wall (*Ḥazon Ish* OḤ 50:9). Others suggested a third potential prohibition, *makkeh bapatish* (lit. "the final hammer blow"), the biblical ban on completing any item in a way that renders it beneficial (*Heikhal Yitzḥak* OḤ 43).

Rabbinic consensus deems these theories legitimate yet not entirely compelling (*Encyclopedia Talmudit* 18:163–74). Their most strident critic was the eminent decisor Rabbi Shlomo Zalman Auerbach (b. 1910), who researched and published on this topic from 1935 until his passing in 1995. Among other points, Rabbi Auerbach claimed that none of the aforementioned prohibitions apply to activities regularly done and undone throughout the day, such as opening circuits (*Minḥat Shlomo* 1:11). Nonetheless, he himself adopted the legal consensus that opening or closing electric circuits – even without the involvement of light – remains rabbinically prohibited for one reason or another.

This entire discussion, however, seemingly applies only to turning a microphone on or off. Speaking into a microphone activated before Shabbat, or by a timer, would only increase or decrease the existing current. While Rabbi Moshe Feinstein (IM OḤ 4:84) believed that increasing a current was prohibited, most scholars disagreed (*Minḥat Shlomo* 1:9). Possibly based on this understanding, several mid-twentieth-century American synagogues, Orthodox and Conservative alike, used microphones on Shabbat (*Tradition* 14:3).

Most Orthodox decisors, however, believe microphones violate other Sabbath restrictions, unrelated to electricity. The major concern stems from a rabbinic decree forbidding activities that cause excessive noise (*hashmaat kol*), even if initiated before Shabbat (Shabbat 18a). These actions were prohibited either because they denigrate the spirit of the day, or because they lead to the wrong impression that something forbidden was done (OḤ 252:5). Lesser concerns include the fear that people may fix a broken amplifier (*Tzitz Eliezer* 4:26).

While hearing aids amplify in a manner similar to microphones, they do not create excessive noise, and they operate quite smoothly. As such, it remains permissible to wear and speak directly into them on Shabbat, especially to preserve the safety and dignity of the hearing-impaired (SSK 34:28).

Over time, the overwhelming majority of Orthodox synagogues banned microphones on the Sabbath, distinguishing themselves from the Conservative movement, whose leaders frequently adopted a more lenient position regarding all electric appliances. However, one prominent contemporary Orthodox rabbi, Yisrael Rozen, has argued that interdenominational polemics led to excessive stringency, with potential problems surmountable through clearly labeled, automated condenser microphone systems installed with precautionary switches (*Tchumin* 15). Supported by the permissive rulings of Rabbis Shaul Yisraeli and Ḥayim David HaLevi, and following a similar mechanism previously advocated by Israeli Chief Rabbi Isser Unterman (*Shevet MiYehuda* 2, p. 57), the Zomet Institute continues to provide such amplification systems for synagogues, highlighting the complex interaction between technology, Shabbat, and denominational divides.

Chapter 25

Shabbat Elevators

Why the continued controversy over their use?

Although fairly widely used in Israel and around the world, Shabbat elevators continue to engender great controversy. A recent prominent example was the 2009 ban promulgated in the name of four prominent *ḥaredi* leaders, including Rabbi Yosef Shalom Elyashiv, just as tourists flooded Israeli hotels for Sukkot, which led to international media attention and mass confusion. Nothing had changed in elevator technology to warrant a new controversy, and it remains unclear what generated that pronouncement. The larger issues regarding elevators on Shabbat, however, are worthy of review.

A person operating elevators violates Shabbat by generating electricity and activating the buttons and floor lights. While stairs represent the easiest (and healthiest) alternative, this remains unfeasible for the young or infirm, or in high-rises. This problem has been addressed by either asking non-Jews to operate the elevator or programming it to run automatically.

Seeking gentile assistance is legally problematic. Generally speaking, one may not request that a non-Jew perform any actions prohibited for Jews (*amira le'akum*), even if an arrangement is made before the Sabbath. While one midrash derives this proscription from the Torah itself (*Mekhilta Bo* 9), most halakhists believe the sages enacted it to preserve the spirit of the day, to prevent the denigration of Shabbat restrictions, or to forbid objectionable behavior by one's representative. Certain dispensations, however, were afforded in cases of need, such as to care for the sick or elderly (OḤ 328:17). The sages further prohibited benefiting from gentile activity performed for the sake of a Jew, even if the non-Jew acted on his own behest. Yet when a non-Jew acts for himself (by turning on the lights upon entering a dark room, for example), a Jew may benefit (OḤ 276:1).

Decisors remain divided as to whether one may ask a non-Jew to operate an elevator so as to allow residents of a tall building to attend synagogue services and Shabbat meals. The Talmud permits asking a gentile to violate rabbinic prohibitions in order to facilitate circumcisions on Shabbat (Eiruvin 67b). While some commentators limited this leniency to circumcisions alone, Maimonides and Rabbi Joseph Karo employed it across the board (OḤ 307:5). One decisor even allowed non-Jews to transgress biblical prohibitions, a position cited by Rabbi Moshe Isserles. Some entirely dismiss this opinion (MB 276:24), thereby precluding reliance on it in our case (SSK 30:54). Rabbi Joseph B. Soloveitchik (d. 1993), however, reportedly permitted Manhattan apartment dwellers to use this dispensation (*Mentor of Generations*, p. 105), while other authorities more hesitantly permit it when done on an ad hoc basis and if arranged before Shabbat (*Yalkut Yosef* Shabbat 2, 307:53). There is greater room for leniency on festivals, when the proscriptions against electricity are narrower and less severe (*Yabia Omer* OḤ 2:26).

As a better solution, Israeli engineers developed automated systems, colloquially known as "Shabbat elevators," which stop on desired floors at fixed intervals. These elevators have become so popular that Israeli law requires all new buildings with multiple elevators to include at least one with this capability. Not all rabbinic decisors have embraced this invention, however. Rabbi Yaakov Breisch, for example, asserted that it violates the spirit of Shabbat (*Ḥelkat Yaakov* OḤ 137).

More significantly, other authorities claimed that each additional rider adds weight that increases the amount of electricity drawn (*Minḥat Yitzḥak* 3:60). The most outspoken proponent of this view is Rabbi Levi Yitzchak Halperin, director of Jerusalem's Institute for Science and Halacha. After seventeen years of painstaking research, he concluded that body weight contributes significantly to an elevator's descent, but not to its ascent. He further asserted that the increased weight during descent can actually transform the motor into a generator for electric lines, especially in extremely tall buildings. Most importantly, he claimed that one descending in an elevator incurs responsibility for the impact of his weight on the lamps and motor (*Maaliyot BeShabbat*). To obviate these problems, Rabbi Halperin developed an alternative mechanic system. (Decisors agree that these concerns do not apply to automated escalators, which are nearly universally permitted.)

Rabbi Halperin's thesis, however, was criticized by Rabbi Shlomo Zalman Auerbach (SSK 23:49) as well as two experts in technology and halakha, Prof. Zev Lev and Rabbi Yisrael Rozen (*Tchumin* 5). Besides questioning whether one's body weight really affects the flow of electricity, they fundamentally contended that the impact of one's weight lacks the intent and causation necessary to constitute a desecration of Shabbat (*melekhet maḥshevet*). Said impact remains at best indirect, rendering it negligible. Accordingly, when left with no choice, one may enter an elevator and exit on any floor selected by non-Jewish passengers for their own purposes. This ruling affirms a position held by Rabbis Yosef E. Henkin (*Kol Kitvei* 2:59) and Isser Unterman (*Shevet MiYehuda* 1, p. 315). The Zomet Institute, run by Rabbi Rozen, authorizes a simpler (and cheaper) Shabbat elevator, neutralizing features such as weighing mechanisms and electric sensors in order to allay some of Rabbi Halperin's concerns.

Some rabbis never categorically accepted the Shabbat elevator solutions proposed by these institutes, as exemplified by the 2009 controversy. I see no reason, however, for those who have previously used these elevators to discontinue doing so, and humbly submit that the fundamentally lenient position taken by Rabbi Auerbach remains compelling.

Chapter 26

Electric Lights Instead of Candles

May lightbulbs be used as Shabbat or Ḥanukka candles?

Since the invention of electricity, halakhic authorities have debated the acceptability of ritual lights deriving from a source other than "classical fire." To understand whether a person may use electric light instead of candles, it is first necessary to appreciate the reasons for these rituals, and the subsequent criterion for the light or fire needed to properly perform them.

Although Shabbat candles remain one of the most widely recognized symbols of the Sabbath, most authorities believe this practice is a rabbinic ordinance. The sages offer three reasons for it (Shabbat 24a–25b). First, the act of lighting candles before the Sabbath lends dignity and grandeur to the sanctity of the day (*kevod Shabbat*). Second, the light facilitates a more enjoyable environment (*oneg Shabbat*), especially at meals; hence the custom to light candles on or near the dining room table (*Tosafot* Shabbat 25b). Finally, the candles prevent the tension and possible mishaps that may occur in a dim or dark environment (*shelom bayit*). Because of this third reason, the sages also decreed that if a person has insufficient funds, Shabbat candles take precedence over Kiddush wine or Ḥanukka candles. Similarly, one must ensure appropriate lighting throughout his residence (MB 263:2).

Today, most homes are well-lit by electric light, diminishing the need for candlelight. Nonetheless, kindling candles still adds grandeur to the Sabbath and remains an essential part of welcoming it. A couple of decisors even suggest turning off the lights before kindling the candles so as to distinguish the candlelight from the electric lighting (SSK 43:34).

Scholars in the twentieth century debated whether one fulfills the mitzva with electric light. Some concluded that Shabbat lights must come from the fire of a wick (*Levush Mordekhai* OḤ 59), ruling out the use of LEDs and possibly fluorescents. Most decisors objected to this requirement, however, claiming that Shabbat candles are intended simply to illuminate. In any case, even the stringent would allow incandescent bulbs, in which an electric current flows through metal filaments, since they generate both light and heat. (Accordingly, rabbis prohibited turning on these "fires" on Shabbat.) While Rabbi Shlomo Zalman Auerbach preferred that these lights possess an independent energy source (such as a battery), the vast majority of decisors – including Rabbis Moshe Sternbuch (*Teshuvot VeHanhagot* 2:157), Yosef E. Henkin, and Joseph B. Soloveitchik – indicated no such preference. Yet since these lights bear no distinguishing feature designating them for the Sabbath, most rabbis advocate their use only when no alternative is available (*Yeḥaveh Daat* 5:24).

The definition of "fire" becomes more important with respect to Havdala candles, since the blessing over their light praises God for creating "the lights of fire." While fluorescent lights do not fit this description, incandescent bulbs do. Some have nonetheless objected to their use, as the glass prevents direct vision of the fire (OḤ 298:15), and the bulb illuminates only displaced light (*Yabia Omer* OḤ 1:17). Others respond that glass per se does not block the fire, but rather is an integral part of the light itself. To that end, the bulb must be transparent, not frosted (*Tzitz Eliezer* 1:20:13). While Rabbi Auerbach raised other objections, many decisors, including Rabbi Ben-Zion Uziel (*Mishpetei Uziel* OḤ 1:8), permitted these bulbs, though favoring a multi-wick candle. One early twentieth-century scholar, Rabbi Chaim Ozer Grodzenski, even preferred using bulbs for Havdala in order to teach people that this relatively new technology should be considered a flame and thus prohibited on Shabbat (*Ḥashmal LeOr HaHalakha* 3:8).

Most scholars, however, took a decisively prohibitive approach when considering electric Ḥanukka candles. Many authorities contended that in addition to requiring a flame, Ḥanukka candles must resemble the miraculous lights that the holiday commemorates. Electric lights, while considered fire for other purposes, certainly do not function like a conventional fire, nor do they have a flame or wick. In fact, most sources advocate using oil and wicks, but allow wax candles too. While Rabbi Yosef Messas (*Mayim Ḥayim* OḤ 1:279) and other scholars permitted electric menoras, most contemporary decisors have rejected this opinion (*Yabia Omer* OḤ 3:35). Rather, if one lacks a regular menora, they prefer that family members light on his behalf or that he partner with someone else by contributing a minimal amount (say, half a shekel) to the person's lighting costs. (The latter solution is frequently employed by travelers staying in someone else's residence.) Nevertheless, all agree that public displays of electric menoras help to publicize the story of Ḥanukka, and while they may not fulfill the mitzva, they contribute to the holiday spirit.

Chapter 27

Dairy Farms on Shabbat

How do they operate?

Operating a dairy farm on Shabbat raises many questions that go well beyond the propriety of milking cows. These include concerns for animal welfare, national security, the state's economy, and the use of gentiles or automated technology to solve modern problems.

The Talmud proscribes milking a cow on Shabbat, yet leaves the nature and severity of the prohibition ambiguous (Shabbat 95a). Since all Shabbat prohibitions are generally subsumed within the thirty-nine categories of forbidden labor, medieval commentators struggled with how to classify this activity. The categorization is significant because it impacts the parameters of the proscription and determines when dispensations might be allowed.

Rashi placed milking within the category of threshing (*dash*), the act of extracting something from where it is grown, such as grain kernels from their chaff. Yet according to most decisors, the prohibition of threshing includes only items grown in the ground (Shabbat 75a). Some commentators asserted that cows fall into this category, since they derive their sustenance from the ground. Others viewed milking as a kind of sorting (*borer*) or shearing (*gozez*). Alternatively, Rabbi Yaakov Tam, the prominent Tosafist, compared squeezing udders to smoothing a surface (*memaḥek*). Given this difficulty of classification, some scholars declared milking a rabbinic offense (Ritva, Ketubbot 60a). Most, however, including Maimonides (MT *Hilkhot Shabbat* 8:7), insisted that milking remained a biblical prohibition. But if one performs this act without collecting the milk (*le'ibbud*), his transgression is at best rabbinic (BH 320:18, s.v. *yesh*).

Dairy cattle suffer greatly if left unattended throughout Shabbat. To alleviate this pain (*tzaar baalei ḥayim*), Jewish law encouraged milking by gentiles (OḤ 305:20). Most scholars allowed Jews to use the milk after Shabbat, especially if the gentile received a nominal fee.

This system worked, more or less, until the twentieth century, when Jews began resettling the Land of Israel and dairy farms (among other agricultural enterprises) were deemed critical to the national economy. Many Zionist ideologues, moreover, promoted Jewish labor (*avoda ivrit*) as central to the nation's political and cultural renaissance. This agenda angered some European scholars, including Rabbi Chaim Ozer Grodzenski, who scorned "irreverent nationalists" for believing Jewish labor overrode Shabbat restrictions (*Aḥiezer* 3:34, 4:7). Yet the use of Arab laborers raised concerns regarding security as well as the spread of animal diseases from Arab farms. Five solutions were proposed, each reflecting broader legal philosophies.

Much to the chagrin of many Zionist farmers, Rabbi Abraham Isaac Kook saw proper Shabbat observance as a cornerstone of the Jewish renaissance. Though generally favoring Jewish labor, he contended that any Jewish state needed gentile workers too, and if current security conditions precluded their employment, then Jews could squeeze the udders as long as they did not retain the milk (*Oraḥ Mishpat* OḤ 64).

Rabbi Ḥayim Hirschensohn insisted that a more realistic solution be found, based upon minority positions and taking Jewish sovereignty into account. He argued that Jews could do the work in an unusual manner (*shinui*) and use the milk after Shabbat (*Malki BaKodesh* 5:3, para. 2).

A more moderate proposal was offered by Rabbi Ben-Zion Uziel. He agreed that farmers could rely upon minority opinions, but only if gentile labor was truly unavailable. To minimize the severity of the action, he recommended that the milking be done privately, with a tool rather than manually, and slowly, so each squeeze could be seen as relieving the animal's pain, as opposed to extracting its milk for consumption (*Mishpetei Uziel* OḤ 1:10)

Rabbi Shaul Yisraeli combined these leniencies with the notion that one may squeeze onto a food rather than into a receptacle. As such, some farmers squeezed the milk onto bread, which could then be used (albeit less profitably) to make cheese (*Amud HaYemini* 1:24–25).

The solution that has become most accepted came from Rabbi Avraham Karelitz (*Ḥazon Ish* OḤ 38:4). Opposing the use of Jewish labor, he suggested automation, with Jewish laborers, when necessary, only doing preparatory work before the milking actually begins. Today, organizations like the Zomet Institute have developed sophisticated machinery employed at many Israeli dairy farms, even those not run by Sabbath observers (*Tchumin* 15).

Some decisors do not love these solutions, and therefore many milk cartons labeled "*mehadrin*" (strictly kosher) contain milk which is not produced on Shabbat. Yet many dairy products do rely on this techno-halakhic solution, which many scholars support to facilitate both Sabbath observance and the continued Jewish renaissance in the Land of Israel.

Chapter 28

Internet Commerce on Shabbat

May a business keep its website open on Shabbat?

Although business transactions are not included within the thirty-nine categories of forbidden Shabbat activities (*melakhot*), they are prohibited on the Sabbath. Some believe the sages forbade such activity since it would inevitably lead to writing. Others contend that conducting business violates the biblical mandate to make Shabbat a day of rest (*Ḥatam Sofer* 5:195). Indeed, the Book of Nehemiah (chapters 10 and 13) records how the prophet banished vendors from cities on Shabbat as part of national repentance (Rashi, Beitza 37a). Based on a passage in Isaiah, the sages further asserted that one honors Shabbat by distinguishing it from weekdays (Shabbat 113a), such as by preparing special food and clothing, and by avoiding discussions about mundane matters, including business (MT *Hilkhot Shabbat* 24:1). Accordingly, one should not read financial reports on Shabbat, even within newspaper articles or advertisements (*She'elat Yaavetz* 1:162). Additionally, one may not be paid for services performed exclusively on Shabbat (*sekhar Shabbat*).

Beyond formal business activities, later decisors also prohibited all property transfers (*mekaḥ umemkar*). As such, people should avoid giving gifts on Shabbat, unless they are meant to be used that day (e.g., wine). One can avoid this prohibition, however, by acquiring the present on behalf of the recipient before Shabbat. Alternatively, the recipient may explicitly intend not to formally acquire the object until after Shabbat, even if it is in his possession. Some exceptions to these rules exist for financial matters related to mitzvot or communal needs, such as charity.

Given these restrictions, under normal circumstances, one may not operate his business on Shabbat. Non-Jewish employees may not be asked to work on the Sabbath, since they are acting on their employer's behalf. Thus, observant Jews have traditionally closed their shops on Shabbat and festivals, sometimes entailing exemplary personal sacrifice.

When Shabbat closings involve tremendous financial loss, however, some scholars developed legal alternatives. When Jews have non-Jewish business partners, contracts are signed to ensure that all Shabbat profits and expenditures accrue to these gentiles. When Jews are the exclusive owners of their businesses, a more controversial arrangement was hesitantly constructed in the nineteenth century by Rabbi Shlomo Kluger to sell Sabbath ownership rights to a non-Jew, usually an employee (*HaElef Lekha Shlomo* OḤ 229). Many scholars vociferously object to this mechanism as violating the letter and spirit of the law, however, and even their lenient colleagues are frequently stringent when such arrangements might be abused or more innocently misunderstood as a broader dispensation to work on Shabbat. These concerns exist particularly when a business is located on a Jew's property or known to be Jewish-owned.

Some Internet sites require ongoing maintenance, and therefore raise similar questions of business operation on Shabbat. Yet many sites can be set to work automatically on Shabbat, especially if they only provide content without generating revenue. Nonetheless, some scholars, including Rabbis Yosef Shalom Elyashiv and Shmuel HaLevi Wosner (*Shevet HaLevi* 10:57), worry that maintaining one's site represents a denigration of Shabbat and might also attract Jewish surfers, particularly if the content is written in Hebrew or intended for a Jewish audience. (Some sites close when it is Shabbat for their sponsors, while others block access when it is Shabbat for the surfer.) Other authorities counter that since there are always additional sites to view, a website owner is not responsible if (Sabbath-desecrating) Jews happen to pick his, especially since he created it for permissible use during the week.

Commercial sites raise more questions, because consumers may purchase items on Shabbat. For that reason, some companies (B&H Photo being the best-known) prevent any web transactions on

Shabbat. Rabbi Shlomo Dichovsky (*Tchumin* 22) and the heads of the Eretz Hemdah Kollel (*BeMareh HaBazak* 1:37), however, contend that in cases of significant potential loss of customers, businesses may keep their sites open if they don't actually process an order or receive any money from credit card companies until after Shabbat. Until that time, the "sale" remains a mere declaration of intent.

More complicated are cases in which a one-time purchaser receives instant access to a product on Shabbat (e.g., music downloads). The business is then receiving direct payment for a service provided on Shabbat itself. Some compare this situation to the Shabbat operation of an ATM (*Tchumin* 19) or vending machine (*Minḥat Yitzḥak* 3:34), which some decisors permit. Many, however, require such companies to close their sites or make a partnership arrangement with a gentile, especially if the primary customers are Jewish (*Orkhot Shabbat* 22:41).

Since these questions entail complex business and legal ramifications, business owners should consult a competent halakhic authority to address their specific case.

Chapter 29

The International Date Line

On what day of the week should I observe Shabbat if I'm traveling from New York to Japan?

Halakhic questions about crossing the International Date Line (IDL) became popular in the twentieth century along with high-speed international air travel. With the sun always setting later while journeying westward, a person traveling for twenty-four hours across the globe's horizon would inevitably return to his departure point at the same time, unless a line somewhere along the way marked a new date for that hour.

The necessity of a calendrical date line was popularized by thirteenth-century geographers who marveled at how a circumnavigator would "paradoxically" gain or lose a date depending on his travel direction. Later, surprised explorers documented how their calendars were off by one day when they landed in distant locations. Various popes and empires subsequently declared date lines in accordance with their needs.

In 1884, a conference established the IDL at 180° from the prime meridian in Greenwich, England, dividing Alaska from Russia in the north and New Zealand from Hawaii (and even closer, Tonga from Samoa) in the South Pacific. As such, dates (i.e., Saturday, January 30) begin at midnight in Tonga, while the previous day (Friday, January 29) simultaneously starts in Samoa. As a result, any calendar *date* exists *at some point on Earth* for forty-eight hours. When a person travels westward across the IDL, he "loses a day" by moving forward one date on the calendar (e.g., from January 29 to 30), while someone traveling eastward "gains a day" and moves one date backward. The arbitrariness of this line was highlighted at the end of 2011, when Samoa switched to the other side (which includes New Zealand and Australia) to improve trade.

Jewish scholars discussed whether halakhic sources had previously determined a date line and if Jewish law should adopt the new convention. The question has major ramifications for Sabbath observance, as rabbinic literature has long established that one calculates the week, including the Sabbath, in accordance with his location (*Shu"t HaRadbaz* 1:76). When is the seventh night of the week in Japan – does it follow the Friday date established by the IDL, or some other line? May one leave Hawaii late Thursday evening to arrive several hours later on a day marked in New Zealand as Saturday?

Amazingly, many historians attribute the first discussion of a date line to halakhic texts. A mishna declares that the latest hour a court may declare a new month (Rosh Ḥodesh) is noontime (Rosh HaShana 20b). Two twelfth-century rabbis, Yehuda HaLevi (*Kuzari* 2:20) and Zeraḥia HaLevi (Baal HaMaor, Rosh HaShana 20b), understood that this rule was to ensure that Rosh Ḥodesh would last twenty-four hours somewhere on Earth. Since noon is eighteen hours after nightfall (which begins the Jewish calendar day), the farthest location that could celebrate a full day of Rosh Ḥodesh would be eighteen hours west of Eretz Yisrael, thereby establishing the date line at 90° east of Jerusalem (today 125° east longitude, which crosses Australia, China, and Russia). Nonetheless, these texts remain somewhat ambiguous; additionally, many commentators interpreted the mishna in a manner entirely irrelevant to our discussion.

In 1941, when several hundred yeshiva students fled Lithuania, relocating first to Kobe, Japan (135° east longitude, 100° east of Jerusalem), and then to Shanghai, they asked scholars when to observe Shabbat and Yom Kippur. Rabbi Avraham Karelitz (*Ḥazon Ish* OḤ 64) adopted the *Kuzari*'s date line, but following indications from lesser-known medieval sources (*Yesod Olam*), he zigzagged it to the easternmost coast of any continuous landmass, thereby keeping Australia, Russia, and China to the west of the line, but moving Japan (and New Zealand) to its east. As such, some students observed Shabbat on Japan's Sunday, while donning *tefillin* on the Saturday of the civil calendar!

Based on the talmudic view that Jerusalem is "the center of the world," Rabbi Yeḥiel Michel Tucazinsky opined that the prime meridian runs through the Holy City, with the date line 180° away (145° west longitude). This would place Japan west of the date line, but also move Hawaii to that side of the day, in contrast with the IDL. Lesser-known figures, such as Rabbi Dovid Shapiro, placed the halakhic date line in the mid-Pacific, close to the IDL.

Many students followed the IDL, based on a ruling given by Rabbi Moshe Kisilav for World War I refugees, which was later endorsed by the eminent Rabbi Menaḥem Kasher. Rabbi Kasher argued that earlier sources were at best inconclusive and theoretical, and that the absence of a direct discussion of these issues in the halakhic literature indicates that Jews always followed the conventional date of the broader society. He contended that Shabbat should be observed on the day locally reckoned as Saturday, which represents the contemporary practice of Jews living in the region.

Chapter 30

Discarding Religious Literature

May I throw away publications that contain religious teachings?

The proper disposal of religious literature has become an acute problem as computer printing has multiplied the number of publications beyond precedent. The value of preserving sacred texts, furthermore, occasionally conflicts with contemporary environmentalism and consumerism, which preach, respectively, that everything is recyclable and disposable.

The Torah forbids the destruction of sacred objects (Deut. 12:4), such as elements of the Holy Temple or any item bearing one of God's names (Makkot 11a). These names (*sheimot*) include the four-letter Tetragrammaton (YKVK) and names like Adonai and Sha-ddai, but not descriptions of God, such as "the Merciful One" (*Raḥum*) (MT *Hilkhot Yesodei HaTorah* 6:1, 5). Many scholars deem names of God in foreign languages to be non-sacred and therefore erasable. This position makes it permissible, contrary to popular practice, to spell God without a hyphen (G-d) (*Shakh* YD 179:11).

The sages ordained that a worn-out Torah scroll be buried (*geniza*) in an earthenware vessel, thereby delaying its inevitable disintegration (Megilla 26b). Receptacles of sacred scrolls, known as *tashmishei kedusha* – such as *tefillin* and *mezuza* cases – also require burial, albeit not in earthenware (OḤ 154:3). This interment prevents degradation of sacred objects and provides an appropriate last rite of honor.

In contrast, the sages permitted a person to simply discard ritual items used to fulfill commandments (*tashmishei mitzva*), such as torn *tzitzit* strings or a *lulav*. With the commandment fulfilled, the object loses its sacredness. The common practice is to discard them in a respectful and indirect manner, but without a formal burial (OḤ 21:1).

The status of religious literature that does not contain God's name was subject to historical debate. Some classified all such as possessing the same inherent holiness as Torah scrolls, since these texts also represent divine teachings (*Magen Avraham* 154:9). Most scholars, however, deem this literature *tashmishei kedusha*, which one must bury and not destroy (MT *Hilkhot Yesodei HaTorah* 6:8). Jews have traditionally interred worn manuscripts in special storage areas, such as the famous Cairo Geniza, which, when discovered in the early twentieth century, revealed a treasure trove of unknown writings.

The invention of the printing press and the production of regularly discarded galleys posed a serious problem for publishers. Since nearly all scholars equated printed material with text written on parchment, many lambasted printers for destroying rough drafts or using them for sacrilegious purposes (*Shu"t Maharshadam* YD 182). In one remarkable eighteenth-century responsum, Rabbi Yaakov Reischer suggested privately burning these galleys rather than allowing them to be used in a denigrating manner, a proposal that drew the ire of his contemporaries (*Shvut Yaakov* 3:10).

In the late nineteenth century, Rabbis Naphtali Berlin (*Meshiv Davar* 2:80) and Yitzḥak E. Spektor (*Ein Yitzḥak* OḤ 5) claimed that writings were holy only if written to produce sacred literature. Material produced for immediate erasure or destruction could therefore be destroyed. This ruling provides a solution not only for galleys, but also for texts displayed on computer screens.

These solutions were not universally accepted, however, and they might not even apply to literature intended to be studied, albeit for temporary use (like weekly Torah publications). As such, some require burial of all contemporary Torah literature, no matter how cheap or common (*Shevet HaLevi* 5:162). In contrast, several decisors – including Rabbis

Ḥayim David HaLevi (*Aseh Lekha Rav* 3:28), Yitzḥak Weiss (*Minḥat Yitzḥak* 1:17–18), and Nachum Rabinovitz (*Siaḥ Naḥum* 74) – suggest that one may place these writings in a bag and throw them away. This ruling is supported by Rabbi Moshe Feinstein's understanding that non-biblical literature (e.g., the Oral Law) cannot attain the status of the Holy Scriptures (IM OḤ 4:39), especially with regard to literature not written in Hebrew (IM OH 2:55). It remains *tashmishei mitzva,* so once one has finished using such texts, he may respectfully dispose of them, as with a *lulav*.

Rabbi Feinstein's grandson Rabbi Shabtai Rappaport further suggested that one recycle this material, especially if it will be reused for new Torah literature. While the Zomet Institute has proposed a procedure for this dignified recycling (*Tchumin* 3), which has been implemented in certain places, it remains to be seen if this practice will become popular.

Chapter 31

Electric Shavers

Is shaving with electric razors permitted?

A distinguished-looking, gray-haired man stroking his beard has long been the dominant image of the Jewish scholar. The legal and cultural basis of this depiction remains a matter of historical intrigue.

The Torah states, "You shall not destroy the side growth of your beard" (Lev. 19:27). While the Talmud limits this prohibition to five sections of a man's face, medieval commentators offer at least six definitions of where they are. While all agree that the center of the chin must remain unshorn, they disagree about the area around the lower earlobe, the ends and sides of the upper jawbone, and the ends of the mustache (Ritva, Makkot 21a). Given this dispute, it has become customary to refrain from improperly destroying any facial hair (YD 181:11). The decisors also debate whether this prohibition extends to the neck (*Shakh* YD 181:7). In any case, the commandment applies to barbers and clients alike (YD 181:4), although many authorities allow Jewish barbers to shave non-Jews.

Medieval commentators offer various explanations for this prohibition. Rabbi Abraham ibn Ezra links it to the ban on the mourning rituals of self-infliction (Lev. 21:5); alternatively, shaving is an inappropriate imitation of gentile destruction of facial hair (Lev. 19:17). Rabbi Ovadia Seforno (1475–1550, Italy) connects the prohibition to a general sentiment that beards are "the glory of one's face" (Shabbat 152a), reflecting the wisdom of age and experience. Indeed, some kabbalistic sources indicate that stroking one's beard improves Torah study!

Maimonides related this commandment to the prohibition of imitating priestly idolatrous practices (MT *Hilkhot Avodat Kokhavim* 12:7). Some decisors understood this rationale as offering room for leniency, such as when "court Jews" must represent the Jewish community to the government (*Taz* YD 181:1). However, many vehemently disagree (*Minḥat Ḥinukh* 51:1), with some using this example to highlight the threat of antinomianism posed by efforts to suggest reasons for the commandments (*Darkhei Moshe* YD 181). Others retort that Maimonides believed his rationale had no legal implications, since the divine command must always be obeyed (*Meshekh Ḥokhma* Lev. 14:9).

The sages understood that the Torah prohibits only the uprooting of facial hair ("destruction") with a blade (*ke'ein taar*). One may trim his beard with scissors, however, or pluck the hair with tweezers, since they have no blade (Makkot 21a). Many decisors, including Rabbi Joseph Karo, permit such actions even if the result is similar to shaving with a razor (BY YD 181:10). On this basis, most authorities allow the use of depilatory cream (*Ḥayim She'ol* 1:52).

Some medieval rabbis, however, assert that close trims remain forbidden (*Ḥinukh* 252). So emphasized the third Lubavitcher Rebbe (d. 1866, *Tzemaḥ Tzedek* YD 93), who also cited kabbalistic traditions from the Arizal that one should never trim any facial hair, except around the lips, if this growth interferes with eating neatly (*Be'er Hetev* 181:5). Other sages, such as Rabbi Avraham Karelitz, criticize depilatory treatment, claiming that beards still symbolize age and wisdom (*Kovetz Iggerot Ḥazon Ish* 1:197). Rabbi Yisrael Meir Kagan (d. 1933) dedicated a book, *Tiferet HaAdam*, to protesting the phenomenon of clean-shaven Jews, which he considered a sign of assimilation. Nonetheless, as Rabbi Moshe Sofer argued in the nineteenth century, most sources allow the trimming or cutting of facial hair, if done in a permissible manner (*Ḥatam Sofer* OḤ 1:159).

Regarding electric shavers, some decisors, including Rabbis Karelitz and Kagan, forbid such a close shave (*Minḥat Yitzḥak* 4:113). Others, like Rabbis Chaim Ozer Grodzenski (cited in *Halikhot Shlomo, Tefilla*, p. 11) and Tzvi Pesaḥ Frank (*Har Tzvi* YD 143), contend that the screen between the blade and the skin prevented the total destruction of the hair (leaving some stubble); therefore, electric shavers are permitted.

Rabbi Moshe Feinstein alternatively argued that the key criterion is the method used to cut the hair, not the result. Since electric shavers employ two blades (the outer screen and the inner blade), they are similar to scissors; as such, it remains permissible to use them, though they may cut the hair at skin level.

Nevertheless, some decisors prohibit certain modern brands, including the "Lift and Cut" shaver, since the inner blade cuts very close to the skin. According to Rabbi Nachum Rabinovitch (*Melumdei Milḥama* 122) and others, however, any shaver that cannot cut long facial hairs as a regular razor can (and therefore requires an attached trimmer) is permissible.

Section III

Social and Business Issues

Chapter 32

Cruelty to Animals

Is foie gras *kosher?*

The tension between benefiting from animals while treating them humanely arises in many areas of public life, with different groups striking this controversial balance differently. After recently returning from an enjoyable family trip to the zoo, which advocates animal preservation and protection, I found on the website of the PETA animal rights group, "Never patronize zoos," since these creatures belong in the wild, not "locked up in captivity."

Through many different mitzvot, Jewish law condemns cruelty to animals. The Torah, for example, forbids muzzling an ox while it works so it can graze freely (Deut. 25:4), and the seven Noahide laws prohibit eating a limb severed from a living animal. The rabbis further decreed that a person must feed his animal before himself (Berakhot 40a).

Many commentators cite the obligation to remove an excessive burden from a donkey, and the supplementary requirement to assist a fallen animal (Ex. 23:5, Deut. 22:4), as demonstrating the prohibition of causing animals pain, *tzaar baalei ḥayim* (Bava Metzia 32b). A major dispute exists regarding whether this law is intended to ensure the animal's welfare, or to guide man's moral development. While these commandments protect the creature's health, they might stem primarily from a concern for the owner's finances. Rabbi Moshe Sofer alternatively suggested that in preventing *tzaar baalei ḥayim,* we emulate the Divine (*Hagahot Ḥatam Sofer*). Following the view that these mitzvot build character, he cited the verse, "His mercies extend to all His works" (Ps. 145:9), obligating compassion toward all creatures.

Nonetheless, as evidenced by the laws regulating the slaughter of animals, the Torah clearly allows one to harm them for legitimate human needs, such as food. Permissible consumption of animals seemingly demonstrates human dominion over other creatures, as the Torah states, "And the fear of you ... shall be upon every beast of the earth ...; into your hand they are delivered" (Gen. 9:2). Based on this principle, Rabbi Israel Isserlein (fifteenth century, Germany) allowed plucking feathers from live chickens, ruling that Jewish law allows *tzaar baalei ḥayim* if it benefits humans (*Terumat HaDeshen Pesakim* 105). According to Rabbi Moshe Isserles, such benefit includes financial gain (EH 5:14). One staunch opponent of this outlook was Rabbi Yitzḥak Bamburger (nineteenth century, Wurzburg, Germany), who waived *tzaar baalei ḥayim* only for health reasons, such as medical experimentation (*Yad HaLevi* YD 196). A middle ground was taken by Rabbi Bamburger's German colleague, Rabbi Yaakov Ettlinger, who permitted painful actions only in cases of "great benefit" with "minimal pain," although these terms remain difficult to define.

While the majority of decisors followed Rabbis Isserlein and Isserles, they themselves urged people to abstain from plucking feathers, since it leads to cruelty. Moreover, most authorities forbid activities such as chicken fighting, where the intended benefit is directly related to the animal's pain (IM EH 4:92). The financial benefit of operating such competitions doesn't justify sadism.

Foie gras is produced by fattening the liver of a duck or goose through "gavage," force-feeding. While this process originated in ancient Egypt, it was particularly popular among certain Eastern European Jews, who used it to obtain schmaltz. Many Jews disdained this food, however, because of the inhumane treatment involved in its preparation, or because they thought the overstuffed animals became so incapacitated that they were no longer kosher (*tereifa*).

Today, *foie gras* is industrially produced by restraining birds while food is poured down their throats, which are held open by a metal pipe; this process is repeated over several days or weeks. Some decisors, such as Rabbi Yosef Shalom Elyashiv, allow this method, contending that it ultimately provides human sustenance, as it did in previous generations. A number of leading rabbis, including Rabbi Ovadia Yosef (*Yabia Omer* YD 9:3), banned the practice as too painful, especially in an age when meat is readily available through gentler means. They further contended that gavage might inflict fatal esophageal wounds, raising questions about the kashrut of the fowl.

Rabbi Moshe Feinstein further prohibited veal production, since the cattle are similarly fattened through severe restriction of their movements (IM EH 4:92). While this ruling has received less attention, the prohibition of *foie gras* has gained a large following among Jews of all stripes. The Israeli Supreme Court cited *tzaar baalei ḥayim* in its 2003 ban of *foie gras* production, which I support.

Chapter 33

Hunting and Experimentation on Animals

Is it permitted to hunt recreationally or conduct medical experiments on animals?

As a native Texan, I certainly understand a person's curiosity about hunting. My gym teacher was an avid hunter, and the recreational gun culture certainly has a prominent place in Texas life. The question also touches on the meaning of *sheḥita,* the ritual slaughtering that produces kosher meat.

After the flood, God permitted Noah – and all humans – to eat meat (Gen. 9:3), rescinding the prohibition imposed on Adam (Gen. 1:30, Sanhedrin 59b). Yet the Torah restricts this consumption. In addition to the prohibition of drinking blood (Gen. 9:4), Jewish law requires that animals be killed by a precise transverse cut in the throat with an extremely sharp knife. This process greatly reduces the animal's pain, since the massive and immediate blood loss renders it unconscious (subsequent movements are spasms).

Furthermore, the animal must be examined to ensure it was healthy enough to live another twelve months. The lungs in particular are meticulously inspected for any sign of fatal illness or injury. Meat is deemed glatt (Yiddish for "smooth") kosher when the lungs are completely smooth, offering greater assurance of the animal's health.

As such, hunted animals are undoubtedly unkosher, since they were not properly slaughtered. The question that remains is whether the permission to slaughter animals for food also permits a person to kill them for other purposes, such as for sport or medical experimentation, to take polar opposite examples. Does such killing violate the Torah's prohibition of cruelty to animals (discussed in the previous essay)?

This issue might relate to the rationale behind *sheḥita*. Maimonides (Guide 3:26, 48) contends that the requirements of kosher slaughter, including the use of an extremely sharp knife and the slitting of the back of the neck, stem from an attempt to minimize the animal's pain. He concludes that killing an animal for sport constitutes *tzaar baalei ḥayim*, prohibited cruelty to animals (Guide 3:17). Many rabbinic sources, however, disparage attempts to find rationales for the mitzvot, and especially to draw legal conclusions on those bases. These scholars maintain that many precepts are meant to discipline our actions and purify our character, but they lack more specific or integral reasons (Tanḥuma, *Shemini* 7). Rabbi Moshe Sofer (nineteenth century, Hungary) also noted that if the laws of slaughter were intended solely to minimize pain, similar regulations should govern the killing of fish and grasshoppers (*Ḥatam Sofer Likkutim* 6:24).

Leaving aside the rationale for *sheḥita*, many decisors determine that killing animals for illegitimate or unnecessary purposes violates the prohibition of *tzaar baalei ḥayim*. Rabbi Yosef ibn Migash (twelfth century, Spain), for example, forbids killing domestic animals and feeding their flesh to dogs (*Shita Mekubbetzet* Bava Batra 20a). While many authorities share this opinion, one notable detractor was Rabbi Yeḥezkel Landau (eighteenth century, Prague). He argued that only cruelty to live animals constitutes *tzaar baalei ḥayim*; the proscription does not include killing them. Yet at the end of his celebrated responsum, he writes that hunting contravenes Jewish values, breeds cruelty, and endangers humans as well, and urges people to refrain from the sport (*Noda BiYehuda Tinyana* YD 10).

Rabbi Yaakov Breisch took this supererogatory spirit to an extreme, contending that one should even refrain from medical experimentation on animals (*Ḥelkat Yaakov* ḤM 34). This position has been widely dismissed as misplaced piety, since the treatments developed as a result of these experiments have definitive use for humans, no less than food itself (*Seridei Esh* 2:91). Nonetheless, many decisors insist on minimizing animal pain (*Tzitz Eliezer* 14:68). Greater caution might be warranted in testing cosmetics and other commercial products, which, while permitted, certainly represents a less pressing need than medical treatments. We should judge each case individually, carefully balancing our rights to benefit from animals with the requirement to avoid unnecessary cruelty.

In recent years, a few high-profile cases have exposed abuses with regard to the handling of animals before *sheḥita*. Yet as long as the actual slaughtering is performed properly, the meat remains kosher. To take a more extreme example (discussed in the previous essay) the continuous and severe restriction of movement of an animal in order to produce veal might constitute *tzaar baalei ḥayim*, yet the food itself is kosher. Nonetheless, the spirit of these laws dictates extra caution, and we should salute any kashrut agencies demanding that animals be treated as tenderly as possible before their slaughter.

Chapter 34

Taxes and *Dina DeMalkhuta Dina*

Must one pay local taxes?

The definitive obligation of Jews to observe local laws and regulations has engaged the Jewish community in recent years because of a number of high-profile white-collar crimes committed by Jews. Beyond its public ramifications, this issue remains fundamental toward understanding our responsibilities to society at large, whether in Israel or in the Diaspora.

On several occasions, the Babylonian Talmud authoritatively quotes Shmuel, the prominent third-century Babylonian sage, as declaring, "*Dina demalkhuta dina* – the law of the kingdom is the law." Perhaps not surprisingly, this principle is cited most prominently in a discussion about tax collection (Bava Kamma 113a). The Talmud prohibits evasion of tax collectors, unless they collect unlawfully, without government mandate, or in a capricious, inequitable manner. Interestingly, the Jerusalem Talmud never mentions *dina demalkhuta*, leading some historians to speculate that the sages did not apply it in an era of suppression and tyranny. In a community with a just political system, however, most authorities believe this principle carries the force of biblical law (*Avnei Miluim* 28:2), and that tax evaders violate the biblical prohibition of theft (*Shulḥan Arukh HaRav*, ḤM *Gezela* 15).

Beyond taxes, medieval authorities debated the scope of *dina demalkhuta*, reflecting in part the different perspectives on the rationale behind recognizing the law of the land. Some scholars asserted that a king's right to enact laws stems from his ownership of the country's territory. Just as an individual property owner may establish rules of entry into his land, a government may regulate the conditions of residence in its territory (Rosh, Nedarim 3:11). This rationale might even justify treating select groups of citizens (such as Jews) differently from everyone else (Maharik 194), though most authorities consider discriminatory regulations unjust and non-binding (BY ḤM 369).

More important, this explanation might limit *dina demalkhuta* to matters strictly related to land and territory, such as real estate regulations and taxes (*Or Zarua* Bava Kamma 3:447). Similarly, if this principle is based on territorial ownership, it might not apply to the Land of Israel, where all Jews are inherently entitled to dwell (Ran, Nedarim 28a). According to an extreme interpretation, *dina demalkhuta* would not apply in the State of Israel (though other halakhic principles might empower the Knesset's authority). Many decisors, however, have contended that even according to this interpretation, basic matters of civil regulation would remain mandatory in the Land of Israel (*Ḥatam Sofer* ḤM 5:44).

In any case, the dominant position among talmudic commentators grounds *dina demalkhuta* in social contract theory. According to this approach, residents of the land (implicitly) consent to the regulations of the local authority for the sake of maintaining order (Rashbam, Bava Batra 54b). As such, these laws would be equally binding in the Land of Israel and elsewhere, and would apply with no distinction between Jewish and non-Jewish sovereigns (MT *Hilkhot Gezela* 5:17–18).

Even within this approach, decisors debate the scope of *dina demalkhuta*. Maimonides, for example, seems to apply the rule only in cases of direct "benefit to the king," although he does not delineate which laws would fall into that category. Some believe the principle covers only matters that directly impact the government's financial interests. Other decisors, however, broaden *dina demalkhuta* to encompass most monetary and civil regulations (BY ḤM 369). Consequently, halakha mandates that one honor traffic laws and health regulations, as well as intellectual property rights, including copyrights (as discussed in the following essay).

Two important limitations pertain to this principle. First, *dina demalkhuta* has no impact on ritual or on personal status. As such, government laws that ban ritual slaughter of animals (*sheḥita*) or circumcision would not be recognized. Orthodox decisors have similarly ruled, based on talmudic precedent (Gittin 10b), that a civil divorce has no effect on halakhic personal status, whereas the Reform movement – partly on the basis of *dina demalkhuta* – recognized such divorces in 1869.

Second, civil monetary regulations (including matters of inheritance and moneylending) are not necessarily binding if they directly contradict Torah law (ḤM 369:11). However, when all parties accept the conventional contractual agreements made in the financial world, then these agreements may become enforceable (*Shakh* ḤM 73:39).

We must emphasize that any attempt within a just society to manipulate halakha in order to shirk one's civic obligations, including paying taxes, constitutes a massive defamation of Judaism. The famed thirteenth-century preacher Rabbi Moses of Coucy once declared that the greatest sanctification of God's name will take place when Jews have an international reputation for honesty in business (*Smag Aseh* 74).

May we earn that reputation quickly in our days.

Chapter 35

Copyright and Intellectual Property

May one share music or videos on the Internet?

The problem of uploading and downloading music, movies, and software on the Internet has received prominent public attention with the closing of sites like Napster, Grokster, and other peer-to-peer file-sharing networks. Such cases raise legal questions regarding intellectual property rights as well as the more abstract issue of how one can steal something intangible.

Jewish values demand that one cite the source of an idea. The sages declare, "Whoever repeats an idea in the name of the one who said it brings redemption to the world" (Avot 6:6). Once credit has been given, however, many sources stress the importance of sharing wisdom, especially Torah knowledge (ḤM 292:20). Some scholars even claim that one may disseminate a halakhic insight against the will of its originator (*Shakh* ḤM 292:35). Others argue that the originator retains veto rights and may withhold publication in case he wants to sharpen his ideas or correct errors (IM OḤ 4:40, para. 19).

Spreading wisdom takes time and other resources. If someone reproduces this knowledge, he often detracts from the original producer's return on his "investment," though the reproducer has technically caused no direct damage, nor has he stolen anything tangible. Besides individual losses, such activity can threaten the entire industry and the possibility of disseminating knowledge altogether (*Ḥatam Sofer* 6:57).

Thus, Rabbi Yosef Shaul Nathanson declared it obvious that Jewish law affords copyright protection (*Shoel U'Meshiv Kamma* 1:44). While the vast majority of scholars concur, they struggle to categorize these intellectual assets within Jewish law.

Many of the earliest responsa written on this topic addressed book publication. When Rabbi Meir Katzenellenbogen (Maharam) of Padua republished Maimonides' *Mishneh Torah* in 1550, Rabbi Moshe Isserles forbade the purchase of a vengeful competing publisher's edition. The rabbi argued that the latter was violating the rabbinic prohibition of *hasagat gevul*, unfair competition (*Shu"t HaRema* 10). While scholars like Rabbi Moshe Sofer supported this claim (*Ḥatam Sofer* ḤM 5:41, 79), Rabbi Mordekhai Benet and others countered that *hasagat gevul* did not apply to books of Jewish wisdom and was generally limited to distinct geographical areas and persons (*Parashat Mordekhai* ḤM 7–8). Moreover, as Rabbi Ezra Basri has noted, many believe the concept of illegitimate encroachment does not extend to intellectual property (*Tchumin* 6).

Some scholars assert that infringement on such property violates the talmudic principle, "If one benefits from another while causing a loss, he [the former] must pay," since the producer loses out on potential sales (*Noda BiYehuda Tinyana* ḤM 24). Yet a few dispute whether this rule applies when the "product" is not physically damaged or is a mere idea. Moreover, unlike copyright law, this halakhic principle might permit a person to copy or download an item he would not otherwise have purchased (*Tchumin* 7).

As Prof. Nahum Rakover has documented, many books published since 1518 have included approbations that incorporated written bans on reproductions without permission. Some dispute the legal weight of those declarations or their long-term impact (*Tzemaḥ Tzedek* YD 195). Yet Rabbi Zalman Neḥemia Goldberg has contended that contemporary copyrights operate on the halakhic principle of *shiyur*, in which a merchant sells a product but retains certain rights (*Tchumin* 6). In the case of the Internet, the seller grants the buyer personal benefit from software or music, but prohibits its unauthorized transmission. Indeed, Rabbi Moshe Feinstein asserted that the unauthorized copying of a recording (even of a Torah lecture) is outright thievery. Others have suggested that copyright declarations might impose a legitimate condition on transactions, especially since halakha generally recognizes standard commercial practices (*minhag sokhrim*). This condition would allow, however, "fair use" exceptions, such as distribution of selections for educational purposes (*Tzitz Eliezer* 18:80).

Some have argued that while these principles might prohibit one from initially uploading or reproducing intellectual property, they would no longer apply once others, by whatever means, have made a product widely available, say, on the Internet. Yet most scholars (*Beit Yitzḥak* YD 2:75) have rejected this argument, since irrespective of the standing of intellectual property within halakha, Jewish law respects copyright laws as part of its broader acknowledgment of civil law (*dina demalkhuta dina*; see the previous essay). A significant majority of countries around the world have banned unauthorized uploading and downloading. Copyright owners and governments have shown intent to uphold these laws through lawsuits against sharing networks, Internet providers, and individual violators. Moreover, when Israelis (or other groups of identifiable Jews) violate these regulations en masse – as has been alleged by several software companies since the early 2000s – it creates a *ḥillul Hashem*, a desecration of God's name. It behooves us to resist the temptation of illegal downloads and respect others' property, physical or intellectual.

Chapter 36

Bankruptcy

Can one escape debt by declaring bankruptcy?

Declaring bankruptcy is morally complex. On one hand, it allows a person to delay or avoid repaying money rightfully owed to others. On the other hand, it prevents creditors from abusing debtors. Modern bankruptcy statutes attempt to balance these opposing forces by aiming to protect the debtor while still recompensing creditors (at least partially). Yet some countries, including the United States, recently enacted stricter bankruptcy laws in order to prevent fraudulent claims and repeat offenders. Jewish law also attempts to balance the needs of debtors and creditors, yet it bases the compromise on different premises.

The Torah commends the provision of loans (Ex. 22:24); lending to the poor is considered even greater than giving charity, since loans avoid the embarrassment that may accompany the acceptance of handouts (*Sefer HaMitzvot, Aseh* 197). In addition, possessions essential to a person's daily living may not serve as collateral, nor may a lender demand the return of a loan if the borrower cannot repay it (ḤM 97:2). Furthermore, according to biblical law, creditors may not charge fellow Jews interest, and loans are relinquished at the end of the seven-year *Shemitta* cycle (Deut. 15:2). Lest these strictures discourage lending, the sages and decisors permitted their circumvention via financial arrangements known as *heter iska* and *pruzbul,* while encouraging people to uphold the magnanimous spirit of these laws. To further minimize disputes, the sages demanded that all loans – even between honest friends – be witnessed or at least documented (Bava Metzia 75b).

While stressing the importance of lending, Judaism absolutely obligates debtors to repay their creditors (Rashi, Ketubbot 86a). Deliberate failure to repay violates biblical law (*Ahavat Ḥesed* 2:24). Borrowers are to use all their assets to repay their loans, even if certain properties (such as food and trade tools) are protected from debt collection (ḤM 97:23–24). Courts can seize recalcitrant debtors' property (97:6, 15). When a person is in debt for reasons other than a loan – for instance, he owes wages or compensation – the "creditor" himself may seize his due, in a non-violent fashion, if he immediately justifies his claim in court (97:14). The obligation to repay is limited, however. For example, debtors may not be subject to involuntary servitude in order to pay back (97:15), since biblical law allows this recourse only in the case of theft (Ex. 22:2).

A borrower can never unilaterally discharge his debt. It remains in perpetuity, even (according to most opinions) if the lender despairs of repayment (ḤM 98:1). Prof. Steven Resnicoff has shown (JHCS 24) that modern-day authorities question whether halakha even permits one to declare bankruptcy (through liquidation or reorganization) in order to avoid debt repayment. Bankruptcy agreements regularly force creditors to settle for partial payment. Rabbi Betzalel Stern (d. 1989) ruled that halakha does not recognize such arrangements, and that a creditor may still demand the rest of his money (*BeTzel HaḤokhma* 3:124). Others, however, cite two halakhic principles that may justify bankruptcy agreements:

The first is *dina demalkhuta dina,* the talmudic concept that one must comply with local regulations. As discussed in previous essays, while some authorities apply this notion only to government finances (BY ḤM 369), others, including Rabbi Moshe Isserles, deem it relevant to all matters of civil law (ḤM 369:11). Rabbi Moshe Feinstein, among others, accepts the broader definition and ostensibly recognizes bankruptcy arrangements involving international corporations (IM ḤM 2:62).

One might contend that corporate bankruptcy is unique, since corporations are creations of civil law and must therefore function according to civil regulation (*Pitḥei Ḥoshen* 2, p. 26); individual bankruptcy, however, would not be included. Others have argued more generally that *dina demalkhuta* does not apply when civil law violates halakha, as it does here by discharging the debt (*Shakh* ḤM 73:39).

The weakness of relying solely on *dina demalkhuta* may be mitigated by a second halakhic principle, *minhag sokhrim* (merchants' practice), which asserts that contractors implicitly accept established commercial procedures. Especially if loan documents comply with local regulations, the lender presumably understood that the borrower had the right, if necessary, to declare bankruptcy. Rabbi Ezra Basri (*Dinei Mamonot* vol. 1) has noted a precedent in a sixteenth-century responsum that forced lenders to accept a discharge agreement made with the majority of the creditors in accordance with customary practice (Maharshakh 2:13, 3:8). It would appear, however, that this dispensation applies only to genuinely impoverished debtors, not to wealthy individuals seeking to circumvent their biblical obligations and moral responsibility through bankruptcy.

Chapter 37

Reporting Criminals

If someone has evidence incriminating a fellow Jew, should he report it to the authorities?

The numerous highly publicized financial crimes and abuse scandals in recent years – such as the notorious case of Bernie Madoff * – within the Jewish community clearly detracts from our mission as a "holy nation" and maligns our religion, the Torah, and God (*ḥillul Hashem*). Our community's soul-searching requires that we examine the laws of collaborating with government authorities. Historically this issue concerned Jews living under hostile rulers. Today, however, it deserves re-examination, given the reality of the State of Israel and the existence of just, democratic governments.

Since the dissolution of the Sanhedrin during Roman rule, the Torah's judicial system has been dormant for many centuries. Nonetheless, as the fourteenth-century Spanish scholar Rabbenu Nissim famously declared, halakha recognizes "the king's justice" (*mishpat hamelekh*), authorizing sovereign rulers to head the army and administer penal laws necessary to maintain society (*Derashot HaRan* 11). Following this logic, many religious Zionist jurists see Israel's penal code as halakhically binding.

* In 2009, Bernie Madoff was sentenced to 150 years in prison for operating a massive Ponzi scheme considered to be the largest financial fraud in US history.

The granting of this power to non-Jewish sovereigns in foreign lands stems from the talmudic principle of *dina demalkhuta dina*, "the law of the kingdom is the law" (Bava Kamma 113a). As discussed in previous essays, some sages based this authority on the sovereign's property rights, and therefore limited its application to financial arrangements, such as paying taxes (akin to paying rent in order to live in the ruler's territory). However, many scholars understood this principle in terms similar to a social contract, which grants the ruler extensive powers to regulate social order.

The legal recognition of a gentile sovereign's penal code was clearly illustrated by the sage R. Elazar's assistance in apprehending Jewish thieves (Bava Metzia 83b). When criticized by colleagues, he replied, "I eradicated thorns from the vineyard," emphasizing the importance of eliminating crime from the community. As Rabbi Yom Tov ibn Asevilli (Ritva, d. 1330, Spain) explained, R. Elazar acted reasonably to enforce fair laws, even as his colleagues deemed this conduct unbefitting for a scholar (*Shita Mekubbetzet*).

Most ancient and medieval Jews, however, assumed that non-Jewish authorities would mistreat them in legal disputes. As such, informing to gentiles was considered a damaging act entitling the victim to compensation (Bava Kamma 117a). More significantly, the Talmud authorizes immediate punitive action – including the death penalty – against informers, who were seen as treacherous pursuers (*rodef*) endangering the alleged wrongdoer and possibly the entire community (*Shu"t HaRosh* 17:1). Indeed, informants were categorized as traitors who deserved the same treatment as apostates (Avoda Zara 26b).

Yet informing remained permissible, even in the Middle Ages, under certain circumstances. If a Jew seeks to avoid paying money owed to a gentile or government authority, another Jew may help collect this debt, provided that doing so will not result in the offender's additional punishment, such as incarceration (ḤM 388:12). Such assistance is even deemed meritorious if one intends to maintain or improve the reputation of Judaism (ḤM 266). Similarly, one may inform on a Jew whose crimes endanger or cast suspicions on the community, or whose violence requires punitive action (ḤM 388:12). As such, contemporary authorities like Rabbis Shlomo Zalman Auerbach and Eliezer Waldenburg have ruled that one must inform the police of domestic and sexual abuse, even if the victim will be placed under the watch of non-religious or non-Jewish caretakers (*Tzitz Eliezer* 19:52).

As Rabbi Michael Broyde has documented (JHCS 43), decisors debate whether the broader restrictions apply to legal systems that do not regularly discriminate against Jews. Rabbi Yaakov Breisch, writing in 1964, ruled that the regulations stand, since the potential for anti-Semitism remains prevalent (*Ḥelkat Yaakov* ḤM 5). Rabbi Yaakov Yeshaya Blau more recently contended that deplorable prison conditions, including abuse by guards and fellow prisoners, make incarceration unfair to all criminals. While recognizing the fundamental fairness of American law, Rabbi Moshe Feinstein also upheld the ban on informing, as gentile courts regularly administer punishments beyond those advocated by halakha (IM OḤ 5:9).

Rabbi Hershel Schachter countered that since Judaism recognizes "the king's justice," the government has the power to determine appropriate punishments for all behavior deemed criminal by Jewish law (JHCS 1). Rabbi Shmuel HaLevi Wosner further contends that all conduct authorized by the halakhic principle of *dina demalkhuta* does not fall into the category of informing (*Shevet HaLevi* 2:58).

I personally support the far-reaching position of Rabbis Waldenburg, Yeḥiel Michel Epstein (AH ḤM 388:7), and Gedalia Dov Schwartz that many democracies maintain fair judicial systems, thereby neutralizing all restrictions on informing. Remaining watchful for individual cases of injustice in both courts and prisons, we can thank God for being citizens of countries that treat Jews equitably – including, alas, Bernie Madoff.

Chapter 38

Selling Weapons

Is it allowed to own a gun store?

The tragic mass shooting in Newtown, Connecticut, in December 2012 drew attention to Jewish attitudes toward weapons and gun control. In a series of articles in *Jewish Ideas Daily,* I have tried to postulate what policies one might derive from Jewish law and values. This essay will focus on a gun seller's responsibility for his customers' weapons use.

The Talmud forbids the sale of weapons to pagans, lest they use them immorally. "One should not sell idolaters weapons or weapon accessories, nor should one sharpen any weapon for them, nor may one sell them stocks, neck chains, ropes, or iron chains" (Avoda Zara 15b). Some sages even pondered whether one may sell them protective gear, such as shields, which may also be used for aggressive purposes. Ultimately, protective wear was excluded from the ban, yet all authorities include raw materials used exclusively to make weapons. The sages also added wild animals or other beasts that threaten the public welfare.

Medieval commentators gave various explanations for these regulations. Some thinkers cited anxiety that hostile neighbors will ultimately turn on the Jewish community (Rashi/Riaz); others referred to the general destruction brought upon the world by unethical weapons use (Maimonides, Commentary on the Mishna, Avoda Zara 1:7). Several noted that the Noahide laws prohibit homicide, and Jews must not aid and abet such crimes (Ritva). Similarly, the Talmud adds that one may not sell a weapon to a Jewish thief likely to use it in the course of a robbery. The sages further prohibited the sale of arms to Jewish middlemen who will resell them to suspect gentiles. As such, no salesperson may simply close his eyes to the harmful use of weapons. One may not sell weaponry to anyone suspicious – Jewish or gentile (YD 151:5).

Yet the Talmud notes that Persian Jews sold weapons to their gentile neighbors, who used them to protect their cities. Some medieval commentators granted these Jews a realpolitik dispensation: We need their help in protecting us, and hopefully they will not use the weapons against us (*Nimukei Yosef*). Yet many medieval commentators understood this clause as a more principled statement: One may sell weapons to groups with whom we have an alliance (MT *Hilkhot Avodat Kokhavim* 9:9) or shared interests (Rabbi Menaḥem HaMeiri), and who will presumably use them responsibly, such as for self-defense. Of course, such evaluations vary with time and place (Riaz on Rif).

Writing in Israel's first decade, Rabbi Yaakov Moshe Toledeno (d. 1960), former chief rabbi of Tel Aviv and religious affairs minister, prohibited Israeli gun merchants from selling to non-Jews (presumably from neighboring Arab villages). Based on past violence and continued animosity, Rabbi Toledeno feared they would use the weapons against Israel's Jewish citizens (*Yam HaGadol* YD 57). In contrast, the current head of Jerusalem's rabbinic courts, Rabbi Eliyahu Abrizal, prohibits selling specifically to known criminals; otherwise, gun sales remain permissible to Jews and non-Jews alike (*Dibrot Eliyahu* 3:13). Rabbi Abrizal seemingly assumes that all other gun purchasers have legitimate intentions, such as self-defense. He might be addressing only the situation created by Israel's relatively successful gun control regulations, leaving unclear how he would rule in a different country.

Rabbi Abrizal buttresses his position by asserting that the seller is guilty of aiding and abetting only if the buyer could not otherwise purchase the gun (or other prohibited object); if it could be purchased elsewhere, the seller is absolved of responsibility (*Darkhei Moshe* YD 151). On this basis, many medieval Jews marketed Christian religious articles (*Shakh* YD 151:7). Yet some medieval decisors argued that Jews remain culpable for facilitating others' sins, especially severe infractions like idolatry. Rabbi Toledeno and others have likewise contended that no such dispensation applies to weapon sales, since a Jew is liable for any role in helping someone commit bloodshed.

Given the debate over the use of this exemption from liability, it remains difficult to justify selling weapons, unless one is confident that local gun control regulations will keep buyers in line. Therefore, Jews worldwide should push for such laws, allowing for self-defense while preventing weapons from falling into the wrong hands.

Chapter 39

Killing Intruders

May one kill a burglar?

The right to self-defense made headlines in Israel in 2007 after Shai Dromi, a Negev farmer, fatally wounded a burglar. Dromi fired only after attempting to scare the intruder away, and then aimed only to wound him. The burglar's ultimate death and the subsequent arrest of Dromi led to a reconsideration of Israeli law on the matter, drawing largely upon Jewish sources. This essay will explore the discussion within Jewish legal theory, though readers should clarify the relevant laws for their own locales.

The right of self-defense is well-established in Jewish law. The sages contend that the verse, "You shall not stand idly by the blood of your neighbor" (Lev. 19:16) demands not only saving someone from drowning or other dangers, but stopping an assailant (*rodef*) from committing murder or sexual assault (Sanhedrin 73a). Even a fetus endangering its mother is considered a *rodef* and must be aborted, despite its lack of malicious intent (ḤM 425:2–3).

More controversially, *rodef* status was extended in medieval times to an informant (*moser*) if his information would unjustly endanger Jews (ḤM 388:10). Rabbi Moshe Isserles even applied this law to money forgers, if their crime would bring punishment upon the Jewish community (ḤM 425:1). Many decisors, however, believe such calculations don't apply in Western democracies that treat Jews fairly (*Tzitz Eliezer* 19:52). (See essay 37, "Reporting Criminals.") Equally significant, Rabbi Yehuda Henkin (*Bnei Banim* 3:33) and Prof. Eliav Shochetman (*Tchumin* 19) have compellingly argued (after the horrific Rabin assassination) that the status of *rodef* cannot be extended to democratically elected government officials, even if one deems their policies misguided and dangerous.

The license to kill an intruder (*haba bamaḥteret*), however, comes from a different biblical passage. "If the thief is seized while tunneling, and he is beaten to death, there is no bloodguilt in his case. If the sun has risen on him, there is bloodguilt in his case" (Ex. 22:1–2). Some biblical commentators understood the difference between the two cases to be a matter of timing: If the thief is killed during the robbery, the killer is not liable, but once the burglar has emerged from the house, one may no longer kill him (*Ḥizkuni*).

The sages, in contrast, understood the verse allegorically: If it is clear (as sunlight) that the thief intends no violence, one may not kill him. (The paradigm of such a non-belligerent intruder is a father stealing from his son; horrible though this situation is, we assume the father would never physically harm his child.) Otherwise, the intruder may be killed with impunity, following the legal principle of "If one comes to slay you, kill him first" (Sanhedrin 72a). The sages noted that people do not remain passive when their property is attacked. As such, a robber expects a confrontation and comes prepared to kill, thereby making him a *rodef* (MT Hilkhot *Geneiva* 9:8).

This rationale led some to contend that a daytime intruder (when the sun literally shines on him) would not be considered a *rodef*, since he hopes to avoid confrontation by entering when the owner is out (Raavad, Nahmanides). While Maimonides disagreed with this conclusion, some have accepted it as normative law (*Baḥ* ḤM 425).

Unlike a classic *rodef* scenario, in which the law requires a person to attempt to save the intended victim (MT *Hilkhot Rotze'aḥ* 1:6), the homeowner is not obligated to kill the intruder (*Hilkhot Geneiva* 9:9). He has permission to do so, and is not liable for his death, but he may also refrain from taking such action (*Afikei Yam* 2:40). Indeed, some maintain that many intruders would flee if confronted, and that the Torah allows killing them only as a punishment for their creating a potentially violent situation (Ran, Sanhedrin 72a).

In 2008, following public outrage over the arrest of Dromi (who was ultimately acquitted), the Knesset adopted a law that no longer required homeowners to prove they were under direct threat, even as it continued to forbid killing if unnecessary to deter a robber. Such is the potential impact of Jewish law on Israeli law.

Chapter 40

Gambling

Does halakha permit gambling?

A glance at the Gamblers Anonymous website and the similar sites highlights the deleterious impact of gambling on our society. Judaism has long recognized the ill effects of such behavior, and it behooves us to examine the sources so they can help us address this problem within our community.

The Mishna disqualifies dice players from serving as witnesses, listing them among others whose greed ruins their credibility. The Talmud offers two reasons for disqualifying dice players (Sanhedrin 24b–25a). Rami Bar Ḥama contends that gambling constitutes theft, since the loser never expects to lose (*asmakhata*). R. Sheshet, on the other hand, maintains that only a full-time gambler is disqualified, since he fails to engage in constructive activity (*yishuv haolam*).

The medieval authorities disagreed about the final ruling in this dispute. Maimonides seems to view gambling as low-level theft, yet he also criticizes gamblers for contributing nothing to society (MT *Hilkhot Gezeila* 6:10–11). While Maimonides' opinion remains ambiguous in other sources (MT *Hilkhot Edut* 10:4), Rabbi Joseph Karo rules stringently, classifying all forms of gambling as theft (ḤM 207:13). Accordingly, contemporary Sephardic decisors debate the propriety of purchasing a lottery ticket. Though Rabbi Ovadia Yosef forbids it (*Yabia Omer* ḤM 7:6), Rabbi Ovadia Hedaya rules leniently, outlawing betting only when one takes money directly from another (*Yaskil Avdi* YD 8:5). This view would permit raffles for non-cash prizes.

Many Ashkenazic authorities contend that normative law follows the more liberal R. Sheshet. Rashi (1040–1105), Rosh (1250–1328), and others explain that gambling is not an *asmakhta,* because everyone knows the dice results are random, so no one thinks his skills give him an advantage in winning. Rabbenu Tam (twelfth century, France) allowed any potentially profitable gaming agreement. Rabbi Moshe Isserles was also lenient (ḤM 370:3). On this basis, former Ashkenazic Israeli Chief Rabbi Avraham Shapira permitted casual playing of the lottery, even for Sephardim (*Tchumin* 5). As Rabbi Chaim Jachter has noted, however, the Ashkenazic tradition permits gambling only when the winner is determined randomly. Sports betting pools (rotisserie leagues), in contrast, might remain problematic, since betters believe their sports knowledge will minimize losses. More important, many classic sources denounce gambling as immoral or, at best, lacking redeeming value, and numerous prominent rabbis therefore discourage or even prohibit onetime casino visits.

Many decisors, Ashkenazic and Sephardic alike, permit light forms of gambling when the proceeds benefit charitable organizations. Here the *asmakhta* issue might not arise, since people feel comfortable "donating" their losses to charity. As such, many mid-twentieth-century Diaspora schools and synagogues held "bingo nights" as fundraisers. (My brothers fondly recall entering their school on subsequent mornings greeted by forgotten signs that read, "No Children Under 18 Allowed.") With increasing awareness of gambling addiction, these events have become less common, as communities recognize the inappropriateness of promoting such behavior in synagogues. As Jews, we must stem the scourge of gambling in our affluent society, particularly among teenagers.

What about on Ḥanukka, however, with its late medieval traditions of dreidel spinning and card playing? Given the Talmud's anti-gambling sentiments, these customs seem to represent an anomaly with suspect origins. Some have speculated that gambling on Ḥanukka recalls an attempt by Hasmonean Jews to hide their rebellious behavior from the Greeks by playing dice.

More likely, however, these customs stemmed from an unholy abuse of the joy of Ḥanukka, which turned into debauchery. As Rabbi Dr. Daniel Sperber has noted, late medieval texts condemn illicit

Ḥanukka parties that included unseemly card playing and gambling. Two of the most prominent Eastern European decisors of the modern era, Rabbi Yisrael Meir Kagan (BH 670:2, s.v. *venohagin*) and Rabbi Yeḥiel Michel Epstein (AH OḤ 670:9), both denounced gambling on Ḥanukka as utterly incompatible with Jewish mores. Thus, it behooves us to think carefully about how to celebrate the holiday without encouraging misconduct.

Chapter 41

Rabbinic Ordination

How are rabbis ordained?

The rabbinate has a fascinating history, having evolved differently in various locales. Already in late antiquity, scholars emerged as the Jewish people's leading spiritual (and occasionally political) figures. Modeled on the biblical elders (Num. 11) and judges (Deut. 16–17), these authorities served as Bible interpreters, authorized transmitters of oral teachings, and legislators. They also constituted the judicial system, including the Sanhedrin, the supreme rabbinic court of seventy-one elders. Smaller courts handled civil suits, criminal cases, corporal punishment and fines, calendrical calculations, and nullification of vows.

To become a certified authority, one required *semikha* (ordination) from an already ordained figure (Sanhedrin 5b). These authorities had to be first-rate scholars, primarily in Jewish law but also in languages, sciences, and general theology (Sanhedrin 17a), as well as bearers of impeccable morals. While the scholars had to have requisite eligibility and knowledge in all areas, their judicial mandate could be limited to specific areas of law (MT *Hilkhot Sanhedrin* 4:8–10). The ordination of an unworthy person was a terrible sin, especially when done for nefarious motives (Sanhedrin 7b). Power struggles over judicial appointments occasionally exploded between the judiciary and the *nasi* (the Jewish political leader in the Roman period), and at times each body retained veto power over selections for the respective offices (Y. Sanhedrin 19a).

Semikha was granted only within the Land of Israel, and following the political turmoil after the Temple's destruction, it ceased, at the latest, by 425 CE. The significance of this institution was understood by despotic Roman emperors like Hadrian, who sought to weaken the Jewish community by forbidding ordination and executing all violators of this decree (Sanhedrin 14a).

In the sixteenth century, when prominent theologians immigrated to Eretz Yisrael amid messianic fervor, Rabbi Jacob Berab of Safed attempted to restore *semikha* through a unanimous declaration by Israel's greatest scholars. While the ordainees included figures like Rabbis Joseph Karo and Moses di Trani, the demurral of Jerusalem's preeminent sage, Rabbi Levi ibn Habib, ended this undertaking (Radbaz MT *Hilkhot Sanhedrin* 4:11). An attempt by Rabbi Yehuda Maimon in 1949 to renew the Sanhedrin in the State of Israel never gained traction.

Already in talmudic times, when Jews moved to Babylonia and classic ordination ceased, the sages authorized scholars to issue rulings (*horaa*) and adjudicate financial disputes in areas like torts, inheritance, and transactions (Bava Kamma 84b, BY ḤM 1). Additionally, the sages permitted social sanctions like excommunication and even corporal punishment, a tool occasionally used by medieval communities with limited autonomy (ḤM 2). These latter powers were frequently held by seven-man political councils (*shiva tovei ha'ir*), who were not necessarily rabbis.

Rabbinic scholars were accorded various positions and titles, including *ḥaver*, *ḥakham*, and *rav*. Gentile rulers sometimes appointed a chief rabbi or parallel figure to collect taxes and occasionally represent the community. This official was not always the greatest scholar, however, and his appointment could be unpopular, which sometimes led to communal strife.

Formal ordination, following a period of study, emerged only in France and Germany in the thirteenth or fourteenth century. This ordination, conferred by one's teacher, certified the student's erudition and virtues (*higgia lehoraa*) and granted him license (*reshut*) to issue rulings in the presence or locale of his teacher (*Shu"t HaRivash* 271). This license could be limited to specific areas of law (YD 242:14), with further certification frequently required for more specialized fields, including divorces (*gittin*) and the judiciary (*dayanut*). Such ordination was not practiced in medieval Spain, where figures like Rabbi Isaac Abrabanel questioned whether it represented an imitation of non-Jewish doctoral titles (*Naḥalat Avot* 6:2). Prof. Mordechai Breuer has more reasonably speculated that this development occurred to help revive Jewish communities and clarify normative practices following the traumas of various plagues and expulsions.

This system of certification created problems, since no distinction was reserved for figures of supreme erudition and piety, while those unworthy of the title could usurp the powers associated with it. Rabbi Israel Isserlein (fifteenth century, Germany) and others attempted to restrict ordinations, lamenting, "The ordained are many, yet the scholars are few" (*Terumat HaDeshen Pesakim* 255). Additionally, the granting of titles to people without clerical positions increased rabbinic competition and led to numerous questions of professional encroachment. In many locations, rabbis had to receive permission from the town's elected rabbinic authority in order to perform clerical functions (AH YD 242:29). In some contemporary communities, such as in England, various titles are used for different functionaries, while Israel's Chief Rabbinate issues various advanced *semikha* certificates to enable ordainees to serve in select positions, such as that of municipal rabbi. In other countries, particularly those without a central rabbinate, such restrictions have been replaced by informal professional regulations and communal standards to promote rabbinic training, collegiality, and effectiveness.

Chapter 42

Rabbinic Salaries

Is it wrong for a rabbi to demand higher pay?

I naturally side with my colleagues, who make significant (and underappreciated) sacrifices in service to their communities. Nonetheless, the historic issue of rabbinic compensation entails a complex web of moral and legal values that deserves continued reflection.

Several classic sources forbid the use of Torah knowledge in seeking acclaim or wealth. As R. Tzaddok famously stated, "Do not use the Torah as a crown for self-glorification or a spade for digging." Hillel further warned that anyone guilty of such misuse would perish (Avot 4:5). Moses himself, the Talmud claimed, exhorted future scholars to teach Scripture free of charge (Nedarim 37a).

In this spirit, many talmudic sages earned their livelihood through various (and sometimes laborious) trades, such as farming, tanning, and wood chopping. Socioeconomic hardships resulted, occasionally creating division between poor scholars and those who were independently wealthy. Tax exemptions and preferences in certain trades helped alleviate these pressures. Most important, scholars were permitted to receive *sekhar tirḥa* and *sekhar battala*, compensation for preparatory efforts and income lost while performing religious services. Thus the sage Karna collected a standard fee from each litigant before issuing his verdicts (Ketubbot 105a), while elementary school teachers could receive compensation for the "day care" aspects of their jobs (Nedarim 37a).

In early medieval times, two major Babylonian yeshivas, Sura and Pumbedita, raised significant funds from local communities and foreign supporters, who in turn received legal guidance from the heads of these academies (*Geonim*). When Spanish Jewry emerged as an independent community in the tenth century, it lured great scholars with large stipends and other benefits (*Sefer HaKabbala*). This extensive public support of scholars, and the "relentless importuning for contributions," as Prof. Isadore Twersky called it, drew the ire of Maimonides, who lambasted the use of scholarship for financial gain as a violation of the talmudic work ethic (commentary on Avot 4:5). Like many scholars before him, Maimonides worked rather than relying on charity.

Nonetheless, in Sephardic lands, rabbis continued to receive stipends from their communities, with Rabbi Simon Duran of Algiers (known as Tashbetz, 1361–1444) even writing a treatise against Maimonides' position. Noting that the Talmud itself allowed certain remunerations, Tashbetz compared contemporary rabbis to ancient priests, who received tithes and other assistance. He also noted that current rabbinic responsibilities had extended well beyond scholarship and included administrative and diplomatic functions, thereby necessitating basic compensation to increase one's stature and devote sufficient time to the job (*Shu"t Tashbetz* 1:142–48).

In Ashkenazic lands, matters developed more slowly. Rabbi Yehuda HaḤasid (1150–1217), leader of the German pietists, opposed communal salaries as a violation of talmudic strictures and an imposition on poor families. His colleague, Rabbi Eliezer of Bohemia, countered that without support – raised during Purim and Simḥat Torah appeals – religious leaders would be forced to abandon their work, leaving communities without spiritual guidance (*Or Zarua* Laws of a Prayer Leader 1:113).

By the fifteenth century, offering communal salaries to rabbis (and in many cases cantors) had become the norm in both Ashkenazic and Sephardic lands. Nonetheless, as Prof. Jeffrey I. Roth has shown, rabbinic emoluments varied greatly. While some communities paid their rabbis a living wage, others offered less, forcing their spiritual leaders to procure other resources. Some rabbinic contracts included minimal salaries supplemented by fees for various rabbinic functions, such as divorces, sermons, and adjudication. While Rabbi Ovadia of Bertinuro found this system unfair, since people in need of these services had nowhere else to turn (commentary on Bekhorot 4:6), it remained the dominant practice for years.

A new problem emerged as rabbis competed to perform these tasks. Rabbi Israel Isserlein (d. 1460), embarrassed by the potential impropriety of these fees, ruled that a newly arrived scholar could offer religious services in his city, even if doing so might detract from the established rabbi's business (*Terumat HaDeshen* 128). Yet a century later, Rabbi Moshe Isserles limited a newcomer's fees (YD 245:22), and Rabbi Moshe Sofer (d. 1839) later ruled that in an era of formal communal appointments, no outsiders could impinge on the official rabbi's salary (*Ḥatam Sofer* ḤM 5:21). Other disputes arose over tenure and inheritance of rabbinic positions (see the next essay).

These debates highlight the conflicting values that continue generating controversy over rabbinic salaries. Rabbis are hard workers who must balance their idealism with supporting their families in a manner that preserves the dignity of their calling and position. While compensation must vary based on many factors, including community finances, very often such a request is an act of prudence, not a lack of piety.

Chapter 43

Inheriting Rabbinic Positions

May a rabbi bequeath his pulpit to his child?

The 2013 elections of Israel's chief rabbis raised questions regarding the entitlement of spiritual leaders to inherit their father's positions. Four of the leading candidates were sons of previous chief rabbis, including the two victors, Rabbis Yitzḥak Yosef and David Lau. While some expressed concerns over nepotism, others noted that rabbinic history (and international politics) is replete with family dynasties.

The Torah declares that two positions are hereditary: the priesthood and the monarchy. Regarding the former, the Torah asserts that the direct descendants of Aaron will serve as *kohanim* (Ex. 29:30), mandating a careful preservation of pedigree that remains intact today. Similarly, the Torah commands the bequeathal of the kingship from father to son (Deut. 17:20). According to some scholars, the monarchy passes to a daughter in limited circumstances (*Minḥat Ḥinukh* 497:2). Decisors debate whether the oldest son automatically inherits the throne, with some arguing that the king decides which child receives the kingship, as proven by David's selection of Solomon, who was not his firstborn. Hereditary succession was also enacted in late antiquity for the position of the *nasi* (political leader), but significantly, only after the passing of Hillel in 10 CE. While similar arrangements existed for Babylonian exilarchs, Nahmanides and others overthrew the Jewish aristocracy in thirteenth-century Barcelona by arguing that children take precedence only when they are equally qualified for the task.

Many sources discourage hereditary succession, especially in matters of spiritual wisdom. Familial succession does not occur in the Book of Judges, and most significantly, Moses handed over the reins of leadership to Joshua, not his own children. While some sources pronounce them unqualified (*Avot DeRabbi Natan* A, 17), other texts indicate that they were capable but passed over because Joshua was worthier (Numbers Rabba 21:14). Indeed, according to a famous rabbinic maxim, the crown of royalty was given to the House of David, and the priestly crown to Aaron's descendants, but the crown of Torah is available to anyone who wishes to take it (Yoma 72b). One talmudic passage even asserts that children of sages are frequently not scholars themselves, because they arrogantly believe wisdom can be inherited (Nedarim 81a).

Medieval decisors debated which communal positions are hereditary. Maimonides writes that inheritance should apply to all positions of authority, as long as the heir displays sufficient fear of God and minimal knowledge (MT *Hilkhot Melakhim* 1:7). Accordingly, some scholars argued that even the position of charity collector should be given to an heir, unless he is far less qualified than others (*Ginat Veradim* YD 3:7). Rabbi Shlomo ibn Aderet (Rashba) noted that popular practice allowed a son to inherit his father's cantorial position, even if his voice was not as pleasant, as long as he was virtuous (*Shu"t HaRashba* 1:300). While this position is codified in *Shulḥan Arukh* (OḤ 53:25), many commentators asserted that Rashba's claim was contingent upon local practice, and that the letter of the law does not require hereditary succession for prayer leaders (*Ḥatam Sofer* OḤ 1:12).

Nonetheless, numerous scholars contended that heirs should be preferred for rabbinic positions, a practice that – as Shaul Stampfer has documented – peaked in nineteenth-century Eastern Europe (*Mikhtav Sofer* YD 23). Some countered that sons (and sometimes sons-in-law) took precedence only among equally qualified candidates, and even then only with the approval of the community (*Shu"t Maharam Schick* YD 228). Yet other scholars adamantly rejected rabbinic inheritance. They argued that the crown of Torah must be awarded based on wisdom and skills alone, especially given rabbis' crucial role in teaching and adjudication (*Shu"t Maharshadam* YD 85). Indeed, in the later medieval and early modern period, many Ashkenazic communities prohibited a son from succeeding his father as rabbi, lest an extended familial hold on power compromise his impartiality as an ecclesiastical judge. In early medieval communities, in contrast, spiritual leadership remained concentrated within the hands of a select group of families, albeit not necessarily through formal inheritance.

In the sixteenth century, Rabbi Moshe Isserles affirmed a son's preferred status, unless the community declared from the outset that rabbinic appointments had term limits and would not automatically fall to children (YD 245:22). This ruling has major implications for contemporary rabbinic appointments, which are frequently made under strict employment conditions that preclude automatic bequeathal (AH OḤ 53:27–28). Rabbis Moshe Sternbuch, Mordechai Eliyahu, Shaul Yisraeli, and others have all affirmed that many rabbinic duties preclude, by default or prearrangement, automatic inheritance of positions. In sum, the election of Rabbis Lau and Yosef was earned through merit and politics, but not mandated by halakha.

Chapter 44

Disciplining Students

May a teacher strike a student or confiscate his property?

The beginning of every school year inevitably revives debates over appropriate disciplinary measures in the classroom. Educators struggle with how to use their limited power and resources in order to help a student learn from his or her mistakes.

One common scenario involves students using their personal effects during inappropriate times or for improper activities (e.g., texting in class). While many teachers respond by seizing students' property, it is questionable whether halakha permits that, even temporarily. If the object is dangerous, such as a knife, halakha demands its removal for the sake of public safety (ḤM 427:8). Yet with respect to more innocuous items, such as those used for entertainment (like an MP3 player), confiscation seems to qualify as stealing. The Talmud strictly prohibits any theft for the exclusive purpose of upsetting the victim (Bava Metzia 61b). Many commentators understand this statement to ban property expropriation under any circumstances, even in jest, briefly, or with intent to provide restitution (*Torah Temima* Lev. 19:11). Maimonides explains that though no monetary loss will result, the Torah desires to prevent people from growing accustomed to taking other people's belongings (MT *Hilkhot Geneiva* 1:2).

However, many authorities, such as Rabbis Shlomo Zalman Auerbach and Zalman Neḥemia Goldberg, justify the confiscation of property on various grounds. They note that a few commentators understand the Talmud as prohibiting non-monetary theft only on a long-term basis, not in the form of temporary confiscations (*Shita Mekubbetzet* Bava Metzia 61b). This permissive rationale is strengthened if the object remains on the teacher's desk or elsewhere within the student's sight, since one may then claim it has not really been taken from him (*Tchumin* 8). Rabbi Yaakov Yeshaya Blau further cites opinions that permit such confiscations for the sake of a mitzva, such as education (*Pitḥei Ḥoshen* 4, p. 24). Some have even argued that since schools establish rules of punishment, students (and their parents) accept them upon enrollment (*Tchumin* 19).

Another justification is based on an *a fortiori* argument: Temporary confiscations are permissible since the Talmud sanctions even physical punishments by teachers or parents (*Mishneh Halakhot* 6:284). While the analogy between monetary matters and battery remains contentious, it highlights the historically controversial leniency of striking children for educational purposes.

Corporal punishment finds it roots in the Book of Proverbs: "He who spares the rod hates his son, but he who loves him chastises him diligently" (13:24). Numerous ethical treatises, including the fifteenth-century *Orḥot Tzaddikim* (sec. 7), promote this type of "tough love." The Talmud even exempts a father or teacher from liability for damages accidentally caused by such punishment (Makkot 8b).

As Prof. Benjamin Shmueli has documented, however, classic rabbinic sources impose many qualifications on this practice. First, the objective must be exclusively educational; any other intentions make the beating strictly forbidden as child abuse. Second, punishment must be either immediate or preemptive, not as retribution for previous misdeeds (*Even Shelema* 6:4). Toddlers who do not understand such a penalty may not be struck (Ralbag, Prov. 19:18), nor may older children if it might backfire (Moed Katan 17a). In fact, excommunications were imposed on those who hit their children at an inappropriate age (Rabbi Akiva Eiger, YD 240:20), and teachers who struck their pupils too often or too harshly were dismissed (Makkot 16b). Maimonides, moreover, demanded that a person not strike a child in anger, and prohibited using harsh instruments such as whips and rods (MT *Hilkhot Talmud Torah* 2:2).

Despite these restrictions, Jewish legal and ethical sources historically allowed for the educational striking of children, a sentiment that continued into the twentieth century (*Mikhtav MeEliyahu* 3:360–61). Yet the type of punishment considered effective was understood to depend on the child and his temperament (*Kitzur Shulḥan Arukh* 143:18).

In the modern era, many scholars deemed corporal punishment undesirable or a last resort. Rabbi Samson Raphael Hirsch, for example, asserted that this method undermines a child's moral development (*Yesodot HaḤinukh* vol. 2, p. 65). Rabbi Eliezer Papo cautioned that in eras when youth rebel against authority, corporal punishment is likely to be counterproductive (*Pele Yoetz,* s.v. *hakaa*). Similar reservations were expressed by Rabbis Moshe Feinstein (IM YD 4:30) and Ḥayim David HaLevi (*Kitzur Shulḥan Arukh, Mekor Ḥayim* 6:126:14). Perhaps the greatest contemporary opponent of corporal punishment was Rabbi Shlomo Wolbe, who contended that in our day, pleasant rebuke and patience constitute the best way to educate a child. I heartily agree.

Section IV
Ritual

Chapter 45

The Evil Eye

Does Judaism recognize it or is it a mere superstition?

The ancient notion of an "evil eye" remains popular in various cultures around the world. Though its meaning varies, it is most commonly considered a powerful force, often unleashed (unintentionally) by jealous onlookers. When sharing good tidings, many Jews use the Hebrew expression *bli ayin hara* ("without an evil eye") to avoid misfortune. There is even a maternity store in downtown Jerusalem called Bli Ayin Hara! Nevertheless, different perspectives on the evil eye, and other alleged forces, have emerged within Judaism, each associated with different customs, and together they reflect an ambivalent and sometimes contradictory attitude.

In the classic Jewish sources, the eye frequently symbolizes God's metaphysical awareness; it also represents the interest humans take in each other. The Bible speaks of God's watchful eye over the Jewish people (Deut. 11:12, Ps. 33:18) and demands that we not close our eyes to the needs of those less fortunate (Deut. 15:9). The Bible also cautions against being led astray by wandering eyes (Num. 15:39), since visual sensations can cause the most sinful temptations (Sota 8a). Within the tannaitic literature, the sages admonish those who possess an *ayin hara,* a jealous outlook (Avot 2:9, 11). Rather, one should adopt an *ayin tova* (good eye), being satisfied with his lot and wishing others the best (*Avot DeRabbi Natan* A, 16).

Beyond the evil and hatred caused by jealousy, numerous talmudic sources, particularly Babylonian, depict the evil eye as having harmful powers in itself. The sage Rav, for example, attributes many illnesses to the evil eye, and the Talmud even maintains that he could enter cemeteries and determine that ninety-nine out of one hundred people buried there had died prematurely due to an *ayin hara* (Bava Metzia 107b). As Prof. Jacob Trachtenberg has noted, these sages affirm that certain eyes possess maleficent powers, or at least that an envious glare, even without ill will, can cause supernatural repercussions.

These beliefs were widespread both in antiquity and in the medieval era amongst the learned elite and the masses alike. Rashi (1040–1150, France) and many other medieval scholars explain that the Bible prohibits head counts so as to avoid inflicting an evil eye (Ex. 30:12). Many medieval philosophers, including non-Jews like Thomas Aquinas, affirm this power. In their Bible commentaries, both Ralbag (1288–1344, France) and Rabbi Yitzḥak Arama (fifteenth century, Spain) elaborate on how eyes can emit certain vapors that wreak havoc on their objects. Others, like Rabbi Ovadia Seforno, contend that escalated individual attention causes God to examine the person's actions, increasing the possibility of divine reproach.

Maimonides challenges the notion of an evil eye (as well as other folklore beliefs) by minimizing its impact on legal matters. For instance, the Talmud forbids excessive admiration of another's crops, lest the evil eye damage them (Bava Batra 2b). Rashi, Nahmanides (Bava Batra 59a), and Rabbi Joseph Karo (ḤM 378:5) affirm this explanation, yet Maimonides reinterprets the prohibition as a protection of privacy (*Shu"t HaRambam* 395). Similarly, the Talmud provides two reasons not to care for lost property in view of strangers, lest the evil eye destroy the property, and lest onlookers steal it (Bava Metzia 30a); Maimonides, however, mentions only the second reason (MT *Hilkhot Gezela* 13:11).

Despite Maimonides' opposition, many customs based on belief in the evil eye have become part of Jewish ritual, such as avoiding double weddings (EH 62:3) and refraining from assigning consecutive *aliyot* to fathers and sons. While Rabbi Yeḥiel Michel Epstein permits one to ignore this custom if he is not concerned with the evil eye (AH OḤ 141:8), most contemporary scholars disagree (MB 141:19).

Some recent authorities clearly continue believing in the *ayin hara*. Rabbi Meshulam Roth (d. 1963) chastised another scholar for dismissing its significance (*Kol Mevasser* 2:7) while Rabbi Ovadia Yosef's office issued detailed measures one can take to avoid it (www. halachayomit.co.il). Others follow Maimonides' lead and relegate this belief to ancient superstition. Nevertheless, most continue to observe customs rooted in this notion, paying homage to the sociological power of the evil eye, even as they deny its metaphysical existence.

Chapter 46

Red Strings

Is it appropriate to wear red strings for their protective powers?

When I visit Jerusalem's Old City, I regularly see an old lady blessing Western Wall visitors as she hands out red strings (*bendeles*) for a small donation. This scene is repeated at many holy sites, especially as New Age spirituality has made these strings fashionable, with celebrities like Madonna sporting them. Despite their popularity in all streams of Judaism, the strings and their alleged protective powers raise a number of legal issues.

The Torah commands that we serve God wholeheartedly, and warns against foreign superstitions, divinations, and sorcery (Deut. 18:13). Consistent with this theme, the Torah (Lev. 18:3, Ex. 23:24) forbids alien rituals, known as "Amorite practices" (*darkhei Emori*), even if they do not constitute actual idolatry (*avoda zara*).

Though difficult to define, these forbidden rites typically draw on purportedly supernatural powers or sorcery to accomplish certain goals. Foreign practices that honor someone or provide some concrete benefit, however, remain permissible (YD 178:1). For this reason, the talmudic sages permitted the pyrrhic burning of a deceased monarch's property in order to pay homage to his irreplaceability (*Tosafot* Avoda Zara 11a).

As Dr. Elly Teman has shown, the red string serves as an amulet in many cultures, although its origin remains unknown. While frequently used for therapeutic purposes – "healing" everything from sore throats to smallpox – it is most often employed as "preventative medicine," to ward off the "evil eye" or difficult pregnancies and births. (Teman speculates that the vitality of the color red, along with the string usually being tied around something, symbolizes its ability to keep danger at bay.) These practices exist within Jewish folklore, with some scholars tracing them to the biblical story in which Rahab spared herself from Jericho's destruction by hanging red strings on her house (Josh. 2).

In cataloging "Amorite practices" – including pulling a child through a cemetery and dancing and clapping around a bonfire – the Tosefta lists wearing a red string around one's finger, an ancient folk practice (Shabbat 7:11). Despite this seemingly explicit source, decisors have defended red strings because a more important talmudic text leaves this example, among many, off its shorter list (Shabbat 67a). Furthermore, the Tosefta says nothing about tying the string around one's wrist, pregnant stomach, or baby carriage. And medieval scholars asserted that only foreign rituals explicitly denounced in the Talmud are forbidden as "Amorite practices" (*Yere'im* 313). While this position opens the door to a series of popular folk traditions, other authorities advocated more restrictions, seeking to avoid all specious alien rituals (*Baḥ* YD 178).

Significantly, the Talmud, followed by later codes, specifically permits medicinal practices (including wearing a fox tooth or grasshopper egg), thus leaving room for the alleged therapy of the red string (OḤ 301:27). The criterion for efficacious medicine, however, varies greatly. Rabbi Shlomo ibn Aderet (thirteenth century, Spain), in defense of widespread folklore practices, contended that as long as a therapeutic ritual had not been proven ineffective, it remained permissible (*Shu"t HaRashba* 1:167, 413). Maimonides and others were more restrictive, insisting that the supposed remedy be proven effective (Guide 3:37).

Yet Maimonides permitted the use of these non-scientific treatments to comfort patients who would be distraught without them (MT *Hilkhot Shabbat* 19:13–14). This paternalism – essentially permitting placebos for the superstitious – drew the scorn of the Vilna Gaon (eighteenth century, Lithuania), who accused Maimonides of rationalistically ignoring deep truths (Gra YD 179:13).

One modern decisor, Rabbi Yair Bachrach (seventeenth century, Germany), argued against banning any long-standing practice within the Jewish community, since such a tradition must have proven itself over the years (*Ḥavvot Yair* 234). Indeed, following this logic, two contemporary rabbis, Moshe Stern (*Be'er Moshe* 8:36, para. 3) and Ephraim Greenblatt (*Rivevot Efraim* 8:51), have defended red strings as an ancient and therefore legitimate custom, effective or not. Others forbid the strings, scorning their popularity as an undesirable "voodoo-ization" of Judaism, with amulets and charms replacing prayer and belief in God's own healing powers.

Chapter 47

Kiddush Levana

Are we praying to the moon?

The blessing of the new moon, known colloquially as *kiddush levana* (and more properly as *birkat levana*), developed over many centuries, thereby accruing layers of ritual that embellish its meaning yet sometimes confuse its message. The practice originated in talmudic times, with the sages declaring, "Anyone who blesses the new moon in the proper time is as if he greeted the Divine Presence" (Sanhedrin 42a).

Far from moon worship, the blessing is one of many recited to acknowledge God's continual control over nature. As the words themselves extol, "Blessed are You, Lord our God, King of the universe, who by His word created the heavens, and by His breath all their hosts. He set laws and times for them, that they not deviate from their appointed task." Rabbi Menaḥem HaMeiri (thirteenth century, Provence) explains that the wonders of nature exemplify God's presence in the world and demand that we praise His greatness. Indeed, the Jerusalem Talmud (Berakhot 9:2), followed by Maimonides (MT *Hilkhot Berakhot* 10:16), codifies *kiddush levana* among other laudatory blessings recited over natural wonders, such as rainbows.

Nonetheless, given the moon worship found in other societies, *kiddush levana* has been modified to highlight our belief in God as controller of the cosmos. Kabbalists, for example, preface the ceremony with Psalm 148, which depicts the heavenly bodies' praise of God's rule. Likewise, a poem immediately following the blessing praises God as the moon's creator, and we conclude with the *Aleinu* prayer, proclaiming

God's Kingship over the world (BH 426:2, s.v. *u'mevarekh*). Furthermore, one should look at the moon only momentarily before reciting the blessing, then look away for the rest of the ritual, showing that we direct our prayers to God (*Taz* 426:4).

A major dispute developed regarding when to recite the blessing. Maimonides and other medieval Spanish authorities, following the simplest reading of the Talmud, ruled that we perform *kiddush levana* starting from the first day of the month, when the crescent phase of the moon's cycle begins. Similarly, the Talmud states that one may not recite the blessing after the fifteenth of the month, when the moon begins to wane. Many authorities, on the other hand, recommended waiting seventy-two hours into the crescent period, when the moon's rejuvenation becomes more visible (BY OḤ 426:2).

However, Tractate Soferim 19:10 advocates reciting *kiddush levana* immediately after the Sabbath, when we are still surrounded by fine aromas and dressed in Sabbath clothing. (The Sabbath itself was not chosen for the proceedings, perhaps because we already acknowledge the divine rulership that day in Kiddush.) Especially with the potentially larger post-Sabbath participation, this timing, first accepted in France and Germany, transformed *kiddush levana* into a more festive ritual. Historian Yaakov Gratner has also speculated that this embellishment might stem from an attempt to recreate the joyful celebrations of the new month in Jerusalem during talmudic times.

Some authorities opposed the recitation of *kiddush levana* after Shabbat, especially in rainy climates, when postponing the blessing might close the window of opportunity to see the frequently cloud-covered moon within the crescent period. Nonetheless, this "schedule" has become widely accepted (OḤ 426:2), and consequently most people wait until the first Saturday night seventy-two hours after the emergence of the new moon.

The festive embellishment of *kiddush levana* complements the blessing's second, more subtle theme that the moon's constant revival symbolizes the Jewish people's coming redemption. As the primary blessing continues, "He told the moon to renew itself as a crown of splendor for those He carried from the womb [Israel], for they are destined to be renewed like it." Many other poems included in the ritual carry this theme, including the famous song, "David, king of Israel, lives and endures.... May it be a good sign and a good omen for us and all of Israel."

One startling custom relating to this motif is that of rising on one's toes while reciting, "Just as I dance before you [the moon] but cannot touch you, may none of my enemies be able to touch me." Besides creating Jewish break-dancing, bopping on one's toes allayed fears that the bodily gestations of actual dancing might be misconstrued as bowing to the moon (*Magen Avraham* 426:9)!

Though *kiddush levana* may initially seem baffling, further study reveals the significance of this ritual and highlights the importance of seeking the meaning behind customs and mitzvot.

Chapter 48

Kippot

What is the source and reason for wearing a kippa?

Religious garb, and head coverings in particular, stir strong religious and sociological emotions. The Muslim hijab, the Catholic miter, and the Jewish yarmulke, to take a few examples, each convey important symbolic messages and shape the identity of the individuals and communities who wear them. The ambiguous legal origins of the *kippa,* as we shall see, only underscore its evocative power.

While the Babylonian Talmud refers to a male head covering known as a *sudra,* it appears that in the talmudic era, not all men covered their heads at all times. Covering one's head, the Talmud explains, expresses reverence for the One above (Kiddushin 31a). Indeed, the word *sudra* connotes those who fear Him (Shabbat 77b). As such, the Talmud implies that head coverings are worn only by those who fear God, such as married scholars (Kiddushin 29b). In particular, the head is covered on occasions requiring greater reverence, such as court decisions (Shabbat 10a), lifecycle ceremonies (Kiddushin 8a), or during the Grace After Meals (Berakhot 51a).

Prof. Yitzhak Zimmer, author of an authoritative historical study of the *kippa,* has further noted that the Jerusalem Talmud never mentions a *sudra* or other coverings. Similarly, an eighth-century geonic text notes that *kohanim* in Eretz Yisrael offered the Priestly Blessing with their heads uncovered, as opposed to their Babylonian counterparts

(*HaḤillukim SheBein Anshei Mizraḥ U'Vnei Eretz Yisrael* 42). Collectively, these sources suggest that male head coverings originated in Babylonia, spreading elsewhere in early medieval times.

By the early Middle Ages, wearing a *kippa* had become customary in all major Jewish populations. Spanish authorities in particular contended that one should always cover his head. They cited, for example, the talmudic prohibition of walking four ells with one's hair uncovered (Shabbat 118b). Similarly, the recitation of prayers and blessings requires a head covering (Soferim 14:12). Other scholars, however, treated these sentiments as pietistic exhortations, not as normative requirements, with several sources indicating that early medieval French Jews, among others, did not always cover their heads (*Kolbo* 11).

The preeminent sixteenth-century decisor Rabbi Joseph Karo mandated head coverings for all males and at all times (BY OḤ 8), and this became the dominant position. Two notable detractors were the sixteenth-century Polish scholar Rabbi Shlomo Luria (*Shu"t Maharshal* 72) and the eighteenth-century Lithuanian sage, the Vilna Gaon (*Bei'ur HaGra* OḤ 8:2). Nonetheless, even these authorities acknowledged the popular practice of constant head covering. Yet many Italian and Moroccan Jews still follow their traditions, which don't require *kippot* at all times.

As Prof. Zimmer speculates, *kippot* helped distinguish Jews from gentiles. A few fifteenth-century German sources, for example, indicate that leaving one's head uncovered imitates gentile habits and leads to assimilation (*Shu"t Mahari Bruna* 34). Similarly, in the seventeenth century, Rabbi David HaLevi Segal ostracized Jews who, like their non-Jewish neighbors, removed their hats once sitting down (*Taz* OḤ 8:3).

Conversely, those seeking to break down the distinction between Jews and non-Jews have historically fought this custom. While the earliest Reform Jews retained their *kippot*, by 1844 this practice was dismissed as an act of talmudic pietism. The American Reform movement in particular downplayed this custom, declaring it unnecessary not only in public but in synagogues as well. Yet recent traditionalist trends within Reform have reintroduced *kippot*.

Some of the most fascinating questions regarding *kippot* shed much light on cultural context. One eighteenth-century rabbi, for example, emphasized the obligation of always wearing a *kippa* while allowing his congregants to remove it when greeting the king and other noblemen. Rabbi Samson Raphael Hirsch, the famed nineteenth-century German leader of neo-Orthodoxy, allowed local youth to remove their head coverings in gymnasium classes.

One decisor who spilled much ink over this topic was Rabbi Moshe Feinstein (twentieth century, United States). He famously allowed American Jews to remove their *kippot* for work purposes, but insisted that they put them back on when returning home (IM OḤ 4:2). He also deemed it better not to remove one's *kippa* if (sinfully) entering an inappropriate place such as a dance club, despite the possible desecration of God's name (IM YD 2:33). Like many other scholars, Rabbi Feinstein recognized that the *kippa* has served an important sociological role for centuries, and refused to allow one to remove himself, even in the most irreverent places, from the community of those who fear God.

Chapter 49

Pe'ot

Why do hasidic men grow sidelocks?

P*e'ot,* sidelocks, often curled around the ears, appear in hasidic and other communities, but not universally throughout the Orthodox world. Many view them as a sign of Jewishness but also as an aberration. This ambivalence reflects the custom's long history, which weaves together halakha, identity, and social realities.

The Torah commands, "You shall not round off the side growth (*pe'ot*) on your head, or destroy the side growth of your beard" (Lev. 19:27). This short verse amazingly encompasses the history of Jewish facial shaving. (See essay 31, "Electric Shavers," for more discussion of this verse.) The rabbis understood the latter part of the verse to prohibit shaving with a razor (which shears and utterly destroys the hair), leaving Jews to grow beards, trimming them with scissors or tweezers, or as in Eastern Europe, to use depilatory cream to burn off facial whiskers. (Being clean-shaven, I regularly thank God for electric shavers!)

For our purposes, the first half of the verse prohibits shearing the hair in front of the ears, extending from the temple to below the cheekbone or, according to some, to the bottom of the earlobes (Makkot 20a). Maimonides and others popularly explain that both prohibitions were intended to distinguish us from idolaters, who shaved these areas (Guide 3:37). Rabbi Abraham ibn Ezra (twelfth century, Spain) alternatively suggested, based on connections to Leviticus 21:5, that these forbidden shaving practices expressed inappropriate mourning. Rabbi Yaakov ben Asher (d. 1343, Spain), however, criticized attempts to offer rationales for these (and other) commandments, contending that we accept them simply because they represent the divine will (*Tur* YD 181).

Medieval scholars struggled to define the scope of the *pe'ot* prohibition. Many, such as Maimonides, maintained that one may cut off this hair with scissors, just not with a razor (MT *Hilkhot Avodat Kokhavim* 12:6). Yet the law follows the opinion of Rabbenu Asher, who required that one leave at least minimal hair uncut, even with scissors (YD 181:3). Much to the rabbis' chagrin, however, some Jews would razor-shave all the hair in this area, or leave a singular strand (*Shu"t Tashbetz* 2:100). Several authorities condemned this behavior as an unfortunate emulation of their non-Jewish neighbors.

Nonetheless, while medieval scholars condemned the cutting of too much hair in this area, they did not require people to grow out this hair either. Maimonides explicitly notes that the masses err in thinking the hair should remain unshorn, like a Nazirite (*Shu"t HaRambam* 244). Moreover, as Prof. Yitzhak Zimmer has documented in a detailed essay on this topic, both Jewish and non-Jewish art and literature historically make no reference to *pe'ot*.

The oldest community to continuously grow *pe'ot* is that of the Yemenites. They called them *simanim*, "signs," perhaps because these sidelocks distinguished them from their Muslim neighbors who also wore beards and head coverings. *Pe'ot* were popularized by the famed sixteenth-century Safed kabbalist Rabbi Isaac Luria (Arizal), who explicitly encouraged Jews to grow them because this "mitzva" can be performed all day for one's entire life. His students also promoted *pe'ot* as a sign of Jewish identity, an idea that quickly spread to Sephardic and Ashkenazic lands alike. Influenced by the Arizal, European hasidic Jews in particular embraced the mystical and symbolic significance of this practice. While some sects wear shorter *pe'ot* tucked behind the ears, others grow them extremely long and twist them into a tight coil. Styles differ in various communities, with members of each identifiable by their *pe'ot*.

Over the centuries, however, an increasing number of Jews violated the biblical shaving regulations. This was particularly true in central Europe under the influence of the Renaissance, Protestantism, the Enlightenment, and the Reform movement, where men were increasingly clean-shaven and, in some eras, wore wigs. As Prof. Zimmer notes, the increased neglect of these regulations by some Jews only amplified facial hair's symbolic importance for traditionalist Jews, and *pe'ot* came to distinguish not only Jews from non-Jews, but also Jews from Jews. Indeed, an Israeli government commission found that certain secular Israeli leaders forced Yemenite children to cut their *pe'ot* during the 1950 mass immigration period, much to the country's shame. This campaign was especially disgraceful given that *pe'ot* were the subject of vicious government decrees by many modern enemies of the Jewish people.

Today, religious Zionist youth are increasingly growing *pe'ot*. Some identify with neo-hasidic spirituality, while others emulate the halakhic stringency found in the ultra-Orthodox world. However one feels about this trend, it clearly indicates the continued symbolic meaning of this hair.

Chapter 50

Praying on a Plane

Does one need a minyan?

On long and crowded international flights, creating a *minyan* (prayer quorum) can cause tension. With crew and passengers alike feeling encroached upon by people who desire (and feel entitled) to fulfill their religious obligations, the 747 can quickly feel like the Knesset!

The sages extol communal prayer, declaring that it is always answered (Deuteronomy Rabba 2:12, Sota 33a) and creates an auspicious moment (Berakhot 8a). Though this practice is only of rabbinic origin, it took on tremendous significance as a public sanctification of God's name (*Shulḥan Arukh HaRav* OḤ 90:17).

Nevertheless, scholars debate whether an individual must pray in a *minyan*. The talmudic sage R. Naḥman did not pray in the synagogue one morning because of some significant burden, leading R. Yitzḥak to emphasize to him the virtues of *minyan* prayer (Berakhot 7b–8a). While some commentators explain that R. Naḥman was exempt because of illness (Rashi), others conclude that communal prayer, while a tremendous value, does not constitute a definitive obligation. Rather, it is simply extremely conducive to efficacious prayer (*Yalkut Yosef* OḤ 90:9).

In *Shulḥan Arukh*, Rabbi Joseph Karo rules that a traveler must extend his stay in town (within certain time limits) to pray in the synagogue (OḤ 90:16), thereby indicating a definitive obligation. Yet elsewhere Rabbi Karo urges one merely to "exert" himself to attend *minyan* (90:9). While some interpreted this language to mean that praying in a *minyan* is wonderful yet non-obligatory (*Yabia Omer* OḤ 6:10, para. 5), most understood it as an exhortation to make great efforts to fulfill this mitzva (AH OḤ 90:13), perhaps even when one has a legitimate exemption (*Minḥat Yitzḥak* 7:6). Others posit an obligation to help establish or maintain a local *minyan*, especially in smaller communities (MB 55:73).

All decisors believe that praying with a *minyan* is preferable, with many condemning those who make little effort to do so (MB 90:52). One may even wake others for *minyan*, if he believes they would want to be woken (*Teshuvot VeHanhagot* 2:50). Women, while exempt from *minyan* attendance, enjoy the same spiritual benefits when praying with the community (*Piskei Teshuvot* 90:8).

Nonetheless, several factors permit one to pray privately, including physical weakness, other pressing mitzvot, direct financial loss (MB 90:29, 53), or the need to arrive early for work (AH OḤ 90:20). While some sources prioritize Torah study over communal prayer (OḤ 90:18), many scholars, including Rabbi Moshe Feinstein, urge yeshiva students to arrange their study to ensure *minyan* attendance (IM OḤ 2:27), even if they feel more inspired praying alone (IM OḤ 3:7).

Especially on flights to and from Israel, some people establish *minyanim* in common areas, like the kitchen. While well-intentioned, such an assembly may not constitute a quorum if the participants cannot hear the *minyan* leader over the din on the plane. More significantly, the sound and tumult of the gathering may wake or inconvenience other passengers, interrupt the flight crew, and endanger the *minyan* attendees during unexpected turbulence. As such, Rabbis Shlomo Zalman Auerbach (*Halikhot Shlomo, Tefilla*, p. 75), Shmuel HaLevi Wosner (*U'Velekhtekha VaDerekh* 7:17), and Hershel Schachter (www.torahweb.org) contend that one should not form a *minyan* on a flight, a position I personally follow. (Mourners saying Kaddish fulfill their obligation with a single daily recitation. If necessary, they can organize a *minyan* before embarking or after landing.) Others believe a *minyan* remains permissible when the airline allows it. Rabbi Chaim P. Scheinberg cautions that one should prepare appropriately so as to not wake another passenger while retrieving prayer articles, including a jacket, hat, *tallit*, or *tefillin* (JHCS 56).

Given the distractions of turbulence and crowdedness, one should try to pray before or after the flight, even with certain dispensations for time requirements (*Piskei Teshuvot* 94:9). If necessary to pray in flight, one must do so in accordance with the time in his current location, keeping in mind changes in time zones. (See www.chaitables.com for calculation assistance.) While the *Amida* is generally recited standing, one should remain seated if standing is unsafe or distracting (OḤ 94:5).

Especially if donning a *tallit* and *tefillin,* it remains courteous and prudent to explain your intentions to your neighbor before you begin. In general, those qualities go a long way in preventing tensions, thereby ensuring that our ritual obligations do not interfere with our ethical imperatives.

Chapter 51

Child + *Sefer Torah* = *Minyan*?

Can a child carrying a Torah scroll complete a minyan?

The alleged ability of a Torah scroll to transform a minor into the tenth person for a *minyan* has tantalized and perplexed scholars and laypeople alike. The mystery includes not only the power of the scroll, but also the role of children in creating ritual quorums.

Conventional wisdom contends that halakha requires a quorum of ten adults to recite prayers of particular sanctity (*devarim shebikedusha*), such as Kaddish and *Kedusha* (Megilla 23b), and three adults to recite the *zimmun* before the Grace After Meals. One talmudic sage, however, includes "even an infant in the cradle" to complete the quorum. While the Talmud seemingly rejects this opinion, it approves an alternative: including in a *zimmun* a "child who understands he is blessing God."

The medieval commentaries disagree as to the scope of this ruling. Regarding a *zimmun*, Rabbi Isaac Alfasi (eleventh century, Algeria) accepted a child above age nine, and other scholars permitted prodigious boys above age six (BY OḤ 199). Rabbi Joseph Karo subsequently ruled that a child may complete the *zimmun*. Sephardim continue to follow this ruling, with most authorities permitting a child over nine to finalize the quorum. Ashkenazim, however, follow Rabbenu Asher ben Yeḥiel

(1250–1327, Germany/Spain), who requires all members of the *zimmun* to be over thirteen (OḤ 199:10).

Matters become more complex with regard to a prayer quorum. Based on the Talmud's cryptic conclusion, the illustrious Rabbenu Tam (twelfth century, France) forbade including a child in a quorum of three, but allowed him to be one of ten. Another scholar, Rabbi Zeraḥia HaLevi, even allowed two children to complete a *minyan* (BY OḤ 55).

Most commentators – including Rabbenu Asher, followed by Rabbi Karo – rejected these opinions, and required all participants to be over thirteen. These scholars contended that Rabbenu Tam himself was lenient only in theory, but in practice never used a minor to complete a minyan. Some Ashkenazic decisors, however, allowed the inclusion of a child in urgent situations, as did Rabbi Moshe Isserles (OḤ 55:4).

A third position allowed a child holding a *sefer Torah*. This opinion stems from the talmudic view that nine men and an *aron kodesh* make a *minyan*, with other sages similarly contending that two people on Shabbat, or two scholars learning Torah together, create a *zimmun*. These opinions suggest that vessels of holiness – the container of the *sefer Torah*, the holy Sabbath, and books of divine wisdom – can themselves complete the atmosphere that allows humans to sanctify God's name. Yet in each case, the Talmud exclaims, "Is the *aron kodesh* a person? Is Shabbat a person?" The Babylonian Talmud rejects these puzzling proposals, insisting that only humans can create the appropriate quorum.

Nonetheless, a number of Ashkenazic scholars permitted this leniency (*Maḥzor Vitry* 81), basing themselves on a parallel source in the Jerusalem Talmud (Berakhot 7:2) and other texts. As Prof. Israel Ta-Shma has documented, this ritual is one of many examples of the influence of customs from the Land of Israel on early Ashkenazic practice. Ta-Shma further contends that such *minyanim* stem from an ancient Jewish mystical belief that a Torah scroll contains the Divine Presence and therefore can create the environment necessary to sanctify God's name in prayer.

Many prominent Ashkenazic figures, including Rashi, dismissed this third opinion, with Rabbenu Tam declaring it nonsense. Some later authorities, including Rabbi Avraham Gombiner (author of *Magen Avraham*), allowed a child to hold the Torah when creating a *minyan* was a pressing need. Yet the majority of decisors forbade the practice, arguing that a child can never complete the *minyan* (MB 55:24).

In the twentieth century, both Rabbis Moshe Feinstein (IM OḤ 2:18) and Yaakov Breisch (*Ḥelkat Yaakov* OḤ 28) permitted this measure if failure to make a *minyan* might lead to the breakdown of the synagogue. Rabbis Shlomo Zalman Auerbach (*Halikhot Shlomo, Tefilla*, p. 64) and Ovadia Yosef (*Yabia Omer* OḤ 4:9), however, prohibited this practice, with the latter even stating that a person should leave the synagogue to prevent any such *minyan*.

Chapter 52

Hebrew Pronunciation

Why do Sephardic and Ashkenazic Jews sound different when they pray?

In 2010, the Israeli Supreme Court censured a Bais Yaakov girls' school for forcing their Sephardic students to adopt Ashkenazic Hebrew pronunciation for prayer. The court deemed this a case of social bias not mandated by Jewish law, highlighting the modern debate over the proper pronunciation of Hebrew.

With the ingathering of Jews into Israel, many questions emerged regarding the propriety of changing one's pronunciation or attempting to create a unified phonetic system. The issue of proper pronunciation has further implications for synagogue rituals, including the recitation of the *Shema* (OḤ 61:15–22) and the Priestly Blessing (128:33).

As a general rule of phonetics, one might intuitively expect distinct sounds for every consonant and vowel. Nonetheless, partially because of the influence of Diaspora languages, Hebrew speakers (at least in recent eras) did not uphold this ideal standard, though the Yemenite tradition probably comes the closest to doing so. Hebrew pronunciation currently varies greatly. Many Sephardic Jews distinguish between the letters *ayin* and *aleph*, but not between the letter *tav* with a *dagesh* (/t/) and without (/s/). Ashkenazic Jews, in turn, distinguish between the vowels of *pataḥ* and *kamatz*, but not between the letters of *tav* and *samekh*, for example.

The talmudic sages recognized the phenomenon of mispronunciation, and struggled with prayer leaders who could not distinguish a *heh* from a *ḥet* (Megilla 24b). While classic codes of Jewish law subsequently stated that one who cannot distinguish guttural letters (including *aleph* and *ayin*) should not serve as *ḥazan*, later authorities waive this restriction if the locals no longer make such distinctions (MB 53:37).

For various reasons of aesthetics and national interest, the famed Hebrew lexicographer Eliezer Ben-Yehuda and the 1913 Hebrew Language Council preferred the contemporary Sephardic pronunciation, ultimately reducing the number of consonant and vowel sounds in modern Hebrew. This change followed Enlightenment attempts to create a "high language" for theater and literature, even as the local vernacular remained.

As Prof. Isaac Gottlieb has documented (*AJS Review* 32:3), rabbis faced the dilemma of multiple groups and prayer enunciations converging in an area where contemporary, reborn Hebrew followed a different system. Rabbi Yitzḥak Weiss, eventual head of the ultra-Orthodox Eda Ḥaredit, contended that one should not cavalierly abandon his heritage, even regarding pronunciation (*Minḥat Yitzḥak* 3:9). He further cited the eighteenth-century German scholar Rabbi Yaakov Emden, who complained that the local Sephardim mispronounced God's name (*Adonoy*) by not distinguishing between a *kamatz* and a *pataḥ*. Weiss insisted that synagogues maintain their pronunciations, and lambasted those who altered theirs for Zionistic reasons. He nonetheless acknowledged, along with other authorities, that if a *ḥazan* uses a different pronunciation, the communal prayer remains valid.

Despite their enthusiasm about the renaissance of the Hebrew language, many Zionist Ashkenazic authorities – including Rabbis Abraham Isaac Kook (*Oraḥ Mishpat* OḤ 16–17) and Meshulam Roth (*Kol Mevasser* 2:12) – also ruled that individuals should not change their family custom, although Rabbi Kook would not censure a congregation for adopting a different pronunciation.

Not surprisingly, Sephardic decisors like Rabbi Ovadia Yosef fiercely defended the accuracy of Sephardic pronunciation. They further asserted that many Ashkenazic scholars acknowledge the superiority of Sephardic pronunciation, with one distinguished eighteenth-century scholar, Rabbi Nathan Adler, even changing his personal enunciation (*Yabia Omer* OḤ 6:11).

Israel's first Sephardic chief rabbi, Ben-Zion Uziel, called for a national rabbinic convention to adopt a unified system (*Mishpetei Uziel* OḤ 1:1). His Ashkenazic counterpart, Rabbi Isaac Herzog, defended switching to Sephardic pronunciation, citing nineteenth-century hasidic emendations of the prayer book as legitimate precedents for liturgical change. Nonetheless, he hesitated to act on this position, lest the shift cause slurring and become confused with non-Orthodox reforms (*Heikhal Yitzhak* OḤ 3).

As generations of Hebrew speakers have since been raised on contemporary Israeli pronunciations, many otherwise conservative decisors have issued dispensations in specific cases. Recognizing the educational value of bar mitzvas, Ashkenazic Rabbis Moshe Feinstein (IM OḤ 4:65) and Yeḥiel Yaakov Weinberg (*Seridei Esh* 1:6) both allowed celebrants to read the Torah using Sephardic pronunciations, while Rabbi Shlomo Zalman Auerbach more recently contended that observant Russian immigrants, struggling to learn the language, should not be taught variant pronunciations (*Halikhot Shlomo, Tefilla*, p. 69).

Most religious Zionist congregations today follow the view of former Ashkenazic Chief Rabbis Isser Unterman (*Shevet MiYehuda* 2, p. 16) and Shlomo Goren (*Torat HaMedina*, ch. 15) that Israeli congregations will slowly but surely adopt the local dialect, completing a new stage in the history of the Hebrew language.

Chapter 53

Praying for Rain

Given the different customs in Israel and abroad, how should one pray while traveling?

The *Amida* contains two prayers for rain. The first, *mashiv haruaḥ umorid hageshem* ("He makes the wind blow and the rain fall"), exalts God's power to provide rain and is therefore included in the second blessing, which praises God's might. All around the world, Jews recite *morid hageshem* from Sukkot until Passover, which more or less brackets the rainy season in Israel. We highlight the Israeli climate since the transition from our dry summers to (hopefully) wet winters best demonstrates God's might in controlling rain (AH OḤ 114:3).

The second rain prayer, *veten tal umatar liverakha* ("Grant dew and rain as a blessing"), asks God to provide the essential sustenance of rain and was added to the ninth blessing of the *Amida*, which discusses people's livelihood (Berakhot 33a). The sages in Eretz Yisrael delayed this petition until fifteen days after Sukkot, out of consideration for pilgrims returning to Babylonia following the festival (Taanit 10a). While some medieval authorities suggested that after the Temple's destruction we should insert this prayer immediately after Sukkot (Ritva), the majority decided to maintain the original date of 7 Ḥeshvan (OḤ 117:1).

Babylonian Jews began requesting rain on the sixtieth day of the fall equinox, which, as Rashi explains, marked the start of their rainy season. In the Gregorian calendar, this date falls on either December 4 or, after a civil leap year, December 5. This law thus represents a unique case in which some Jewish communities proceed according to the secular date and others according to the Hebrew one (great trivia question!).

Although Rashi lived in northern France, whose climate differs greatly from Babylonia's, he asserted that Diaspora Jews should continue asking for rain when their Babylonian brethren did, since we generally follow the practices enshrined in the Babylonian Talmud. Many authorities, like R. Menaḥem HaMeiri (*Beit HaBehira* Taanit 10a), ruled that Diaspora communities may follow either the Babylonian date or the one used in the Land of Israel. Historical sources testify that select localities, including Provence (southern France), began reciting the prayer on 7 Ḥeshvan. Most authorities, however, ruled that each region cannot simply adapt their prayer schedule to local weather. These decisors cited the case of Nineveh, which required rain in the summer. In that season, Rebbi ruled, residents should request rain in their personal petitions but not recite *veten tal umatar* (Taanit 14a).

Rabbenu Asher, known by the acronym Rosh, vociferously objected to following the talmudic dates. He argued that our prayers must reflect our needs, especially regarding life-sustaining forces such as rain. He further cited Maimonides, who, at least in an early work, argued that failure to localize the rain prayer schedule makes our petitions dishonest (Commentary on the Mishna, Taanit 1:3). Rosh further maintained that the talmudic ruling regarding Nineveh applied only to a small, distinct area, not to an entire region or nation (*Shu"t HaRosh* 4:10).

Rosh tried to convince his colleagues in his native Germany to petition for rain from Sukkot until the early-summer holiday of Shavuot, but to no avail. His failure continued after he moved to Spain, where, despite a terrible drought in 1313, the rabbis refused to change their custom. They contended that to prevent division, Diaspora communities should maintain a uniform practice (Ritva, Taanit 10a). Indeed, even Maimonides seems to have ruled in his later, authoritative *Mishneh Torah* (*Hilkhot Tefilla* 2:16–17) that Diaspora communities must follow one of the two talmudic dates (although his ruling is ambiguous). Rosh eventually gave up, and while select Diaspora communities continued using 7 Ḥeshvan, ultimately the Northern Hemisphere accepted the Babylonian practice (OḤ 117:1–2). One late nineteenth-century authority even claimed that a heavenly voice ruled against Rosh's reasoning (AH OḤ 117:4). This rhetoric represents a polemic against the Reform movement, which, led by Abraham Geiger, changed the rain liturgy to reflect the contemporary climate.

While the debate subsided in Europe, at least within Orthodox circles, it heated up when Jews immigrated to the Southern Hemisphere. Indeed, the first halakhic query from the New World, in 1637, concerned when Jews should pray for rain in Brazil (another great trivia question!). There Sukkot ushers in the summer, and settlers feared rain would harm their crops. Rabbi Ḥayim Shabbetai of Salonika ruled that these Jews should never add *veten tal umatar*, since rain after Sukkot would be harmful and praying for precipitation after Pesaḥ would deviate from universal practice. As Arnold and Daniel Lasker have documented, this debate continued in other countries, with a particularly acrimonious dispute in Australia in the nineteenth century. While some followed Rabbi Shabbetai's ruling, other authorities contended that Australian Jews should follow the Northern Hemisphere schedule. The latter position ultimately prevailed, and my students in Yeshivat Hakotel from Australia, South Africa, and Uruguay attest that Jews in the Southern Hemisphere today say this prayer in December.

The authorities disagree about whether Israelis traveling abroad before December 5 should continue requesting rain or adopt the local practice (MB 117:5). Some contemporary rabbis alternatively suggest omitting the prayer in its regular spot but including it in personal petitions within the blessing of *shome'a tefilla* (*Pitḥei Teshuvot* OḤ 117:3). I lean toward Rabbi Moshe Feinstein's position, that while we do not follow Rosh's ruling, his logic remains extremely compelling (IM OḤ 2:102). Therefore, a traveling Israeli should not stop asking for rain, since he and his family still need it in their homeland.

Chapter 54

Cemetery Prayers

To whom are we praying?

The phenomenon of Jews praying in cemeteries has existed since antiquity, and while its propriety has been the subject of historical debate, today it is commonplace in most communities. Nevertheless, there are contrasting justifications, each imposing various meanings and limitations on this practice.

The Torah definitively discourages Jews from "seeking out the dead," attempting to contact those in the next world through sorcery or other "abominable" methods (Deut. 18:11). The sages, however, narrow this proscription to a form of necromancy or divination wherein a person starves himself, then enters a cemetery to commune with an "impure spirit" and gain knowledge (Sanhedrin 56b).

Tellingly, the Torah states that Moses' burial place remains unknown (Deut. 34:6), a verse ironically and unfortunately ignored by some unscrupulous tour guides! Many midrashim explain that God concealed Moses' grave lest it become a site of worship for Jews and non-Jews alike (*Lekaḥ Tov* Deut. 34:6). Similarly, R. Shimon ben Gamliel deemed tombstones unnecessary for scholars, contending that "their teachings serve as their remembrance" (Y. Shekalim 2:5). Maimonides codified this opinion as law, adding, "One should not visit graves" (MT *Hilkhot Avelut* 4:4).

In modern times, the Vilna Gaon (*Maaseh Rav, Kuntres Hilkhot HaGra,* mitzvot 15), Rabbi Azriel Hildesheimer, and Rabbi Chaim Soloveitchik (*Nefesh HaRav,* p. 254) all opposed visiting gravesites, even on a memorial day (*yahrzeit*), lest this practice lead to inappropriate worship and, more fundamentally, because cemeteries engender and signify impurity (*Ish HaHalakha*, pp. 36–40). Others, like Rabbi David Tzvi Hoffman (Germany, d. 1921), expressed concern that elaborate tombstones and memorials waste money that would be better spent on worthier pursuits, such as giving charity in the memory of the deceased (*Melamed Leho'il* YD 2:139). Indeed, many communities historically discouraged excessive memorials, emphasizing that simple stone markers suffice (*Shu"t HaRadbaz* 4:243).

As Dr. Yeḥezkel Lichtenstein has documented, a dominant position in Jewish law and thought permits, and at times encourages, praying in cemeteries. The Talmud records several stories of various sages doing so, and further asserts that Caleb prayed at the tomb of the patriarchs (Num. 13) to protect himself from his fellow spies' evil counsel (Sota 34b).

In the talmudic period, communal cemetery visits were most prevalent in times of distress, such as during droughts (Taanit 16a). The rabbis debate the purpose of these pilgrimages, which initially developed as folk customs without textual support (Ritva). One sage suggests that the gatherings symbolically communicated to God that "we are as if dead before You," and, as such, could take place even at non-Jewish cemeteries. Others understood this practice more radically, as a request for the deceased to intercede on behalf of the living. These sentiments echo talmudic descriptions of the dead maintaining a presence in the world. Based on these sources, ritual observance is typically forbidden in cemeteries, since it insults the deceased (*loeg larash*), who can no longer perform mitzvot (Berakhot 18a).

This latter interpretation raises controversial questions about intercessory prayer, in which the departed or angels are asked to beseech God on a person's behalf. Maimonides deemed such prayers heretical in his Thirteen Principles of Faith. Not surprisingly, he adopted the first explanation of cemetery visits, that they convey people's sense of lifelessness (MT *Hilkhot Taanit* 4:18) – a position codified in *Shulḥan Arukh* (OḤ 579:3).

Despite the permissibility of non-Jewish cemeteries, these rituals were historically performed at Jewish gravesites (*Magen Avraham* 579:11), and various explanations were proposed. Some depicted cemeteries as places with greater spiritual presence (*Derashot HaRan* 8); others stressed the fundamental importance of recalling the merits of the righteous and one's beloved (*Ktav Sofer* YD 178).

Many, however, advanced the idea that such visits serve as an opportunity for intercessory prayer, and some even noted that the living repay the dead for their services by praying for the elevation of their souls (*Sefer Ḥasidim* 710). The Zohar extols Jews who come to cemeteries in remorse and repentance, making their request worthy of additional support (*Aḥarei Mot* 70:1). Indeed, cemetery visits became particularly prominent on fast days, times of mourning, and during the High Holy Days.

Despite the widespread allowance of cemetery visits (*Baḥ* YD 170), many worried about abuses. In one extreme sixteenth-century case, Rabbi David ibn Zimra chastised worshippers who opened graves (!) to communicate with the dead (Radbaz MT *Hilkhot Taanit* 4:4). And in the nineteenth century, Rabbi Abraham Danzig warned against praying to the dead and ignoring God entirely (*Ḥokhmat Adam* 89:7).

Given the excesses of cemetery supplications and the theological concerns raised by intercessory prayers, I vehemently oppose praying to the deceased. Instead, one should use cemetery visits to think about mortality, ponder the heritage of the deceased, and pray to God that we create our own righteous legacy.

Chapter 55

Adopting Foreign Rituals I

May one place a memorial wreath at a military funeral?

The State of Israel has adopted many international rituals, such as moments of silence and laying wreaths on graves. While these practices may evoke strong emotions, they also raise important questions regarding the appropriateness of mimicking non-Jewish traditions.

After condemning the unethical practices of the ancient Egyptians and the Canaanites, the Torah warns, "You shall not walk in their ways" (Lev. 18:3). Instead, the Israelites must loyally follow God's commandments and become a holy nation (Ex. 23:24; Lev. 18:30, 20:23).

Commentators have interpreted this exhortation, colloquially known as *ḥukkat hagoyim*, in various ways. Some suggest that it prohibits the sexual debauchery of those ancient societies (*Sifra Aḥarei Mot* 9:8, *Yere'im* 313). Others assert that these verses provide additional proscriptions of sorcery (Rashi, Shabbat 67a), thereby increasing the severity of performing these prohibited actions (*Tur* YD 178). Alternatively, Scripture here issues a general ban on imitating foreign cultures – not only their rituals, but even their seemingly innocuous dress and hairstyle fashions (*Sifra Aḥarei Mot* 9:9).

This prohibition would certainly apply to idolatrous societies, since Jews should cultivate a unique appearance signifying their distinct worldview (MT *Hilkhot Avodat Kokhavim* 11:1). Most, however, have applied the admonition to all non-Jewish cultures, including those of monotheists (*Shu"t Tashbetz* 3:133), claiming that its intent is to prevent acculturation and unwanted influences (*Ḥinukh* 262). Dispensations, however, are issued to "court Jews," whose frequent interaction with officialdom requires them to follow general etiquette (YD 178:2).

Scholars debate the scope of prohibited behaviors, especially in light of a talmudic passage permitting the honorific burning of beds and other artifacts of kings after their demise, despite its similarity to idolatrous practices (Avoda Zara 11a). Following a different talmudic justification of this pyrrhic rite, based on a biblical precedent (Sanhedrin 52b), the Vilna Gaon forbade all gentile customs, unless they have Jewish origins or could have reasonably emerged without non-Jewish influence (Gra YD 178:7). Others banned only rituals done in consonance with idolatry, or those that are foolish or haughty (*Tosafot* Avoda Zara 11a).

Rabbi Moshe Isserles, however, established the normative position of proscribing only foreign rituals that are idolatrous or pointless (YD 178:1). The latter customs are prohibited because we suspect they have (forgotten) idolatrous origins (Ran, Avoda Zara 11a), or because they are adopted solely for the sake of acculturation or immodest desires (Maharik 88). Yet any reasonable, non-idolatrous norm, ranging from honorific rites to professional uniforms, remains permissible when adopted for practical purposes, not to mimic (*Baḥ* YD 178).

The contemporary application of this law is complicated, since motivations are difficult to gauge and societal norms remain subject to time and place (*Minḥat Ḥinukh* 251:1). For example, both the Bible (Zeph. 1:8) and rabbinic literature (*Sifrei Re'eh* 81) speak of the merit of Jews distinguishing themselves by their clothing. While some have therefore insisted on parochial garb, others maintain that Jews must merely avoid clothing worn by non-Jews for religious services (*Perisha* YD 178:2). Indeed, a number of texts indicate that Jews in talmudic times dressed the same as their neighbors (Maharik 88), a practice that continued in many places during the medieval period (*Otzar HaGeonim* Nazir, p. 200) and persists in the modern period (*Shiyurei Birkei Yosef* YD 178).

Wherever all Jews dress distinctively, it may be forbidden to depart from that norm (*Ḥokhmat Adam* 89:1). Yet as Rabbi Moshe Feinstein has noted, in many contemporary societies fashion doesn't distinguish between religions, and therefore it remains permissible to dress in accordance with current styles, provided that they conform with standards of modesty (IM YD 1:81).

One unique artifact, of course, is the male yarmulke. In societies where men walk bareheaded, some claim that removing one's yarmulke violates the prohibition of *ḥukkat hagoyim* (*Taz* OḤ 8:3). Rabbi David Tzvi Hoffman, however, permitted such removal when necessary to comply with decorum for financial or legal purposes, including to take an oath in a courtroom (*Melamed Leho'il* YD 2:56).

Based on *ḥukkat hagoyim*, Rabbis Ovadia Hedaya (*Yaskil Avdi* YD 4:25) and Betzalel Zolty (*Noam* 2) castigated the laying of memorial wreaths at funerals as unwanted emulation of non-Jewish rituals. Rabbi Ovadia Yosef, however, defended the practice by citing other rites, including the use of horse-drawn caskets, which Jews adopted because they found them meaningful (*Yabia Omer* YD 3:24). Similarly, Rabbi Yehuda Henkin contends that one should stand for a moment of silence during a memorial ceremony (*Tchumin* 4). All scholars, however, urge Jews to observe more traditional mourning rituals as well, such as the recitation of Psalms and the lighting of candles.

Chapter 56

Adopting Foreign Rituals II

May one incorporate non-Jewish music into prayer rituals?

In the previous essay, we discussed whether laying wreaths at funerals is permitted or if it falls under the biblical prohibition of imitating non-Jewish behavior (*ḥukkat hagoyim*). We noted that the dominant position among scholars is to proscribe only foreign rituals that are idolatrous or pointless. The adoption of nonsensical practices presumably reflects a desire to imitate foreign culture; moreover, these rituals may have (forgotten) idolatrous origins.

This prohibition casts a wide net. The sages (*Sifra Aḥarei Mot* 9:9) forbade hairstyles apparently associated with cultic figures (BY YD 178). Maimonides even claimed that the Bible prohibits shaving with a razor because such was the custom of idolatrous priests (MT *Hilkhot Avodat Kokhavim* 12:7). Others sharply criticized his interpretation, because it links God's commandments to cultural norms that vary with time and place.

Some decisors also included non-Jewish names in this prohibition (*Shu"t Maharam Schick* YD 169). Others, however, noted that even in talmudic times, Jews used names from their surrounding cultures (*Shu"t Maharshadam* YD 199). Contending that this phenomenon stems from the use of the local dialect, Rabbi Moshe Feinstein permitted foreign names, yet he discouraged the adoption of those associated with other religions, such as Mary or Lucas (IM OḤ 5:10).

Some decisors even protested the use of the Gregorian calendar, since the alleged birth date of Jesus is its starting point, and its months are named after Roman gods (such as January for Janus). Rabbi Ovadia Yosef defended its prevalent use as stemming from the pragmatic need to work with the international civil calendar (*Yabia Omer* YD 3:9). Furthermore, Jesus was clearly born before the year 1. Nonetheless, Rabbi Yosef encouraged writers to note when using the calendar that it is a non-Jewish one. To that end, writers in Hebrew sometimes add "*leminyanam*" ("according to *their* calendar"), while English writers frequently add CE (Common Era) to dates, as opposed to AD, which has a Christian connotation.

As Rabbi Michael Broyde has documented (JHCS 30), figures like Rabbi Yitzḥak Hutner opposed Jewish celebration of the American Thanksgiving holiday, because it was created by Christians and is celebrated according to their calendar (*Iggerot Paḥad Yitzḥak* 109). Most leading rabbis, including Rabbi Joseph B. Soloveitchik, deem it a civic holiday with no definitive religious affiliation (*Nefesh HaRav*, p. 231), though some have suggested occasionally skipping its observance, lest it become comparable to a religious obligation (*Bnei Banim* 3:37).

More problems arise with the appropriation of rites with definite non-Jewish associations. According to some authorities, even biblical rituals became prohibited if associated with non-Jewish rites. For example, the Torah ultimately bans worship via a sacrificial monument (*matzeva*), even though it was regularly used by the biblical forefathers, because it became a major part of idolatry (*Tosafot* Avoda Zara 11a). Some have further contended that Jews do not worship with their arms outstretched, despite biblical precedent, because it is too similar to foreign methods (*Be'er Sheva* 71).

The sages similarly debated whether rituals with definitive Jewish origins remained permissible when analogous practices were found amongst idolaters (Sanhedrin 52b). The Talmud mentions a number of rites, including elements of the daily sacrificial order, which were altered to distinguish them from non-Jewish practices (Tamid 30b). Likewise, while many congregations adorn their synagogues with greenery on Shavuot, the Vilna Gaon banned this custom as too similar to church holiday decorations (*Ḥokhmat Adam* 89:1).

These strictures became extremely prominent in nineteenth-century polemics against synagogue innovations introduced by the Reform movement. To modernize the service, Reform leaders moved the *bima* (Torah reading platform) and added organ accompaniment. Orthodox opponents denounced the innovations as *ḥukkat hagoyim* (*Melamed Leho'il* OḤ 1:16). Some also criticized "cantorial garb" as imitating non-Jewish clergy, though this attire remains popular in many circles (*Pitḥei Teshuvot* OḤ 53:15).

Historically, it seems clear that non-Jewish music has influenced Jewish song, ranging from medieval Jewish poetry to hasidic melodies to the Maccabeats. Some authorities vehemently oppose this influence, and even ban the use of secular tunes in prayer. Others are more liberal, especially if a song's origins are no longer known (*Birkei Yosef* OḤ 560:6).

Many strictly forbade the incorporation of non-Jewish religious tunes (MB 53:82). However, a nineteenth-century chief rabbi of Rome, Yisrael M. Ḥazan, permitted Jews to learn choral music and use it in Jewish services (*Krakh shel Romi* 1). While Rabbi Eliezer Waldenburg criticized this practice (*Tzitz Eliezer* 13:12), Rabbi Ovadia Yosef largely defended it, though he raised concerns that worshippers may begin thinking about or singing the original, inappropriate lyrics (*Yeḥaveh Daat* 2:5). All decisors affirm that any "imported" tune should suit the content and context of the given prayer – which, alas, many prayer leaders forget.

Chapter 57

Entering a Church or Mosque

Is one allowed to enter a non-Jewish house of worship?

In advocating monotheism, the Torah warns of the spiritual perils of idolatry (*avoda zara*). As such, it is not surprising that beyond the prohibitions of worshipping other gods or making idols, Jewish law mandates many activities to distance ourselves from forbidden forms of service.

The Mishna states that a Jew may not enter a pagan town unless the pathway traversing it leads elsewhere as well (Avoda Zara 11b). Some commentators, such as Rashi, understood this restriction as intended to prevent suspicions that the traveler is entering the town to worship. A similar talmudic passage prohibits Jews from bending down to drink from a well with an idol behind it (Rashba, Avoda Zara 12a). Other commentators limited this restriction to festival seasons (YD 149:1–2). Concerns of this sort were also raised regarding removing one's hat or prostrating before a religious or political figure wearing an idolatrous symbol. Some scholars, however, believed it would be obvious that one was only honoring the personage (150:3).

In this context, many commentators refer to a talmudic statement urging Jews to avoid even coming within four ells of a prohibited temple (Avoda Zara 17a). Based on these sentiments, scholars deemed it forbidden to enter or otherwise benefit from such a temple. Some claimed that Jews may not flee into such a temple even to save their lives (Ritva, Avoda Zara 11b); other authorities disagreed but only in this extreme situation (*Shu"t HaRosh* 19:17).

What constitutes foreign worship (*avoda zara*)? Which religions fall into that halakhic category? Prof. David Berger summarily defines *avoda zara* as "the formal recognition or worship as God of an entity that is in fact not God." Many ancient pagan cults and Eastern religions engage in such worship, which has implications for tourists traveling to the Far East. Islam, however, is monotheistic and lacks icons, so a Jew may enter a mosque (*Yabia Omer* YD 7:12).

Jewish scholars, including such medieval figures as Rabbi Menaḥem HaMeiri and the Tosafists, have long understood Christianity as monotheistic and thus distinct from paganism. Nonetheless, because of the Christian deification of Jesus, Christianity falls into the forbidden category. As Berger puts it, Christianity is "non-pagan *avoda zara* in a monotheistic mode." Thus both Maimonides (Commentary on the Mishna, Avoda Zara 1:4) and Rabbi Yehuda HaḤasid (*Sefer Ḥasidim* 435) – in the uncensored versions of their texts – forbid entry into churches, a position affirmed throughout the centuries.

Scholars have debated the parameters of this rule. For example, nineteenth-century Italian Jews reportedly entered churches to learn choral music for use in the synagogue, while Rabbis Joseph Carlebach and Eliezer Berkovits, who lived in Germany prior to World War II, allowed entry into a church for educational purposes. These positions were widely criticized by a strong consensus of decisors, including Rabbis Moshe Feinstein (IM YD 3:129, para. 6) and Eliezer Waldenburg (*Tzitz Eliezer* 4:91).

Medieval sources allowed Jews to cut through the courtyards of non-Jewish temples, even if an idol was located there, since doing so would not seem suspicious (*Darkhei Moshe* YD 149:1). This precedent would certainly allow a Jew to use a church parking lot or, according to Rabbis J. David Bleich (*Tradition* 44:2) and Moshe Sternbuch (*Teshuvot VeHanhagot* 2:410), to enter a church basement for civic purposes like voting or donating blood. Rabbi Feinstein, however, forbade a yeshiva from renting church classrooms, because he likened rooms designated for religious instruction to a sanctuary (IM YD 3:77, para. 1).

One sensitive situation emerges when state ceremonies, such as coronations or funerals, are performed in churches like England's Westminster Abbey. Rabbi Ovadia Yosef strictly forbade participation, contending that Jewish law does not permit such attempts to ingratiate oneself with local officials (*Yeḥaveh Daat* 4:45). Yet various chief rabbis and other Orthodox rabbinic leaders have attended these ceremonies, including Pope John Paul II's funeral and Prince William's wedding. As precedent, Rabbi Michael Broyde recently cited medieval sources that permitted "court Jews" to violate certain biblical prohibitions in order to ensure Jewish political safety. Others, however, have retorted that such dispensations are thankfully not necessary in a pluralistic era when Jews can respectfully express admiration and gratitude to non-Jewish leaders while upholding their own parochial obligations.

The legal question of a Jew entering a church, mosque, or other house of foreign worship, it should be noted, remains independent of any evaluation of that religion's moral standards or social agenda. This point was exemplified in the 1960s by Rabbi Joseph B. Soloveitchik, who strongly advocated cooperation with the Catholic Church in the war against poverty and other social issues, though he believed one should not enter a church.

Chapter 58

Non-Jews and Torah

May a Jew teach Torah to a gentile?

In contemporary society, non-Jews learn Jewish texts in many forums, including university classrooms and Internet sites. Sometimes this study occurs even without Jewish instruction, such as in South Korea, where schoolchildren read talmudic stories. This phenomenon is the latest development in the historical discussion regarding the propriety of teaching Torah to non-Jews.

The Torah states, "Moses has commanded us the Torah, an inheritance for the community of Jacob" (Deut. 33:4). Deeming this inheritance the exclusive property of Jews, the sages prohibited gentiles from learning Torah (Sanhedrin 59a) and Jews from teaching it to them (Hagiga 13a). This prohibition was also stridently reinforced in the Zohar (*Aḥarei Mot* 18:4). Although the Talmud does mention that non-Jews were occasionally taught Torah (Bava Metzia 119a), some of those cases clearly involved government coercion (Bava Kamma 38a).

Scholars offered different rationales for this ban, which broadly impacted its scope. Some thinkers understood non-Jewish study as a betrayal of the unique bond between Jews and God or a misappropriation of national treasure. On this basis, a few scholars stringently contended that the prohibition included teaching potential converts (*Shu"t Rabbi Akiva Eiger, Pesakim* 41). Some authorities even banned teaching the Hebrew alphabet (*Shiyurei Berakha* YD 246:4), although other sources indicate that this step was intended to prevent abuses by hostile anti-Semites (*Sefer Ḥasidim* 238). Such polemical considerations, however, could also lead to leniencies. One medieval source, for example, suggested that gentiles may learn the Prophets and Hagiographa, because these sections of the Bible attest that God has not abandoned the Jewish people (*Shiltei Gibborim*, Rif, Avoda Zara 20a).

The sentiment that some exposure to Torah study was necessary to spread important values led many scholars to similarly limit the prohibition. The Talmud itself contends that gentiles may learn material necessary to properly observe the seven Noahide laws. In this spirit, Rabbi David Tzvi Hoffman argued that one may teach non-Jews the narrative portions of the Torah, which inspire belief in the grandeur of God (*Melamed Leho'il* YD 2:77). Rabbis Naphtali Berlin (*Meshiv Davar* 2:77) and Tzvi Hirsch Chajes (*Shu"t Maharatz Chajes* 32) went further, contending that only aspects of the Oral Law were off-limits, not Scripture.

Rabbi Samuel Eidels alternatively suggested that the prohibition included only the "reasons and secrets" of the Torah, not basic texts or laws (Maharsha, Ḥagiga 13a), with Rabbi Eliyahu Mizraḥi maintaining that even this restriction could be waived if one had no choice (*Shu"t HaRe'em Mizraḥi* 57). Other scholars asserted that non-Jewish Torah study was problematic only if consistent or exhaustive.

Maimonides applied the prohibition only to gentiles who deny the divinity of Scripture, since their study might distort the Bible and confuse the Jewish community. Christians, he writes, who believe in the divinity of Scriptures may therefore learn Torah: At best they'll come to believe in the Jewish interpretation, and at worst they'll cause no harm (*Shu"t HaRambam* 149).

Rabbi Menaḥem HaMeiri connected this edict to a similar one in the same talmudic passage, which prohibits gentiles from observing the Sabbath (*Beit HaBeḥira* Sanhedrin 59a). He believed both prohibitions stemmed from concerns that "insider knowledge" might allow the gentile to pass as a Jew and undermine Jewish ritual. Yet gentiles genuinely seeking wisdom (or to observe other commandments) may study. Like Maimonides before him, Rabbi HaMeiri asserted that gentiles who perform mitzvot (even beyond the Noahide laws) deserve reward.

The increased social intermingling between Jews and gentiles in the modern era introduced new dilemmas. Jewish classes were frequently attended by non-Jews, for instance, as was the case with Jewish schools that accepted children who were not halakhically Jewish. Almost all scholars, including Rabbis Hoffman and Moshe Feinstein (IM YD 2:132), contended that mixed audiences were no problem when the intent was not to teach non-Jews. This argument was later cited to permit teaching Torah on public airwaves in the Diaspora.

The question took a new turn when scholars began debating the propriety of translating the Talmud into the vernacular. Some opposed such translations not only because anti-Semites might ridicule these texts, but because the ban on teaching Torah to non-Jews seemed to preclude making Jewish sources accessible to the gentile world (*Yehuda Yaaleh* OḤ 1:4).

Yet Rabbi Yisrael Salanter advocated both the translation of the Talmud and its introduction into the university curriculum. Apparently this famed pietist aimed to enhance Judaism's reputation in the broader world in which Jews had become engaged. Rabbi Yeḥiel Yaakov Weinberg himself taught at a university before World War II. He contended that the proscription applied only to gentile study geared toward forming competing religious ideals and rituals (*Seridei Esh* 2:55–56). It remained perfectly permissible, however, to teach even an exclusively non-Jewish audience if the goal was simply to spread Jewish wisdom.

Chapter 59

Cremation

May a deceased's ashes be buried in a Jewish cemetery?

Cremation has greatly increased over the past few decades in many Western countries, with well over half of all corpses cremated in countries like Canada, Australia, and the United Kingdom. Many people choose this option because it is relatively inexpensive, they believe it simplifies the funeral process, or they dislike the thought of their bodies decomposing. Others do so under the influence of Buddhism or Hinduism, which mandates cremation. While Jewish law unequivocally bans this method, the rabbinic debate over how to handle the ashes represents a fascinating balance of values.

Recognizing the divine image in all human beings, the Torah prohibits leaving a body (or body part) unburied, even that of a criminal who has received the death penalty (Deut. 21:23). Several ancillary laws derive from this commandment, including the prohibitions of mutilating a corpse, deriving benefit from it, or delaying its burial. The Torah further demands that one take responsibility for a *met mitzva,* a corpse with no one to bury it (Deut. 21:1), even if doing so costs money or requires a *kohen* to become impure (Yevamot 89b). As such, even if a person desires not to be buried, Jewish law instructs us to ignore that request.

What constitutes burial? The Bible records the interment of several figures. According to one midrash, a grief-stricken Adam was at a loss in handling the corpse of Abel until he saw birds laying one of their own to rest, whereupon he decided to bury his son (*Pirkei DeRabbi Eliezer* 21). On many occasions, the Bible emphasizes a family plot, such as the Cave of Machpelah, tomb of the patriarchs and matriarchs (Gen. 23, 25:9, 27:30, 50:13).

The Torah also records the embalmment of Jacob and Joseph (Gen. 50), as necessitated both by Egyptian custom and by their desire to be buried ultimately in the Land of Israel. Some scholars have argued that embalming might therefore be permitted in honor of the deceased, especially to preserve the body until it is interred in a family plot. Others allow such preservation only if it involves no incisions (e.g., injecting preservatives or aromas via orifices or the bloodstream). Yet most contemporary decisors forbid any form of embalmment, unless absolutely necessary to preserve the body for burial (*Emek Halakha* 1:48–49). This prohibition includes freeze-storage of the body and above-ground crypts (IM YD 3:143–144).

A major debate regarding cremation in Jewish law erupted in the late nineteenth century following the emergence of new methods. As David Malkiel has documented, a few Italian scholars argued that cremation did not violate Jewish law as long as the ashes were properly buried. (In fact, Rome's chief rabbi, Ḥayim Castiglioni, was himself cremated upon his request!) In addition to the embalmment of Jacob and Joseph, these authorities noted that several biblical kings were burned after death, including Saul (I Sam. 31:12) and Asa (II Chr. 21:19). They further cited Rabbi Shlomo ibn Aderet (d. 1310), who permitted lime seed to be placed on a corpse to hasten its decomposition so the bones could be transported to a faraway family plot (*Shu"t HaRashba* 1:369).

Nonetheless, a nearly unanimous consensus of scholars firmly banned cremation. They argued that the body's incineration was its ultimate desecration, citing a talmudic perspective on the burning of King Jehoiakim's remains as the ultimate punishment (Sanhedrin 82a). The medieval allowance of lime seed represented an exception under extreme circumstances, while the biblical stories of kings were aberrations, or alternatively interpreted as ceremonial burnings of clothing and other objects in line with many pyrrhic rites in antiquity. Some, moreover, wrote that cremation reflected a heretical denial of either the World to Come or physical resurrection.

As Rabbi Dr. Adam Ferziger has shown, opposition to cremation was so intense that many scholars in Germany and elsewhere, led by Rabbi Meyer Lerner of Altona, declared that cremated bodies were not entitled to burial within Jewish cemeteries. These authorities considered cremation the ultimate rejection of Judaism, and thought that refusal to bury the ashes would significantly discourage the practice. Others deemed this sin no worse than Sabbath desecration or many other common transgressions and therefore allowed burial, albeit in a separate section of the cemetery (*Melamed Leho'il* YD 2:114). (All agreed, however, that bodies consumed by fire or in martyrdom had full burial rights.)

This debate was revived in 2005 when the first cremation society was founded in Israel. In addition to religious opposition, many Israelis were offended by the concept in light of the Holocaust. Indeed, cremation remains unpopular in Israel, though the trend continues to make alarming inroads within the global Jewish community.

Chapter 60

Bar Mitzva

Is a thirteen-year-old, no matter how immature, really obligated in mitzvot? Must the celebration be held on his actual birthday?

The tension that underlies this question usually arises in awkward bar mitzva speeches when the pre-pubescent boy's voice cracks as he declares, "Today I am a man!" (Note to parents: Scratch that line!) Furthermore, the modern conception of adolescence puts forth that teenagers do not assume full adult responsibilities until a later age, such as eighteen or twenty-one.

Classic Jewish sources also recognized that children mature at different ages. The Bible, for example, often speaks of twenty as the appropriate age for taking on communal responsibility, such as serving in the army (Num. 1:3) or in the Temple (1 Chr. 23:24). Even the teaching that determines thirteen as the bar mitzva (Hebrew for "obligated in commandments") age, or the legal age of majority, acknowledges that intellectual and emotional maturity develops over a period of years. The Mishna states, "Five years is the age to begin studying Scripture, ten for Mishna, thirteen for the obligation of the commandments, fifteen for Talmud study, eighteen for marriage, twenty for seeking a livelihood..." (Avot 5:21).

While this mishna might seem to definitively affirm thirteen as the age of majority, medieval and modern commentators alike, including Rabbi Menaḥem HaMeiri, have noted that this passage (along with the sixth chapter of Avot) is a very late emendation, postdating ancient and many medieval manuscripts. A conflicting mishna, moreover, contends that the growth of two pubic hairs obligates a child in mitzvot (Nidda 6:11). While Rabbenu Asher argued that thirteen had always been the accepted age of puberty (*Shu"t HaRosh* 16:1), the medieval Tosafists contended that physiological differences in previous eras might sometimes have advanced the age of majority to nine or ten (Sanhedrin 69a).

After a thorough survey of numerous texts, Prof. Yitzḥak Gilat concluded that the talmudic sages had no definitive age of majority. Rather, the age of obligation depended on the nature of the mitzva. A young child was obligated to perform purely physical actions, such as dwelling in a sukka or donning phylacteries. Commandments requiring greater intellectual capabilities, such as making vows, became obligatory after age eleven or twelve. One could not receive judicial punishments, however, until age twenty, indicating that moral culpability was reserved for adults.

Be that as it may, thirteen became the standard age of majority toward the end of the talmudic period. The sage Rava cited a legal assumption (*ḥazaka*) that a boy of thirteen or a girl of twelve had developed two pubic hairs, thereby eliminating the need to examine each child (Nidda 46a). This determination also eliminated the variability between different mitzvot and the subjectivity of each child's physical maturation. Not all decisors accepted Rava's assumption, however, particularly regarding the notion of children fulfilling biblical commandments for others, such as reciting Kiddush (MB 55:31). But most agree that for rabbinic obligations, such as leading prayers or reading from the Torah, we rely upon Rava's premise (53:25).

Children below the age of majority remain obligated to fulfill many mitzvot for the sake of educational training and religious inculcation. Many Talmudists place this obligation on parents, since covenantal commitments exclude insufficiently mature children. Others, however, contend that children themselves are obligated to fulfill these mitzvot, yet remain absolved of penal or judicial culpability for their actions.

Bar mitzva parties are intended to celebrate the child's entrance into the world of mitzvot, just as the meal following a *brit mila* commemorates the child's entrance into the covenant. As such, the celebration should ideally coincide with the actual birthday. However, when accompanied by Torah learning, the festivities may take place after that day (*Yam shel Shlomo* Bava Kamma 7:37). While holding the party before the birthday is not forbidden, it misses the point of the celebration entirely.

The popular abuse of bar mitzva celebrations as an excuse for ostentatious birthday parties led Rabbi Moshe Feinstein to move for eliminating these gatherings altogether, since they lacked the proper decorum for a mitzva celebration (IM OḤ 1:104). Other decisors affirmed the educational value of such parties, and contended that they should be held for boys and girls alike (*Yeḥaveh Daat* 2:29). Yet all urged their adherents not to go overboard. As contemporary rabbis like to say, "Our bar mitzvas need to place more emphasis on the mitzva and less on the bar!"

Chapter 61

Bat Mitzva

Why do bat mitzva celebrations differ so greatly within the Jewish community?

At one of my first bat mitzva parties, at some point between dessert and the limbo dance, a family friend leaned over and said to me, "Did you know my grandpa invented the bat mitzva ceremony?" I had never heard of his famous grandfather, Rabbi Mordecai Kaplan, but I was surprised that the bat mitzva celebration is so new and, as I later discovered, quite controversial.

Historically, there was no difference between boys and girls regarding the significance of reaching the age of adulthood. At this age, a bar or bat mitzva becomes legally responsible for performing mitzvot. As discussed in the previous essay, many sources even establish the identical criterion for becoming a bar or bat mitzva, namely the growth of two pubic hairs, though other texts state that puberty begins at age twelve for girls and thirteen for boys (*Nidda* 45b).

Despite the significance of this transition, few sources mention the requirement to celebrate the occasion. The basis for this practice derives from a talmudic sage whose blindness exempted him from certain mitzvot. He declared that he would grandly celebrate gaining full covenantal responsibilities (Kiddushin 31a). Subsequently, Rabbi Shlomo Luria (sixteenth century, Poland) maintained that becoming a bar mitzva should be marked by a festive meal with singing and learned discourses (*Yam shel Shlomo* Bava Kamma 7:37).

Another ritual, with more definitive talmudic support, is the blessing recited by the bar mitzva boy's father, known as "*Barukh ShePetarani.*" Customarily recited following the child's first *aliya*, the father proclaims, "Blessed is He who has absolved me of responsibility for this one" (Genesis Rabba 63:10). Until the bar mitzva, the father is punishable for his child's sins, since they stem from the father's failure to educate him. With the child's maturation, however, the father loses legal culpability as his son gains legal responsibility (*Magen Avraham* 225:5).

This transformation applies to both genders, so why have fathers not traditionally recited the blessing for girls? While various explanations have been given, authorities such as former Israeli Sephardic Chief Rabbis Ovadia Yosef (*Yabia Omer* OḤ 6:29) and Yitzḥak Nissim have ruled that fathers should indeed recite it when their daughters become bat mitzva. One contemporary author, Rabbi Getsel Ellinson, has suggested that *mothers* say this blessing, as they might have prime educational responsibilities (and therefore legal culpability) for their daughters.

The creation of a parallel public ceremony for girls, however, has become the most contentious issue surrounding the bar and bat mitzva discussion. The modern bat mitzva ceremony began in America in 1922, when Rabbi Kaplan, founder of the Reconstructionist movement, invited his twelve-year-old daughter, Judith, to participate in the Torah reading. It took until the egalitarian 1960s, however, for the bat mitzva ceremony to become the norm in non-Orthodox movements. It has even been popularly adopted in Reform circles, which previously preferred "confirmation" ceremonies at age fifteen or sixteen, when Jewish education programs were completed. Some historians contend that bat mitzva ceremonies served as an impetus for egalitarian prayer services within these movements.

Many Orthodox rabbis, on the other hand, reject any form of bat mitzva ceremony, associating it with non-Jewish influences and antinomian egalitarian values. Rabbi Moshe Feinstein, for example, deemed synagogue celebrations inappropriate, since they stemmed from non-Orthodox origins (IM OḤ 1:104) and marked no significant ritual change, such as the donning of *tefillin* or leading services (OḤ 2:97). He did, however, permit a shul Kiddush to commemorate the event, while like-minded decisors allowed for more private gatherings and celebratory Torah study sessions.

Other Orthodox rabbis, such as Yosef and Nissim, encouraged public celebrations and festive meals, even if not part of synagogue ritual. Rabbi Yeḥiel Yaakov Weinberg (d. 1966) contended that in an age of female self-expression and achievement, such celebrations were necessary to foster dedication to mitzvot and traditional values. As for claims that these festivities constitute an unsuitable appropriation of foreign culture, he retorted that events that inspire piety should not be banned on such grounds (*Seridei Esh* 2:39). Many bat mitzva banquets include sermons or *siyum* ceremonies, celebrating the completion of a program of Torah study. When done with good taste and modesty, they instill a sense of religious maturity, which includes knowledge, commitment, reverence, and joy.

Section V

Women

Chapter 62

The Obligation to Pray

Must women pray three times a day?

Prayer plays a definitive role in the Bible, with humanity's encounter with the Divine frequently manifested in supplication and dialogue. Biblical characters pray for many things: Abraham demands the salvation of Sodom (Gen. 18), Jacob prays for protection (28:20–22), Moses pleads for atonement for the Jewish people (Ex. 32:11–13, 31; Num. 14), Hannah entreats God for fertility (I Sam. 1:10–11), and Hezekiah begs for his health (II Kings 20:2–3). Prayer, moreover, seems to transcend the bounds of particular religions, as seen in the Book of Jonah (1:14) and in Isaiah's (56:7) utopian vision of the Temple becoming a house of prayer for all peoples (IM 2:25).

As Moshe Greenberg has noted, many biblical prayers follow this structure: First one formally addresses God, then states his petition, and then argues why God should fulfill his wishes. As Rabbi David Kimḥi (known as Radak, d. 1235, Provence) points out, the word *tefilla* in the Bible connotes judgment, implying that through prayer one entreats God to judge him favorably and overlook his evil actions (*Sefer HaShorashim*). While many medieval philosophers struggled with the perception that God could be swayed by such entreaties, they too affirmed the centrality of prayer in Judaism, albeit as a more contemplative practice (*Sefer HaIkkarim* 4:18).

Given this background, it might come as a surprise that – according to numerous medieval commentators – the obligation to pray is not biblical. Since the Torah states several times that Jews must serve (*laavod*) God (e.g., Ex. 23:25), Maimonides, following certain tannaitic precedents (*Sifrei Ekev* 41), contended that daily prayer (including praise for God, petition for one's needs, and thanks for His goodness) is a biblical commandment (MT *Hilkhot Tefilla* 1:1–2). Nahmanides, however, cites talmudic definitions of prayer as a rabbinic requirement (Berakhot 21a), and sees prayer as a gift allowing one to supplicate for his needs (*Hassagot LeSefer HaMitzvot* 5). Nahmanides acknowledges, however, that praying in times of crisis is a biblical commandment (Num. 10:9). Rabbi Joseph B. Soloveitchik understood this debate on an existential level: Maimonides viewed everyday life itself – with all its fears and moments of despair – as a time of crisis, while Nahmanides assumed a biblical obligation only in times of acute distress, like war.

In any case, all authorities agree that the *form* of prayer, as well as daily prayer times, stems from rabbinic origins. The sages debated whether the morning, afternoon, and evening times were intended to parallel the sacrificial rite or the respective entreaties made by the nation's forefathers (Berakhot 26b). One ramification of this dispute is the status of the evening prayer, since there was no nightly sacrifice in the Temple, though the entrails of the afternoon offering burned throughout the night (*Ḥiddushei Pnei Yehoshua* Berakhot 26b). While most medieval commentators considered the evening service optional, over time the Jewish people accepted it as mandatory (Rosh, Berakhot 4:2).

Since these prayers were instituted to help us petition God, a unique element of their structure – as distinct from the daily sacrificial order – was the ability to "make up" (*tashlumin*) for missed services. Early authorities debate the scope of this dispensation (Rabbenu Yona, Berakhot 18a), establishing that one may make up only the immediately preceding time period's prayer in a case of unintended omission (OḤ 108:3). Similarly, a person may pray in any language, developing an intimate relationship with his Maker, because prayer is a gift from God (Sota 33a).

No wonder, then, that women are obligated in prayer (Berakhot 20a). Rashi and Nahmanides, who believed the entire institution of prayer was of rabbinic origin, contended that this obligation stemmed from the gift of prayer, since women would otherwise be excused from such time-bound commandments (as they are from reciting the *Shema*).

As such, these commentators deemed men and women equally obligated in prayer (*Magen Avraham* 106:2). Some decisors obligated women to recite the *Amida* three times a day (AH OḤ 106:7), with others reducing that number to two, since women never took upon themselves the obligation of the evening service (MB 106:4).

Yet Maimonides and Rabbi Isaac Alfasi, followed by Rabbi Joseph Karo (OḤ 106:2), asserted that daily prayer was a bona fide biblical obligation unbound by time. As such, women remained obligated in one daily prayer. Some, like Rabbi Ovadia Yosef, understood this position to obligate women to recite the *Amida* once a day (*Yabia Omer* OḤ 6:17), while others believed women could fulfill this obligation with a minimal utterance of praise, petition, and thanks (*Magen Avraham* 106:2). (Scholars have noted that young mothers in particular struggle to find time for lengthy prayer.) While some justify this practice (*Divrei Yatziv* OḤ 62), citing stories of formidable scholars whose wives did not formally pray (*Halikhot Beitah* 6:1), all agree that it remains praiseworthy for women to recite the *Amida* at least once a day.

Chapter 63

Tallit and *Tefillin*

Why do Orthodox women not wear these articles during prayer?

The widespread Orthodox practice is for women not to don *tefillin* (phylacteries) or wear a *tallit* (fringed prayer shawl) while praying. Following the controversial arrests in recent years of non-Orthodox women who prayed at the Western Wall while wearing these articles, it behooves us to understand the underlying dispute within Jewish law.

Talmudic law exempts women from performing time-bound positive commandments, such as blowing a shofar on Rosh HaShana or dwelling in a sukka (Kiddushin 29a). The Talmud derives this principle from the commandment of *tefillin,* which is deemed "time-bound" since *tefillin* are not worn on the Sabbath or holidays (34a). Some explain the exemption of women from these obligations as a pragmatic matter, removing the pressure that time-bound commandments would place on women already consumed with household duties (*Sefer Avudraham, Birkhot HaMitzvot* 3). Others contend that women have superior spiritual wisdom (*bina*) and therefore do not require time-sensitive religious imperatives (Rabbi Samson Raphael Hirsch, Lev. 23:43). Whatever the rationale, the Talmud notes many exceptions to this rule, with women obligated in such time-bound commandments as Sabbath and Passover rituals.

The sages disagree about whether women may nonetheless perform mitzvot from which they are exempt (Rosh HaShana 33a), thereby providing spiritual satisfaction (Ḥagiga 16b) and earning reward (Kiddushin 31a). Normative law resolutely adopted the permissive approach. Some decisors even discuss whether certain commandments (like shofar blowing) have become obligatory because women regularly observe them (*Yabia Omer* OḤ 2:30).

Maimonides (MT *Hilkhot Tzitzit* 3:9) and Rabbi Joseph Karo (BY OḤ 589:6), however, asserted that this voluntary observance does not warrant a blessing, whose formula includes, "Blessed are You … who has commanded us …," since women were not commanded to perform these actions (Rosh, Kiddushin 1:49). Others retorted that women may recite the blessing, since they are commanded in mitzvot in general and receive reward for their observance (*Tosafot*, Ran, Rosh HaShana 33a). While Ashkenazic decisors adopted the permissive position (OḤ 589:6), Sephardic practice remains divided, with some permitting the blessing (*Birkei Yosef* OḤ 654:2) and others demurring (*Yabia Omer* OḤ 1:42).

Given this background, one might expect the donning of *tefillin* or a *tallit* to be a viable option for women. In fact, the sages even recorded an opinion that women must wear *tzitzit* (fringes). Normative law ultimately deemed it a time-bound commandment, applying only by day, but seemingly optional for women (Menaḥot 43a). The Talmud reports that Michal, daughter of King Saul, donned *tefillin* without reproach (Ritva, Eiruvin 96a). Additionally, Rabbi Samson of Coucy and others specifically list *tefillin* among the optional commandments women may perform (*Hagahot Maimoniyot Tzitzit* 3:9). Nonetheless, various factors exclude these rituals from popular female practice.

One such factor is an early Bible translation implying that *tefillin* and *tzitzit* constitute men's clothing (*Targum Yonatan* Deut. 22:5). While a few decisors agreed with this sentiment (*Levush* OḤ 17:2), many rejected it, since the prohibition of cross-dressing applies only to articles of clothing worn for style or appearance, not to fulfill a commandment (*Shu"t Maharam Schick* OḤ 173).

Among other reasons historically given for women not wearing *tefillin* (*Piskei Riaz* Rosh HaShana 4:3), the primary objection stemmed from the fact that this commandment requires a "clean body." As such, one may not wear *tefillin* if he might fall asleep or flatulate (OḤ 38:2). (This requirement is why most people do not wear *tefillin* throughout the day.) Rabbi Meir of Rothenburg contended that women could not maintain such cleanliness, perhaps because of menstrual blood. While some authorities disagreed, most concluded that women should not don *tefillin,* and either deemed Michal an exception (AH OḤ 38:6) or cited talmudic criticism of her action (BY OḤ 38:3). While Rabbi Eliezer Berkovits as well as non-Orthodox rabbis claimed women could still choose to carefully perform this mitzva, the vast majority of Orthodox decisors have forbidden this practice, since it is an optional commandment that women have not historically fulfilled (*Eliya Rabba* OḤ 38).

This sentiment has also greatly impacted women's wearing *tzitzit,* which is required only if wearing a four-cornered garment, such as a *tallit.* Since women do not regularly don such garments, Rabbi Moshe Isserles (OḤ 17:2) asserted that their doing so would be an act of religious arrogance (*yuhara*). This position became widely accepted within Orthodox circles (AH OḤ 17:3) and was reinforced in the face of the feminist critique (IM OḤ 4:49). This last factor has undoubtedly contributed to the controversy over these rituals at the Western Wall.

For a more comprehensive halakhic analysis, please see my "Women, *Tefillin,* and the Halakhic Process," *Torah Musings,* February 24, 2014, available at www.torahmusings.com.

Chapter 64

Kaddish

May women recite Kaddish?

Although the Kaddish prayer is popularly associated with death, the text itself never mentions bereavement. Instead, it is a call to sanctify God's name – "May His great name be magnified and sanctified" – with respondents proclaiming, "May His great name be blessed, for ever and ever" (*Sifrei* Haazinu 306). Drawing its key lines from passages in Psalms (113:2), Daniel (2:20), and Ezekiel (38:23), the prayer has strong eschatological connotations, with many versions explicitly summoning the Messiah. The power of this prayer is praised in the Talmud (Berakhot 57a) and in the *Heikhalot* literature, which elaborate on its mystical impact and its ability to draw a person close to God.

Different versions of Kaddish are recited depending on liturgical context. One form of Kaddish marks the end of sections of prayer services, another form concludes a funeral and the completion of the study of a talmudic tractate (OḤ 551:10), and another is recited after communal Torah study. Many sources indicate that Kaddish originated in the latter setting (*Midrash Mishlei* 14:28) and was introduced at funerals only because biblical verses are recited during the interment (*Teshuvot HaGeonim Shaarei Teshuva* [Coronel ed.] 94). On this basis, it has been speculatively suggested that Kaddish was initiated as post-study prayer during the second-century Hadrianic persecutions, when Torah learning was banned. Following clandestine study sessions, Jews would pray for their salvation and the coming of the Messiah.

The first source to connect Kaddish to mourning is Tractate Soferim, a disputably eighth-century text, which discusses how a cantor recites Kaddish to comfort mourners (19:9). Many early medieval writers, including Maimonides, never mention a mourner's Kaddish, even as they ordain the recitation of Kaddish on other occasions.

A mourner's Kaddish emerged as standard practice in early medieval Ashkenazic writings (*Or Zarua* Laws of Shabbat 2:50). They record mystical traditions in which a young child saves his impious father from the judgment of Hell by reciting Kaddish, thereby sanctifying God's name. Interestingly, other prayers – including the *Shema* (*Maḥzor Vitry* 144) – are deemed equally efficacious, as is the recitation of the *haftara* (*Kol Bo* 114). Rabbi Moshe Isserles adds that a mourner should lead the services and recite sacred blessings (such as *Barkhu*) instead of reciting Kaddish, which was instituted for minors, since they are not permitted to perform those functions (YD 376:4).

While some claimed that Kaddish is recited exclusively by a son following the death of his father (*Shu"t Binyamin Ze'ev* 201), it became customary that all deaths warrant the recitation of Kaddish by the deceased's nearest relatives (*Mishpetei Uziel* OḤ 1:2). If no relatives are available, one may hire someone to perform this function (*Kaf HaḤayim* 55:30).

Initially, only one mourner was allowed to recite each Kaddish, leading to detailed rules of priority (BH 132:1, s.v. *kuntres*) as well as pressure to add (sometimes excessive) additional Kaddish opportunities (AH OḤ 55:4). Eventually, to avoid disputes, the custom developed for all mourners to recite Kaddish together on each occasion (*Pitḥei Teshuva* YD 376:6).

In the seventeenth century, a father requested that his only child, a daughter, recite Kaddish for him in a *minyan* (composed of men) in his home. Rabbi Yair Bachrach responded that on a technical level, a woman may recite Kaddish, since she is equally obligated to sanctify God's name and her doing so provides equal tranquility to the departed. Yet he ultimately opposed the establishment of private quorums, lest such innovations weaken existing customs (*Ḥavvot Yair* 222). For various reasons, many concurred with this conclusion, with some suggesting that women perform other mitzvot for the benefit of the deceased

(*Sdei Ḥemed, Avelut* 160). Other decisors did allow special home services (*Be'er Hetev* 132:5). Furthermore, a number of responsa acknowledge that in European communities, women and girls recited Kaddish in the synagogue itself (IM OḤ 5:12).

Accordingly, Rabbi Yosef E. Henkin (d. 1973) contended that since Kaddish had developed such sentimental value, and was recited among other mourners, women could perform this ritual (*Teshuvot Ibra* 2:4). As Dr. Joel Wolowelsky has reported (*Judaism* 44:3), Rabbi Joseph B. Soloveitchik further permitted a woman to recite Kaddish even if she was the lone mourner. These permissive positions were opposed by many decisors, who argued that (1) women were not allowed to participate in this part of the service (*Minḥat Yitzḥak* 4:30), (2) the classic mystical sources spoke only of men's recitation (*Mishpetei Uziel* OḤ 3:13), (3) women's recitation was immodest in public settings (*Aseh Lekha Rav* 5:33), or (4) it would encourage antinomian, non-Orthodox trends (*Yaḥel Yisrael* 2:90). Rabbi Ahron Soloveichik countered that it is technically permissible for women to recite Kaddish, and preventing them from doing so will push women away from traditional Judaism (*Od Yosef Yisrael Bni Ḥai*, p. 100).

Chapter 65

Megilla Reading

May women chant publicly?

Communal debates regarding whether a woman may recite *Megillat Esther* on behalf of other women can sometimes become divisive. This is most regrettable, since Purim shows how Jewish unity is crucial to our ultimate salvation (Est. 4:16). This essay intends to facilitate a more informed dialogue while encouraging each community to account for its unique sensitivities in implementing its position.

While women are generally exempt from performing time-bound commandments, the Talmud asserts that women are included in the commandment to read the Megilla because "they too were a part of the miracle" (Megilla 4a). This rationale, also applied to certain commandments of Passover and Ḥanukka, means either that men and women both benefited from the miracle, since both were in danger, or that women (in this case, Esther) were active in our salvation (*Tosafot*). As such, everyone agrees that, at the very least, women must hear the Megilla reading (Y. Megilla 2:4).

The Talmud explicitly states that, as opposed to the mentally incompetent or children, women may read the Megilla (Arakhin 2b). As such, a number of medieval commentators – including Rashi (Megilla 4a) and Maimonides (MT *Hilkhot Megilla* 1:1) – asserted that women may do so even for others, including men. This conclusion stems from the principle that people who are equally obligated in a mitzva may perform the ritual on behalf of one another (*Beit HaBeḥira* Megilla 4a).

As Rabbi Dr. Aryeh Frimer has documented, a few medieval texts dispute this ruling for ancillary reasons. Some invoked the prohibition of a man's listening to a woman sing (*kol isha*) (*Kol Bo* 45). (See essay 70, "*Kol Isha*.") Indeed, some contemporary decisors cite *kol isha* as one reason women may not chant from the Torah (*Nishmat Avraham* YD 195:1). (See essay 67, "*Aliyot*: May women read from the Torah?")

A number of scholars, however, responded that the Talmud never mentioned *kol isha* as a reason to exclude women from chanting from the Torah, thereby explaining why other medieval authorities omitted it from their discussion of reading the Megilla (*Shevet HaLevi* 3:14). Rather, chanting for the sake of a mitzva was not prohibited, because it will not lead to inappropriate sexual behavior in such a context (*Seridei Esh* 1:77).

A third medieval opinion states that women may not publicly read the Megilla for the same reason the Talmud excludes them from public Torah reading (Megilla 23a), namely, that their participation represents an affront to *kevod hatzibbur*, the dignity of the congregation (MB 689:7), or, more broadly, *zilu behu milta*, an act of impropriety (*Tosafot* Sukka 38a).

This latter view stems, in part, from an attempt to interpret an alternative talmudic-era text, the Tosefta (Megilla 2:7), which seemingly negates any obligation of women to read the Megilla. To reconcile these sources, the medieval Tosafists cited a fourth opinion: Women are obligated to hear the Megilla reading, but not to read it. As such, they cannot chant the Megilla on behalf of men, and when they read for themselves, they should recite a slightly different blessing (*Tosafot* Megilla 4a).

While this opinion was dismissed by many medieval scholars, who believed that the Tosefta text was either corrupted (Rashba, Megilla 4a) or rejected (*Or Zarua* Laws of Megilla 2:368), Rabbi Moshe Isserles (OḤ 689:2) cited it approvingly. Rabbi Joseph Karo, on the other hand, cited both views regarding women reading for men. While some Sephardic scholars adopt the stringent position (*Kaf HaḤayim* 689:14), Rabbi Ovadia Yosef contends that in principle the law follows the lenient one. He therefore ruled that if no man present can properly recite the Megilla, a knowledgeable woman may read on behalf of all (*Yeḥaveh Daat* 3:51).

All the aforementioned medieval sources indicate that women may read for women. In recent centuries, several arguments were leveled against this position. One eighteenth-century figure interpreted the Tosafists as asserting that women may not read for each other, because it represents a breach of propriety (*Korban Netanel* Megilla 1:30). Rabbi Yehuda Henkin, however, has contended that parallel medieval texts (*Tosefot HaRosh* Sukka) disprove this interpretation (*Bnei Banim* 2:10). Yet it was endorsed by Rabbi Yisrael Meir Kagan, who further noted kabbalistic disapproval of women's public readings (*Shaar HaTziyun* 689:15). Others, like former Israeli Chief Rabbi Avraham Shapira, have noted that women's Megilla readings go against traditional practice, or that it remains preferable for women to join the congregation, in consonance with the principle that the miracle is best publicized en masse.

Nonetheless, major scholars including Rabbis Henkin, Yosef (*Yabia Omer* OḤ 8:56), and Aharon Lichtenstein have permitted women's Megilla readings because they accord with the vast majority of sources. These decisors add that especially in women's seminaries, or wherever additional readings are held for mothers of young children, there is no reason women should not read for each other, provided that they recite the text properly.

Chapter 66

Meḥitza

Why and how did this issue become a dividing line between Orthodox and Conservative synagogues?

Mixed seating was undoubtedly one of American Jewry's most controversial and divisive issues. In my hometown of Houston, for example, our decades-old Orthodox synagogue did not have a Shabbat morning service with a *meḥitza* (a partition that divides the genders) until a 7 am (!) service was added in 1969 to accommodate the new day school principal. The congregation fully abandoned mixed seating only in the early 1990s, following years of acrimonious debate and synagogue votes on the subject. Similar battles took place in numerous cities, with outcomes frequently including denominational switches, legal battles, and broken friendships.

Since both the Orthodox and Conservative movements claim allegiance to ancient practice, some tried to resolve this debate by examining relics of ancient synagogues. Yet academics sharply disagree on how to interpret the ambiguous evidence, with ideological inclinations tending to bias critical judgments.

It remains clear, however, that medieval and early modern synagogues had separate sections for men and women, with the latter seated in a gallery or adjacent room. (As Prof. Avraham Grossman has documented, many medieval women attended services regularly, both on the Sabbath and during the week. This seems to have been the case as well in talmudic times, as seen in Sota 22a and Avoda Zara 38a–b.)

While Orthodox decisors claim that this historical precedent creates an inviolable custom, their liberal detractors maintain that the legal system is flexible.

The first rabbinic text that explicitly forbids the intermingling of genders during prayer appears only in about the ninth century (*Tanna DeVei Eliyahu* 9), while the first definitive depiction of a permanent women's section surfaced in an eleventh-century fragment found in the Cairo Geniza. While the Temple in Jerusalem had a "Women's Courtyard," men entered this area as needed, such as for the Torah reading on Yom Kippur and the *Hak'hel* ceremony on Sukkot (Sota 41b). Also, women crossed the main "Israelite Courtyard" to offer sacrifices (*Bikkurim* 1:5). Some consider this "traffic" proof that gender separation was not mandated in the Temple; according to defenders of Orthodoxy, however, these examples demonstrate that intermingling was only temporary and for specific needs.

Most Orthodox proponents of a *meḥitza* point to a different Temple ceremony to show the necessity of gender separation. In describing the seating during the festive Water Drawing Ceremony of Sukkot, the sages taught, "Originally, women were inside [the Women's Courtyard] and men were outside, and they came to frivolity. [The sages] instituted that women would sit outside and men inside, but they still came to frivolity. They therefore instituted that women sit above and men below" (Sukka 51b). The Talmud further cites a verse from Zechariah to justify this addition to the Temple infrastructure.

Orthodox proponents of the *meḥitza* cite this enactment against frivolity as the basis for requiring gender separation in synagogues as well, since Jewish law frequently calls these houses of worship "mini-sanctuaries." While Rabbi Moshe Feinstein posited a biblical-level requirement of a physical barrier (IM OḤ 1:39), Rabbi Joseph B. Soloveitchik asserted that such a divider is a rabbinic mandate, with Torah law requiring only physical separation (*The Sanctity of the Synagogue*, p. 141). Conservative opponents retort that the Sukkot separation was a rabbinic enactment only for a specific ceremony. Others have accused Orthodox scholars of trumping up severe prohibitions for polemical purposes, an allegation that Rabbi Gil Student has attempted to refute (BDD 17).

In 1851, the first American Reform synagogue introduced mixed pews after purchasing its new temple from a church. Prof. Jonathan Sarna has argued that this innovation, and its subsequent spread to other denominations, stemmed from convenience as well as a desire to modernize by emulating the decorum of the Christian majority. While certain Conservative rabbis from the Jewish Theological Seminary opposed mixed seating, their more liberal colleagues prevailed, especially as the nascent feminist movement turned the issue into a fight for egalitarianism. Additionally, the modern motto of "Families that pray together stay together" became a formidable sociological argument for mixed pews. Orthodox rabbis stood firm, however, deeming such practices completely unacceptable. While graduates of Orthodox rabbinical schools continued, until the 1980s, to take positions in synagogues with mixed seating, over time they frequently demanded a *meḥitza*. Thus, the partition separating men and women came to symbolize the denominational divide.

Chapter 67

Aliyot

May women read from the Torah?

Since the founding of Congregation Shira Hadasha in Jerusalem and similar "partnership *minyanim*" around the world, the issue of women reading from the Torah and receiving *aliyot* has received much attention in the Orthodox community. This practice has been rejected by the vast majority of Orthodox scholars, including several who are relatively sensitive to women's issues, such as Rabbis Shlomo Riskin and Yehuda Henkin. This essay will try to briefly delineate the major areas of contention.

Most scholars agree that there is no problem for women, including those in a state of *nidda* (ritual impurity caused by menstruation), to touch a Torah scroll. As the Talmud states, words of Torah cannot become impure (Berakhot 22a). On this basis, Maimonides (MT *Hilkhot Tefillin U'Mezuza VeSefer Torah* 10:8) and Rabbi Joseph Karo (YD 282:9) explicitly state that a woman may touch a Torah scroll. Based on an obscure early medieval text, however, some Ashkenazic authorities record a custom that menstruating women should refrain from prayer and other rituals (*Baraita DeMasekhet Nidda*). Yet many scholars, including Rabbis Moshe Isserles (OḤ 88:1) and Shneur Zalman of Liadi (*Shulḥan Arukh HaRav* OḤ 88:2), note that this tradition is not required by law, and was regularly waived for important communal rituals like High Holy Day services or family celebrations. Others add that most communities no longer observe this custom.

The central debate relates to whether the talmudic proclamation that women may not publicly read from the Torah is still applicable. The

Talmud states, "All are included among the seven [who are called to the Torah on Shabbat], even a minor or a woman, but the sages said, 'A woman is not to read from the Torah on account of *kevod hatzibbur* (the dignity of the community)'" (Megilla 23a). As noted by Rabbi Mendel Shapiro, who wrote the initial article in support of women's Torah reading, the Talmud implies that the problem of a female reader is only that it is an affront to communal dignity; otherwise, it would be permitted. In responsa on other matters, a number of decisors have similarly interpreted this talmudic passage to assert that no additional legal obstacles exist. Rabbi Ovadia Yosef, for example, writing about women's Megilla readings, argued from this passage that there is no prohibition of hearing a woman sing (*kol isha,* discussed in essay 70) when she chants the Torah (*Yeḥaveh Daat* 3:51). Likewise, describing the Eastern European practice of one or two female mourners entering the men's section to recite Kaddish, Rabbi Moshe Feinstein noted that the text in question seemingly shows that minimal, temporary intermingling of the sexes is permissible (IM OḤ 5:12).

Not everyone agrees with these assessments, however. Rabbi Shlomo Zalman Auerbach and others contended that in addition to *kevod hatzibbur,* there is in fact a problem of hearing a woman sing (*Nishmat Avraham* YD 195). And for Rabbi Yaakov Ariel, the term *kevod hatzibbur* means that it remains immodest for women to perform a role that will cause sexual distraction.

In his article, Rabbi Shapiro asserts that the nature of Torah reading allows women to read for others, even if they do not share the same obligation to hear this reading. Rabbi Riskin, however, has countered that subsequent evolution of the ancient institution of public Torah reading prohibits women from reading on behalf of others.

Even if one agrees with Rabbi Shapiro that *kevod hatzibbur* is the dominant factor, many dispute whether it may be waived. Advocates of partnership *minyanim* contend that it is an outdated sociological assessment that looks askance at unknowledgeable men who require women or children to fulfill their ritual roles. These proponents also point out that other talmudic laws based on communal dignity have been waived, and that various commentators have suggested that women may read the Torah in limited circumstances, such as if no men can, in private family *minyanim*, or as long as a woman is not the exclusive reader. Rabbi Dr. Daniel Sperber has further argued that preventing women from reading violates the halakhic concept of *kevod habriyot* (human dignity), which should outweigh other concerns, particularly in a community that has consented to women reading.

Opponents of these changes, including Rabbis Eliav Shochetman and Michael Broyde, say that the exceptions mentioned in earlier sources were theoretical rulings meant for extenuating circumstances and were never put into practice. Furthermore, many scholars believed that the ban on women receiving *aliyot* could never be waived, even in extreme circumstances, such as in a town populated entirely by *kohanim*, who normally receive only the first *aliya*. As such, the talmudic passage with which we began creates a bona fide rabbinic prohibition, as implied by Maimonides' formulation of the law (*Maaseh Roke'aḥ* MT *Hilkhot Tefilla* 12:17). Rabbi Dr. Aryeh Frimer further claims that the notion of *kevod habriyot* can never be employed by a group simply because it dislikes a rabbinic edict when the alleged indignity comes from the rabbinic law itself.

Whatever the merits of each side, Rabbi Henkin has contended that women's *aliyot* remain outside the consensus of Orthodox scholars, and that any congregation that institutes such a practice will soon become non-Orthodox.

Time will tell.

Chapter 68
Zimmun

Is a woman permitted to lead the Grace After Meals?

Jews must recite the Grace After Meals (*Birkat HaMazon*) after consuming a satiating amount of food within a limited time (Deut. 8:10). While some sages believed women are equally included in this biblical imperative (Berakhot 20b), others disagreed, contending that certain passages within the blessings regarding the Land of Israel (Rashi) or circumcision (*Tosafot*) exempted women from reciting them. Ultimately, the rabbis concluded that women are required to recite the Grace After Meals. While Rabbi Moshe Isserles ruled that they should omit those passages irrelevant to them (OḤ 187:3), the universal contemporary practice is that women recite the same text as men (MB 187:9).

The talmudic dispute over whether women's inclusion in this ritual stemmed from a biblical imperative or rabbinic decree was never resolved in normative Jewish law (OḤ 186:1). This issue remains significant, since only a person obligated to fulfill a commandment on a level equal to or higher than others may discharge that obligation on their behalf (as is today customarily done for Kiddush). Since historically *Birkat HaMazon* was frequently recited aloud by one person to cover everyone else at the meal, women were not permitted to recite these blessings on behalf of men (186:1). In any case, it was difficult for listeners to concentrate on the extended blessings, so today individuals recite the text quietly to themselves (MB 183:27).

When three or more people eat together, they should also recite grace simultaneously to amplify the public exultation of God (Berakhot 45a), with an additional name of God inserted by a quorum of ten or more (OḤ 192:1). This practice, known as a *zimmun*, entails a convener inviting others to join him in praising God. The Talmud states that women are not included in a regular *zimmun* but should form their own quorum (Berakhot 45b). Everyone agrees that women may answer the *zimmun* recited by a quorum of men (*Shu"t HaRosh* 4:16). The commentators, however, debate what active role women might play in a quorum.

The straightforward reading of the text indicates that women eating separately from men are obligated to form a quorum (Rosh, Berakhot 7:4). Although some female members of scholarly families did perform this ritual (*Mordekhai* Berakhot 155), most medieval women did not. This phenomenon, likely the result of female illiteracy, led some scholars to postulate that a *zimmun* was merely optional for women (*Tosafot* Berakhot 45b). Indeed, Rabbi Yeḥiel Michel Epstein claimed that he had never heard of women forming separate quorums (AH OḤ 199:2).

Nonetheless, the practice remains perfectly legitimate (OḤ 199:7) and, according to the Vilna Gaon, obligatory. As such, Rabbi Yosef Ḥayim of Baghdad (d. 1909) advocated teaching girls how to recite a *zimmun* when they eat separately (*Ben Ish Ḥai, Koraḥ* 13). Others further claimed that women may separate from a larger meal to create their own quorum (*Shaar HaTziyun* 199:9). Rabbi Shlomo Zalman Auerbach even contended that two men eating with three women should respond to the female convener's blessings (*Halikhot Beitah* 12:7).

Greater controversy surrounds the inclusion of women in a quorum with men. Several medieval authorities assert that one woman counts toward a quorum of three (*Tur* OḤ 199) or even ten (*Mordekhai* Berakhot 155). This position stems from a significant leniency regarding the formulation of quorums. When a minority of participants have not eaten bread, it does not hinder the recital of a *zimmun*, provided that they partook of at least minimal food or beverage while the majority consumed bread (MB 197:22). Consequently, these medieval scholars contended that a woman who ate grain-based foods is no less involved in the meal than a man who consumed no bread, and therefore she may help complete the quorum.

Yet historically, normative practice rejected joint quorums, for the following reasons: (1) Women have a lower-level obligation in reciting *Birkat HaMazon* (*Shu"t Maharam* OḤ 4:227); (2) men and women recite different texts (Rashi, Arakhin 3a); (3) women do not establish a steady presence (*keviut*) at the table (*Teshuvot HaRaavad* 12); and (4) a joint quorum, in which one pays attention to the presence of the other gender, will lead to promiscuity (Ran, Megilla 6b).

In the 1980s, Rabbi Eliezer Berkovits (*Jewish Women in Time and Torah*) proposed rethinking the ban on joint quorums, since (1) we may rely on the position that men and women are equally obligated in *Birkat HaMazon* (or that this factor is irrelevant to *zimmun* participation); (2) the text today is uniform for men and women; and (3) prevailing social norms allow for joint dining between the sexes, especially within the family. The latter point was already made in the nineteenth century (*Shoel U'Meshiv Kamma* 3:155), and there is some historical evidence that a few scholars allowed mixed quorums at home (*Gan HaMelekh* 75). Based on these points, a more modest proposal was recently floated to allow a *zimmun* within the nuclear family alone (*Akdamot* 26). This proposed reform drew the sharp response of several traditionalists, however, leaving its prospects in serious doubt.

Chapter 69

Brit Mila

Is there an equivalent ceremony for women?

The commendable desire for a meaningful celebration of the birth of a daughter has led to the restoration of bygone ceremonies and the innovation of others, some decidedly more appropriate and some less so. I have been blessed with three daughters and a son, and I believe the different celebrations we had for each were equally joyful both for us and for our community.

Frequently overlooked, however, are the potential theological implications of the absence of a ritual that inducts girls into Judaism. The Hebrew term for circumcision, *brit mila,* recalls God's commanding Abraham to circumcise himself as a sign of the covenant (*brit*) between them, which includes his descendants as well (Gen. 17). God nearly kills Moses for failing to circumcise his son (Ex. 4), and the Torah establishes that only circumcised Jewish men may partake of the Paschal sacrifice (Ex. 12).

In fact, circumcision and the Passover sacrifice are the only two positive commandments that incur the punishment of *karet* (excision from the Jewish people) for deliberate non-performance, signifying their powerful role in instilling Jewish identity to this day. Similarly, male converts must undergo circumcision. Midrashim portray the covenantal blood of circumcision as a quasi-sacrifice and as protection from Hell. Early medieval sages, including Rabbi Naḥshon Gaon (ninth century), write that one must name dead newborns and remove their foreskins to assure their place in the afterlife, and while many medieval authorities opposed this postmortem rite, it has become normative practice (YD 263:5).

Though women are biologically excluded from *brit mila* (Judaism has never advocated the abhorrent mutilation of female genitals found in other cultures), ancient and medieval sources indicate that they occasionally served as surgeons and/or *sandakot* ("godmothers") for this ritual (Avoda Zara 27a; Raavya, Shabbat 1:279). Yet given the central role circumcision plays in forming Jewish identity, the absence of an equivalent physical symbol to represent the covenant for women can raise uncomfortable questions about their status.

As Prof. Shaye Cohen has documented, among the earliest to ask these questions were Christian theologians. Paul, Justin Martyr, and others argued that believers need not physically circumcise themselves, since God desires only the "spiritual circumcision of the heart." They supported this claim by asserting that since women were not circumcised, the ritual must not be essential. Ironically – and unknowingly – early Reform Jews who sought to abolish "barbaric" circumcisions similarly contended that uncircumcised baby boys should still be registered as Jews, like their "uncircumcised" sisters.

More traditional thinkers offered various explanations for the absence of a female *brit mila*. The first-century philosopher Philo interpreted circumcision as symbolically teaching a person to reduce his sexual appetite. Maimonides (twelfth century, Spain) went further and famously asserted that circumcision reduces men's excessive sexual drive by weakening the organ (Guide 3:49). Following Aristotle, Maimonides contended that all sensual pleasure – including eating and drinking, along with sex – harmed the soul, and removing the foreskin reduced this enjoyment. He also claimed that all monotheistic followers of Abraham share this obligation, ruling that Muslims must circumcise themselves as well. This assertion angered scholars who understood this covenant as an exclusive bond between the Jewish people and God (*Pitḥei Teshuva* YD 263:14).

The theme of reducing excessive male sexual desire was taken in conflicting directions by readers of Maimonides. Rabbi Jacob Anatoli (thirteenth century, Naples), for example, controversially argued that a woman was subservient to her husband's orders, and therefore had no need for the additional discipline provided by circumcision. Rabbi Samson Raphael Hirsch (nineteenth century, Germany), on the other hand, venerated women as more pious than men; therefore, he argued, they require no bodily symbols to remind them of their spiritual and moral duties. Rabbi Joseph Bekhor Shor, the twelfth-century Bible commentator, took a different approach. Creatively, he maintained that menstrual blood functions as the female equivalent of the blood of circumcision. The blood itself, it seems, becomes covenantal by virtue of observing the laws of family purity.

Perhaps the simplest and most elegant answer was offered by an anti-Christian polemicist from central Europe, Rabbi Yom Tov Lippman Muhlhausen (d. 1421). He contended that circumcision is one of many commandments that obligate only a segment of the population. Just as priests, Levites, and Israelites all have their exclusive mitzvot, so do men and women. For example, while men perform *brit mila*, women offer sacrifices after childbirth (Lev. 12). Observing the Torah is a communal enterprise, and only as a united group do we fulfill – and embody – our covenantal responsibilities.

Chapter 70

Kol Isha

May women sing zemirot *when men are also present at the meal?*

The prohibition of *kol isha* that greatly restricts the ability of women to sing in the presence of men regularly engenders passionate response. In recent years, the issue has taken on a public dimension when some religious Israeli soldiers refused to participate in state ceremonies at which female singers perform. In private contexts, the issue regularly emerges at Shabbat tables when Jews of various religious practices begin to sing the customary Shabbat songs.

In two talmudic passages, the third-century sage Shmuel states, "*Kol be'isha erva*," loosely translated as "A woman's voice is indecent." One of these sources (Berakhot 24a) appears after a talmudic ruling that a woman's thighs and other uncovered body parts inappropriately distract a man from properly reciting the *Shema* prayer. Many medieval commentators (BY OḤ 75:3) deduce from this juxtaposition that one is also forbidden to recite the *Shema* while listening to a woman sing (*kol isha*). According to this approach, the sages prohibited *kol isha* because it leads to illicit or distracting thoughts (*hirhurei aveira*).

Indeed, a few medieval sources indicate that *kol isha* applies primarily during the recitation of the *Shema* and may even be circumvented if a man feels he can control his thoughts (Rabbenu Yona, Berakhot 17a). Accordingly, a few contemporary rabbis have tried to justify the neglect of this law in certain Modern Orthodox circles by arguing that *kol isha* is prohibited only when it distracts from worship. This position has been largely rejected, however, as I will explain below. Nonetheless, some rely upon these sources when confronted with *kol isha* in professional or other contexts, a policy that might have medieval precedent (*Mordekhai* Berakhot 80).

The overwhelming majority of Orthodox rabbis contend that the second source of *kol be'isha erva* clearly forbids men from listening to women sing in non-ritual contexts (Kiddushin 70a). In the course of a larger discussion regarding intermingling of the sexes, the Talmud once again cites Shmuel's statement, unrelated to *Shema* or other rituals. Rabbi Joseph Karo codified this prohibition in his list of licentious behavior, such as giddy flirting (EH 21:1). Independent of any additional problems it might cause, such as illicit thoughts, *kol isha* remains problematic because it represents, in its own right, frivolity between the sexes.

Classifying *kol isha* as inappropriate interaction, however, opens the door for leniencies in contexts where a woman's singing cannot be deemed as licentious. Rabbi Moshe Feinstein (IM OḤ 1:26), for example, permitted girls under twelve to sing in front of men, since we are not concerned about frivolity between them. (A few sources might indicate that the entire prohibition does not apply to single women of any age, since they are technically "available" for creating non-frivolous, licit relationships. The preponderance of decisors, however, reject that position.)

A major modern debate revolved around the permissibility of listening to female performances on the radio or on television. Rabbi Eliezer Waldenburg (*Tzitz Eliezer* 5:2) contended that since there is no physical interaction, such listening does not constitute licentious behavior. Rabbi Yaakov Breisch, however, argued that any pleasure from a woman's voice, even with no contact, remains prohibited (*Ḥelkat Yaakov* OḤ 30). Rabbi Ovadia Yosef took a middle position, allowing radio listening only if one doesn't know who's singing or has never seen her picture (*Yabia Omer* OḤ 1:6).

This background brings us to the question about *zemirot*. After World War II, a French co-ed youth group asked Rabbi Yeḥiel Yaakov Weinberg about the propriety of participants singing *zemirot* together (*Seridei Esh* 1:77). Rabbi Weinberg recalled that while women had refrained from singing *zemirot* in his native Lithuania, leading rabbis in Germany, where he had headed a yeshiva, invited women to join the men at the table in song. He justified this tradition by citing scholars who felt that religious songs could not lead to licentiousness or illicit thoughts. After all, the prophetess Devorah had led the nation in hymns following a military victory (Judges 5). Rabbi Weinberg further argued that in an age when well-educated women displayed tremendous self-respect, prohibiting their participation would only insult these teenagers and distance them from Judaism.

Many rabbis strongly reject this position. Some dispute Rabbi Weinberg's legal argument, while others marginalize the ruling as an emergency measure intended exclusively for his times (*Tzitz Eliezer* 14:7). Other scholars, such as Rabbis Joseph B. Soloveitchik (as reported by Rabbi Chaim Jachter) and Ḥayim David HaLevi (*Mekor Ḥayim LiVnot Yisrael* 5:10), permitted joint singing of *zemirot*, and much of the religious Zionist community (including my family) follows this opinion.

Chapter 71

Separate Seating

Must buses be gender segregated?

The issue of the "denigration of women" (*hadarat nashim*) in public greatly engaged Israeli society in 2011 and 2012. Unfortunately, numerous phenomena were included under this umbrella headline. There is a big difference, from the perspectives of both halakha and democracy, between allowing religious soldiers to excuse themselves from concerts given by female singers and forcing non-religious women to sit in the back of a bus or violently harassing them for entering a certain neighborhood while dressed immodestly.

Clearly many of these phenomena are deplorable and require redress on three levels: (1) rectifying the massive desecration of God's reputation (*ḥillul Hashem*) created by extremists like the Sicarii group and their neighbors who fail to condemn their actions; (2) creating greater understanding of the relationship between halakha, democracy, and tolerance; and (3) clarifying the halakhic sources related to these matters. This third level will be the focus of this essay.

Jewish law forbids not only illicit sexual relations, but also actions that might lead to such behavior or are immodest or inappropriate in their own right. This prohibition includes intimate physical contact between the sexes (Lev. 18:6, 19), illicit thoughts (Ketubbot 46a), and leering (*Sifrei Shelaḥ* 115). Accordingly, scholars forbid many contemporary recreational activities, including mixed swimming (*Shevet HaLevi* 3:185) and dancing (*Kitzur Shulḥan Arukh* 152:13). Many interpreters similarly understood the prohibition of cross-dressing to preventing illicit behavior (Rashi, Deut. 22:5).

These restrictions apply to men and women alike (*Ḥinukh* 188, 387), with each obligated to avoid illicit sexual arousal or causing it in others (*lifnei iver*). The sages, however, understood that men are more prone to such arousal than women. Therefore, men are warned not to stare at women (Shabbat 64b). Women, at the same time, are expected to dress modestly, in consonance with Jewish norms (*dat yehudit*), even as the exact standards are subject to debate and locale (Ketubbot 72a).

Be that as it may, if men find themselves around immodestly dressed women, the sages exhorted them to avert their glances or distract their thoughts (Bava Batra 57b). Due to the inevitability of these situations, Rabbi Moshe Feinstein allowed people to work in the summer on a crowded, urban street – or even sit on the beach for health reasons – if they feel they can focus their thoughts appropriately (IM EH 1:56). Some authorities have expressed concern that people will abuse this dispensation, particularly by lingering in an immodest area such as a beach (*Yeḥaveh Daat* 5:63). Nonetheless, the basic sentiment that men need to control their thoughts in immodest situations has been affirmed by many decisors (*Ateret Paz* 1:3 EH 6).

The sages remained wary of a man walking behind a woman, lest he notice her bodily movements (Berakhot 61a). Instead, they recommended that he move aside or in front of her. Yet the recent attempt to dictate separate sides of the street for opposite genders is historically unprecedented. Moreover, several decisors note that today men and women commonly walk the streets together, so it is no longer stimulating (*Tzitz Eliezer* 9:50).

Similar claims were made regarding the talmudic prohibition of greeting another man's wife (Kiddushin 70b). Rabbi Moshe Schick, for example, asserted that such courtesies are no longer inappropriate (*Shu"t Maharam Schick* EH 53). To support his claim, he drew upon a significant medieval declaration in which scholars, following talmudic precedent, allowed men to be served by a woman (such as a waitress), since their intentions are honorable (*Tosafot* Kiddushin 82a).

The general notion of separate seating is well-founded in halakha. To prevent licentious behavior, the sages dictated separate galleries for the Temple festivities on Sukkot (Sukka 51b). This measure historically served as a source for the partition in the synagogue (*Ḥatam Sofer* ḤM

5:190). Scholars disputed, however, whether separate seating is necessary on other occasions as well, such as weddings. While the medieval German pietists required separation (*Sefer Ḥasidim* 393), Rabbi Mordekhai Jaffe (sixteenth century, Poland) deemed it unnecessary in cultures where men and women habitually mingle (*Levush* OḤ *Minhagim* 36).

Regarding buses, Rabbi Moshe Feinstein allowed travel on public transportation, though passengers of the opposite gender regularly sit or stand next to one another, since this proximity does not stimulate sexual thoughts (IM EH 2:14). Rabbi Shlomo Braun ruled likewise regarding air travel (*She'arim Metzuyanim BaHalakha* 4:152:8). Rabbi Binyamin Zilber has further noted that besides being economically impractical, advising people to travel in private cars or taxis does not necessarily spare them from immodesty; ultimately, one must know himself and act appropriately in any given situation (*Az Nidberu* 7:75). While he himself has ruled that one must avoid physical contact on public transportation, he has argued that this is in any case frequently doable (5:48).

As such, it remains difficult to assert that halakha requires separate seating on a bus or demands that people change seats on planes to accommodate those who want to sit next to someone of the same gender. One may argue that people are entitled to privately arrange for such accommodations, but Jewish law does not require them.

Chapter 72

Modest Dress

Do norms of tzniut *change over time?*

The 2012 publication by Rabbi Shlomo Aviner of detailed guidelines for modest female attire (*tzniut*) led to a storm of controversy. In addition to establishing relatively stringent standards (including prohibiting certain fabrics), Rabbi Aviner delineated methods of testing one's adherence to them (e.g., checking the transparency of clothing against sunlight). This uproar followed a similar one triggered by Rabbi Aviner's declaring that ideally, women would not vote or take active roles in politics, even as he conceded that given the current reality, women may participate.

Many objected to the notion that modesty laws should be spelled out so technically, as if explaining how to clean an oven before Passover. The prophet Micah teaches, "Walk modestly with your God" (6:8). This overarching value (for men and women alike) should not be reduced to detailed discussions about the propriety of bright orange shirts or unbraided hair. The Ne'emanei Torah Va'Avodah movement further deemed the publication of "modesty codes" counterproductive: "The obsessive attention to articles of clothing is in itself immodest, and all this publicity distorts halakha, which seeks to reduce a person's engagement in matters of human urges." Instead, say these critics, modesty norms are best taught informally at home or in school. Defenders of such detailed guidelines retort that we are bombarded daily with immodest images in a society that promotes an uninhibited, provocative lifestyle. As such, it is important to anchor our dedication to modesty in clear, unambiguous standards.

This reaction, in turn, relates to a central question: Do societal changes impact notions of modest behavior? At the height of the women's suffrage movement in the early twentieth century, Jewish scholars debated whether women should receive voting rights. Many scholars opposed women's voting, with some, such as Rabbi Abraham Isaac Kook, arguing that involvement in public affairs would corrupt women's integrity while leading to family strife over political differences (*Maamarei HaRaaya*, p. 189). Rabbi Ben-Zion Uziel strongly disagreed, citing a basic moral claim of "No taxation without representation." Furthermore, he found nothing immodest about women voting (or even being elected to office), since intermingling of the sexes is inappropriate only when frivolous, not when dealing with weighty political and economic affairs. He added that husbands and wives could disagree amicably regarding political matters, just as parents and grown children do (*Mishpetei Uziel* ḤM 4:64). Eventually, women's suffrage became fully accepted even within ultra-Orthodox circles, albeit sometimes for purely pragmatic reasons. Most readers of this essay, I suspect, believe that granting women the right to vote promoted human dignity without impinging on standards of modesty.

When it comes to guidelines for female attire, the Talmud prohibits exposure of any areas that should normally be covered, adding that a man should not pray in the presence of such exposure, lest he become distracted. Some of these norms are mandated by Jewish law (*dat Moshe*) and remain unalterable, while others represent the customary behavior of Jewish women (*dat Yehudit*), which under certain circumstances may change with the times (Ketubbot 72a). Contemporary scholars sometimes debate how to classify certain attire restrictions. For example, the overwhelming majority of twentieth-century Orthodox decisors, including Rabbis Moshe Feinstein (IM EH 1:53, 57) and Ovadia Yosef (*Yeḥaveh Daat* 5:62), believe that biblical norms require a married woman to cover her hair. Yet as Rabbi Michael Broyde has documented (*Tradition* 42:3), a few scholars, including Rabbi Yosef Messas (*Collected Letters* 1884), declared this practice dependent on contemporary norms. Once modest women in society no longer covered their hair, then modest Jewish women could follow suit, because uncovered hair was no longer provocative.

A similar dispute relates to which areas of the body should be covered. The Talmud, for example, asserts that a woman's "thigh" should not be improperly revealed (Berakhot 24a). Decisors debate whether this term includes the entire leg, until the ankle (AH OḤ 75:3), or only the area above (and including) the knee (MB 75:2). While Rabbi Aviner preferred the former position, other scholars have adopted the latter, in part because they believe this level of exposure remains fully modest within contemporary society. Yet even they recognize the limitations of modern standards, especially in many Western societies, which devalue modest dress.

Given the sensitivity of these matters and their impact on both appearance and self-image, it behooves the Jewish community to engage in a scholarly and thoughtful dialogue regarding the best way to establish guidelines and promote modesty. One prays that such dialogue will enhance human dignity and allow men and women alike to walk modestly in the ways of God.

Chapter 73

Funerals

May women deliver eulogies?

Under pressure from the Israeli Supreme Court, the Chief Rabbinate in 2012 issued a halakhic ruling permitting women to deliver eulogies. This declaration was the culmination of a legal battle led heroically by the ITIM organization following highly publicized incidents in which women were forcefully prevented by the municipal burial society (*ḥevra kaddisha*) from eulogizing their beloved. These incidents highlight the widely divergent views within Jewish sources regarding the participation of women in funerals.

In antiquity, many cultures featured lamentations at funerals, a phenomenon also found in Jewish sources. Jeremiah, for example, proclaims, "Summon the dirge singers… send for the skilled women…. Let them quickly start a wailing for us, that our eyes may run with tears…" (Jeremiah 9:16–17). Citing this verse, the sages noted that such singers attended the funerals of the greatest scholars (*Pirkei DeRabbi Eliezer* 17). Elsewhere the rabbis detail the rich, poetic lyrics recited by the women of Babylonia (Moed Katan 28b). One sage even asserted that a husband, within his marriage contract, becomes obligated to provide a dirge singer for his wife's funeral (Ketubbot 46a). This requirement was codified by Maimonides (MT *Hilkhot Avelut* 12:1) as well as by Rabbi Joseph Karo, though the latter limited it to societies that observed this custom (YD 344:3). Rabbi Yeḥiel Michel Epstein concurred that the marital contract obligates one to provide appropriate ceremonies in accordance with contemporary practice (AH YD 344:2).

Supporters of female eulogists reasonably contend that dirge singers serve as a precedent for women participating in burial ceremonies. This rationale is particularly compelling if the deceased would have wanted his female loved ones to eulogize him, since Jewish law assigns great weight to the last requests of the dying. In fact, dirge singing would seem *more* problematic than eulogies, because halakha prohibits female singing (*kol isha*) in public. One decisor used the example of dirge singers to argue that *kol isha* applies only to love songs meant to arouse the listener, but not to more prosaic singing (*Sdei Ḥemed*, vol. 4, *Kuf*, 42). Many, however, contended that while such songs would normally be prohibited, the somber context of the funeral inhibits any unseemliness (*Tiferet Yisrael – Yakhin*, Moed Katan 68). Whatever the explanation, eulogies involve no *kol isha*, seemingly strengthening their halakhic propriety.

Opposition to female eulogizers stems partly from general considerations of modest behavior. Bnai Brak's Rabbi Shmuel HaLevi Wosner, along with many ultra-Orthodox decisors, prohibits women from addressing mixed audiences (*Shevet HaLevi* 3:14). Yet in many religious Zionist or Modern Orthodox communities, such lectures are perfectly acceptable, with women serving as Knesset members and professors, as well as in other jobs that include public speaking. Indeed, even Rabbi Moshe Feinstein permitted women to lecture in front of male audiences, albeit only on an ad hoc basis and outside a synagogue (IM OḤ 5:12).

Opponents of female eulogies also draw from another controversial law regarding women and funeral etiquette. The talmudic sages debated whether women should head a funeral procession or follow the bier. The latter opinion, apparently, was motivated by concerns of immodesty (*Tosafot*). Yet according to both views, women would attend the actual burial, even as care was taken to prevent inappropriate intermingling (*Darkhei Moshe* YD 359).

In the sixteenth century, however, Rabbi Joseph Karo ruled that women should follow the bier only during the procession, without entering the cemetery. This latter restriction originates in the Zohar. Echoing a notion found in the Talmud (Berakhot 51a), the Zohar contends that women mystically endanger men within cemeteries because of Eve's role in the exile from the Garden of Eden (YD 359:2). In some communities, the combined factors of mysticism and modesty led some women to forgo funeral processions altogether.

This position, however, did not go unchallenged. Scholars noted that regardless of mystical concerns, the Talmud clearly permitted women to participate in the funeral procession (*Beit Leḥem Yehuda* YD 359:2). When the Zohar and Talmud conflict, the latter takes precedence. Moreover, many medieval communities seem to have been lenient, while carefully avoiding inappropriate intermingling. Therefore, say these authorities, there is no legal impediment to women attending the burial, especially when their absence would cause emotional pain (*BeMareh HaBazak* 3:73). In any case, this discussion applies only to graveside participation, but not to eulogies delivered in a funeral home.

Recognizing no definitive ban, in law or custom, on women delivering eulogies, Ashkenazic Chief Rabbi Yona Metzger permitted this practice. This ruling was definitely correct, especially for communities where men and women have regular social and professional interaction. Unfortunately, Rabbi Metzger allowed for municipal burial societies to determine local procedure, thereby preventing an appropriate resolution in all cities. One hopes that future chief rabbis will ensure that the sensitivity of Jewish law be reflected at all funerals and other life-cycle events.

Chapter 74

Torah Study

Are women allowed to study Talmud?

In a famous biblical passage recited daily in the *Shema* prayer, the Torah commands, "And you shall teach them [the commandments] to your children" (Deut. 11:19). The sages derived from this verse the obligation to both learn and teach Torah (Kiddushin 29b), and further extolled Torah study as the greatest mitzva (Pe'ah 1:1). The Bible also states that one should study Torah every day and night (Joshua 1:8). While this mitzva is minimally fulfilled by reciting the *Shema*, the sages greatly commend those who establish fixed times for daily study.

The sages, however, understood that women were excluded from the commandment to study Torah formally, at least in its most comprehensive form (Kiddushin 29b). Rabbi Eliezer even forbade fathers to teach Torah to their daughters, comparing such an activity to the teaching of "*tiflut*" (Sota 21b). While commentators dispute the meaning of this term, many followed Maimonides' interpretation: that unlettered women will trivialize the Torah's wisdom (MT *Hilkhot Talmud Torah* 1:13). (Rabbi Eliezer was so adamant that he refused to answer an intelligent query from a woman who was one of his primary patrons [Y. Sota 3:4].) While Ben Azzai countered that fathers *must* teach their daughters, he garnered minimal support (*Otzar HaMelekh* 1:13), with the historical consensus siding with Rabbi Eliezer.

Yet several limitations were placed on this purported prohibition. Numerous commentators allowed women to study Scripture, at least on a basic level, though the Oral Law remained prohibited (*Taz*

OḤ 47:10). This license helps explain female participation in the Torah-mandated *Hak'hel* ceremony every seven years, when the Torah was read publicly (*Baḥ* YD 246). Furthermore, women must recite the blessings over Torah study each morning, indicating that they may be rewarded for their voluntary study (*Bei'ur HaGra* OḤ 47:14).

Equally significant, several medieval scholars obligate women to learn any material necessary for their halakhic observance (YD 246:6). This goal may be accomplished in different ways, with many communities historically limiting women's education to practical instruction from their mothers with very minimal textual study (AH YD 246:19), as remains the case today among Satmar Hasidim (*Divrei Yatziv* YD 139).

Yet other decisors asserted that while the Talmud bars fathers from teaching their daughters, a qualified woman may elect to learn Torah on her own (*Perisha* YD 246:15). This self-motivation proves that she will not turn the Torah's wisdom into nonsense, say these authorities, and makes her actions praiseworthy. Rabbi Ḥayim David Azulai (eighteenth century) added that this dispensation explains why the Talmud commended the famous Bruria's wisdom and knowledge (*Tov Ayin* 4). Indeed, despite limited educational opportunities, many learned women (usually related to great scholars) appear in rabbinic literature throughout the ages (*Halikhot Bat Yisrael* 9:7). In light of this historical phenomenon, scholars have questioned whether Rabbi Eliezer's statement represents a bona fide prohibition or just a word of caution (*Aseh Lekha Rav* 2:52). Some contend that he prohibited teaching only young children, not mature, sophisticated daughters (*Torah Temima* Deut. 11:19).

As women worldwide began receiving general educations, a number of Jewish schools for girls developed, particularly in nineteenth-century Germany, on the theory that women needed more knowledge than previously necessary to maintain religious commitment. This sentiment culminated in the early twentieth century with the famed Rabbi Yisrael Meir Kagan's endorsement of Sarah Schenirer's fledging network of Bais Yaakov schools (*Likkutei Halakhot* Sota 21). Noting that secularly educated women were abandoning Jewish tradition, he asserted that their contemporaries required greater exposure to Scripture and rabbinic ethical literature. This limited curriculum is maintained in many girls' schools, with the belief that the Talmud should remain closed to the average female (IM YD 3:87).

Other scholars, however, including Rabbis Zalman Sorotzkin (*Mozna'im LaMishpat* 1:42) and Joseph B. Soloveitchik, asserted that women – especially those with secular educations – must be exposed to the most sophisticated rabbinic literature. Rabbi Soloveitchik implemented this educational philosophy in his own schools, asserting that a talmudic curriculum was an "absolute imperative" and that the continued neglect of such teaching "has contributed greatly to the deterioration and downfall of traditional Judaism" (*Community, Covenant and Commitment*).

Rabbi Aharon Lichtenstein has further argued that even in more traditional circles, female students are indirectly exposed to talmudic teachings through the Bible commentaries of Rashi and Nahmanides as well as in legal works, and there is no reason to categorically deny women more intense exposure (*Ten Daat* 3:3). This curricular development, he added, follows the traditional understanding that women are obligated to receive instruction geared toward mitzvot performance. Yet it recognizes that the education necessary today to inspire women toward a religious lifestyle must afford greater opportunities for rigorous and sophisticated study. I heartily agree.

Chapter 75

Positions of Communal Authority

Can a woman serve as prime minister of Israel?

While the prominent roles of women in recent Israeli governments have reignited interest in this question, the issue of female politicians has engaged Israeli society since the beginning of the *yishuv* (the modern, pre-state Jewish community in the Land of Israel). The debate has also extended beyond the Knesset to communal positions like synagogue presidents and kashrut supervisors, raising concerns of feminism, pragmatism, tradition, and self-fulfillment.

The major sources excluding women from public office revolve around the possibility of a ruling queen. Following the Torah's mandate, "Place a king over yourself" (Deut. 17:15), the Midrash infers, "A king, but not a queen" (*Sifrei*). Maimonides extended the prohibition to all positions of authority (MT *Hilkhot Melakhim* 1:5). A medieval midrashic compendium, *Pesikta Zutrati* seemingly buttresses his opinion, as do Cairo Geniza manuscripts of the original midrash.

Yet what about Deborah the prophetess, who led the Jewish people in the Book of Judges? Some medieval authorities rejected this case as a precedent, since Deborah was uniquely chosen by divine revelation (*Tosafot* Bava Kamma 15a). Others contended that she served as a judge, not a political leader. This opinion would allow women to occupy judicial positions, but not political office. Many authorities, however, argued that Deborah justifiably served as a political leader, since her constituents agreed to her appointment (Nahmanides, Shevuot 30a).

In 1918, the Jewish Agency granted women the right to vote and hold office, which generated a fierce debate within the rabbinic community. Leading rabbis denied women both rights. These decisors argued that women may receive only ad hoc acceptance as judges and leaders, not permanent appointments. Rabbi Ḥanokh Agus maintained that women are excluded from the mitzva of appointing a king and therefore have no role in politics (*Marḥeshet* 1:22). Beyond the formal halakhic issues, Rabbi Abraham Isaac Kook contended that modesty barred women from the cutthroat political arena (*Maamarei HaRaaya*, pp. 189–94). Furthermore, he opined, allowing women to vote would cause marital disputes when husbands and wives supported opposing candidates.

These arguments drew heavy criticism from Rabbi Ben-Zion Uziel, who deemed it immoral to impose the responsibilities of citizenship on women without granting them the right to vote (*Mishpetei Uziel* ḤM 4:6). For him, Rabbi Kook's concerns were absurd and denied women the political voice they deserved as intelligent beings created in God's image. Indeed today, whether for ideological or pragmatic reasons, all segments of the Orthodox community encourage women to vote.

More significantly, Rabbi Uziel asserted that women could hold public office, like Deborah, since democratically elected officials are accepted by the community, in contrast to leaders in monarchies or feudal systems. He dismissed claims that political dialogue would lead to immodesty, noting that the seriousness of public deliberation precluded levity. Other supporters of this position included Rabbis Yehuda L. Maimon and Ḥayim Hirschensohn, with the latter accusing his interlocutors of disguising ideological beliefs as legal reasoning (*Malki BaKodesh* 2:4). Taking different sides of this issue, the religious Zionist parties the Jewish Home (HaBayit HaYehudi) and Meimad have included female candidates, while *ḥaredi* party lists like Shas and UTJ do not.

A potentially different permissive approach distinguishes between communal positions. In addition to women, the Talmud excludes converts from posts with coercive power, such as wielded by bailiffs and inspectors of weights and measures (Kiddushin 76b). Positions without "lordship" (*serara*), however, remain permissible (*Shakh* YD 269:15). Some have argued that in democratic societies – where officials may be voted out of office, share power with others, and have distinct checks and balances placed on that power – these offices do not constitute *serara* (*Amud HaYemini* 1:12). Moreover, as Rabbi J. David Bleich has suggested, synagogue officials possess no coercive powers (perhaps to their chagrin!), and therefore women and converts should not be excluded from these positions (*Tradition* 15:4).

Rabbi Moshe Feinstein used this argument to permit a woman to serve as a kashrut supervisor (IM YD 2:44–45). While he ultimately objected to female politicians and synagogue presidents for different reasons, he conceded that a righteous and qualified woman was preferable to an unqualified man. Indeed, following the failure of Tzipi Livni to form a coalition with Shas in 2009, the party's spiritual leader, Rabbi Ovadia Yosef, stated that one should vote for a religious party (like Shas!), or at least support the secular candidate most supportive of religion, independent of his or her gender (www.halachayomit.co.il). In addition to indicating Shas' willingness to work with Livni or other women in the future, the ruling highlighted the complex mingling of halakha with Israeli politics.

Chapter 76

Female Rabbinic Ordination

Can a woman be a rabbi?

The issue of women receiving rabbinic ordination has recently animated debate in the Orthodox community, particularly in America. While no widely recognized decisors of Jewish law have endorsed such an innovation, it remains on the agenda of some Orthodox activists. To facilitate greater dialogue, Rabbi Michael Broyde and I wrote a thirty-four-page article surveying the various halakhic and policy issues at stake (*Ḥakirah* 11). Here, I will briefly summarize two of the major legal issues, while the article (available on the web) greatly elaborates on these and additional aspects.

The historic institution of *semikha* (rabbinic ordination), which ceased in late antiquity, recognized a scholar as a bearer of the Oral Tradition and as a potential member of the Sanhedrin, who could adjudicate in all realms of Jewish law (MT *Hilkhot Sanhedrin* 4:1–3). In contrast, the contemporary notion of *semikha*, which originated in medieval times, represents a more limited mandate from a teacher to permit his student to issue rulings in Jewish law in his areas of expertise (YD 242:14). According to some, such authorization was unnecessary following the teacher's death (*Shu"t HaRivash* 271), even as the consensus is that such certification is always required (*Shu"t HaRadaḥ* 18:10). No *semikha* is needed, however, to teach Torah or explicate decided matters of basic Jewish law (YD 242:8–9). (See essay 41, "Rabbinic Ordination.")

Despite the limited power of *semikha* today, some authorities required that recipients have the same qualifications as bearers of the ancient version of ordination, including the ability to perform all judicial functions of the Sanhedrin (MT *Hilkhot Sanhedrin* 4:8–10). These decisors worried that less qualified recipients would not command communal respect (*Shu"t HaRema* 24) or would errantly act beyond their authorization (*Ḥatam Sofer* EH 2:94). This criterion excludes women from ordination, since they are generally ineligible to perform judicial functions (Shevuot 30a).

Most authorities, however, maintain that contemporary ordination may be issued to any pious, suitably erudite student (YD 242:14) and may be limited or expanded, based on his areas of expertise. Numerous sources attest that sufficiently knowledgeable women (even without ordination) may issue Jewish legal decisions (*Ḥinukh* 77, 152), and despite limited educational opportunities, there have been such learned women throughout history (*Halikhot Bat Yisrael* 9:7). According to this criterion, women are theoretically eligible for ordination.

Yet as Prof. Mordechai Breuer has documented, limitations or conditions were frequently added to this form of ordination. Some figures claimed that ordination could be given only at a certain age, or they restricted recipients' activities in order to prevent undue rabbinic competition. For other authorities, standard *semikha* inherently included certain posts, including that of pulpit rabbi (AH YD 242:29). As such, any attempt to ordain women would need to resolve this issue and explicate the nature of their ordination.

Another question involves the halakhic permissibility of women serving in positions of authority (*serara*). As discussed in the previous essay, when the Torah declares, "Place a king over yourself" (Deut. 17:15), the sages inferred, "A king, but not a queen" (*Sifrei*). While some authorities limited this prohibition to the monarchy (*Ḥinukh* 497), Maimonides, following different versions of the midrash, extended the ban to all positions of authority (MT *Hilkhot Melakhim* 1:5). This extension parallels the talmudic exclusion of converts from offices that possess coercive power, such as bailiffs and inspectors of weights and measures (Kiddushin 76b).

Yet what about Deborah the prophetess, who held a position of authority (Judges 4:4–5)? Some medieval authorities rejected this case as a precedent, since Deborah was uniquely chosen by divine revelation (*Tosafot* Bava Kamma 15a). Others contended that she served as a judge, not a political leader, and litigants can agree to be judged by those normally forbidden from this position (*Ḥinukh* 87).

Many authorities, however, argued that Deborah justifiably served as a political leader, since her constituents consented to her appointment (Nahmanides, Shevuot 30a). This notion was cited by Rabbi Ben-Zion Uziel, Israel's first Sephardic chief rabbi, in asserting that women may be elected to the Knesset (*Mishpetei Uziel* ḤM 4:6). Alternatively, many rabbinic positions lack the coercive powers forbidden to women, and therefore they may serve, in function if not in name, as rabbis in these posts (*Binyan Av* 1:65).

Beyond these disputes, other issues surround the ordination of women, such as modesty, departure from tradition, the potential threat to communal unity, the impact on polemical disputes with non-Orthodox movements, and practical questions regarding the involvement of women in certain rituals. Given that no semblance of consensus currently exists on these matters, I humbly suggest that the controversial agenda of female ordination be shelved, with greater energies dedicated to increasing women's education and expanding their meaningful contributions to the community.

Chapter 77

Army Service

Why do some religious women enlist while others enroll in national service?

The inclusion of women in the army roiled the state in its early years, and remains controversial within the religious community. The IDF estimates that close to 30 percent of religious female teens join the army, though the vast majority of the religious Zionist rabbinate opposes such enlistment.

Under certain circumstances, the Torah clearly mandates warfare, as exemplified in the books of the Prophets. Most authorities distinguish between an "optional war" (*milḥemet reshut*) intended to expand the nation's borders beyond its biblical mandate, and "obligatory wars" (*milḥemet mitzva*), which include battles against the Amalekites and the seven Canaanite nations, and responses to enemy attacks and threats (MT *Hilkhot Melakhim* 5:1). Though the former category is inapplicable today, since such wars require the approval of the long-disbanded Sanhedrin (supreme rabbinical court), the king may initiate "obligatory wars" and demand national conscription. Since Israel acts to protect its citizens and secure its sovereignty over the land, many twentieth-century rabbis, including Rabbi Isaac Herzog (*Tchumin* 4), deemed IDF activity a *milḥemet mitzva*.

In addition to exempting the tribe of Levi – the nation's spiritual leaders – from engaging in warfare (Num. 1:47), the Torah grants exemptions from optional wars to those particularly fearful of battle. It further excuses newlyweds and those who have just built a home or planted a vineyard (Deut. 20:5–8). Yet the fearful must still contribute to the war effort, such as by working in food supply lines, whereas the others are entirely exempt (MT *Hilkhot Melakhim* 7:9–11), in line with the general proscription of their leaving their homes (Deut. 24:5). Later authorities debated whether these exemptions, intended to mitigate individual hardships and prevent halfhearted fighting, barred these people from being drafted but allowed them to volunteer to serve (*Haamek Davar*), or if they should be prohibited from enlisting (*Minḥat Ḥinukh* 581:3). The founders of the Jewish state debated whether these exemptions should apply to the Israeli army, and while this discussion resumed after Operation Cast Lead in early 2009, when a reservist in his first week of marriage was nearly fatally wounded, no such exemption has been enacted.

Regardless, in the case of a mandatory war, these exemptions do not apply. As the Mishna states, "Regarding an obligatory war, all go out, even the groom from his chamber and the bride from her wedding canopy" (Sota 44b). Although Rabbi Shlomo Goren postulated that the groom should be drafted as a last resort (*Meshiv Milḥama* 2, p. 449), Rabbi Avraham Karelitz recognized no such distinction (*Ḥazon Ish, Moed* 114:3).

Regarding our question, the Mishna seems to include brides amongst those who participate in a mandatory war, implying that women may be drafted (*Minḥat Ḥinukh* 604:3). Furthermore, as Rabbis Yehuda Shaviv (*Tchumin* 4) and Aryeh Bina (*BeTzomet HaTorah VeHaMedina* 3) noted in their theoretical analyses of this issue, Maimonides implies that women may participate in such wars (*Minyan HaMitzvot*, introduction).

Despite these sources, leading rabbinic figures in the religious Zionist community – starting with Israel's first chief rabbis, Isaac Herzog and Ben-Zion Uziel – have opposed female conscription. They cite commentaries that interpreted the Mishna as rhetorically depicting a bride who will not enjoy the company of her drafted husband (*Torah Temima* Deut. 20:7), or that women are to serve only in non-combat support roles, such as providing food (Radbaz MT *Hilkhot Melakhim* 7:4). Many writers further noted that a number of biblical narratives seemingly exclude women from active warfare.

More poignantly, the Talmud cites the biblical prohibition of women wearing men's clothing (Deut. 22:5) as the basis for women's not going out to war and bearing arms (Nazir 59a). As Rabbi Yehuda Henkin has observed (*Tchumin* 28), the prohibition of cross-dressing remains subjective to contemporary norms (YD 182:5). As such, in societies where men and women alike regularly wear uniforms and bear arms, this law might no longer apply. Yet many understood this talmudic statement and others as categorically barring women from warfare (*Haamek Davar* Deut. 22:5), unless their intervention is necessary to save lives, as in the case of Yael killing Sisera (Judges 4:21). Others, moreover, understood this proscription as intended to protect women from illicit sexual behavior within the army (Rabbenu Baḥya). Indeed, concerns for women's dignity (*tzniut*) and inappropriate sexual interactions have driven much opposition to female enlistment.

Nonetheless, a few religious institutions today have established programs to spiritually prepare female soldiers, especially those serving in capacities such as education and intelligence, which might fulfill the criterion of support roles mentioned in earlier sources. Moreover, as Rabbi Shlomo Aviner, a vehement opponent of female conscription, has argued, once a female enlists, the nation must provide all means – and prayers – necessary for her welfare.

Section VI

Israel

Chapter 78

Residing in Israel

Is it a mitzva?

The choice to live in Israel, an option with which we are uniquely blessed today, encompasses many dimensions, including cultural, historical, and nationalistic ones. While related to many of these elements, the particular legal obligation has been subject to various formulations over the centuries.

Scripture indicates the centrality of Israel to God's vision for the Jewish people. From the covenant with Abraham to the sacrificial rite enunciated in Leviticus to the military conquest planned and implemented in Deuteronomy and Joshua, the Bible emphasizes the importance of Jewish settlement in the Promised Land. As such, the subsequent exile from the land, forewarned by the later prophets as divine punishment for sinful behavior, was bemoaned in Lamentations and subsequent Jewish thought and liturgy.

Nahmanides formulated this biblical legacy as a twofold normative directive (*Hashmatot LeSefer HaMitzvot, Aseh* 4). On the national level, the Jewish people must conquer the land and establish sovereignty over its borders. Even when we cannot do so, as in times of exile, Jews as individuals remain commanded to dwell in the Holy Land. As proof, Nahmanides cites such talmudic statements as "A person should live in Israel, even in a city full of idol worshippers, and not outside of Israel, even in a city of Jews, as the mitzva of living in the Land of Israel is equivalent to all the mitzvot in the Torah" (Tosefta Avoda Zara 4:3).

Historians have argued that this pronouncement and others emerged following the failure of the Bar Kokhba rebellion and subsequent Roman persecutions (second to third centuries CE). While many Jews fled to Babylonia and other safe havens, the sages remaining in the former Judean province continued to exalt the land's centrality. However, some Babylonian scholars, like Shmuel and R. Yehuda, contended that living within the epicenter of Jewish life was more important. They even forbade immigration to the Land of Israel, proclaiming that "Living in Babylonia is like living in Eretz Yisrael" (Ketubbot 111a). All agree that to earn a living, find a marriage partner, or study Torah, one may dwell outside the land, at least temporarily.

Interestingly, Maimonides omitted residence in Eretz Yisrael from his enumeration of the mitzvot. According to some commentators, Maimonides considered this commandment dormant until the Messianic era (*Megillat Esther*). They cited a famous passage, also attributed to R. Yehuda, asserting that following the exile, God made the Jews swear not to attempt to retake the land by force or rebel against their host countries, who in turn swore not to persecute the Jews (Ketubbot 111a). While religious anti-Zionists quote these lines fervently, many have responded that the homiletic passage was never cited in subsequent legal literature. Moreover, both the Balfour Declaration and the UN permitted the Jewish people to return to the Holy Land, while the non-Jews didn't keep their promise not to persecute us! Other sources have explained that Maimonides omitted the commandment because it was included in other commands (*Avnei Nezer* YD 454), while Rabbi Tzvi Yehuda Kook asserted that Eretz Yisrael remains so central to the entire Torah that it cannot be encompassed within one mitzva.

Rabbi Moshe Feinstein offered an intermediate position, suggesting that while one fulfills a commandment (*mitzva kiyumit*) by making *aliya*, there is no obligation to do so (IM EH 1:102). Two twentieth-century colleagues, Rabbis Ovadia Yosef (*Yeḥaveh Daat* 4:49) and Eliezer Waldenburg (*Tzitz Eliezer* 7:48:12), demurred and affirmed Nahmanides' position, especially given the viability of *aliya* to the State of Israel. Rabbi Yosef added that the mitzva overrides parental objections, an assertion that Rabbi Waldenburg felt he – and youth groups – could not unequivocally endorse (*Tzitz Eliezer* 14:72).

Maimonides, who himself moved to Eretz Yisrael toward the end of his life, did emphasize the significance of the land, citing many talmudic statements praising its habitation (MT *Hilkhot Melakhim* 5:9–12) and noting that only here may one perform many judiciary, ritual, and agricultural commandments. Analogously, the Talmud rules that a person may demand a divorce if his spouse refuses to move to the Holy Land with him, thereby negating his ability to perform these virtuous actions. The financial and political inability to fulfill these commandments, along with safety concerns, led the medieval Tosafist Rabbi Ḥayim HaKohen to deem this rule inapplicable in his time (*Tosafot* Ketubbot 110b).

Despite these factors, three hundred of his thirteenth-century colleagues immigrated to the Land of Israel. Indeed, the self-sacrifice of centuries of our ancestors to dwell here might provide the greatest inspiration to settle in the center of the past, present, and future of the Jewish people.

Chapter 79

Selling Land to Non-Jews

Does halakha permit it?

The pronouncement of Safed Chief Rabbi Shmuel Eliyahu in 2010 against the selling or renting of land to non-Jews elicited heated responses, with some denouncing it as undemocratic and racist, and others defending it as bold and patriotic. A nationwide group (including several municipal rabbis) declared their support for this ban, which in turn led to massive condemnation, including by prominent rabbis. Unfortunately, polemical sound bites generate more heat than light. This essay will seek to calmly provide the Jewish legal background for this debate and articulate the various sides of the argument, even as I state from the outset that I strongly opposed the ban.

When enjoining the Israelites to uproot the seven nations residing in the Promised Land, God declared, "You must doom them to destruction: grant them no terms and give them no quarter (*lo teḥanem*)" (Deut. 7:2). While the last clause clearly denies the inhabitants any mercy during war (MT *Hilkhot Avodat Kokhavim* 10:1), the sages understood this verse as further proscribing the offering of accolades, gifts, or territory within the Land of Israel (Avoda Zara 20a).

One major question regards the scope of this expanded prohibition. Rabbi Joseph Karo (BY ḤM 249:2), followed by more recent figures, such as Rabbi Avraham Karelitz (*Ḥazon Ish, Shevi'it* 24), applied it to all gentiles. Many, however, contended that it pertained only to idolaters (*Tosafot* Avoda Zara 20a), thereby excluding Muslims, for example (*Baḥ* ḤM 249). This distinction would stem from the perceived goal of these commandments: to distance Jews from idolatrous influence (*Sefer HaMitzvot, Lo Taaseh* 50–51). The prohibitions would certainly not apply to a *ger toshav*, a non-Jew who has accepted the seven Noahide laws (Raavad MT *Hilkhot Avodat Kokhavim* 10:6).

Rabbi Menaḥem HaMeiri (*Beit HaBeḥira* Avoda Zara 20) and Rabbi Abraham ibn David of Posquières (Raavad, MT *Hilkhot Avodat Kokhavim* 10:6) asserted that the ban applied only to the immoral seven nations that inhabited Israel in antiquity, not to ethical people guided by religious norms. Similar sentiments were adopted by Rabbi Barukh Epstein (*Torah Temima* Deut. 7:2), though this remains a minority position, as noted by Rabbi Yaakov Warhaftig (*Tchumin* 2).

Beyond this dispute, many qualifications minimize the scope of prohibited activities. Regarding accolades, the talmudic passage cited above states that one should recite a blessing when seeing a person of unique wisdom or beauty, since this is ultimately praise of God for His wondrous creations (OḤ 225:10). Following the medieval philosophers who lauded Aristotle and other gentile thinkers, Rabbi Eliezer Waldenburg contended that one may praise great inventors of medicine and technology (*Tzitz Eliezer* 15:47). Rabbi Moshe Feinstein deemed it appropriate even to hold a dinner honoring a gentile for his communal service (IM YD 2:117).

Similarly, the sages limited the prohibition of gifts to cases in which there is no reciprocity, and therefore asserted that one may give a gift to a non-Jewish acquaintance with whom he enjoys a mutually beneficial relationship (*Taz* YD 151:8). Moreover, to keep the peace, Jews should care for impoverished or sick gentiles (YD 151:11).

The prohibition of granting territorial claims led to major controversies. One concerned the temporary sale of Jewish agricultural land (*heter mekhira*) to gentiles during the Sabbatical year (*Shemitta*), thereby allowing Jews to continue supporting themselves by farming in Eretz Yisrael. Beginning in the late nineteenth century, scholars debated the propriety of this sale. Some, like Rabbi Naphtali Tzvi Berlin, denounced it as a legal fiction.

Proponents of the sale, however, offered several justifications. Rabbis Yehoshua Trunk (*Yeshuot Malko* YD 55) and Eliyahu Rabinovitch-Teomim (*Eder HaYakar* 9) asserted that, as in the case of gifts, the prohibition did not apply when it benefited a Jew. Rabbi Karelitz retorted that this dispensation was inapplicable here, since any sale inherently provided financial benefit, yet it would still remain prohibited. Yet Rabbi Abraham Isaac Kook argued that the prohibition did not apply if the non-Jew already resided in the land, especially if he was a monotheist. Rabbi Kook further noted that this sale was merely temporary and would strengthen long-term Jewish settlement (*Shabbat HaAretz*, ch. 12). (Regarding *heter mekhira,* see essay #90.)

However, the more recent debate over relinquishing liberated territories (discussed at length in the next essay) clearly entails a long-term transfer of land. Yet Rabbi Ovadia Yosef (*Tchumin* 10) and others argued that a peace deal with the Arabs (non-idolaters) might strengthen the Jewish people's hold on the remaining parts of the land. Moreover, these decisors claimed, the principle of saving lives overrides the "no quarter" prohibition. But Rabbi Shlomo Goren retorted that this principle does not trump the settling of Eretz Yisrael, for which we are commanded to fight and risk our lives (*Torat HaMedina*, ch. 8).

Within the contemporary Israeli scene, many members of the religious community who passionately oppose territorial concessions also adamantly insist on employing the various dispensations to support the Sabbatical sale. These Jews reasonably contend that their position remains legally consistent in supporting the long-term Jewish settlement of the land. Yet one must always distinguish between what is religiously inspired and what is halakhically required, especially in controversies that combine political perspectives with spiritual values.

Likewise, with regard to this controversy, one must appreciate the political background from the perspective of the ban's proponents. Safed – a city of Jewish historic, religious, and national significance – serves as the central provider of medical, economic, and educational resources in the Galilee region, whose Arab and Muslim population has rapidly increased relative to its Jewish inhabitants. Some local rabbinic figures have found this trend (also characteristic of cities like Lod and Acco) troubling, especially since popular groups like the northern branch of the Islamic Movement support Hamas and similar causes. These rabbis further fear that fraternization with friendlier Arab neighbors might lead to intermarriage. Concomitantly, some political activists claim that international Palestinian sympathizers have attempted to purchase strategically located real estate (like Jerusalem's Nof Tzion project) to prevent Jewish settlement, even as the Palestinian Authority continues to forbid land sales to Jews.

Critics have responded that even if legitimate political concerns exist, one cannot deny property rights to non-Jewish Israeli citizens. (In one notorious case, a Holocaust survivor was harassed after renting his apartment to three Druze students, themselves IDF veterans, who are pursuing degrees at Safed College.) Furthermore, say the ban's opponents, just such discrimination was directed at Jews for centuries. If the Galilee needs to boost its Jewish population, the appropriate response is government incentives and more Zionist education, not discrimination.

Beyond these criticisms, the ban was condemned in rabbinic quarters for legal reasons. Rabbis Yosef Shalom Elyashiv and Aharon Steinman, leading *ḥaredi* decisors, insisted that it would lead to anti-Semitism and similar discrimination against Diaspora Jews. These figures further declared the ban hypocritical, since many of the municipal rabbis behind it support the *heter mekhira*. Rabbi Ḥayim Steiner, a defender of the ban, retorted that *heter mekhira* is entirely different, since it is a temporary sale that actually sustains Jewish settlement. And Rabbi Eliyahu pointed out that Rabbis Elyashiv and Steinman had previously declared a similar ban in Bnei Brak, albeit more quietly.

More fundamental critiques, with which I identify, came from other segments of the religious Zionist camp. Rabbi Ḥayim Druckman, head of Yeshivot Bnei Akiva, contended that one may prohibit real estate deals with "enemies of the state." Yet it remains unacceptable to issue a blanket prohibition against all gentiles, including many loyal citizens, such as college students, IDF veterans, and health care providers.

In a statement supported by the Tzohar rabbinic organization, Ramat Gan Chief Rabbi Yaakov Ariel cited the State's self-imposed obligation to ensure equal rights for its citizens. He endorsed the classic stance of Israel's first Ashkenazic chief rabbi, Isaac Herzog, who declared (before the State's establishment) that as long as real estate deals were not intended to harm Jews or undermine Israeli control over the territory in question, they remained permissible (*Tchumin* 2).

Rabbi Aharon Lichtenstein of Yeshivat Har Etzion launched a more trenchant critique, contending that the Safed rabbis had greatly oversimplified Jewish law. It remains unquestionable, he noted, that there is a halakhic basis for prohibiting the sale of land to gentiles within Israel. Yet as we saw, a few figures limited the prohibition to the seven Canaanite nations, while many other scholars applied different dispensations to the rule, including a strong (albeit not exclusive) tradition – originating with the medieval school of the Tosafists – that severely narrowed this and similar laws. These points and others were made years earlier by Rabbi Ḥayim David HaLevi in sweeping essays that presented a halakhic stance in tune with democratic values (*Aseh Lekha Rav* 4:1, 8:68, 9:30).

In short, genuine political problems may exist in various parts of the country. But the solutions lie in education and political wisdom, not in overreaching halakhic statements that distort – and disgrace – Jewish law and its adherents.

Chapter 80

Land for Peace

What's the Jewish view of this complex issue?

Based on anecdotal evidence, I would venture that I'm not the only Israeli who thinks that those engaged in the debate regarding "land for peace" frequently do not speak the same language. The many complex issues, including differing historical narratives, theological perspectives, and geopolitical outlooks, make it difficult, yet all the more essential, for each side to understand the other.

Before discussing the legal debate surrounding this perennial issue, one must distinguish between theoretical discourse and its practical implications. This essay will focus on the former, asking whether territorial concessions are hypothetically legitimate. One might answer affirmatively, but assert that contemporary geopolitical realities render any deal imprudent or dangerous. Alternatively, one could claim that land concessions might prove strategically astute, yet still condemn them as betrayals of our religious covenant. (In reality, the latter claim occurs much less frequently.) Unfortunately, the mixing of religion and politics in Israel occasionally conflates these two distinct steps, creating much confusion and discord.

The theoretical debate revolves around the balancing of two important values: the commandment to settle the Land of Israel and the primacy of saving lives. In general, all commandments are pushed aside in order to save a life, excluding the proscriptions of murder, idolatry, and illicit relations (Sanhedrin 74a). As such, Rabbi Ovadia Yosef (*Tchumin* 10) and Rabbi Joseph B. Soloveitchik, among others, consistently contend that under satisfactory military and political conditions, Israel may cede control over contested territories to prevent further bloodshed. These authorities argue that just as doctors determine whether a person can fast on Yom Kippur, military and political experts should determine the viability of any peace settlement. (Shas' irresolute stance on this issue reflects constant political reassessment, not changes in the party's halakhic position.)

Scholars such as Rabbis Avraham Shapira and Shaul Yisraeli (*Tchumin* 10), former heads of Yeshivat Mercaz HaRav, counter that the commandment to conquer and settle the land inherently calls for endangering one's life. As Rabbi Yosef Babad (nineteenth century, Galicia) noted, warfare necessarily entails casualties on both sides, yet the Torah (Deut. 7:2) commands us to eradicate the seven nations that inhabited the land (*Minḥat Ḥinukh* 425:3). These decisors further cite Nahmanides' codification of this mitzva (*Hashmatot LeSefer HaMitzvot, Aseh* 4), which includes a communal obligation to gain sovereignty over the land, as well as the talmudic interpretation of this verse, which forbids relinquishing control of any portion of Eretz Yisrael to gentiles (Avoda Zara 20a). While this commandment (discussed at length in the previous essay) does not demand the pursuit of aggressive warfare – especially if such is doomed – it does prohibit withdrawal from conquered areas, especially for the sake of questionable security benefits. This prohibition remains particularly applicable to border areas, which the Talmud categorizes as extremely important to protect (Eiruvin 45a).

Supporters of the opposing position, however, cite sources that downplay the contemporary obligation to settle the land (as discussed in essay 78, "Residing in Israel"). They further retort that without the appropriate spiritual leadership, no contemporary warfare falls within the category of the biblical commandment to go to war. They also interpret the prohibition of relinquishing territory to apply only with respect to idolaters (*Sefer HaMitzvot, Lo Taaseh* 51), and then only when Israel maintains absolute control of the land, which is not the case under current geopolitical conditions.

More poignantly, they argue that the commandment to settle the Land of Israel, while permitting self-endangerment, does not obligate it, especially when faced with inopportune circumstances. The approaches of Jeremiah, during the last days of the First Temple (Jeremiah 28–29), and R. Yoḥanan ben Zakkai, at the end of the Second Temple (Gittin 56b), both set historical precedents for surrendering sovereignty in order to preserve Jewish life in the land. These examples, however, might be seen as desperate attempts at preservation when defeat was inevitable. Indeed, the Talmud condemns King Hezekiah's concessions to Assyria when the prospects of military success were good (Pesaḥim 56a).

Although not inherently connected, messianism sometimes plays an implicit role in this debate. Rabbis who perceive the state's founding and military victories as miraculous events heralding a messianic process (*atḥalta digeula*) tend to view territorial concessions as defying the divine plan, although concessions may also be interpreted as painful birth pangs (*ḥevlei Mashiaḥ*) in this process. Religious Zionists like Rabbi Soloveitchik, who did not attribute eschatological meaning to Israel's founding, and certainly religious anti-Zionists, like Degel HaTorah founder Rabbi Elazar Shach (d. 2001), tend to view these matters more pragmatically. Rabbi Yosef quotes Rabbi Chaim Soloveitchik, who, when told that the unprecedented bloodshed of World War I must be redressed by the coming of the Messiah, forcefully responded, "Better to delay the redemption in order to save the life of even one Jew. The commandment of saving lives overrides all commandments, including the coming of the Messiah."

One hopes that greater understanding of each other's perspectives will bring peace among ourselves, even if not with our neighbors.

Chapter 81

Fleeing Israel at Wartime

Must Israeli citizens remain in a war zone?

During the 2012 Operation Pillar of Cloud, ultra-Orthodox yeshiva students in southern Israel were ordered by *ḥaredi* scholars including the Belzer Rebbe and Rabbi Aharon Leib to flee northward toward cities like Bnei Brak. By and large, their religious Zionist counterparts in Hesder yeshivas remained in cities like Sderot or Netivot, unless they were drafted into the army. Now that the dust has settled, it behooves us to contemplate the appropriateness of each response, while praying that this discussion remain theoretical.

In addition to military action, the Torah commands a spiritual response to times of crisis. "When you are at war…you shall sound trumpets, that you may be remembered before God and be delivered from your enemies" (Num. 10:9). Beyond prayers and fasting, Jewish law demands certain restraints on lighthearted activity, such as grand feasts, to reflect the gravity of the hour (OḤ 574:4).

Likewise, the sages called for sexual abstinence in times of famine (Taanit 11a). The medieval commentators debated whether this call was an actual ordinance or merely a pietistic recommendation (*Tosafot*), and concluded that such piety was inappropriate for those who had not yet fulfilled the commandment of procreation or for whom abstinence would cause excessive marital strain (*Shaarei Teshuva* 574:1). While Rabbi Moshe Isserles contended that this stringency was appropriate in other types of crises, such as war (OḤ 240:12), Rabbis Ḥayim Benveniste (*Hagahot Tur*) and Avraham of Buczacz (*Eshel Avraham* 240) argued that such abstinence applied only during famines, when one cannot properly feed newborns. Procreation, on the other hand, might be viewed as a central means of repopulation during war or oppression, as in the case of Moses, who was born despite the enslavement in Egypt. As such, during the Yom Kippur War, Rabbi Eliezer Waldenburg did not require abstinence (*Tzitz Eliezer* 13:21).

Upon the outbreak of war, the Torah calls upon the High Priest to rouse the courage and confidence of the soldiers by ensuring divine support. Yet if a soldier remains petrified, the Torah mandates that he return home, lest he ruin morale (Deut. 20:8), even as Jewish law requires him to fulfill support functions, such as manning food supply lines (MT *Hilkhot Melakhim* 7:9). Many medieval commentators, including Maimonides, contended that the Torah viewed fear of the enemy as lack of faith in God (*Sefer HaMitzvot, Lo Taaseh* 58). Later scholars asserted that this prohibition pertains not to a natural fear of the enemy, but rather to a state of fright so acute that it harms one's battle-readiness.

While the Torah remains unequivocal regarding soldiers, it does not address the propriety of non-combatants – including spiritual leaders – fleeing a war zone. In the early nineteenth century, the chief rabbi of Pressburg, Rabbi Moshe Sofer, fled the city upon the invasion of Napoleon. He later expressed pain at having abandoned his congregants during a time of war. In his talmudic novella, he laid out both sides of the argument and gave historical precedent for each, without delivering a final ruling (*Ḥiddushei Ḥatam Sofer* Ḥullin 46a). On the one hand, a rabbi is responsible, like every human being, for his own safety and is therefore entitled to flee. At the same time, a spiritual leader is responsible for strengthening his followers with his faith and solace.

This dilemma was borne out during the Holocaust. As has been well-documented, some rabbinic leaders attempted to flee with their students or communities, while others stayed to support their flock and ultimately suffered the same tragic fate. In some controversial cases, rabbis escaped even as their communities were annihilated. This phenomenon led to bitter condemnation in posthumously published statements by Rebbetzin Eva Halberstam and Rabbi Yissachar Shlomo Teichtel, both killed during the *Shoah*. Some scholars, such as Esther Farbstein, have defended the rabbinic refugees for remaining as long as they did and for fleeing to save their lives and the ideals that they represented.

During the first Gulf War, in 1991, many yeshiva students from the Diaspora went home, in part at the behest of their parents, believing that their continued presence was an act of self-endangerment unnecessary to strengthen the country. This phenomenon was condemned by Rabbis Yaakov Ariel of Ramat Gan (*Tchumin* 12) and Yona Metzger of Tel Aviv (*Sufa BaMidbar* 41), who felt that it was demoralizing, and that yeshiva students were uniquely responsible for bolstering the home front. In the same essay, however, Rabbi Ariel deemed it permissible for citizens to head for a safer location within Israel, since such measures helped prevent unnecessary loss of life, which would have undermined the war effort. This line of reasoning would also justify the abandonment of several *ḥaredi* yeshivas near Gaza in the 2012 operation, even as the Hesder students' efforts to strengthen the morale of their southern neighbors remain commendable.

Chapter 82

Torah Study and Military Service

Are yeshiva students exempt?

The heated disagreements over the exemption of *ḥaredi* men from serving in the Israeli army have highlighted severe schisms within Israeli society. Many citizens deem the historical arrangement neither ethical nor realistic. Without entering the political fray, we will try to provide halakhic background to this debate by elucidating the alleged basis for exempting yeshiva students.

The Torah speaks very harshly of evasion of national service. When the tribes of Reuben and Gad asked to settle on the east bank of the Jordan River, before the Israelites began their conquest of the Land of Israel, Moses exclaimed, "Are your brothers to go to war while you stay here?!" (Num. 32:6). He ultimately consented to their request, but only after they pledged to join their brethren in battle.

The Torah exempts certain people from serving in battle: the fainthearted, newlyweds, and those who have just built a home or planted a vineyard (Deut. 20:5–8). These exemptions, however, apply only to military campaigns intended to expand Israel's borders, not to mandatory wars (*milḥemot mitzva*), which are necessary to conquer the land or defend it against its enemies. As the Mishna states, "Regarding an obligatory war, all go out, even the groom from his chamber and the bride from her wedding canopy" (Sota 44b).

Following the loss of national sovereignty, Jews, as a group, were infrequently drafted into the army. This changed after the Emancipation, and as Dr. Judith Bleich has documented, the phenomenon of Jews serving in non-Jewish armies greatly divided rabbinic scholars. Some figures, including Rabbis Samson Raphael Hirsch (*Ḥorev* 609) and Moshe Glasner (*Tel Talpiyot* 104), enthusiastically supported such patriotic service. Others, including Rabbis Yeḥezkel Landau (*Noda BiYehuda Tinyana* YD 45) and Meir Eisenstadt (*Imrei Esh* YD 1:74), expressed grave reservations about the impact on religious observance as well as the halakhic propriety of the aggressive warfare frequently practiced by those armies. While expressing similar concerns, Rabbi Moshe Sofer noted that governments were entitled to "tax" citizens with military service (*Ḥatam Sofer Likkutim* 6:29). If quotas were imposed upon the Jewish community, he insisted on using a lottery to choose draftees, making no distinction between observant and non-observant Jews. However, citing talmudic-era exemptions from taxes toward municipal fortifications, he argued that rabbinic students and clergy were excused from military service, a sentiment found in many other cultures, including his own.

The notion that spiritual leaders are exempt from warfare might have biblical support in the exclusion of the tribe of Levi from the military census (Rashbam, Num. 1:47), even as the Talmud never mentions such an exemption. Maimonides, in noting the unique role of the Levites as "the Lord's corps," asserts that they did not go to war (MT *Hilkhot Shemitta* 13:12–13). He adds that "any person throughout the world whose spirit has uplifted him ... to stand before God, to serve Him ... and has cast aside the many considerations that men have sought" will share the same lot as the Levites. Based on these sentiments, Rabbi Yeḥiel Michel Tucazinsky and other rabbinic figures maintained that dedicated rabbinic students should be excused from military service, especially since their studies provided central spiritual support for the national cause (*BeTzomet HaTorah VeHaMedina* 3).

Many rabbinic decisors countered that defending Israel's inhabitants is a positive commandment allowing for no broad exemptions. They contended that Maimonides' statement was a homiletical exhortation for spiritual excellence, including even non-Jews ("any person throughout the world"), and that he never mentioned such an exemption, for

Levites or others, when he codified the laws of war. Furthermore, they argued, the historic tax exemption does not mean scholars should opt out of protecting their homeland and brethren. As Rabbi Shlomo Zevin wrote to other rabbinic leaders in 1948, in the spirit of Moses, "It is your obligation to encourage young and healthy scholars to fight. Will you send your brothers to war, and yourselves sit at home?" (*Tradition* 21:4).

Some have retorted that even leading religious Zionists like Rabbi Isaac Herzog supported the exemption of yeshiva students during the state's earliest years. Yet this was when yeshiva study desperately needed resuscitation after the Holocaust, and the exemption applied to four hundred students. Today, in contrast, 10 percent of the draft-age populace claims exemptions, and Torah study flourishes, including in many yeshivas (like my own) dedicated to producing students who will also serve as soldiers. Prof. Benjamin Brown also points out that even Rabbi Avraham Karelitz, the legendary ultra-Orthodox leader who lobbied David Ben-Gurion for yeshiva exemptions, did not believe the discharge should be applied to every *ḥaredi* Jew, perhaps for fear that widespread abuse would ultimately lead to this privilege being revoked from those who truly learn with vigor.

Of course, Torah study represents a supreme value, and the State of Israel should be saluted for creating arrangements that allow students to flourish as soldiers and scholars. But no definitive precedent exists for issuing blanket exemptions to all who learn Torah exclusively.

Chapter 83

Redeeming POWs

Must we release hundreds of terrorists to fulfill this mitzva?

The dilemma over what price to pay for redeeming captives has, alas, engaged the Jewish people since antiquity. The capture of soldiers, such as the 2006 abductions of Gilad Schalit, Ehud Goldwasser, and Eldad Regev and the subsequent demand to release terrorists in an exchange, only further complicates this quandary. This essay will try to present the debate's parameters in the hope of facilitating dialogue.

The Bible highlights stories about redeeming captives, including Abraham's rescue of Lot (Gen. 14) and Moses' and David's liberation of prisoners of war (Num. 20, I Sam. 30). The Talmud praises the redemption of captives (*pidyon shevuyim*) as a great mitzva – superior even to giving charity – because it liberates a person from the emotional (and sometimes physical) pain of captivity (Bava Batra 8a–b). Consequently, money dedicated to other causes (such as synagogue construction) may be reallocated toward ransom funds, with some authorities even permitting the sale of Torah scrolls for this purpose (*Tosafot*). Maimonides lists no fewer than seven biblical commands that are fulfilled by liberating a captive (MT *Hilkhot Matanot LeAniyim* 8:10), while Rabbi Joseph Kolon conversely compares one who needlessly delays this process to a murderer (YD 252:3).

Nonetheless, in the name of *tikkun olam* (mending the world), the sages forbade the ransoming of a captive for more than his market value (Gittin 45a). Some believed that this decree aimed to ease the financial burden on the public, while allowing a wealthy individual or community to voluntarily pay dearly to free a captive. Most medieval commentators, followed by Rabbi Joseph Karo, adopted an alternative talmudic explanation: This ordinance was intended to discourage further kidnappings and ever higher ransoms. According to this rationale, excessive payments were forbidden even to people with deep pockets (YD 252:4).

Despite this rule, the Talmud recalls several instances of captives being redeemed for exorbitant sums, including one case in which a family defied the rabbinic stricture (Gittin 45a). While families will understandably do all they can to save their loved ones, such actions may remain illegitimate from a communal perspective. This, to my mind, is a fundamental principle of decision-making in this realm: Leaders must use their intelligence to set fair policy and not become caught up with the emotional trauma of the situation. The Schalit, Regev, and Goldwasser families do not deserve condemnation for their campaigns, though they may have led to higher ransom demands. Yet the government must avoid populism (as must the media) and choose wisely.

In any case, exceptions were made to the "market value" rule. While Rabbi Menaḥem HaMeiri contended that a person may not overpay even to redeem himself, the normative halakha allows him to do so (YD 252:5). Despite Maimonides' protest (MT *Hilkhot Ishut* 14:19), similar dispensations were granted for redeeming one's spouse (*Tosafot* Ketubbot 52a). Indeed, the marriage contract obligates men to redeem their wives, and the halakha further rules that, in general, communities should give preference to freeing female captives so as to prevent ignoble acts against them (Horayot 13a). While the community may force a wealthy member to pay for the fair-rate redemption of his other relatives (YD 252:11–12), it remains forbidden for a person to voluntarily overpay.

The Talmud relates that after the Roman conquest, R. Yehoshua ben Ḥanania paid an exorbitant price to redeem a promising youth who grew up to become the great sage R. Yishmael. Some medieval authorities explained that it was futile to try preventing subsequent kidnappings in wartime (*Tosafot* Gittin 45a). As such, some believe the sages' rule does not apply to standard prisoner swaps following contemporary wars, especially since these exchanges follow conventional protocols. Rabbi Ḥayim David HaLevi even justified lopsided deals to free soldiers, since Israel's enemies will continue capturing and/or killing members of its armed forces in any case (*Aseh Lekha Rav* 7:53). Other authorities retorted that today such a policy will only encourage kidnappings and strengthen terrorist groups. Indeed, one might argue that Regev and Goldwasser are dead because Hezbollah wanted the same benefits it received from previous kidnappings.

A more controversial interpretation asserts that one may redeem scholars for inflated sums, since their value to the community is immeasurable and irreplaceable. Yet in one celebrated incident, Rabbi Meir of Rothenburg (thirteenth century, Germany) died in captivity after refusing to be redeemed at Emperor Rudolph I's inflated ransom price, lest other despots imprison his fellow scholars (*Yam shel Shlomo* Gittin 4:66).

Other commentaries contended that ransom limitations did not apply where captives' lives are endangered, as in R. Yishmael's case (*Tosafot* Gittin 58a). Nahmanides (Gittin 45a) and others disagreed, contending that one may not save a captive's life by threatening the lives of future captives. By the sixteenth century, however, Jewish communities throughout the world had created funds to redeem as many captives as possible, fearing for both their lives and the future of the nation (*Shu"t HaRadbaz* 1:40). Yet the contemporary Israeli situation presents a competing claim, since the ransom fee is not money, but terrorists who may threaten other lives. For many years, this factor prevented Israeli governments from agreeing to disproportionate prisoner exchanges.

Israeli policy on this issue shifted in 1979 and then most famously in the 1985 "Jibril deal," which released 1,150 Arab prisoners for three live Israeli soldiers captured during the Lebanon War. Rabbi Shlomo Goren vociferously criticized the deal for endangering soldiers by providing incentives for future kidnappings. He further warned of the prisoners' returning to terrorism, fears borne out by Ahmed Yassin (future founder of Hamas, assassinated by Israel in 2004) and other released terrorists. However, when Rabbi Goren republished his essay on the topic (*Torat HaMedina*, ch. 29), he agreed with Rabbi Shaul Yisraeli (*Ḥavvat Binyamin* 1:16) that the government must take full responsibility for its soldiers, just as one may pay an exorbitant price to redeem himself. Yet Rabbi

Yisraeli stipulated that such exchanges are permissible but not mandatory, and are subject to political and military considerations. The debate continued during subsequent prisoner exchanges, culminating in the 2011 deal to release 1,027 captives in exchange for Schalit.

At that time, Rabbi Ovadia Yosef contended that we must give priority to the life of a soldier, who is endangered in his service on behalf of the state, over the uncertain threat to the public. This position was supported by the director of Israel's General Security Service (today known as the Israel Security Agency) who likewise averred that Israel will remain under the same security threat, irrespective of an additional group of terrorists on the street. Rabbi Shlomo Aviner, on the other hand, argued from experience that freed terrorists kill many more Israelis. Instead of capitulating to demands for their release, said Rabbi Aviner, we must use military means to free soldiers. This position was supported by previous chiefs of military intelligence, who fiercely oppose such exchanges. These experts believe that while the army should never leave soldiers behind on the battlefield, the government cannot bring them home at any price. This approach was recently advocated by a military commission on prisoner exchanges, which urged Israel to take a stricter position on such exchanges.

Let's pray that this discussion remains theoretical.

Chapter 84

Retrieving Corpses for Burial

To what extent should soldiers risk their lives for the bodies of fallen comrades?

As the 2008 funerals of Ehud Goldwasser and Eldad Regev poignantly showed, the burial of fallen soldiers arouses great national emotions. It is undoubtedly to Israel's credit that we care so much about each loss. Yet as the final Winograd report noted, these tragic events demand a rational examination of the extent to which Israel should sacrifice to bring a soldier to his final resting place.

The Torah commands us to bury the dead (including just a body part), even in the case of an executed criminal (Deut. 21:23). To preserve the corpse's dignity, it is also forbidden to derive benefit from it or delay its burial. The law further demands that one take responsibility for a *met mitzva*, a corpse with no caretaker (21:1), even if doing so entails an expense or defiles a *kohen* (Yevamot 89b). A soldier killed in enemy territory would seemingly qualify as a *met mitzva*.

To a certain extent, medieval Jews grappled with a similar situation in redeeming the corpses of Jews killed in captivity. Frequently the local authorities refused to release the body until the Jewish community paid a ransom. Jewish leaders balanced the desire to bring the deceased to burial with the risk of encouraging kidnapping and harsher treatment of captives (BY YD 252).

Contemporary Israel knows this dilemma all too well. Some argue for releasing Arab prisoners in return for Israeli corpses, while others retort that doing so will lead to further kidnappings, and that freeing terrorists endangers the population. It is undoubtedly virtuous to bring our dead soldiers home for a dignified burial. Yet there might be limits to the price we pay for these noble deeds.

A battlefield situation, however, adds a dimension that makes it incomparable to both the medieval and contemporary deals made to redeem dead captives. In the latter cases, the debate revolves around the financial or political price to be paid. In the former, we directly endanger other soldiers by asking them to retrieve bodies under fire or in dangerous territory. As Rabbi Yaakov Ariel has noted, while the mitzva of burial is important, it certainly does not trump that of preserving one's own life (*Tchumin* 25).

Of course, one does not always know if a downed soldier has been killed or merely wounded. With a bona fide corpse, however, the commandment of preserving life (*pikuaḥ nefesh*) certainly overrides that of *met mitzva*. Indeed, after a 2004 terrorist explosion in the Philadelphi Route led to Israeli soldiers combing the sand in dangerous territory to retrieve their comrades' body parts, Rabbi Zalman Neḥemia Goldberg asserted that in this circumstance one should not endanger himself to bury a *met mitzva* (*Maayan* 44:4).

Nonetheless, the IDF ethos remains different, with numerous legends told of heroic attempts to retrieve bodies under fire. Moreover, at least three former IDF chief rabbis have endangered their own lives to retrieve corpses. Most notably, Rabbi Shlomo Goren repeatedly crossed enemy lines or entered minefields for this task (*Meshiv Milḥama* 3, p. 12).

As Rabbi Yehuda Zoldan points out in a penetrating essay on this topic, a biblical precedent might exist for this bravery (*Tchumin* 25). After the Philistines mutilated the corpses of King Saul and his sons and left them to rot, the residents of Jabesh-Gilead brazenly snuck into enemy territory to retrieve their bones (I Sam. 31:8–13). Of course, the denigration of a king is a unique affront to the nation and demands an exceptional response. Nonetheless, one might argue that in the era of modern media, any captured corpse represents the entire country. This sensitive symbolism, however, might in turn stem from our unique and possibly overstated concern for burial.

The most compelling and frequent argument made to defend IDF policy is that soldiers left on a battlefield, captured or otherwise, harm the morale and fighting power of other soldiers, and therefore endanger the nation. This assessment might be particularly true if the soldiers left behind held important documents or weapons (*HaTzava KaHalakha*, p. 194). Others note that burials help bring closure to the bereaved. Corpse or body-part retrievals also assist in identifying the deceased and prevent cases of *agunot*, probable widows unable to remarry because of the indeterminate status of their husbands (*Noam* 19). These are serious considerations about which reasonable people can disagree. Do we risk one man's funeral for the sake of another man's burial? If so, how much of a risk are we willing to take?

While I remain conflicted regarding the 2011 exchange to free Gilad Schalit (discussed in the previous essay), I find it much more difficult to justify releasing terrorists in order to redeem the corpses of soldiers. I understand the importance of maintaining soldiers' morale by affirming that the state will never leave them behind, even once deceased. Yet this consideration, I humbly submit, is outweighed by the danger to Jewish lives as well as the demoralizing effect of undermining justice by releasing murderers. Better to honor those dead soldiers by remembering them among the countless martyrs throughout Jewish history who never received a Jewish burial.

Chapter 85

Reinterment

If graves are discovered during construction, may they be moved?

Israel, with its historically rich terrain, frequently runs into this problem as it seeks to build a new layer of history. One recent controversy occurred in 2010 during the construction of an emergency room in Ashkelon's Barzilai Medical Center. This fortified emergency wing is intended to provide urgent care for the region's growing population, especially during wartime in nearby Gaza. Construction stopped, however, after builders uncovered ancient bones, likely those of pagans or Romans. The stoppage caused tremendous delays and additional expenses, and an alternative building site was deemed less fortifiable and less appropriate for urgent care. May the bones be buried elsewhere?

The Torah asserts that humans were created in the image of God (Deut. 21:23), and therefore assigns tremendous value to treating corpses and their final resting places with dignity (*kevod hamet*). Thus, one may not benefit from a corpse (YD 349:1) or disgrace or mutilate it (*nivul hamet*). The Talmud also forbids exhuming a corpse purely for financial reasons, such as to identify heirs (Bava Batra 154b). We would not allow the relocation of a cemetery simply because it was situated on prime real estate. Exhumation is generally prohibited even if the intent is to immediately move the remains to a more respectable location (*Tur* YD 363).

One explanation for the prohibition of reinterment invokes a mystical notion that the dead experience pain when their remains are exposed. Some commentators readily dismiss this concern (*Shu"t HaRashba* 1:369) while others allegorically assert that the soul is pained by the body's decomposition (*Sefer Ḥasidim* 1163). Alternatively, the soul fears that divine judgment is repeated when its corpse is removed from a grave (BY YD 363:1). Some decisors, however, accept this reason only while the body decomposes, but not when mere bones remain (*Noda BiYehuda Kamma* YD 89).

Most authorities confirm, however, that the law's primary goal is to prevent the corpse's denigration, a biblical prohibition (*Ḥakham Tzvi* 47–50; IM YD 1:242, 2:159). As such, the Talmud and subsequent sources permit reinterment under circumstances that befit the dignity of the deceased. For example, if the deceased requested to be buried in a family plot but circumstances necessitated an initial burial elsewhere, one may reinter the remains in the desired spot (YD 363:1).

Similarly, when graves are unprotected from robbery or flooding, one may move the remains to a more secure location, as Rabbis Meshulam Roth (*Kol Mevasser* 2:9) and Yitzḥak Weiss (*Minḥat Yitzḥak* 9:129) and many others have ruled regarding Diaspora cemeteries, especially those located among hostile neighbors. Rabbi Ovadia Yosef similarly permitted the transfer of a cemetery from Yamit following its evacuation, a process repeated after the Gaza disengagement (*Yalkut Yosef* Mourning 22:11). Unless the deceased explicitly directed otherwise, Jewish law also allows for a body buried in the Diaspora to be reinterred in Israel, even at the behest of the children alone, since burial in Israel is meritorious (*Pitḥei Teshuva* YD 363:2).

In addition, the Talmud allows for reinterment when a grave causes public damage (Sanhedrin 47a–b), such as when it is found next to a public road (YD 364:5). This dispensation might stem from the belief that such a destructive grave dishonors the deceased. Alternatively, it might mean that communal needs sometimes override the dignity of the dead (*Ḥazon Ish, Ohalot* 22:26–29). As Rabbi Yisrael Rozen has documented (*Tchumin* 18), Rabbi Akiva Eiger and others understood this clause to permit reinterment for any important communal necessity, even if an entire cemetery must be moved (*Pesakim* 45). Historically, this dispensation was applied to cases of synagogue expansions or major municipal projects (*Ḥavvat Binyamin* 1:25, para. 5). Furthermore, one should not spend excessively to preserve the dignity of a cemetery (YD 368:1).

Even after the removal of the corpse, questions remain regarding the use of the vacated area and its continued sanctity (*Kesef Mishneh, Hilkhot Tumat Met* 8:5). Rabbi Joseph Karo permits this use once the premises have been cleared of bodily remains and gravestones (YD 364:1). While Rabbi Moshe Isserles contended that one may not benefit from the dust of the area, others applied this restriction only to the dirt covering the corpse. In any case, they claimed, travel over the former gravesite does not constitute prohibited benefit. This is the basis for removing bones discovered during road construction.

In the Barzilai case, prominent *ḥaredi* decisors initially declared that the lifesaving benefits were not sufficiently direct to justify removing the remains in question. Yet based on the above sources, Israel's Chief Rabbinate, supported by the Tzohar rabbinic organization, correctly concluded that the fortified emergency room sufficed as an urgent public need and warranted the dignified reburial of the ancient bones.

Chapter 86

Shabbat Protests

Does halakha mandate protesting the opening of public facilities on Shabbat?

Israel has been plagued with this issue for several years, including extended protests in 2009 and 2011 over the opening on Shabbat of the Karta parking lot near Jaffa Gate. These protests (which quickly turned into riots) tarnished Jerusalem's image and distorted Jewish values. While such tactics thankfully did not gain widespread religious support, even within the ultra-Orthodox community, it behooves us to examine the sources that would lead one to protest, albeit respectfully.

Immediately before famously commanding, "Love your neighbor as yourself," the Torah lists a series of interpersonal ordinances, including the commandment of rebuke: "You shall not hate your kinsfolk in your heart; reprove your fellow and incur no guilt because of him. You shall not take revenge or bear a grudge" (Lev. 19:17–18). As *Ḥizkuni* (thirteenth century, France) noted, these mitzvot encourage people to discuss their differences and mend fences. Instead of loathing someone privately, we must air grievances and clarify matters, thereby preventing vengefulness.

In addition to repairing relationships, the commandment to rebuke imposes accountability on people for their friends' behavior ("incur no guilt because of him"). As Maimonides codifies, one who sees someone sinning bears responsibility for preventing further wrong-doing. Thus the Torah enjoins us to tactfully reprove misconduct, even repeatedly (MT *Hilkhot De'ot* 6:6–8).

The talmudic sages recognized the difficulty of this delicate task. They chastised the false modesty of those who gossiped about misconduct yet shirked this commandment to rebuke, claiming themselves unworthy, when in fact they feared arousing hatred. On the other hand, these rabbis questioned whether anyone in their era was skillful enough to properly reprimand or humble enough to accept rebuke (Arakhin 16b). The sages determined that when in doubt as to whether rebuking someone will succeed, one must try, but should always stop if threatened with curses or physical abuse.

Difficult dilemmas ensue when any attempt to censure seems doomed. Some say that in such cases halakha forbids rebuke, since it will only antagonize the wrongdoer. The sages declared, "Just as one is commanded to say that which will be obeyed, one is commanded not to say that which will be disobeyed" (Yevamot 65b). Similarly, the Talmud advises rabbis not to scold unwitting sinners (*shogeg*) if they will continue sinning nonetheless (*mezid*), thereby increasing the severity of their offense (Beitza 30a). Based on these sentiments, two prominent thirteenth-century authorities, Rabbi Moses of Coucy (*Smag Aseh* 11) and the unknown author of *Sefer HaḤinukh* (339), prohibited the reprimand of sinners impervious to admonishment.

According to other talmudic sources, however, upright Jews, as promoters of goodness within society, must speak out against injustice and sinfulness. Furthermore, only God knows who will heed rebuke, so we must not deprive anyone of the opportunity to repent (Shabbat 55a). Based on these sources, Rabbi Eliezer of Metz (twelfth century, France) declared that while one may discount unwitting sinners who will ignore rebuke, wanton sinners must face censure, even if it might increase their culpability (*Yere'im* 223).

An alternative approach, advocated by Rabbi Yosef ibn Habib (early fifteenth century, Spain) and adopted by Rabbi Moshe Isserles (OḤ 608:2), contended that given the desecration of God's name and the potential negative influence on society, all wanton sins in public must be condemned at least once. However, with the modern emergence of Jewish sectarianism and secularism, prominent decisors like Rabbis Yeḥiel Michel Epstein (AH OḤ 608:7) and Yisrael Meir Kagan (BH 608:2, s.v. *aval*) claimed that such criticism makes sense only among those with shared cultural assumptions.

Debates over Shabbat demonstrations have largely centered on this dilemma of whether one aims to persuade others or to make a statement. Despite thirty-three fruitless weeks of protests against the opening on Shabbat of Petaḥ Tikva's Heikhal Theater in 1984, Rabbis Yitzḥak Zilberstein and Simḥa Kook defended these demonstrations as expressions of rights and values (*Tchumin* 8). Petaḥ Tikva's chief rabbi, Rabbi Moshe Malka, a reluctant participant in the effort, countered that the extended reprimand only emboldened secularists and harmed the Torah's image in Israeli society (*Tchumin* 7).

Beyond the futility of such protests, I would add that they distract the religious community from developing a meaningful Shabbat culture capable of generating broader interest. Especially when officials make accommodations for religious sensitivities, the community must focus on educational initiatives that will encourage all Jews to reclaim their heritage of Shabbat – and Jerusalem.

Chapter 87

Censuses

May the State of Israel conduct a census?

Jewish leaders continue to obsess over demographics in Israel and abroad. The topic influences debates ranging from the viability of a two-state solution to the assimilation crisis. Yet the notion of counting the entire nation or even a segment thereof remains entangled in halakhic controversy.

The Talmud states repeatedly that it is forbidden to count the Jewish people directly. The clearest biblical source for this prohibition seemingly stems from the half-shekel payments made by each Israelite before the building of the Tabernacle. "When you take a census of the Israelite people... each shall pay the Lord an atonement for himself on being enrolled, that no plague may come upon them" (Ex. 30:12). While talk of atonement (*kofer*) implies protection from previous sins, most understand the payment as necessary to offset any harm done by the census itself.

The most common explanation of this harm is that the counting of individuals might draw the "evil eye" (Rashi). Some equate the evil eye with divine judgment, which favors groups, whereas individuals receive more attention to their personal vices (Rabbi Ovadia Seforno), as on Rosh HaShana (Rabbenu Baḥya). Others understand the evil eye naturalistically (Rabbi Isaac Abrabanel). In any case, since at least the early medieval period, Jews have refrained from counting heads to check for the requisite ten members of a prayer quorum (*Sefer HaIttim* 174). Instead, they count by reciting a ten-word biblical verse (*Kitzur Shulḥan Arukh* 15:3).

Some talmudic sages traced this prohibition to the prophecies in Genesis (32:12) and Hosea (2:1) that the Jewish people would be as countless as grains of sand (Yoma 22b). These rabbis also prohibited head counts even for the sake of a mitzva. As such, the Temple priests were counted by numbering their outstretched fingers (MT *Hilkhot Temidim U'Musafim* 4:3–4). The Talmud praises King Saul for conducting his two military tallies (I Sam. 11:8, 15:4) by counting personal items, such as pottery shards (Radak, 15:4). To avoid this prohibition, some ancient leaders based population estimates on the number of participants in the Paschal sacrifice (Pesaḥim 64b).

Scholars struggled to explain how King David could commit such an elementary error as conducting a forbidden census (Berakhot 62b), which was punished with a plague that killed seventy thousand (II Sam. 24:15). Some claimed this census was a purposeless act of hubris (Nahmanides, Num. 1:3). Others more generously asserted that David thought a direct count was prohibited only in the desert, but not once the Jews entered the Land of Israel (Nahmanides, Ex. 30:12). Still others suggested that the firmness of the prohibition became clear only after this incident (*Levush HaOra* Ex. 30:12).

Some concluded that a census is allowed only when done indirectly and for the sake of a mitzva (*Tosafot Rid* Yoma 22b). Other sources, however, indicate that any population survey remains permissible if conducted for a good reason (Numbers Rabba 2:17), with others arguing that an indirect count alone circumvents the prohibition (Maimonides, Commentary on the Mishna, Yoma 2:1).

The census question resurfaced with the modern-day resettlement of the Land of Israel. While the issue was raised as early as the beginning of the nineteenth century (*Kovetz She'elot U'Teshuvot Ḥatam Sofer* 8), it became a cause célèbre in the twentieth. In 1937, Rabbi Ben-Zion Uziel permitted a membership tally in preparation for labor union elections, arguing that written surveys were a sufficiently indirect method of counting, and that the polling was necessary to prevent foul play (*Piskei Uziel BeShe'elot HaZeman* 40).

Similar sentiments were echoed by Rabbi Yeḥiel Yaakov Weinberg, who submitted that a census was essential for economic planning and national security (*Seridei Esh* 1:140). Rabbi Menaḥem Kasher added that the inclusion of non-Jewish citizens eliminates the prohibition, plus any large-scale census is inevitably inexact (*Torah Shelema* vol. 21, appendix). Rabbis Ḥayim David HaLevi (*Aseh Lekha Rav,* 6:306) and Shaul Yisraeli (*Amud HaYemini* 1:13) alternatively deemed it easier to circumvent this proscription when one does not intend to count the entire Jewish people.

Nonetheless, great reservations about the census were expressed by Rabbis Eliezer Waldenburg (*Tzitz Eliezer* 7:3) and Shlomo Goren (*Torat HaMedina,* ch. 20), even as they marshaled arguments in divergent directions. The fiercest opposition came from anti-Zionist figures, including Rabbi Yaakov Kanievsky and the Eda Ḥaredit, who saw no need for a state census and discouraged participation (*Tchumin* 4). While the assistance of the Chief Rabbinate and the use of computer technology have helped allay some concerns, the national census remains a contentious topic, particularly among those who reject not only the necessity of a census, but also the Zionist State.

Chapter 88

Civil Courts

Does halakha permit recourse to Israeli civil courts?

In recent years, the relationship between segments of the religious community and Israel's civil courts has been fraught with tension over Supreme Court rulings perceived as antagonistic to religious values or institutions. This friction stems partly from those in the judiciary who are determined to enforce the democratic nature of the state and those in the religious community whose sole interest lies in promoting Israel's halakhic character. This clash, however, is rooted in a larger question regarding whether Jewish law recognizes non-halakhic legal systems.

The sages asserted that within God's commandment to establish a judicial system, the Torah prohibited Jews from adjudicating their conflicts in non-Jewish courts. "And these are the statutes that you shall place before *them*," the Torah proclaims (Ex. 21:1), but not before gentile judges (Gittin 88b). This prohibition exists, according to the sages, even if non-Jewish law accords with halakha (*Shu"t HaRan* 73), and notwithstanding the Noahide law that gentiles should establish their own legal systems. Medieval Jewish communities, which were regularly granted judicial autonomy by the local government, subsequently demanded full allegiance to their courts (*batei din*), even as their constituents sometimes turned to the civil legal system for financial or social gain.

As suggested by a parallel prohibition of adjudication before improperly trained Jewish judges (*hedyotot*), some sources indicate that the ban on non-Jewish courts (*arkaot shel goyim*) stems from a fear that gentile judges will not adjudicate the case properly (Y. Avoda Zara 2:7). Other sources suggest that foreign law will not reflect the spirit of Jewish culture (Tanḥuma, *Mishpatim* 3). Most frequently, scholars regarded recourse to non-Jewish courts as an act of treason that denied the Torah's wisdom and displayed mistrust of its legal system. This disloyalty was comparable to blasphemy (MT *Hilkhot Sanhedrin* 26:7). As such, the ban on non-Jewish courts applies even if their judges adjudicate in accordance with halakha (*Shu"t HaRan* 73).

As Rabbi Yaakov Ariel has argued, the inverse situation in contemporary Israel is equally problematic, as Jewish judges adjudicate according to norms based on British, Turkish, and local laws, but not halakha (*Tchumin* 1). At best, this state of affairs might be analogous to a case in which judges lack training in Jewish law. Rabbis Avraham Karelitz (*Ḥazon Ish* ḤM Sanhedrin 15:4) and Ovadia Yosef (*Yeḥaveh Daat* 4:65) contended that the fact that the judges are Jewish only increased the gravity of employing an alternative legal system. Most decisors, however, agree that one may use civil courts even within Israel if (1) one's interlocutor refuses adjudication in a *beit din*, (2) the threat of financial loss is imminent without civil intervention, or (3) the religious court is not empowered to enforce its decision.

With the founding of the State of Israel, Rabbi Shlomo Goren suggested that one might validate Israeli courts based on a historic model accepted by the sages: In the Roman province of Syria, where no scholars were qualified to adjudicate according to Jewish law (Sanhedrin 23a), halakha recognized the decisions reached by ad hoc courts composed of distinguished citizens who ruled based on personal judgment (ḤM 8:1). Although supported by prominent Orthodox Israeli legal scholars, this solution was rejected by Chief Rabbi Isaac Herzog and other decisors. They convincingly contended that an established legal system based on non-halakhic principles was not comparable to an ad hoc court based on personal discretion. Herzog suggested instead that each Israeli tribunal include at least one judge with knowledge of Jewish law, although that proposal was never adopted (*Teḥuka LeYisrael Al Pi HaTorah* 1, p. 163).

Further complicating this dispute is the talmudic principle of *dina demalkhuta dina* ("the law of the land is the law"). This axiom mandates not only payment of taxes and observance of zoning and safety regulations, but also cooperation with the judicial bodies created to enforce those laws. A similar ruling applies to criminal law, which rabbinic decisors agreed should be enforced by government authorities. (See essays 37 and 40 for further discussion.)

Other areas of law, however, definitively require halakhic adjudication. The resulting tension is particularly acute for religious Zionists, who support state institutions *and* maintain absolute fealty to halakha. Hence Justice Minister Yaakov Neeman's controversial declaration in 2009 that he hoped Israeli law would ultimately become Jewish law. As with many of this country's internal disputes, this deeply rooted conflict will probably simmer for years to come.

Chapter 89

The Temple Mount

Are Jews allowed to enter?

Following the Six-Day War, Israel's Chief Rabbinate promulgated a ban on Jews ascending the Temple Mount. This decision, along with the continued effective control of the site by the Waqf, has severely limited the Jewish civilian presence on the mount. As a result, many Jews and non-Jews ignore its significance in Judaism. The recent attempt to rectify this situation by organizing group visits to the mount has ignited a passionate legal debate.

Several biblical commandments regulated entrance to the various sections of the Temple, including the establishment of a guard system to enforce these rules (Num. 18:1–4). The Torah (Lev. 19:30) further commands a general reverence for the Temple, interpreted by the sages to include respectful behavior within permissible areas, such as not carrying a stick or wallet, wearing leather shoes, or walking around for mundane purposes (Berakhot 54a).

Medieval commentators debated whether these restrictions became dormant following the Temple's destruction. Raavad (twelfth century, Provence) contended that although the rest of Eretz Yisrael retained its sanctity, the Temple Mount was desacralized by its non-Jewish conquerors (Nahmanides, Makkot 19a; MT *Hilkhot Beit HaBeḥira* 6:14). Rabbi Menaḥem HaMeiri (*Beit HaBeḥira* Shevuot 16a) understood this position to allow for Jews to walk on the Temple Mount, and he reports that they have historically done so. Indeed, as noted by Gedalia Meyer and Henoch Messner (*Ḥakirah* 10), talmudic stories (Makkot 24b) and medieval travelogues indicate that Jews ascended the Temple Mount until Muslim conquerors banned entrance by non-Muslims in the twelfth century.

Maimonides, however, insisted that the entire compound has retained its sanctity, and that sacrifices may still be offered there, even without the Temple (MT *Hilkhot Beit HaBeḥira* 6:14). In fact, as Rabbi Tzvi Hirsch Chajes points out, several talmudic passages indicate that many Temple rites – particularly the Passover sacrifice – continued into late antiquity (*Darkhei Horaa*, p. 261). Rabbi Tzvi Kalischer, moved by messianic aspirations, attempted to renew such activity in the nineteenth century (*Derishat Tziyon*). Yet his proposal was shot down by figures like Rabbi Yaakov Ettlinger, who contended that sacrifices were not permissible without finding the altar's exact location, priests with proven pedigree, and various Temple apparatuses (*Binyan Tziyon* 1).

Maimonides' ruling, which demands continual reverence for the Temple Mount and restricts entry to it (MT *Hilkhot Beit HaBeḥira* 7:7), was widely accepted by medieval (*Kaftor VaFeraḥ* 6) and modern (MB 561:5) authorities. According to Rabbi Abraham Isaac Kook, even Raavad believed that the area remains holy, but that entry is punishable only when the Temple stands (*Mishpat Kohen* 96). As Rabbi Eliyahu Bakshi-Doron noted, these laws also prohibit tour guides from encouraging unrestricted visits to the site by non-Jewish tourists (*Tchumin* 11).

Yet the sages permitted entry into some of the sacred areas following appropriate ritual preparation, including immersion in a *mikve*, a ritual bath (Kelim 1:8), even for people who had contracted impurity through contact with corpses (MT *Hilkhot Beit HaBeḥira* 7:15). Moreover, the current rectangular Temple Mount complex, which was expanded in the Herodian era to about 150,000 square meters, includes sections not within the original Temple area, which formed a square (500 *amot* x 500 *amot*) with sides of roughly 250 meters (Middot 2:1). Maimonides himself walked and prayed in the permissible areas when he visited Eretz Yisrael in 1165 (*Iggerot HaRambam* 1, p. 224).

As such, two sixteenth-century rabbis, David ibn Zimra (*Shu"t HaRadbaz* 2:691) and Yosef di Trani (Maharit, *Tzurat HaBayit*), attempted to delineate the exact Temple location and permitted Jews to walk on certain areas of the mount. Yet their calculations are highly disputed, leading many scholars – including Rabbi Yisrael of Shklov, leader of Jerusalem's Jewish community in the nineteenth century (*Pe'at HaShulḥan* 2:11) – to prohibit entrance to the Temple Mount (which was regularly banned by the ruling authorities anyway). This position was adopted by numerous authorities following the Six-Day War, including Rabbis Ovadia Yosef (*Yabia Omer* YD 5:26), Yitzḥak Weiss (*Minḥat Yitzḥak* 5:1), and Eliezer Waldenburg (*Tzitz Eliezer* 10:1).

Others contend that this stringency has led to neglect of the sacred space. Most prominently, Rabbi Shlomo Goren dedicated a book, *Har HaBayit*, to determining the permissible areas of entry. While the efforts of Rabbis Mordechai Eliyahu (*Tchumin* 3) and She'ar Yashuv HaKohen to build a synagogue on the Temple Mount have been thwarted, other scholars – such as Rabbis Nachum Rabinovitch and Ḥayim Druckman – recently advocated Jewish entry (after strict halakhic preparation) into areas they claim are indisputably outside the restricted zones. Yet other religious Zionist leaders – including Rabbis Avraham Shapira and Shlomo Aviner – have opposed such entry, maintaining that modern-day Jews are spiritually unprepared for the Temple's holiness.

Chapter 90

Produce in a *Shemitta* Year

May Jewish farmers sell their land to non-Jews in order to cultivate it?

The Torah greatly emphasizes the importance of *Shemitta,* which along with canceling all debts, obligates Jews to let the Land of Israel lie fallow during this sabbatical year. The Torah even implies that God will exile the Jews for violating the *Shemitta* restrictions (Rashi, Lev. 26:34).

Scholars cite many reasons for this mitzva. The Torah itself highlights the potential social benefits of letting the poor (as well as the animals) enjoy the fruits of the abandoned fields (Ex. 23:11, Lev. 25:6–7). Maimonides stresses that this practice, as well as the cancellation of debts, helps restore financial stability to the less fortunate (Guide 3:37).

Maimonides also claims that leaving the land fallow improves its quality. Indeed, many farmers historically used this strategy, although today crop rotation has become the preferred method. Many medieval rabbis, however, scoffed that this reason seems insufficient to justify the significance the Torah attaches to the mitzva.

Rabbi Abraham ibn Ezra detects a more spiritual benefit, noting that the break from work allows people to dedicate themselves to Torah study and other holy pursuits (Deut. 31:10). Universities have adopted this ideal by granting professors sabbaticals for research and exploration.

Sefer HaḤinukh (84) takes a more theological approach. The "Sabbath of the land" (Lev. 25:6), like the weekly day of rest, testifies to God's creation of the world and His subsequent "rest." Moreover, it attests that divine grace, and not human toil, ultimately makes produce grow. This theme strikes a chord in contemporary society, in which technology and industrialization can easily lead one to believe that humans alone control their environment.

Sefer HaḤinukh also contends that *Shemitta* builds character by teaching us to let go, to give without regard to recompense. Similarly, the cessation of work both displays and reinforces one's trust in God as the source of one's livelihood. The Torah itself testifies to this element of the mitzva: "And should you ask, 'What are we to eat in the seventh year, if we may neither sow nor gather in our crops?' I will ordain My blessing for you in the sixth year, and it will yield a crop sufficient for three years" (Lev. 25:20–21).

Despite the notion that *Shemitta* is intended to help the underprivileged, the rabbis found that its laws actually harmed this population. The threat of debt cancellation caused lenders to stop lending to the poor, leading Hillel to famously enact the *pruzbul* arrangement, which allowed people to collect their debts after the *Shemitta* year (Gittin 34b). Lack of income combined with foreign taxation caused the great talmudic rabbi, R. Yehuda HaNasi, to even contemplate abolishing the mitzva, although R. Pinḥas ben Yair talked him out of it. Be that as it may, some talmudic sages (Moed Katan 2b), followed by most medieval scholars (*Tur* YD 331), believe that *Shemitta* today is only a rabbinic decree, with a few even asserting that our observance of these laws is merely a pious custom (*Beit HaBeḥira* Gittin 36b).

This factor was critical for many rabbinic authorities who searched for dispensations to help grapple with the economic problems posed by *Shemitta* when Jews returned to Eretz Yisrael in the late nineteenth century. Deeming it economically untenable to leave the Land of Israel fallow, several scholars – led by Rabbis Shmuel Mohliver and Yitzḥak E. Spektor – endorsed the *heter mekhira* mechanism in 1888 (5649), which allowed Jews to formally sell the land to non-Jews for the year, enabling themselves to continue working it. Many decisors, including Rabbi Naphtali Berlin, opposed this legal fiction (*Meshiv Davar* 2:56), while others, such as prominent Jerusalem Rabbis Shmuel Salant and Yehoshua Diskin, fluctuated in their support, depending on their assessment of the economic strain. Over time, the primary representatives of each side of the debate became Rabbi Abraham Isaac Kook, who favored the *heter mekhira*, and Rabbi Avraham Karelitz (author of *Ḥazon Ish*), who opposed it.

The *heter mekhira* rests on the following halakhic assumptions: (1) *Shemitta* today lacks the status of a biblical commandment, as discussed above. (2) Land in Eretz Yisrael owned by a non-Jew need not remain fallow. This was the opinion of Rabbi Joseph Karo (*Avkat Rokhel* 22–25), which was historically followed (*Pe'at HaShulḥan* 23:29), even as his Safed colleague Rabbi Moshe di Trani attacked it in a famed sixteenth-century polemic. (3) Even a Jew may work fields owned by a non-Jew during *Shemitta* (*Avnei Nezer* YD 2:458). (4) Despite the prohibition of selling territory in Eretz Yisrael to a non-Jew (discussed in essays 79–80), temporary sales are permitted if intended to strengthen Jewish settlement of the land (*Yeshuot Malko* YD 55). (5) This legal fiction is executed properly and with full intent.

Each of these premises has strong support within the halakhic literature, even as some, including the *Ḥazon Ish* (Shevi'it 24:4), challenged many of them. Rabbi Kook himself supported this dispensation only when economically necessary. In any case, given the continued controversy over the *heter mekhira*, some scholars have sought other solutions.

Obviously one can simply buy non-Jewish produce, such as by importing it from abroad. Yet many scholars have argued that doing so strengthens Israel's competitors and sometimes even supports anti-Zionists. One recent alternative is to use produce grown hydroponically. Since these fruits and vegetables grow in enclosed areas and without soil, many decisors, including Rabbi Shlomo Zalman Auerbach, exclude them from the *Shemitta* restrictions intended for fields. This position has received widespread support, yet other authorities argue that *Shemitta* encompasses any agricultural methods regularly used in contemporary society, including hydroponics (*Minḥat Yitzḥak* 10:116).

Another complex solution, promoted by both Rabbis Kook and Karelitz, entails an economic arrangement known as *otzar beit din* (the court's warehouse). This system, which appears in the Tosefta (Shevi'it 8:1–2) but was not recorded in the Talmud or by Maimonides, allows the rabbinic court to seize control of the fallow land, hire workers (e.g., the owners and their laborers) to harvest its produce, and then sell it, charging only for the labor. The advantage of this mechanism is that it allows one to harvest while observing the commandment, thereby maintaining the sanctity of the land and its fruit. As such, consuming this food is a mitzva, which also means that any leftovers must be disposed of respectfully.

Yet this solution has its problems: (1) It was not used throughout the generations. (2) It allows payment only for labor, not for the fruit itself. While some decisors think one may "charge extra" for labor during a *Shemitta* year, many disagree. (3) The *beit din* must lay out money for labor without knowing if sales will cover these expenses. (4) Planting remains forbidden, so this arrangement does not help provide vegetables toward the end of the *Shemitta* year.

In recent years, the Institute for Torah and the Land of Israel established the Otzar HaAretz program, which provides designated shops with produce grown hydroponically or harvested through an *otzar beit din* arrangement. When necessary, however, Otzar HaAretz also relies on the *heter mekhira*. This is a positive development, helping us observe the *Shemitta* year while maintaining the Israeli economy.

Section VII

Kashrut

Chapter 91

Waiting Between Meat and Milk

Is there a normative amount of time?

The confusion stems from an unresolved rabbinic debate that has led to a plurality of legitimate practices reflecting historical developments and geographical divisions.

While the prohibition of eating meat and milk together originates in the Bible, the notion of waiting after consuming meat only appears in the Talmud. The first explicit discussion of this tradition emerges in the amoraic period (200–500 CE), and ostensibly derives from a pious attempt to avoid consuming milk while meat remains stuck in one's teeth or its fatty taste lingers in one's mouth. (The alleged fear of digesting both types together rarely appears in rabbinic sources.) Although some medieval scholars applied these concerns only to fleshy beef, not to chicken or meat extracts (like broth), the rabbinic consensus makes no such distinction (YD 89:3).

The Talmud discusses whether one must wipe his hands or wash his mouth before consuming the opposite type of food (Ḥullin 104b). Later in this passage, a recent immigrant from Babylonia, where this custom seemingly emerged, asked R. Yoḥanan of Eretz Yisrael how long he waits to drink milk after consuming meat. He responded, "I don't wait!" Bewildered by R. Yoḥanan's answer, the Talmud reinterprets it to mean that one need not wait between cheese and meat.

Based on this statement, many scholars see no need to wait after consuming dairy, beyond simply rinsing one's mouth. The first authority to mention waiting after eating cheese was Rabbi Meir of Rothenburg (thirteenth century, Germany), who took on a personal stringency after once finding cheese stuck between his teeth. Although Rabbi Shlomo Luria spurned this practice (*Shakh* YD 89:17), his sixteenth-century contemporary, Rabbi Moshe Isserles, ruled that one should wait to eat meat following the consumption of hard cheese, because its thick and fatty texture might be as problematic as meat (YD 89:2). This ruling refers to uncooked cheese that is aged for six months, like Parmesan.

The aforementioned section of the Talmud records Mar Ukva's confession that while his pious father waited twenty-four hours between meat and dairy, he himself waits only "until the next meal." Mar Ukva did not quantify this standard, leaving an ambiguity that was interpreted differently by commentators around the world. Maimonides – followed by Spanish and Provençal sages – ruled that one must wait "*about* six hours" (MT *Hilkhot Maakhalot Asurot* 9:28), basing himself on the ancient practice of consuming two meals a day (Shabbat 10a). While Rabbi Joseph Karo understood this expression to mean a full six hours (YD 89:1), others, like Rabbi Menaḥem HaMeiri (*Magen Avot* 9), spoke of waiting five to six hours, colloquially known as "into the sixth hour." A compromise interpretation asserted that without clocks, Maimonides could not demand an exact time, and therefore five and a half hours suffices.

The medieval sages of Germany and northern France, in contrast, took "until the next meal" literally (*Tosafot* Ḥullin 105a). They maintained that once a person recited the Grace After Meals, cleared the table, and rinsed his mouth, he could immediately begin a dairy meal. Their fifteenth-century successors, such as Rabbi Israel Isserlein, called for waiting one hour, as Dutch Jews still do. As Ashkenazic Jewry moved to Eastern Europe, however, many sages urged their followers to observe Maimonides' ruling. This stringency ultimately became the dominant Ashkenazic practice (*Shakh* YD 89:8), even as we remain lenient for those whose health or diet requires a shorter waiting period (*Pitḥei Teshuva* YD 89:3).

German Jewry, followed by its British descendants, took a middle ground, waiting three hours. This period might represent the amount of time between meals in these countries, or it may be a compromise between the different opinions. Textual references to this custom, however, remain very sparse; Dr. Aviad Stolman traced the first record of the practice to a 1492 manuscript. (An alleged earlier citation by Rabbenu Yeruḥam appears to be a scribal error.) Much to the chagrin of contemporary authorities, many Jews of Eastern European and Sephardic origin adopted this custom, sometimes out of convenience. While Rabbi Shlomo Zalman Auerbach believed Jews should abandon this custom, it appears well-established in select communities.

When a person has no family custom, I would recommend waiting at least five hours. The three-hour option, however, might fit the religious needs of someone who "keeps a modicum of kashrut" and help maintain a legitimate minimum standard, especially for one of Ashkenazic background. Each individual should consult a local rabbi to determine the most appropriate practice for him.

Chapter 92

Eating Meat and Fish

Is this rabbinic decree still valid?

The talmudic prohibition of consuming meat and fish together touches upon several issues that relate to the intersection of science and Jewish law.

The Talmud warns against eating meat and fish cooked together and states that the combination causes health problems and bad breath (Pesaḥim 76b). Because Jewish law strictly forbids activities that directly harm one's health (MT *Hilkhot Rotze'aḥ* 11:5–6), the combination is deemed forbidden. Legal scholars thus classified this prohibition along with other activities forbidden for health reasons (YD 116).

What is the health hazard here? While Rashi understood that this combination can cause the biblical disease of *tzaraat,* others believed it to trigger a more general disorder. Some contemporary writers posit that people might focus on removing the relatively larger bones found in meat and therefore neglect to remove the smaller fish bones, putting themselves at risk of choking. This idea, however, is not found in earlier sources. In any case, though scholars have long acknowledged that nowadays this combination is harmless, it remains forbidden.

Since the early medieval era, scholars have cautioned against following talmudic medical advice if deemed unreliable (*Otzar HaGeonim* Gittin, p. 152). The Talmud reports, for example, that fishermen say fish is best eaten just as it turns putrid (!), yet the medieval Tosafists quickly dismissed this counsel as no longer accurate, at least outside Babylonia (Moed Katan 11a). In fact, practitioners of talmudic medicine – which reflects ancient scientific understanding – were threatened with excommunication, since their harmful actions could discredit the Talmud (*Yam shel Shlomo* Ḥullin 8:12).

The examples above point to a broader question regarding how changes in nature (or our understanding of it) should impact Jewish law. As Rabbi Neria Gutel has meticulously documented, medieval scholars remained divided and inconsistent about when they could change norms based on flawed scientific assumptions.

For example, the Talmud (Ḥullin 42a, 57b) lists several types of wounds that were believed to kill an animal within twelve months, thereby making it non-kosher (*tereifa*). Maimonides declared this list exclusive and unchangeable, even if, as some have noted, it is partially inaccurate from a biological perspective in both what it includes and what it omits (MT *Hilkhot Sheḥita* 10:12–13). Some scholars dismissed such charges of inaccuracy as flawed and nefarious (*Shu"t HaRashba* 1:98). Others contended that the list stems from oral traditions that are not to be altered.

Regarding other scientific misconceptions, however, halakhic norms may change in light of contemporary knowledge (IM EH 2:3, para. 2). One famous example is the prohibition of drinking water left uncovered overnight, lest snakes have poisoned it (Avoda Zara 30a). Medieval rabbinic authorities contended that with this danger no longer present, the law became null (YD 116:1). As a rule, a senior legislative body is required to abolish rabbinic decrees (Eduyot 1:5). Yet scholars asserted that this one was nullified automatically, since it was limited to areas where the danger existed (*Shu"t Binyamin Ze'ev* 222).

Interestingly, while Rabbi Joseph Karo codified the prohibition of eating meat and fish together (YD 116:2), Maimonides never mentioned it (MT *Hilkhot Maakhalot Asurot* 9:23). Some asserted that he considered the combination dangerous only if the meat and fish were cooked together, not simply in the same oven (*Yam shel Shlomo* Ḥullin 7:15); this interpretation became a minority position (*Darkhei Moshe* YD 116:3). Others more convincingly argued that Maimonides believed the original concern was limited to certain types of fish in a given locale (*Be'er Sheva* 35). Indeed, Rabbi Avraham Gombiner (seventeenth century, Poland) declared this prohibition obsolete, like many other talmudic health decrees (*Magen Avraham* 173:1).

While others shared this sentiment (Maharsham 4:124), most did not adopt it in practice (*Yad Efraim* YD 116). Some nineteenth-century scholars asserted that one must take all precautions regarding potential health concerns (*Shu"t Maharam Schick* YD 244), with others contending that we cannot overturn this rabbinic decree (*Ḥatam Sofer* YD 2:101). Other authorities in turn questioned these positions, yet ultimately ruled that we must follow the *Shulḥan Arukh* (*Divrei Malkiel* 2:53, para. 12).

Nonetheless, many scholars believe that especially given the negligible health fears, the taste of a minimal amount of fish is nullified by larger quantities of other permissible substances (*Yabia Omer* YD 1:7–8). As such, many Worcestershire sauces in which anchovies constitute less than one-sixtieth of the product may be used with meat. Those with problematic quantities will frequently have "Kosher-Fish" stamped on the label.

Chapter 93

Eating Milk and Fish

Can a scribal error change Jewish law?

In the previous essay, we discussed whether the ancient prohibition of consuming meat and fish together remained valid given that talmudic health concerns regarding this mixture no longer apply. That topic raised questions regarding the legal standing of contemporary science. The alleged prohibition of eating fish and cheese together, observed in certain Sephardic communities, explores the impact of inaccurate texts on Jewish law: Can a scribal error in an authoritative text change Jewish law?

While Jewish law proscribes various mixtures of milk and meat, it excludes fish from either category, deeming it neutral (Ḥullin 103b). As such, any potential problem of eating fish with meat or milk does not involve kashrut. The Talmud prohibits the combination of meat and fish for health reasons, as codified in *Shulḥan Arukh,* in the section relating to hygienic practices (OḤ 173:2). Similar sentiments are never expressed regarding milk and fish, and two passages (Pesaḥim 76b, Ḥullin 111b) imply that it is entirely permissible (*Shakh* YD 87:5).

The first legal text to allegedly ponder such a prohibition was *Beit Yosef,* a sixteenth-century commentary written by the famed Rabbi Joseph Karo of Safed. After noting fish's neutral status, *Beit Yosef* continues, "Nevertheless, one should not eat fish in *milk* because of danger, as explained in OḤ 173:2." Yet this proof text deals with *meat*! As such, Rabbi Moshe Isserles (*Darkhei Moshe* YD 87), followed by many other prominent decisors, contended that a scribe miscopied the word "milk" instead of "meat" (*Taz* YD 87:3). This error would further explain why

Rabbi Karo never prohibited milk with fish in the *Shulḥan Arukh*. These authorities concluded that fish may be consumed with dairy products, a position adopted by almost all Ashkenazic authorities (AH YD 87:15).

Ancient manuscripts regularly suffered from poor penmanship, slipping of the eyes, and misunderstandings by unlearned or confused copyists. The resulting problems became more pervasive following the twentieth-century discovery of the Cairo Geniza, which provided a treasure trove of variant texts.

Medieval authorities would change norms based on alternative readings in different manuscripts. Maimonides, for example, dismissed a certain halakhic position advocated by earlier authorities because he believed their decision was based on faulty talmudic texts (MT *Hilkhot Malveh VeLoveh* 15:2). Yet reasonable people can disagree on how to weigh the alleged evidence of variant manuscripts, with Maimonides' regular interlocutor, Raavad of Posquières, upholding the ruling of the earlier scholars (*Maggid Mishneh*).

As Rabbi Moshe Bleich has documented, separate questions relate to whether the composition of authoritative legal codes, such as Rabbi Karo's *Shulḥan Arukh*, precludes the subsequent use of variant texts (*Tradition* 27:2). One issue relates to the discovery of rabbinic positions regarding halakhic disputes. Some argue that had authorities seen these earlier statements, they might have changed their own opinions (*Yabia Omer* OḤ 5, introduction). Others retort that normative practices should not be altered (*Moadim U'Zemanim* 4:274).

In other instances, widespread practices became established on the basis of texts that, judging by manuscript evidence, were inaccurate. As Rabbi Dr. Daniel Sperber has noted, figures like Rabbi Yisrael Meir Kagan struggled with this phenomenon (MB 551:32). In theory, the law should follow the position found in accurate manuscripts. Yet once a practice has become the norm, it might take on independent stature (*Minhagei Yisrael* 3).

In our case, the alleged textual error was noted immediately, so the practice was more easily dismissed. Yet some authorities, mostly Sephardic, defended this prohibition. Rabbi Ḥayim Benveniste contended that Karo's proof text was intended only to show that the consumption of fish and milk was prohibited like other actions deemed unhealthy

(*Hagahot* BY YD 87). Others claimed they knew doctors who believed this combination posed a genuine health risk (*Pitḥei Teshuva* YD 87:9), at least within certain locales (*Kaf HaḤayim* OḤ 173:3).

One eighteenth-century scholar famed for his rabbinic and scientific knowledge, Rabbi Yitzḥak Lampronti, found no historical evidence of any medical danger, but asserted that we should maintain the traditional practice. This sentiment was shared by Rabbis Ovadia Yosef (*Yeḥaveh Daat* 6:48) and Ḥayim David HaLevi (*Tchumin* 17). The latter, after noting the medical and textual rationale for abandoning this practice, nonetheless contended that since it is not a big inconvenience, Sephardim who observe this stricture should continue to do so.

Chapter 94

Swordfish

Was it once kosher?

I first heard about the swordfish controversy as a college student, when a local Orthodox rabbi told me the Conservative movement might be correct in declaring it kosher. I forgot about the remark, since I was never a big fish eater (I started eating tuna only a few years ago). Yet a recently acquired taste for fish (*aliya* will do that to you!), plus a fascinating article by Prof. Ari Zivotofsky of Bar-Ilan University (*BDD* 19), has revived my interest.

While the Torah specifies that kosher fish must have both scales and fins (Lev. 11:9–10), an ancient tradition, later codified as halakha, asserts that all fish with scales have fins as well (Nidda 51b, YD 83:3). As such, much of the halakhic literature has focused on defining halakhically acceptable scales – a complex project, since scales vary greatly. Among other criteria, kosher fish must contain scales that are attached to the body but capable of being peeled without damaging the skin (YD 83:1). Scales that shed when fish mature or leave the water, or that develop only later in life, are also acceptable.

Nonetheless, it remains difficult to identify which fish fulfill these criteria. For starters, the myriad species must be carefully examined by competent authorities. Moreover, as Zivotofsky emphasizes, contemporary scientific classifications do not easily correspond to what one would think would be the parallel halakhic distinctions. Furthermore, similar fish in different regions can have distinct characteristics or names, even as different fish can have similar names (e.g., salmon is kosher, but rock salmon is not). With other species, such as birds, legal traditions derived from previous generations help determine an animal's status. With fish, however, the inconsistency of names and traits leaves the decisor with nothing but the specimen in front of him to tip the scales (sorry, I couldn't resist!).

Rabbi Ḥayim Benveniste (seventeenth century, Turkey) issued the first ruling on the "fish with the sword." He recorded that Jews eat the fish, though it lacks scales on land, since "when it comes out of the water, due to its anger, it shakes, and the scales are thrown off" (*Knesset HaGedola* YD 83:74). The kosher status of the swordfish was continuously affirmed over the next centuries in important halakhic works like *Peri Meggadim*, *Darkhei Teshuva*, and *Kaf HaḤayim*. Significantly, swordfish appears on the 1933 kosher fish list of the Agudath HaRabonim of the United States (*Xiphias gladius*). While the list was challenged for including certain types of sturgeon and eel, its inclusion of swordfish was accepted.

Rabbi Dr. Moshe D. Tendler, a microbiologist and prominent scholar at Yeshiva University, first questioned the kashrut of the swordfish in 1951, noting that he had examined it under a microscope and found no scales, and that Rabbi Benveniste must have permitted a different fish. Rabbi Tendler added that his distinguished father-in-law, Rabbi Moshe Feinstein, and his teacher, Rabbi Joseph B. Soloveitchik, agreed with his conclusions. However, another prominent student of Rabbi Soloveitchik, Rabbi Hershel Schachter, claims that his teacher in fact permitted swordfish! Be that as it may, based on Rabbi Tendler's research, many American kashrut agencies banned swordfish, a position affirmed by the prominent Israeli decisor Rabbi Eliezer Waldenburg (*Tzitz Eliezer* 9:40).

Not everyone agreed with Rabbi Tendler, though. Rabbi Isser Unterman (d. 1976), who later became Israel's chief rabbi, contended that swordfish indeed have scales while in water, and that, moreover, a 350-year-old tradition affirms that the fish is kosher (*Shevet MiYehuda* 2, p. 118). Zivotofsky further claims that Prof. Yehuda Felix, a widely respected researcher of biblical and talmudic science, currently identifies the swordfish as the fish permitted in a talmudic-era text (Tosefta Ḥullin 3:27), though his earlier article in the *Encyclopedia Talmudit* (7:201–6) equivocated.

The heated dispute within Orthodox circles took a new turn in the 1960s when Conservative Rabbi Isaac Klein published a sharp responsum affirming the tradition of permitting swordfish. According to Rabbi Klein, premier scientists had confirmed that juvenile swordfish possess scales. While both sides marshaled scientific and halakhic arguments, the debate now took on a polemical element that entrenched each position. To this day, the Conservative movement allows swordfish consumption, while Orthodox kashrut agencies in Israel and the United States forbid it. One hopes that Zivotofsky's continued research into the halakhic and scientific aspects of this dispute will allow for a calm and scholarly re-examination of this embattled fish.

Chapter 95

Kosher Birds

What are the signs?

The Torah provides detailed signs of kosher animals. Fish require fins and scales, while terrestrial mammals with four legs must have split hooves and chew their cud. Yet the Torah never explains how to identify kosher birds. Instead, it lists twenty-four classes of birds that may not be eaten (Lev. 11:13–19). While a few medieval commentators believed that other forbidden birds might exist (*Tosafot* Ḥullin 61a), it was widely assumed that any unlisted species remain permissible (MT *Hilkhot Maakhalot Asurot* 1:15). Unfortunately, we cannot definitively identify the biblically forbidden birds, making it difficult to classify the various species.

To resolve this conundrum, the sages enumerated four characteristics of kosher birds, which, unfortunately, led to conflicting interpretations and further dispute (Ḥullin 59a). First, a kosher bird is not a predator (*dores*). While the rabbis provided two physical indicators of predators (they spread two toes to each side while standing on a rope, and they can eat mid-flight), the medieval commentators continued to disagree on how to define predatory behavior (BY YD 82). Some focused on the method of killing, stating that predators either claw their prey to death or inject it with venom. Others highlighted the method of consumption, requiring the bird to hold its prey down with its claws and break off small pieces, or to consume the prey while it is alive.

The other three features of kosher birds are the following: an "extra" toe (sometimes a defensive spur, as chickens have); a peelable gizzard in the digestive tract; and a crop, a muscular food-storage pouch near the throat.

The commentators disagree if all four criteria are needed for the bird to be kosher, or if the presence of some (or all) of the last three indicate that the bird is not a predator (*Beit HaBeḥira* Ḥullin 61a). This confusion led a twelfth-century scholar, Rabbi Abraham ben Isaac of Narbonne, to bemoan, "We are groping and searching for God's word and not finding it" (*Sefer HaEshkol, Simanei Behema* 180a). This frustration, in truth, already existed in the talmudic period, when Jews errantly ate a non-kosher bird, causing much consternation (Ḥullin 62a). The Talmud further documents that acrimonious debates led those scholars who forbade a particular bird to declare that those who eat it will "pay the price" in the World to Come (65a).

To solve this problem, some scholars, including Rabbi Joseph Karo, sought to codify the normative characteristics of kosher birds (YD 82:2–3). These authorities also drew on other indicators found in rabbinic literature, including the shape of the bird's eggs (86:1). Yet Rabbi Karo himself also favored an established tradition to attest to the permissibility of a given species. This requirement was unequivocally adopted by Rabbi Moshe Isserles, who contended that we can never rely on identifying characteristics alone. One may, however, rely on the bona fide traditions of other locales (82:4).

Transmitting these traditions over the centuries and from place to place has been no simple matter. Before contemporary scientific categorization, it was very difficult to accurately depict (orally or in writing) a given bird, especially since bird names differ in various areas. While some scholars wrote pamphlets painstakingly classifying sundry birds and fowl, other rabbis felt that written lists were not helpful (*Darkhei Teshuva* 82:34).

As professors Zohar Amar and Ari Zivotofsky have brilliantly documented, there was a fascinating debate regarding the status of fowl discovered in the New World, such as turkey and the Muscovy duck, which lacked any tradition attesting to their permissibility (JHCS 46). One distinguished European scholar, Rabbi Shlomo Kluger (d. 1869), asserted that any bird originating in America cannot be kosher, since no Jews historically lived there to establish a tradition of kashrut (*HaElef*

Lekha Shlomo YD 112). This sentiment led some scholars to initially prohibit Muscovy duck, even as it gained popular acceptance and ultimately rabbinic sanction because it readily crossbreeds with kosher species, which, according to some talmudic interpretations, indicates that it is kosher (*Meshiv Davar* 2:22).

For some reason, turkey has been considered kosher without controversy for hundreds of years. Some asserted that its de facto consumption (*Meshiv Davar* 2:22) and similarity to chicken (*Dvar Halakha* 53) create a sufficient "tradition" of kashrut. Others even contended, though with much dissent, that the consumption of turkey proves that we may rely on the talmudic indicators without requiring a bona fide tradition (*Shu"t Maharam Schick* YD 98–100).

In any case, birds from the New World represent an interesting example of the intersection between ancient traditions and new discoveries.

Chapter 96

Yashan and *Ḥadash*

May Israelis eat grain products from outside Israel?

In addition to commemorating significant historical events connected to the Exodus, the Jewish pilgrimage holidays mark turning points in the agricultural year. Passover heralds the beginning of the spring harvest (*Ḥag Ha'Aviv*), which is marked by the Omer sacrifice of the first grains of barley on the festival's second day (Lev. 23:11). Shavuot marks the bringing of the first fruits (*Ḥag HaBikkurim*) with the obligation to offer two loaves of bread from the new wheat crop (23:16–17). On Sukkot (*Ḥag Ha'Asif*), at the end of the harvest season, we give thanks for all this produce and begin praying for rain for the coming year (23:39).

Regarding the Omer sacrifice, the Torah states: "Until that very day, until you have brought the offering of your God, you shall eat no bread or parched grain or fresh ears; it is a law for all time throughout the ages in all your settlements" (23:14). Many understood that this law prevents benefiting from the harvest before acknowledging God as its source (*Ḥinukh* 303).

Accordingly, grains of the five major species – wheat, barley, oats, rye, spelt – that took root before Passover may not be consumed until the Omer offering is brought during the holiday. While some believe these grains must be planted at least two weeks before Passover in order to be presumed to have taken root before the holiday, normative practice asserts that they need be planted only by the thirteenth of Nisan, giving them several days to take root (AH YD 293:7–9). Grain that *didn't* take root before Passover may not be consumed until the Omer offering is brought the *following* Passover. (One may benefit from this grain, however, such as by feeding it to animals.) This produce is colloquially known as *ḥadash*, "new."

The difficulties of *ḥadash* are minimized in Israel (and other Mediterranean countries), since its agricultural cycle has only a single winter harvest. Farmers plant in the fall, and most crops are harvested around Passover, hitting the market only after the holiday. Yet in much of the Diaspora – including Yemen, North America, and many countries in Europe – a large percentage of the crop grows during the summer, with the seeding taking place after Passover (especially when the festival occurs early on the Gregorian calendar).

This timing poses no problem according to those talmudic sages who asserted that the proscription of *ḥadash* applies only to grains grown in the Land of Israel, as do many mitzvot related to agriculture (Kiddushin 36b). Other sages, however, apply the prohibition worldwide, as implied by the conclusion of the aforementioned verse: "in all your settlements" (Orla 3:9). While another position relegates *ḥadash* outside of Eretz Yisrael to a rabbinic prohibition, thereby potentially allowing for leniency if necessary, the Talmud does not determine which of these views is the law (Menaḥot 68b).

Maimonides (MT *Hilkhot Maakhalot Asurot* 10:4) and many other medieval Spanish scholars, followed by Rabbi Joseph Karo (OḤ 489:10), asserted that this prohibition applies to all lands. As Rabbi Binyamin Lau has documented, this ruling was not a problem in Spain, since its agricultural cycle approximates that of Eretz Yisrael, whereas Yemenite scholars – loyal to Maimonides' code – lamented that the masses consumed products in a marketplace dependent on grains planted after Passover.

Rabbinic authorities in northern Europe also struggled with this dilemma, which was accentuated by the region's widespread beer consumption. Some, like Rabbi Meir Rothenburg (*Hagahot Maimoniyot Maakhalot Asurot* 10:4) and Rabbenu Asher (*Shu"t HaRosh* 2:1), privately behaved stringently but refrained from condemning the masses who acted otherwise. Following earlier scholars, Rabbi Moshe Isserles contended that because grain sources varied, one could assume he was partaking of a previous year's harvest or of crops planted before Passover (*Shu"t HaRema* 132). Recognizing the socioeconomic pressure to consume any available grain, Rabbi Isserles added that one should not condemn those who acted inappropriately (YD 293:3).

The lenient practice, however, was buttressed by two additional arguments. Some argued that *ḥadash* outside of Eretz Yisrael was only a rabbinic decree applying to areas with climates similar to its own (AH YD 293:5–6, 20–23). Alternatively, Rabbi Yoel Sirkes (seventeenth century, Poland) maintained, unlike earlier scholars (*Tosafot* Kiddushin 36b), that the *ḥadash* prohibition does not apply to grains grown by a non-Jew (*Shu"t HaBaḥ* 42). While many strongly disagreed – including his own son-in-law (*Taz* YD 293:3) as well as the Vilna Gaon – this position was supported by others (*Mishkenot Yaakov* YD 67) and celebrated by the Baal Shem Tov as a laudatory defense of popular practice.

While some urged the pious to act stringently (MB 489:45), this was clearly not the widespread practice for many centuries. In recent decades, some rabbinic figures have contended that given the global food supply, we should stop relying upon these dispensations, which were issued in times of socioeconomic necessity. This argument is particularly popular in Israel, where stores may import *ḥadash* products from around the world, despite *ḥadash* restrictions imposed on local food producers. Others, however, retort that the lenient position is entrenched within the legal canon and need not be challenged. Thus, whether in Israel or the Diaspora, Jews may consume grains grown from around the world without fear of transgression.

Chapter 97

Gelatin and Milk

Why are many products labeled kosher for some but not others?

In principle, if a product is kosher, it should be permissible for all. However, as in other areas of Jewish law, there are disputes over certain ingredients and industrial processes. Occasionally, these disagreements stem from differences between Ashkenazim and Sephardim, such as with *kitniyot* (legumes) on Passover or the necessity of meat being glatt kosher. More complex disputes, however, relate to gelatin and milk.

Gelatin is a protein substance derived from animal collagen, the tissue that connects bones, tendons, and skin. It is a valuable industrial ingredient because it binds while remaining transparent, flexible, and digestible. Gelatin is used in medicines ("gelcaps"), drinks, yogurts, and other products, but it is most famous as the ingredient that contributes to the silkiness of desserts such as marshmallows, chocolates, and Jell-O (the name stems from this central ingredient).

Classically, gelatin came from the skin and bones of non-kosher animals, such as pigs or animals that were slaughtered inappropriately (*neveila*). Though Rabbi Chaim Ozer Grodzenski contemplated whether hard, dry bones of non-kosher animals were permissible (*Aḥiezer* 3:33, para. 5), most gelatin derives from skin or soft bones that still contain meat and marrow.

Several decisors declared gelatin permissible because of its complex production process, which includes boiling water, acids, and heat.

Rabbi Tzvi Pesaḥ Frank contended that since the substance becomes inedible ("like dry wood") during this process, it loses its status as a non-kosher product (*Har Tzvi* YD 83). Alternatively, Rabbis Ovadia Yosef (*Yabia Omer* YD 8:11) and Eliezer Waldenburg (*Tzitz Eliezer* 4, introduction) contended that the raw material is radically altered by the process, thereby giving it a new identity (*panim ḥadashot*).

These claims were strongly challenged by Rabbi Aharon Kotler, who deemed gelatin absolutely forbidden, since its use as a central ingredient revitalized its original identity as a prohibited food (*Mishnat Rabbi Aharon* 1:16). Fellow American decisors Rabbis Moshe Feinstein (IM YD 1:37, 2:27) and Yosef E. Henkin, while more moderate in their opposition, ultimately considered the production process insufficient to negate gelatin's non-kosher origins.

The Israeli Chief Rabbinate relies on the lenient opinions in issuing its basic (but not *mehadrin*) kosher certification, yet labels products permissible only for those who consume gelatin. Most American kashrut organizations do not certify standard gelatin products, but do permit a relatively recent form of gelatin made from kosher animals. Its use remains somewhat limited, however, because of the additional costs of producing this material. Even within the stringent group, many decisors allow medicinal gelcaps (*Edut LeYisrael* p. 177).

On a related note, all milk from kosher animals should theoretically be permissible, no matter who performs the milking. The sages, however, feared that non-kosher milk (from camels or horses, for example) might get mixed with kosher milk, and therefore decreed that milking must be performed or supervised by a Jew (Avoda Zara 35b). As such, unsupervised milk (*ḥalav akum*) is considered non-kosher (YD 115:1).

In the seventeenth century, Rabbi Ḥizkia de Silva declared such supervision unnecessary in areas where non-kosher milk was not produced. While this leniency received much support (*Shu"t HaRadbaz* 4:74), it was challenged by many scholars, including Rabbi Moshe Sofer, who contended that the sages allowed no exceptions to their decree, which itself was made to prevent a remote possibility (*Ḥatam Sofer* YD 2:107). Historically, various communities adopted different positions on this question (*Darkhei Teshuva* 115:6).

As milk production became more industrialized and mass-produced in the twentieth century, Rabbi Feinstein issued a landmark responsum contending that governmental regulation and inspection (including severe penalties) provided sufficient supervision, though inspectors oversee the process only at production dairies, not on the actual farms (IM YD 1:47–49). While this position was endorsed by Rabbi Joseph B. Soloveitchik and most American kashrut organizations, other decisors, like Rabbi Yosef, required Jewish supervision at all stages (*Yeḥaveh Daat* 4:42). Some also feared that any leniency would lead to the neglect of the law in locales where there are careless inspectors or where non-kosher milk is readily available, such as in parts of Eastern Europe (*Ḥelkat Yaakov* YD 3:37). When available, Rabbi Feinstein himself advocated using supervised milk, which has become increasingly prevalent in Diaspora communities.

Given the preponderance of dairies in Israel, the Israeli Chief Rabbinate rejects this leniency and requires Jewish supervision at all factories (*Tchumin* 23), even as it reluctantly accepts the more moderate dispensation of Rabbi Frank (*Har Tzvi* YD 103–4) with respect to powdered milk. American dairy products imported into Israel, however, frequently rely on this lenient opinion, and therefore bear a Hebrew label stating that they are kosher only according to certain standards.

Section VIII

Jewish Identity and Marriage

Chapter 98

Conversion Standards

May one convert with the intention of not being fully observant?

Controversies over appropriate standards for conversion to Judaism have abounded since the Enlightenment and continue to proliferate today. Medieval Jewry did not struggle with this issue, since observance of halakha was a given, certainly for a proselyte. This combination of religious and social norms followed the model of Ruth, who declared to her mother-in-law Naomi, "Your people shall by my people, and your God shall be my God" (Ruth 1:16). (Conversion to a minority religion whose adherents regularly suffered persecution was also relatively rare, especially in countries that banned converting to Judaism.) Modern Jewish life, with its variety of cultural lifestyles in open societies, has undone this norm, launching great debates within the rabbinic world. This has been particularly true in recent years in the State of Israel, where many fully integrated Israelis of Jewish ancestry from the former Soviet Union and elsewhere have immigrated under the Law of Return, though they are not Jewish under halakha because they were not born to Jewish mothers.

The formal conversion procedure is fairly simple: immersion in a *mikve* (*tevilla*), circumcision for men, and in Temple times, an animal sacrifice (Keritot 8b–9a). The essential criterion for conversion, however, remains the commitment to perform the commandments, and for the right reasons (Yevamot 46b–48a). The sages, for example, did not want people to convert for financial or political gain or for the sake of marriage

(Yevamot 24b). A potential convert was warned of the hardships Jews might suffer, as well as the punishments if they sin. Once deemed sincere, they were taught various elements of Jewish law (*hodaat mitzvot*) and were required to accept the yoke of Heaven (*kabbalat mitzvot*). Maimonides added that they be instructed in the theological underpinnings of Judaism as well, a requirement not specified by the Talmud (MT *Hilkhot Issurei Biah* 14:2).

This conception of conversion raises a problem with converting children, who presumably cannot take on this responsibility. The Talmud, however, asserts that the rabbinic court serves as their guardian and can accept this categorical benefit for them (Ketubbot 11a). Once the children reach the age of majority, they can reject their Jewishness, but they are presumed to consent if they continue practicing Judaism.

This paternalistic approach was challenged in the modern era, lest child converts be raised in non-observant homes, thereby setting them up to sin and be liable for punishment. Rabbis Abraham Isaac Kook (*Daat Kohen* 147–48) and Yosef Shalom Elyashiv (*Kovetz Teshuvot* YD 2:55) contended that the court may not convert a child unless it is confident that he or she will grow up to be religious. While agreeing that the fulfillment of this condition is preferable, Rabbi Chaim Ozer Grodzenski felt that it remains meritorious for a child to convert, as long as she will be generally observant, for although she may sin, she will accrue many benefits (*Aḥiezer* 3:26–28).

Rabbi Ovadia Yosef believed in converting children from non-observant homes if their parents undertook to educate them in a religious setting, making them likely to become fully observant (*Yabia Omer* EH 2:3–4). This position was shared by Rabbi Moshe Feinstein, who further contemplated the possibility that it is always meritorious for the child to enjoy the sanctity of the Jewish people, while her sins will be exculpated because she acts out of ignorance (IM EH 4:26). On this basis, Rabbi Nachum Rabinovitch and others have advocated conversion programs (with parental consent) for the many non-Jewish Israeli children (usually children of immigrants) enrolled in religious Israeli primary schools. This proposal, however, has not received widespread interest.

A more complex case involves adult conversions in which the court doubts the convert's intent to become fully observant. The Talmud asserts that if a potential convert accepts all but one aspect of Jewish law, the court should reject him (Bekhorot 30b). As such, many decisors, including Rabbi Feinstein, have argued that converts must commit to full observance (IM YD 1:157).

To prevent intermarriage, Rabbi Grodzenski leniently permitted conversion as long as the convert intends to observe basic Jewish law, even if he will fall short in many areas. This decisor's reasoning – that the Talmud excluded only those who explicitly intended to disregard certain laws – was more radically applied by Rabbi David Tzvi Hoffman. Again to prevent intermarriage, he allowed a non-Jewish woman to convert, though her husband was a *kohen* and thus prohibited from marrying her (*Melamed Leho'il* EH 3:8). Other scholars, such as Rabbi Avraham Kahane-Shapiro, criticized these rulings as unfounded hairsplitting and burying one's head in the sand (*Dvar Avraham* 3:28).

Most lenient was Rabbi Ben-Zion Uziel, who asserted that even if we know a potential convert will not be fully observant, we can accept a generic commitment to Jewish law and hope he will eventually become observant (*Piskei Uziel BeShe'elot HaZeman* 65). This approach has been advocated by such contemporary Israeli figures as Rabbi Chaim Amsallem, who want to preserve the Jewish identity of Israelis who have Jewish lineage (*zera Yisrael*) and are fully integrated into Israeli society, though they are not halakhically Jewish.

Nonetheless, most decisors have rejected this position, even as they debate what level of observance we must demand. Many religious Zionist scholars have contended that while we require an intensive educational program prior to conversion, followed by a genuine declaration of mitzva acceptance at the time of immersion, the court may proceed even if it anticipates only the level of observance found among traditional Israelis. These thinkers believe that relatively low conversion standards are imperative to prevent intermarriage and the division of the Jewish people within the State of Israel. Toward this goal, programs have been established to help soldiers convert within the living structure of the army, where basic Shabbat and kashrut observance are maintained. However, other decisors, particularly but not exclusively within the *ḥaredi* sector, have rejected such programs, leaving conversion standards a matter of divisive debate.

Chapter 99

Nullifying Conversions

Can a court revoke a proselyte's status?

In 2008, Israel became embroiled in its most recent conversion controversy after a senior rabbinic court headed by Rabbi Avraham Sherman nullified a conversion performed by a different court of the Israeli rabbinate, and further called into question thousands of conversions performed in the context of the Israeli army and special conversion courses established by the state and overseen by Rabbi Ḥayim Druckman. While various lawsuits, Supreme Court rulings, and agreements with Sephardic Chief Rabbi Shlomo Amar have partially neutralized that decision, it raised larger questions regarding conversion standards (discussed in the previous essay) and one court's power to nullify another's decision.

A *beit din* cannot whimsically declare a legitimate conversion null and void. Unlike a country club, whose board can revoke membership rights, no legislative body can simply declare a convert non-Jewish once he has properly undergone conversion. The question is what constitutes "properly undergoing conversion," and what happens when a conversion is performed under non-ideal circumstances.

Sometimes the problems are easily rectified, such as if the convert did not immerse in a *mikve* or undergo circumcision. Other times, the entire conversion is invalidated, which nullifies any marriage the convert entered into with a Jew. Such is the case with non-Orthodox conversions, which, as Rabbis Moshe Feinstein (IM YD 1:157) and Yaakov Ariel (*Tchumin* 17) have argued, are halakhically unacceptable, because the movements behind them reject basic Jewish theological and legal axioms. To accommodate all sensitivities, the Ne'eman Commission established conversion schools composed of teachers from the various streams of Judaism, even as the formal court remained exclusively Orthodox. This process, however, has achieved limited support and success.

Matters have become particularly complex regarding conversions done under Orthodox purview but according to disputed standards. The Talmud states that one should not accept converts for the sake of marriage, or when the Jewish people flourishes politically or economically, as under Kings David and Solomon, as these newcomers might primarily seek to reap the material benefits of citizenship (Yevamot 24b). For this reason, the Cutheans and others were rejected as Jews, since they attempted to join the Jewish people for political gain while remaining idol worshippers (II Kings 17:33). Commentators therefore questioned how Persians joined the Jewish people once Mordekhai and Esther gained the upper hand against Haman (Est. 8:17), with some scholars asserting that they never formally converted (*Tosafot* Yevamot 24b).

The talmudic sages debated what happens if such a conversion takes place under these non-ideal circumstances. While R. Neḥemia deemed the procedure invalid, the rabbinic majority concluded that, after the fact, the conversion remains valid (Yevamot 24b). Elsewhere the Talmud asserts that even if the convert begins sinning, he remains a Jew (albeit a sinful one) and is treated like other sinful Jews (Bekhorot 30b). On this basis, Maimonides ruled that Samson and King Solomon remained married to their convert wives even though these women strayed from observance (MT *Hilkhot Issurei Biah* 13:17).

Nonetheless, those who present themselves to the court under false pretenses can have their conversions nullified because of fraud. In the 1970s, for example, Rabbi Betzalel Zolty invalidated a conversion after the court discovered that the converts were Christian missionaries seeking to infiltrate into Israel via the Law of Return (*Torah SheBe'al Peh*, vol. 13). More recently, Rabbi Yisrael Rozen, then head of Israel's special conversion courts, nullified a conversion after the Interior Ministry discovered that the convert had been romantically involved with a gentile throughout and after the conversion process (*Tchumin* 23).

The most controversial conversion nullification took place in 1972. Overruling several courts, IDF Chief Rabbi Shlomo Goren nullified the (undocumented) conversion of a distinctly non-observant Polish man that had allegedly taken place thirty years earlier. His Jewish wife had subsequently left him without obtaining a divorce, and then remarried and had two children. By invalidating his conversion, Rabbi Goren also invalidated the first marriage, which legalized the "second." This ruling was celebrated by many politicians because it allowed her children to marry without the stigma of *mamzerut* (bastardy). Yet it was derided by many rabbinic scholars, including Rabbi Yosef Shalom Elyashiv, as logically flawed and against all protocol. Regardless of who was right, this case shows that scholars across a wide ideological spectrum believe that in very limited circumstances, a conversion may be nullified, even as this move has historically been extremely rare.

The recent controversy relates to conversion standards and who determines them. Rabbi Sherman asserted that Israeli population registries must follow the ruling of leading *ḥaredi* decisors, including Rabbis Elyashiv and Elazar Shach, who had declared that any conversion lacking full-fledged commitment to observance was meaningless (*Tchumin* 31). He further contended that a convert's fidelity to halakha (*kabbalat mitzvot*) remains subject to future scrutiny and that his court had supervisory jurisdiction over all others in the state's system.

This assertion was sharply criticized by Rabbi Shlomo Dichovsky, who contended that we do not endlessly badger converts with examinations of their behavior (*Tchumin* 29). Others further declared that the state's conversion courts followed standards acceptable to many decisors while promoting Zionist interests, as discussed in the previous essay. As such, this controversy quickly became a battle over control of the rabbinate and its vision for the future.

Chapter 100

Converting Out of Judaism

Am I Jewish if my Jewish mother converted to Christianity before I was born?

Frequent apostasy, often forced, propelled the status of apostates into one of medieval Jewry's most significant controversies. Scholars struggled to define Jewishness in a manner that recognized the sociological implications of apostasy yet preserved the inborn nature of Jewish identity.

Three major positions developed in rabbinic sources. The first, a distinctly minority opinion, contended that an apostate loses his status as a Jew. Proponents of this view highlighted the talmudic declaration that descendants of the ten lost tribes of Israel were to be considered gentiles (Yevamot 17a). Accordingly, once apostates become "completely absorbed into their surroundings," they lose their Jewish status. Consequently, a spouse deserted by such a person does not require a *get* (divorce writ) to remarry, since their initial marriage automatically dissolves (*Beit HaBeḥira* Yevamot 16b).

Despite this potential benefit, the vast majority of scholars contended that apostasy cannot rescind Jewish identity. Regarding the national sin of the Golden Calf, the Talmud declares, "Even though [the people] have sinned, they are still [called] Israel" (Sanhedrin 44a). Rashi applied this principle to individual sinners as well. Support for this position may be found in the Talmud's assertion that even a genuine convert who later adopts a different religion remains Jewish (Yevamot 47b).

From this perspective, the lost tribes represent a unique case, addressing the historic exile of a whole community that no longer maintains viable pedigree. In general, however, Jewish identity is inalienable. An apostate, no matter how distant he becomes from his people and its traditions, remains part of the Jewish nation.

Many scholars took a middle position, agreeing with Rashi regarding matters of personal status, but denying the apostate other legal privileges. As Rabbi Aharon Lichtenstein and Prof. Yaakov Blidstein have documented, several medieval rabbis ruled that an apostate forfeits his inheritance (*Shu"t HaRosh* 17:10), and others permitted Jews to charge him interest on loans, usually prohibited to fellow Jews (*Sefer HaYashar, Ḥiddushim* 743).

Nonetheless, regarding the central question of personal status, most scholars ruled that the apostate retains his Jewishness. On the one hand, this position eased his path to repentance. Especially in cases of forced conversions, rabbis permitted remorseful apostates to return to the community immediately, and at most required only a symbolic immersion in a *mikve* or other minor penance. On the other hand, this ruling sometimes tragically stranded women as *agunot* (abandoned wives unable to marry) if their technically still-Jewish husbands – fully absorbed into frequently hostile non-Jewish society – would not issue them a formal divorce allowing them to remarry.

A few sages took an interesting fourth position that directly addresses this question. They contended that while the apostate remains a Jew, we treat his children as gentiles. This approach, sometimes attributed to the author of *Halakhot Gedolot* (eighth century), might stem from the children's assimilation at birth into gentile culture. Rabbi Yaakov ibn Habib (sixteenth century) gave a different explanation, postulating that while the apostate was "conceived and born in holiness" to faithful Jews, his children, the offspring of sinners, were not (*Shu"t HaRe'em Mizraḥi* 47).

Yet few accepted this opinion, contending that the "holiness" of Jewish identity granted at birth stems from formal biological criteria, not parents' spiritual commitment. As long as their biological mother was Jewish, the children of apostates retain their Jewish identity, and require no formal conversion process should they return to the fold (*Pitḥei*

Teshuva YD 268:10). In the case where one's mother has converted to Christianity before his birth, his Jewishness would be affirmed by the overwhelming majority of rabbis.

One notable exception is Rabbi Moshe Feinstein, who ruled that a child born to a non-Jewish father and an apostate mother requires full conversion (IM EH 1:8). Although Rabbi Feinstein creatively advocates this position in a fascinating excursus (*Dibrot Moshe* Yevamot 1:13), the rabbinic consensus rejects this opinion (*Tzitz Eliezer* 13:93). Therefore, our case would not erupt into rabbinic and interdenominational disputes regarding conversion standards.

However, one who is born into the Christian community will need to prove his or her mother's Jewishness. As with all cases of personal status, a local rabbi should be consulted to certify one's Jewish lineage in order to prevent any future doubts.

Chapter 101

Karaites

Are they considered Jews? May a Jew marry a Karaite?

The status of Karaites intrigues all visitors to Jerusalem's Old City when they pass by the ancient Karaite synagogue next to Yeshivat Hakotel. The restored synagogue, overseen by the Old City's single Karaite family, was built between the tenth and twelfth centuries, in the heyday of Karaism. While the majority of today's thirty thousand adherents – mostly of Egyptian origin – live in Israel (primarily in Ashdod and Ramle), the Karaites once comprised a noteworthy minority of the Jewish people in places like Persia, Spain, and Egypt. They produced a rich literature of biblical interpretation, grammar texts, and legal works, although much of it is no longer extant.

Historians usually attribute the founding of Karaism to Anan ben David, an eighth-century Babylonian Jew who opposed the authority of the Babylonian Talmud and the Oral Law. Like the Sadducees and Boethesians before him, Anan rejected rabbinic Judaism, which contradicted, to his mind, the plain sense of the Torah. Nonetheless, different Scriptural interpretations led to various Karaite practices and communities. Yet there were some uniform characteristics, particularly regarding the calendar. The sect follows a lunar-based calendar rather than the intercalated rabbinic one. Karaites also do not mark the post-biblical holidays of Purim and Ḥanukka. Most famously, they celebrate the holiday of Shavuot on a different date than Rabbanites. In the context of Passover, the Torah commands us to declare a holiday seven weeks "from the day after the Sabbath" (Lev. 23:15, 21). The Karaites take this verse literally, celebrating Shavuot on the seventh Sunday after Passover. The sages, in contrast, understood the "Sabbath" here as the first day of Passover, which resembles Shabbat in its ban on creative labor. They therefore established Shavuot on 6 Sivan, seven weeks from the second day of Passover.

Other differences include variances in rituals and dietary laws. Most Karaites eat meat and milk together, since the Torah explicitly forbids only boiling a sheep in its mother's milk. They deny the mitzva of *tefillin*, since they interpret Scripture's ordinance that "These words shall be on your heart ... bind them for a sign upon your hand ... and between your eyes" (Deut. 6:6, 8) as a metaphor beseeching Jews to absorb the Torah's message, not to wear a scroll on one's head and heart. Similarly, the Karaites do not affix *mezuzot* to their doorposts.

Given these major differences in ritual, one might deem it impossible for observant Jews to marry faithful Karaites, even if the latter technically remain Jews. Indeed, in the earliest responsum on this topic, Rabbi Natronai Gaon (ninth century, Persia) rules that one may not marry a Karaite who maintains his beliefs (*Otzar HaGeonim* Yevamot, p. 113). Yet Prof. Simḥa Assaf has proven that Karaites and Rabbanites – who often lived in the same areas – did indeed intermarry, frequently with complex marriage contracts (*ketubbot*) stipulating respect for each other's religious practices.

Nonetheless, as professors Michael Corinaldi and Yaakov Shapiro have documented, two mainstream rabbinic positions emerged regarding the status of Karaites, both of which demanded that Karaites fully accept halakha. According to the more lenient opinion, exemplified by Maimonides, Jews raised in a Karaite home – like infants taken captive by non-Jews – cannot be punished for their wayward behavior (MT *Hilkhot Mamrim* 3:2–3). If they repent, they are to be embraced. Indeed, in the early fourteenth century, Rabbi Ishtori HaParchi noted that a large group of Egyptian Karaites had adopted rabbinic practices and fully assimilated into the community.

The more stringent position questions whether Karaite descendants may marry other Jews. Noting that Karaites failed to write proper divorce documents, a certain medieval Rabbi Shimshon (whose identity is disputed) ruled that we must treat all Karaites as potentially illegitimate offspring (*safek mamzerim*) of illicit second marriages, and therefore they may not marry into the mainstream community (EH 4:37). Many Ashkenazic decisors adopted this opinion, while Sephardic rabbis tended to allow Jews to marry repentant Karaites, although exceptions to this generalization exist in both directions.

A later and more extreme Ashkenazic position that ironically opened the door for leniency was proposed by Rabbi Yaakov Emden (eighteenth century). He contended that after centuries of living among non-Jews and not practicing rabbinic Judaism, Karaites were no longer Jews (*She'elat Yaavetz* 2:152). As non-Jews, they no longer retained their blemished lineage, and like any other gentile, could convert to Judaism by accepting (Rabbanite) mitzvot, and thereby marry a Jew!

In the twentieth century, the State of Israel allowed Karaites to immigrate to Israel under the Law of Return. The rabbinate, however, remains sharply divided over Karaite marriage to Jews. While prominent Ashkenazic Rabbis Avraham Sherman (*Tchumin* 19) and Eliezer Waldenburg (*Tzitz Eliezer* 5:16) denounced such unions, two former Sephardic chief rabbis, Ovadia Yosef (*Yabia Omer* EH 8:12) and Eliyahu Bakshi-Doron (*Tchumin* 18, 20) were lenient, especially when Karaite descendants had no loyalty toward their ancestors' rituals. While such cases do not make the headlines, they nonetheless represent a fascinating chapter in the ongoing struggles over personal status and marriage in Israel.

Chapter 102

Intermarriage

Where in the Bible is it prohibited?

To preserve their membership and transmit their values to future generations, many faiths ban or limit intermarriage. Orthodox Christian churches, for example, forbid marriage to those who have not undergone baptism. Other groups allow intermarriage if subsequent children will be raised in their faith, while some practice exogamy, whereby men may marry non-believers (on the assumption that the husband will determine the family's faith), while women may not.

Jewish intermarriage regularly makes the news due to high-profile interfaith marriages, including that of a Jew to Chelsea Clinton in a ceremony that included Jewish rites. This phenomenon highlights the general acceptance and assimilation of American Jewry, as well as the global trends of pluralism and multiculturalism. One might view these developments as the culmination of the Enlightenment, beginning with Napoleon's 1806 demand that Jews drop their ban on marrying gentiles, even as the "Sanhedrin" of scholars he assembled insisted that these marriages would not be recognized under Jewish law.

Since its 1844 Braunschweig convention, the Reform movement has permitted intermarriage if the government allows the child to be raised as a Jew, even as the movement officially discouraged it, at least until recent years, by forbidding rabbinic participation in interfaith nuptials. While intermarriage has increased exponentially in the last few decades, a recent study of American university students sponsored by the Hillel Foundation shows that few children born of these unions identify themselves as Jews (37 percent of those with a Jewish mother, 15 percent of those with a Jewish father).

The Bible condemns intermarriage as a threat to monotheism, lest Jews be corrupted by pagan spouses (Ex. 34:15–16). These fears are supported by many biblical stories, including those describing the illicit relations of Israelite kings. The prophets Ezra (9:2) and Nehemiah (13:23–28) fought such marriages, as did scholars in the Maccabean era. Additionally, particular prohibitions focus on marrying members of nations that historically mistreated ours (Deut. 23:4, 8).

While the Torah explicitly prohibits marriage to members of the seven nations who occupied the Land of Israel (Deut. 7:3) before the Israelite conquest, the sages debated whether this proscription includes all gentiles, or if a rabbinic edict expanded the prohibition (Avoda Zara 36b). While Rabbi Yaakov ben Asher followed the latter opinion (*Tur* EH 16), Maimonides, citing Nehemiah, codified the view that marital relations (indicating some form of commitment) with a non-Jew violate a biblical prohibition, while more casual liaisons come under the rabbinic edict (MT *Hilkhot Issurei Biah* 12:1). The rabbis specifically banned relations between a Jewish male and a non-Jewish female during the Maccabean period, when Hellenism generated tremendous assimilation (Sanhedrin 82a). Some further assert that casual intercourse with a non-Jew violates the general biblical prohibition of licentiousness (*Shu"t Maharam Schick* EH 37, 155). All agree, however, that any nuptials between a Jew and a non-Jew are not legally binding (EH 44:8).

One biblical story that highlights the severity of the prohibition of intermarriage concerns Pinḥas' execution of Zimri for publicly consorting with the Midianite princess Cozbi (Num. 25:6–8). The Talmud (Sanhedrin 82a) justifies Pinḥas' extra-judicial behavior in order to eradicate such debauchery (*kana'im poge'im bo*). (The commentators debate whether the openness of the depravity was what mandated Zimri's punishment [*Beit Shmuel* EH 16:4]; marriage, because of its pronounced nature, certainly constitutes a public relationship [*Kitvei Maharatz Chajes* 2, p. 996].) While the sages severely limited such zeal and ultimately deemed it improper to be taught publicly (*halakha ve'ein morin ken*), it nonetheless demonstrates the severity of this illicit behavior, which is punishable by spiritual excommunication (EH 16:2). Indeed, the Talmud homiletically condemns men who consort with gentile women as unworthy of their circumcision, i.e., their mark of Jewishness (Eiruvin 19a). As such, many talmudic edicts, especially relating to dietary norms, were enacted to prevent excessive social intermingling (Avoda Zara 35b).

The modern phenomenon of intermarriage has caused a recent development in conversion laws. According to halakha, a person may not convert for the sake of marriage, since this ulterior motive might indicate insincere acceptance of Judaism (YD 268:12). Yet in the modern era, Jews seeking to marry gentiles can do so civilly, or easily convert to their partners' religion.

Given those possibilities, Rabbis Shlomo Kluger, Chaim Ozer Grodzenski (*Aḥiezer* 3:26–28), and Moshe Feinstein (IM YD 3:109, para. 3) permitted the spouse to convert, on condition that other conversion requirements (including a commitment to Jewish law) are met. Some have further contended that if the couple is already civilly married, we do not deem this a conversion for marriage, since they live together anyway; others, however, retort that via conversion they will now enjoy the social sanction given to their matrimony (*Seridei Esh* 2:75). While Rabbis Abraham Isaac Kook (*Daat Kohen* 155) and Eliezer Waldenburg (*Tzitz Eliezer* 5:15) sternly warned that this deviation from talmudic norms would only encourage intermarriage, most rabbis today advocate conversion in this situation, highlighting the complex ways in which intermarriage has impacted contemporary Jewish life.

Chapter 103

Non-Jews in Jewish Cemeteries

May a gentile be buried next to his or her Jewish spouse?

In many societies, burial grounds convey cultural affinities, including familial, tribal, socioeconomic, and national ties. Because of urbanization, the modern era has seen a shift from catacombs and local graveyards to larger cemeteries, as well as the professionalization of burial and cemetery services, with people buying plots in which to be laid to rest.

Within Jewish communities, a *ḥevra kaddisha* (holy society) ensures that all corpses receive proper purification (*tahara*) and burial, and it sets aside graves exclusively for its community's members. Frequently attached to synagogues, organizations, or guilds, membership in the *ḥevra kaddisha* is reserved for Jews. This practice has been attributed to biblical times, as Ruth notes that her conversion will warrant burial with her new nation (*Targum Rut* 1:17).

Exclusivity, however, should not be mistaken for indifference toward non-Jewish corpses. Within a list of kindnesses extended to gentiles for the sake of peace, the Talmud states, "We must bury the non-Jewish dead along with the Jewish dead" (Gittin 61a). Nahmanides (Deut. 21:22) points out that Joshua insisted on burying the defeated Canaanite kings (Josh. 10:27), implying that the abandonment of any corpse violates a biblical prohibition (*Minḥat Ḥinukh* 537:3).

Yet this talmudic imperative does not include burial in the same cemetery as Jews (Rashba, Gittin 61a). Some commentators contend that the designation of a Jewish cemetery stems from a legal opinion that requires separate burial areas within the Jewish community itself (Ran, Gittin; 28a in Rif).

The Talmud asserts that one should not bury an evil person next to a righteous one (Sanhedrin 47a). Subsequent halakhic authorities deduced from here that people should be buried next to those of similar religious stature; the very pious, for example, should be separated from those less saintly (YD 362:5). The Talmud even states that there were two cemeteries for executed criminals, with placement dependent on the severity of the death penalty each received.

While Rabbis Moshe Sofer (*Ḥatam Sofer* YD 2:341) and Abraham Isaac Kook (*Daat Kohen* 201) believed that burial according to spiritual level was biblically mandated, earlier sources deem the practice a mystical custom (*Minhagei Maharil* Semaḥot 10), and Maimonides omits it entirely. In any case, it was not always observed (*Minḥat Elazar* 2:41), perhaps because of the difficulty in determining the relative righteousness of each person. Those whose sins warranted social sanctions were sometimes buried separately, but any Jew other than an apostate retains the right to be buried within a Jewish cemetery (*Tzitz Eliezer* 10:41:2).

In modern times, burial in such a cemetery becomes more complicated due to greater social intermingling and the existence of "hyphenated identities" with competing cultural affiliations. The State of Israel has encountered this challenge, especially in burying non-Jewish soldiers and citizens, such as Amos Yarkoni in 1991 (*Yabia Omer* YD 7:36). Subtle, sometimes controversial separations have been created, with non-Jewish graves placed at the edge of the cemetery or separated from their neighbors by decorative bushes. Rabbi Yehuda Shaviv, citing a potential talmudic precedent (Bava Batra 10a), has suggested that this practice may not be necessary in military cemeteries, which are built for the burial of comrades in arms without distinction (*Tchumin* 14). This idea was also endorsed by Rabbi Shlomo Goren (*Tchumin* 26), who noted a seventeenth-century opinion that allows Jews and non-Jews who died together to be buried in the same courtyard (*Baḥ* YD 151).

While the Reform movement allowed for interfaith interment in the early twentieth century, the American Conservative movement recently authorized separate sections within Jewish cemeteries for interfaith couples, reflecting the growing social pressure of intermarriage within that denomination.

Orthodoxy, with its unwavering opposition to intermarriage, has maintained that intermarried Jews should be buried with Jews of similar religious character (*Kolbo al Aveilut* 1:194). Non-Jewish spouses or offspring are not permitted burial within the Jewish cemetery (*Melamed Leho'il* YD 2:127). Therefore, following pressure from political parties supported by immigrants from the former Soviet Union, former Israeli Chief Rabbis Yisrael Meir Lau and Eliyahu Bakshi-Doron allowed intermarried Jewish spouses to be interred, upon request, in non-Jewish cemeteries (*Tchumin* 17). When a cemetery is controlled by those who allow for interfaith interments, Rabbi Moshe Feinstein demanded that a separate section, cordoned off by a low wall, be created for those who wished to follow classical burial rules (IM YD 3:147).

As documented by Rabbi Moshe Yeres (*Tradition* 23:3), an equally complex case involves non-Jews who died before completing their conversion. Most decisors allow their burial within a Jewish cemetery, at least ex post facto. More controversial, however, is the burial of converts who are not accepted as such by Orthodox standards. Rabbi Yeḥiel Yaakov Weinberg insisted that such people be buried in a separate section (*Seridei Esh* 2:99), yet Rabbi Feinstein contended that one should not engage in a divisive fight over the matter, but should merely ensure that more traditionalist Jews be buried elsewhere (IM YD 1:160). These rulings highlight the complex social dynamic of cemeteries, symbolically marking how Jews remain both united and divided, even in death.

Chapter 104

Non-Marital Sexual Relations

Are they always forbidden?

In various forums, ranging from conferences about the "singles crisis" to the Israeli TV show *Serugim,* the religious community has begun to confront the regrettable phenomenon of pre-marital relations. Despite the understandable emotional hardships, particularly for older singles, the arguments to bypass the halakhic restrictions against this behavior have failed to gain rabbinic support, and for good reason.

While the Torah explicitly commands us to procreate (Gen. 1:28), it never definitively demands marriage. While many biblical narratives relate to this institution (including levirate relationships), marriage and divorce laws appear only indirectly (Deut. 24:1–4). "If a man takes a wife…," the verse states, without clarifying whether this action is required.

The Talmud is equivocal as to whether marriage is commanded (Kiddushin 41a) or optional (*Moed Katan* 18b). Moreover, the blessing recited at weddings, known as *birkat erusin,* speaks about sexual prohibitions and the sanctity of marriage, as opposed to the traditional formulation recited over mandated actions: "Blessed are You…who has sanctified us with His commandments and commanded us to…" (Ketubbot 7b). Yet Maimonides (MT *Hilkhot Ishut* 1:2) and many other scholars (*Smak* 183) posited an obligation to marry. Others formulated it indirectly – one does not have to get married, but if one wants such a legal relationship, marriage is required (*Ḥinukh* 552). Some commentators, however, recognized no such mitzva (Rosh, Ketubbot 1:12). At best, marriage may be viewed as a facilitator (*hekhsher mitzva*) of procreation, which can be achieved through other relationships.

While this latter interpretation would explain some of the quirks regarding the blessings of the wedding ceremony (Ritva, Ketubbot 7b), it remains questionable what other relationships may legitimately serve the purpose of procreation. The Torah clearly prohibits prostitution (Deut. 23:18) and other promiscuous behavior (Lev. 19:29). Adultery is condemned as well, and in any case, it is unclear if the offspring of such illicit affairs fulfills the commandment to procreate (*Minḥat Ḥinukh* 1).

In medieval times, Rabbenu Asher suggested that a legitimate alternative (or supplement) to marriage was concubinage. The Bible, which permitted polygamy, tells of numerous men – including the nation's forefathers and Kings David and Solomon – establishing casual yet ongoing marriage-like relationships with concubines. Although some talmudic sources indicate that a formal ceremony is necessary to establish such a relationship (Y. Ketubbot 5:2), most require no such act (Sanhedrin 21a), with almost all agreeing that the woman receives no alimony (*ketubba*) in case of separation (Raavad MT *Hilkhot Ishut* 1:4). While a few scholars believed that divorce was necessary in such an instance (*Shu"t HaRosh* 35:10), even the majority, who did not, contended that during the concubinage the woman must remain committed exclusively to the man, usually living in his domicile. More casual flings were strictly prohibited as outright depravity (Nahmanides, *Hassagot LeSefer HaMitzvot shoresh* 5).

Medieval responsa clearly attest that concubinage was common in certain Jewish communities, such as in Spain (*Shu"t HaRan* 68). Yet many scholars prohibited such relationships. Maimonides (MT *Hilkhot Melakhim* 4:4) believed that the Bible permitted concubines only to kings, while Rabbi Meir Abulafia asserted that the sages prohibited concubinage to protect Jewish women from mistreatment (*Yad Rama* Sanhedrin 21a). Indeed, numerous talmudic sources indicate that relations with concubines were viewed as shady (Genesis Rabba 74:7). The Spanish Rabbenu Yona condemned such arrangements as illicit (*Shaarei Teshuva* 3:94–95), noting that the sages prohibited seclusion (*yiḥud*) with single women to prevent sexual acts (Avoda Zara 36b). Even his cousin Nahmanides, who wrote him a letter defending the legality of concubinage, concluded his treatise on the subject by warning of its hazards, including the fact that concubines regularly failed to immerse in the *mikve* (*Shu"t HaRashba* [attributed to Nahmanides] 284). Indeed, immersion in ritual baths might reduce the severity of the action, but does not make it permissible (*Shu"t HaRivash* 425).

While scholars continued to debate these relationships (EH 26:1), concubinage became extremely uncommon as people came to see its legal and moral pitfalls, and as the ban against polygamy spread (*Yam shel Shlomo* Yevamot 2:11). Two attempts were made to revive these associations in the modern era. Rabbi Yaakov Emden (d. 1776) suggested establishing such relationships to prevent more serious extramarital liaisons (*She'elat Yaavetz* 2:17). And Rabbi Yaakov Moshe Toledeno (twentieth century) proposed that concubinage, whose dissolution requires no divorce (according to most, as mentioned), might serve as an alternative to marriage, thereby sparing women from suffering at the hands of recalcitrant husbands, should separation become necessary. Both of these suggestions were rejected by the rabbinic consensus, however, in favor of preserving the sanctity of the marital covenant, which is characterized by commitment and fidelity.

Chapter 105

Civil Marriage

Does halakha recognize it?

The impact of civil marriage on personal status under Jewish law has engaged scholars for centuries. This discussion has broad ramifications, since anyone legally betrothed must obtain a halakhic divorce before remarrying. Otherwise, any "second marriage" would be considered adultery, and the offspring would be illegitimate (*mamzerim*).

Ideally, a competent scholar should supervise Jewish weddings to ensure that all procedures, documents, and blessings are in order. Unlike in other societies, where the clergyman or clerk has power vested in him by God or the state, officiating rabbis merely ensure that the nuptials are performed appropriately. At its core, Jewish marriage remains a simple contractual agreement between two parties, which can be created without rabbinic involvement.

The Jewish marital process involves two stages, usually combined today in one ceremony: *kiddushin* (betrothal) and *nissuin* (nuptials). The latter is accomplished by the bride and groom coming under the wedding canopy together and/or entering a room or their home in seclusion, thereby indicating their shared domicile. This was the method of legal marriage before the Torah was given (MT *Hilkhot Ishut* 1:1), and remains the manner in which the Torah recognizes marital bonds between non-Jews, for whom adultery and other illicit relations are also forbidden (Sanhedrin 57b).

The formal betrothal ceremony, which initiates the legal relationship and requires two lawful witnesses, may be accomplished in three ways. The first entails the groom giving the bride an object of monetary value, and is performed today almost universally with a wedding band. Yet betrothal may also be enacted through a written document or through sexual relations (Kiddushin 2a). The latter method, which when performed in one's own home might combine both stages of the marital process (EH 33:1), was deemed unseemly by the sages (Kiddushin 12b). Nonetheless, such betrothals might remain in force, leaving open the possibility that even those who forgo a Jewish wedding ceremony become legally married once they live together with the intent of being husband and wife.

The Talmud declares that people do not want their sexual relations to be deemed licentious, and therefore we assume that they acted with intent to make them licit (Gittin 81b). Therefore, some commentators conclude that two singles who engage in sexual intercourse intend to wed and become legally married. Maimonides deemed this notion preposterous, and limited the talmudic assumption to a few circumstances in which a quasi-relationship had already been established (MT *Hilkhot Gerushin* 10:19) or when dealing with righteous people (MT *Hilkhot Naḥalot* 4:6). In his mind, non-marital intercourse remains just that, unless explicitly stated otherwise.

One medieval ramification of this question regarded a female Jewish apostate who, after marrying another apostate under Christian or Islamic law, sought to return to the Jewish community. Based on Maimonides' opinion, Rabbis Isaac Perfet (*Shu"t HaRivash* 6) and Israel Isserlein (*Terumat HaDeshen* 209) declared that weddings under non-Jewish religious auspices have no legal impact, since we assume that the choice of such a ceremony was a declaration not to be married under Jewish law. Especially since such people are unlikely to observe family purity laws, which carry severe punishment, we have no reason not to view their current relationship as illicit and non-marital, thereby allowing the woman to remarry without a hard-to-obtain divorce document (EH 26:1).

Not all scholars said the same of civil marriage, however. Some believed that elements of a civil ceremony (like the ring ceremony or a marriage certificate) might suffice to create a recognized union (*Otzar HaPoskim* EH 26). Rabbi Yosef Rosen contended that the marriage methods declared at Sinai did not nullify the mechanism used until then, i.e., simply living together for the sake of marriage (*Tzofnat Paane'aḥ* [Warsaw ed.] 26). Rabbi Yosef E. Henkin more compellingly argued that people who declare their intent to marry and then consummate that marriage by cohabitation have fulfilled the basic requirements of Jewish law, even if they did not specifically intend to wed under Jewish law (*Perushei Ibra* 3–5).

Most decisors, however, contend that civil marriage does not create a halakhic marriage. They note, for example, that the civil ceremony is declarative, not performative, and that sexual relations no longer serve as a betrothal method. More important, Rabbi Moshe Feinstein maintained that the couple's choice of a non-halakhic ceremony reflects a desire not to be married under Jewish law (IM EH 1:74). Based on these considerations, Rabbis Ovadia Yosef (*Yabia Omer* EH 6:1) and Meshulam Roth (*Kol Mevasser* 1:22) have indicated that no divorce procedure is necessary. Yet most scholars, including Rabbi Yeḥiel Yaakov Weinberg (*Seridei Esh* 1:108), prefer that a woman be formally divorced (*get leḥumra*) before "remarriage," though they waive that condition if deemed unfeasible.

Chapter 106

Civil Marriage in Israel

Should Israeli law allow for the option?

Although marriage outside the framework of Jewish law is far from ideal, a civil marriage option may be the most effective way to help this country become a more Jewish and a more democratic state. Allow me to explain.

We have previously discussed the halakhic status of non-marital cohabitation (concubinage) as well as civil marriage. We concluded that according to normative Jewish law, the former is forbidden, while the latter is no substitute for halakhic marriage. Some decisors believe that ex post facto, a couple who marry under civil law create a sufficient legal bond to require a divorce should they split up. Yet the current consensus maintains that such arrangements do not create bonafide marital bonds, and therefore, when necessary, we waive the divorce requirement.

Since its founding, Israel has granted jurisdiction over marriage and divorce to the Chief Rabbinate. As such, civil marriages between Jews are not performed in this country. In recent years, however, Israeli courts have ordered the Interior Ministry to recognize civil marriages performed abroad. As such, the government will recognize, for example, the marriages of non-Orthodox immigrants from America, or of Israelis who go to Cyprus for the weekend to tie the knot.

The latter option is frequently exercised by couples who cannot marry under Jewish law, such as if one partner is not halakhically Jewish, or when a *kohen* desires to wed a divorcée. (Alternatively, these couples simply live together out of wedlock.) Yet it is also chosen by numerous secular Israelis who have found the process of working with the rabbinate to be unprofessional and demoralizing. While many employees of the rabbinate undoubtedly serve with dignity and kindness, the rabbinate has unfortunately gotten a bad name.

To alleviate this situation, the Tzohar rabbinic organization has established a marriage project that provides a more user-friendly, religiously uplifting experience for secular couples. Knesset legislation was passed to ensure that all couples, regardless of residence, can register at a Tzohar-friendly municipal rabbinate. Yet Tzohar (rightfully) works within the strictures of halakha, and thus some couples (including many children of immigrants from the former Soviet Union) may not marry even through this program.

Many scholars maintain that although this policy denies these citizens the right to marriage, it remains important to preserve the Jewish identity of the country by preventing the state from sanctioning non-halakhic relationships. They further note that a civil marriage option in Israel would allow for intermarriage, making the Jewish state the only Jewish community in the world to facilitate such weddings.

Yet former Sephardic Chief Rabbi Eliyahu Bakshi-Doron favors this option. He has marshaled several arguments against imposing halakhic marriages upon the Israeli public, many of which have to do with contemporary trends of divorce and infidelity (*Tchumin* 25). Once a couple is halakhically married, any extramarital relationship is adulterous, with offspring of that affair deemed *mamzerim* (illegitimate). This problem can become particularly acute, since even divorcing couples may seek other companionship before receiving a *get* (divorce writ) from the rabbinate. Accordingly, it remains preferable, in the long run, for such couples to remain halakhically unmarried.

Rabbi Bakshi-Doron denounces any attempt to solve this problem by subtly arranging invalid weddings for secular couples (such as by using unacceptable witnesses for the ceremony). He notes that according to many decisors (*Ḥatam Sofer* EH 3:100), any public wedding attended by many people becomes, per force, legitimate. More fundamentally, along with Rabbi Moshe Sternbuch (*Teshuvot VeHanhagot* 4:289), he finds such deception immoral and unfathomable.

Rabbi Bakshi-Doron further questions the halakhic standing of weddings when the couple has no interest in the ceremony and desires only to receive civil benefits. Historically, numerous decisors, such as Rabbis Abraham Isaac Kook (*Ezrat Kohen* 41) and Ben-Zion Uziel (*Mishpetei Uziel* EH 2:49), felt that marriages intended primarily to secure immigration rights (like residency papers or citizenship) were invalid. While other scholars demurred (*Mishneh Halakhot* 10:238), Rabbi Bakshi-Doron believes everyone would agree when the couple is ideologically opposed to Orthodox conceptions of marriage.

Many share Rabbi Bakshi-Doron's belief that a civil marriage option would remove much of the animosity created by religious coercion, and instead facilitate more meaningful religious experiences for those who choose a rabbinic wedding. According to some surveys, 80 percent of non-religious couples eligible to wed halakhically would do so even if they had a civil alternative. This affirmation of Jewish identity would be strengthened by a rabbinate that would be forced to provide pre-marital counseling and wedding ceremonies that were both halakhic and meaningful. It is worthwhile to forsake the symbolism created by state-mandated religious coercion and replace it with substantive Jewish identity.

Chapter 107

Marriage for the Mentally Disabled

What are the issues involved?

The right of the mentally disabled to marry has sparked passionate debate around the world. On the one hand, some societies are wary of the risks to such couples as well as their offspring. On the other hand, this paternalistism might deny the mentally disabled a basic right to self-fulfillment, especially in light of studies showing that marriage frequently improves their social acclimation.

The Torah considers an action meaningful only if performed with basic cognizance. Therefore, the Talmud regularly exempts three categories of people from commandments: the deaf-mute (*ḥeresh*), the mentally incompetent (*shoteh*), and the child (Arakhin 2a).

Nonetheless, the sages declared that one should begin to train his children to perform commandments before they become formally obligated in their strict observance (Sukka 42a). Training in various commandments begins at different ages, depending on the development of the child as well as the nature of the precept (*Tosafot* Sukka 28b). Because the deaf-mute was presumed incapable of ever achieving the acumen or discipline to perform mitzvot, many decisors declared that his parents have no obligation to train him (*Minḥat Ḥinukh* 5:2). Yet those who have acquired a minimal ability to speak fall outside this category and should be taught according to their capabilities (*Maharsham* 2:140). Marriage requires consent (Kiddushin 2b), and therefore all three groups may not marry. One exception is the child bride, whom the Torah allows to be betrothed by her father or, upon his death, by her mother or brother. Such betrothals were seemingly common in antiquity (*Mordekhai* Ketubbot 179), yet some sages forbade them, lest they lead to unhappy marriages when the bride matured (Kiddushin 41a). The phenomenon continued into the medieval era, largely to help ensure the economic security of the daughter (*Tosafot*). Thankfully, it is no longer practiced today.

The sages additionally legitimized the nuptials of deaf-mutes, lest they fall into promiscuity or sexual abuse (Yevamot 112b). Similar dispensations, however, were not granted for the *shoteh*, who was deemed too unstable for marriage.

Mental incompetence takes many different forms, with the sages diagnosing a *shoteh* based on behavior patterns (as opposed to a medical-therapeutic viewpoint). A *shoteh* includes one who goes out alone at night, spends the night in a cemetery, tears his garments, and destroys everything given to him (Hagiga 3b-4a). While some medieval scholars understood that a *shoteh* must exhibit precisely these characteristics, Maimonides (MT *Hilkhot Edut* 9:9) and others deemed them mere examples of bizarre conduct stemming from psychological illness (BY EH 121).

Scholars debate whether a *shoteh* is defined differently depending on the realm of law under discussion, and if a person can be declared competent in some areas but not others (IM EH 1:120). Some contend that one may be incapable of testifying about past events, but can handle financial or marital responsibilities when cognizant (*Shu"t Maharit* EH 2:16). This status would apply to people who display irrational behavior only periodically.

Since divorces are effective only when both parties are fully cognizant, this factor becomes critical when a married person develops a mental illness and then the spouse seeks a divorce. In one famous eighteenth-century case, known as the Divorce of Cleves, European scholars fiercely debated whether to recognize a divorce document issued by a husband who had become mentally unstable soon after his wedding (*Shaagat Aryeh*, addendum). Yet even if such a person is not disqualified from marriage as a *shoteh*, many decisors recommend avoiding such nuptials to prevent such predicaments (*Meshaneh Halakhot* 9:260).

A different category is that of the simpleton (*peti*), who possesses limited cognitive abilities (*Sma* ḤM 35:21). As Rabbi Zalman Neḥemia Goldberg has noted (*Tchumin* 7), such individuals are legally entitled to wed, as long as they comprehend (even with guidance) the nature and obligations of marriage (*Beit Shmuel* EH 44:4). Rabbi Shlomo Aviner has included people with mild cases of Down syndrome in this category, though others have demurred (*Assia* 12). As Rabbi Shai Peron has documented, questions regarding supervision, birth control, and family purity laws have led to further reservations, even as he and others have offered concrete suggestions pursuant to alleviating these concerns and facilitating such marriages. Israel's Chief Rabbinate has reportedly allowed the marriage of a few couples in which both parties have Down syndrome. While this topic remains a matter of debate in the legal world, it represents a significant example of praiseworthy attempts to responsibly integrate those with mental disabilities into mainstream lifestyles.

Chapter 108

Prenuptial Agreements and *Agunot*

Can the tragedy of get *refusal be prevented?*

Over the past two decades, considerable effort has been made to relieve the problem of *iggun,* in which one member of a divorcing couple (usually the woman) may not remarry because the other refuses to agree to a divorce. Various solutions have been proposed, some of which have been challenged on halakhic grounds, while others have been deemed ineffective. This article will focus on the most promising initiative, a prenuptial agreement that mandates continued financial support by the recalcitrant spouse, as proposed in the arbitration agreement of the Beth Din of America (www.theprenup.org) and the "Agreement for Mutual Respect" employed in Israel (www.kdam.info).

The notion of a prenuptial agreement to ensure an ethical divorce settlement was first enacted by the rabbis in the form of the *ketubba,* the marriage contract that continues to be signed today (Ketubbot 82b). This contract, which obligates the husband to provide a financial package upon divorce, ensured basic economic support for the wife. However, the financial arrangements of a *ketubba,* as declared in its standard formulation, were largely neutralized because of an important medieval development. According to talmudic law, a man may divorce his wife against her will, and he may take multiple wives. Around the year 1000 CE, Rabbenu Gershom prohibited both these practices (EH 1:10). Over the centuries, this decree – known as *Ḥerem DeRabbenu Gershom* – was universally adopted, with men permitted to remarry without a divorce writ (*get*) only in limited circumstances, following the written consent of one hundred rabbis (*Heter Me'a Rabbanim*).

As such, the economic premises of the *ketubba* became vacated, since halakha demanded mutual consent for divorce, which presumably would not occur without each side consenting to the financial settlement. For this reason, Rabbi Moshe Isserles contemplated whether a *ketubba* remained necessary (EH 66:3), and while Jewish law continued to require it, its real-world monetary value was frequently left undetermined, since it had minimal practical impact (IM EH 4:91–92).

Accordingly, a divorce document forced upon either side (*get me'useh*) is void. Talmudic law, however, contends that in certain cases (of illicit behavior, for example) a person is advised, obligated, or forced to divorce his or her spouse. When coercive measures are mandated, they may include corporal punishment to force the recalcitrant spouse to consent. Medieval scholars significantly disagree about when courts may authorize a divorce (*Tosafot* Ketubbot 70a). Maimonides and many early medieval authorities allowed a wife to force a divorce by declaring her husband repugnant to her (MT *Hilkhot Ishut* 14:8). Yet Rabbenu Tam (*Sefer HaYashar, Teshuvot* 77) and others demurred, and to avoid this dispute (*Tur* EH 154), a stringent position was adopted, which empowers courts to apply coercive measures only in limited cases (EH 154:21). Taken together, these developments strengthened the legal bonds of marriage and made it more difficult to divorce.

The well-known problem of recalcitrant spouses emerged in the modern era with the advent of civil divorce (especially in societies with no-fault divorce laws) and the stripping of punitive powers from ecumenical courts in the Diaspora. Most commonly, a couple will divorce under civil law, yet the husband will withhold a *get* until he receives favorable financial or custody arrangements, thereby preventing his ex-wife from remarrying under Jewish law. (Because of the *heter me'a rabbanim* option, the phenomenon of recalcitrant women occurs much less frequently.)

To discourage such extortion and abuse, some scholars proposed the imposition of financial penalties upon such a husband.

While some authorities permitted them, since the husband ultimately consents, others worried that imposing a fine (*kenas*) constitutes illicit coercion, even as such a divorce would remain valid ex post facto (EH 134:4).

To circumvent this disagreement, Rabbi Mordechai Willig drafted a prenuptial agreement that removed any reference to divorce or financial penalties. Instead, at the time of marriage, the husband undertakes to provide continued reasonable financial support once the marriage has irretrievably broken down (e.g., once a civil divorce has been granted), as determined by the Beth Din of America. Because the *beit din* serves as a recognized court of arbitration, this agreement may be enforced in secular courts as well. In truth, a somewhat similar proposal was previously adopted in the 1950s by Moroccan scholars (*Tevuot Shemesh* EH 66) and in many ways echoes a seventeenth-century marriage contract that claimed its origins in eleventh-century Ashkenazic quarters (*Naḥalat Shiva* 9:14). This agreement, which has prevented cases of *agunot* and has held up in secular courts, has received approval – at least for use in America – by leading decisors, including Rabbis Ovadia Yosef, Hershel Schachter, Asher Weiss, Zalman Neḥemia Goldberg, and Gedalia Dov Schwartz.

Within Israel, rabbinical courts retain exclusive rights to issue divorce documents. When halakhically mandated, they may coerce recalcitrant husbands by revoking passports or professional licenses, and through imprisonment. For various disputed reasons, including claims that the courts impose coercive measures too slowly, these powers have not eliminated *agunot*.

To address this problem, the prenuptial "Agreement for Mutual Respect" obligates the recalcitrant party, under halakha and general Israeli law, to pay additional support payments once his spouse has initiated divorce proceedings and efforts at marital reconciliation (if so desired) have failed. While this document invokes the same halakhic mechanism as the American prenup, it has not yet garnered the same widespread support, in part because some fear it undermines the rabbinical court system by providing a (halakhically licit) incentive via civil law for the recalcitrant spouse to agree to divorce (*Tchumin* 21–22). Its advocates, however, believe it represents the best opportunity, under current circumstances, to prevent the suffering of an *aguna* and the concurrent desecration of God's name (*ḥillul Hashem*). Efforts have been made to reconcile these different approaches, and one hopes that the Chief Rabbinate will agree upon a solution that can rid Israel of this terrible phenomenon.

Chapter 109

Orthodoxy and Homosexuality

What is the halakhic position?

Now that non-Orthodox streams of Judaism have accepted homosexual members and clergy, homosexuality has become a particularly sensitive and contentious issue within the Jewish community. Orthodoxy, given its conservative approach to Jewish law, has steadfastly defended the biblical prohibition, yet maintains varying approaches to understanding it and dealing with violators.

The Torah prohibition of male homosexual penetrative intercourse is set within a list of illicit sexual behaviors. The verse states, "You shall not lie with a man as one lies with a woman; it is an abomination (*to'eva*)" (Lev. 18:22). Willful, forewarned violators of this prohibition are condemned to death (20:13). Additionally, such transgression falls into a category of cardinal sins (*gilui arayot*) that a person may never proactively commit, even to save his own life (YD 157:1). The Noahide laws similarly prohibit gentiles from engaging in such behavior (Sanhedrin 58a).

While the Torah does not mention lesbianism, the sages include it, along with other illicit sexual practices, in the ban on Egyptian practices (*Sifra Aḥarei Mot* 9:8). While some scholars deem female homosexual activity a biblical transgression (*Kiryat Sefer, Issurei Biah* 21:8), most understand it as rabbinically proscribed (*Perisha* EH 20:2).

Some forms of non-penetrative male homosexuality might constitute a less severe violation, but all are strictly prohibited (EH 20:1). While as a matter of legality, it remains preferable for someone to transgress a less severe prohibition, any such violation is merely the lesser of two sins, so to speak.

Various explanations have been offered for the injunction against homosexuality. Many note that this type of intimacy precludes reproduction, whereas man is to populate the world (*Ḥinukh* 209). This rationale partially reflects a utilitarian view of sexual activity, which deems procreation its central purpose. This explanation, however, suffers from the fact that the Torah permits physical intimacy even when procreation is impossible, as in the case of sterile people (Rabbenu Baḥya, Lev. 18:6).

As stated, the Bible characterizes homosexuality as a *to'eva*. The sages read this term as a contraction meaning, "You go astray in it" (*to'eh ata bah*) (Nedarim 51a). In this sense, *to'eva* should be translated as an "aberration" (as opposed to an abomination). In this light, some commentators explain that homosexuality causes deviations from heterosexual marital norms, thereby breaking down the family structure (*Tosafot* Nedarim 51a). Others understood homosexuality as a deviation from human nature (*Lekaḥ Tov* Lev. 20:13). As Rabbi Chaim Rapoport has noted in his important book on this subject, *Judaism and Homosexuality: An Authentic Orthodox View* (2004), these rationales, even when taken together, remain incomplete and disputable, and therefore one must rely on the fact that the ultimate foundation for the commandment remains with divine wisdom.

One major bone of contention regarding this prohibition lies in the origins of homosexual orientations. Some authors understood it as entirely unnatural and a wanton rebellion against biblical wisdom (IM OḤ 4:115). However, many recent scholars, including the late Lubavitcher Rebbe, understand homosexual inclinations as innate, involuntary desires. This position reflects greater affinity with contemporary science and social perspectives, which generally accept the notion that however it originates, people do not "choose" their sexual-affectional attraction. In this regard, it is significant that the Torah does not prohibit homosexual orientation, but rather forbids a person to act on it.

Yet how can the Torah forbid one to act on his natural sexual inclinations? Conservative rabbis like Rabbi Elliot Dorff find this tension theologically untenable and have therefore sought ways to permit homosexual activity, despite the verses in Leviticus. Some Orthodox activists, on the other hand, contend that homosexuality must be "reversible" or "curable"; otherwise God would not forbid it.

Many Orthodox rabbis, however, recognize a continuum of sexual attraction. In a famous 1974 article, Rabbi Norman Lamm posited that while homosexual acts remain prohibited, the actors are not culpable for actions that stem from involuntary inclinations (*ones*). Most Orthodox thinkers have rejected this thesis, since one always retains the free will to abstain from sexual activity. Nonetheless, they acknowledge the tremendous challenge of celibacy, and recognize that sexually active homosexuals (especially those with no anti-religious agenda) should not be viewed as defiant rebels worthy of ostracism (*mumar lehakhis*). Rather, they must be approached with understanding and compassion, and should be treated as respectfully as other contemporary Jews whose level of observance falls short of halakhic standards (*mumar lete'avon* or *tinok shenishba*).

While it is sometimes difficult to maintain amid society's many cultural clashes, this position retains intellectual honesty while showing proper respect and compassion. To my mind, it is a proper approach to this complex issue.

For more on this topic, please see my "Homosexuality and Halakha: Five Critical Points," co-written with Rabbi Michael Broyde and published in the *Jewish Press*.

Section IX

Shabbat and Holidays

Chapter 110

Bicycle Riding

Why do some religious Jews ride their bikes on Shabbat, while others prohibit it?

Most decisors forbid bicycle riding on Shabbat, but for different reasons, all reflecting the complexity of this activity. In general, we can divide the potential problems into two categories: (1) technical transgressions of the law, and (2) violations of the spirit of Shabbat.

Bicycle riding makes grooves in the dirt, which violates the prohibition of plowing (*ḥoresh*) on Shabbat. While Rabbi Azriel Hildesheimer (OḤ 49) forbade bike riding for this reason, most decisors dismissed this consequence as unintentional, undesired, and infrequent. They noted that strollers and wheelchairs also occasionally create grooves, but remain permitted. (However, one may push these items – and ride a bike, for that matter – only within an *eiruv*, an enclosure that transforms public areas into a private domain, thereby eliminating the prohibition of carrying [*hotzaa*]. Most Israeli cities, and many Jewish communities around the world today, have built *eiruvim* to overcome this problem. See essay 112, "Metropolitan *Eiruvim*," for more details.)

Many scholars ruled stringently regarding bikes because they frequently break and require tire or chain repairs that are forbidden on Shabbat. Many rabbis compared this restriction to the talmudic decree prohibiting horseback riding, lest the rider pull off a tree branch to strike the animal. Yet other rabbis, including Rabbi Ovadia Yosef, contended that we do not institute such preventive decrees today, and therefore rejected this reasoning (*Leviat Ḥen* 107).

Another argument against bike riding is that it's not *Shabbosdik,* i.e., it violates the spirit of Shabbat. While some scoff at this notion, its gravity is well-grounded in talmudic sources. The rabbis declared that we honor the Sabbath (*kevod Shabbat*) not only with special clothing, but also by limiting discussions to sacred matters, walking at a leisurely pace (Shabbat 113a), and refraining from weekday activities (*uvdin deḥol*). This notion of making Shabbat special finds expression in the Torah itself, which demands that we designate Shabbat as a day of rest (*shabbat shabbaton*). In a celebrated passage, Nahmanides asserts that one who violates the spirit of the Sabbath transgresses a biblical precept (Nahmanides, Lev. 23:24). He bases himself on a number of talmudic-era passages that, as Prof. Yitzhak Gilat has documented, prohibit many practices (including horseback riding) simply because they are not appropriate on the Sabbath (*Sifra Aḥarei Mot* 5:7).

What makes something *Shabbosdik* or not? Regarding bike riding, many rabbis contended that the strain of the activity as well as its recreational purpose make it inappropriate for Shabbat. One notable dissenter was Rabbi Yosef Ḥayim of Baghdad (1832–1909), known as the Ben Ish Ḥai. His argument was buttressed by the absence of the "*Shabbosdik* factor" in numerous medieval discussions regarding riding animals led by non-Jews on Shabbat. Rabbi Yosef Ḥayim added that rabbis should focus on more clear-cut violations of the law (*Rav Pe'alim* 1:25).

Yet the rabbinic majority rejected this position, and bike riding remains prohibited in most communities. In a fascinating passage, Rabbi Ovadia Yosef firmly defended the lenient position, yet concluded that since the majority of rabbis did not permit the practice, we should forbid it (*Leviat Ḥen* 107). Clearly, the severity of bike riding does not approach that of driving on Shabbat or similar activities.

I suspect that in many communities, the bike riders come from traditional families that maintain some modicum of halakhic Shabbat observance. Elements of the traditional Sephardic population, for instance, might not travel by car on Shabbat, but will bike. For similar reasons, many non-observant Israelis don't drive on Yom Kippur; on that day, bicycles rule the roads.

Less mechanically complex than bikes, scooters are less likely to break on Shabbat and require less physical exertion. In many ways, they are comparable to tricycles, which many rabbis permit children to ride on Shabbat (SSK 16:18). Nonetheless, scooters remain recreational vehicles that might detract from the spirit of Shabbat, so many communities encourage their children above the age of bar/bat mitzva to refrain from riding them.

Chapter 111

Inviting Non-Observant Jews

May one invite a non-observant Jew to shul on Shabbat if he'll drive there?

In Israel as well as in the Diaspora, non-observant Jews – some traditional and others avowedly secular – are increasingly interested in taking part in traditional Shabbat experiences. This wonderful phenomenon helps strengthen Jewish identity and unity. Yet it also raises questions about whether more-observant Jews may invite their less-observant brethren to Shabbat services or meals, knowing their participation will likely entail driving or other activities forbidden on Shabbat. May one encourage Shabbat observance even if doing so involves Shabbat desecration?

The desire to increase Shabbat observance and not cause its desecration stems from one broad value: "All Jews are responsible for one another" (Sanhedrin 27b). This concept is reflected in many biblical commandments that depict all Jews as comrades, such as, "You shall not hate your kinsfolk…; reprove your fellow and incur no guilt because of him. You shall not take revenge or bear a grudge against your countrymen; love your fellow as yourself" (Lev. 19:17–18). Jews bear an obligation to help each other do good and avoid sinning.

This sentiment is embodied in another commandment, "You shall not place a stumbling block before the blind (*lifnei iver*)" (Lev. 19:14), in which the sages included giving bad advice or facilitating another's sin (Pesaḥim 22b). Thus, one may not give a fellow Jew a ham sandwich (Avoda Zara 6a); one may not even give an apple if the recipient will not recite the blessing beforehand (OḤ 169:2). Accordingly, many decisors – including Rabbis Shmuel HaLevi Wosner (*Shevet HaLevi* 8:256) and Yosef Shalom Elyashiv – believe that such Shabbat invitations transgress this prohibition, with Rabbi Moshe Feinstein (IM OḤ 1:99) even asserting that they might further violate the prohibition of inciting sinful behavior (*mesit*) (Deut. 13).

However, the Talmud states that one violates *lifnei iver* only if the transgressor is "across the river," i.e., incapable of sinning without one's help. Yet if the ham sandwich is readily available, one violates no biblical prohibition by facilitating its consumption. Some commentators counter that in this case one still violates a rabbinic prohibition of aiding and abetting (*mesaye'a*). Medieval commentators, for example, debated whether Jews were permitted to sell non-Jewish religious articles to Christians, since the latter could always find suppliers within the gentile community (YD 151:1). Our case might be similarly contingent on this debate, since non-observant Jews are free to travel elsewhere.

Some scholars rule stringently on this matter, since any public toleration of Shabbat violations constitutes an affront to Judaism. Yet others contend that such concerns are overridden by the fact that participation in Shabbat rituals strengthens Jewish identity. Several decisors further argue that Shabbat invitations do not even violate the prohibition of aiding and abetting, albeit for various reasons. Some contend that the sages prohibited only direct, physical assistance at the time of the actual sin; a verbal invitation, usually extended before the Sabbath, might not fulfill those criteria. A few scholars have noted that mutual responsibility only goes so far, and therefore the entire prohibition of aiding and abetting does not apply to those who have chosen to be non-observant (*Shakh* YD 151:6). Others have rejected that claim, yet assert that there is no greater act of taking responsibility for another Jew than showing him how to observe the Sabbath (*Seridei Esh* 2:9).

A different argument for leniency acknowledges that such Shabbat invitations are theoretically prohibited, yet contends that this relatively minor transgression may be performed to facilitate broader religious commitment (*BeOhola shel Torah* OḤ 5:22). This claim, in part, relates to a larger discussion regarding whether one may sin to prevent himself or others from committing worse offenses (Shabbat 4a).

In medieval times, for example, scholars allowed outright Shabbat violation in order to prevent a Jew from apostasy and intermarriage (OḤ 306:14). In that case, however, the effect of the "rescue" is immediate, whereas the impact of Shabbat invitations is less direct, not immediate, and far from guaranteed.

Taking these considerations into account, Rabbis Yaakov Kamenetsky (*Emet LeYaakov* ḤM 423) and Shlomo Zalman Auerbach (*Minḥat Shlomo* 2:4) argued that one may frame the invitation in a manner that would not necessarily lead to Shabbat violation. Accordingly, one may invite guests for a whole Shabbat, and even if they are unlikely to stay that long, he may encourage them to come for a Friday night meal, arriving before Shabbat begins, even as we assume they will drive home later. Rabbi Moshe Sternbuch allows even Shabbat day invitations, however, because he believes Jews do not violate the *lifnei iver* prohibition if they intend to bring others closer to Judaism (*Teshuvot VeHanhagot* 1:358). This leniency, which I personally find compelling, was adopted by the Beit Hillel rabbinic organization, even as it stressed that it should be used sparingly and cautiously.

Chapter 112

Metropolitan *Eiruvim*

May one build an eiruv *within a large city?*

An *eiruv* is a legal construct that allows Jews to move objects – including prayer shawls and strollers – within a public area on the Sabbath. The area, which can range greatly in size, becomes legally joined through two mechanisms. First, one must demarcate the territory by enclosing it within either physical barriers or – in limited cases discussed below – symbolic doorposts (made of strings and poles). Second, people within the area must establish a legal relationship that symbolically unifies their ownership of the territory. This step is accomplished through residents sharing possession of a designated object (frequently a box of matza) and renting the territory from the local government, which must authorize joint use of the area for these purposes.

Building an *eiruv* has generated two types of controversies. In the Diaspora, the process of receiving government permits for construction and space rental occasionally runs into opposition from local residents. Fortunately, courts have repeatedly understood that an *eiruv* facilitates the religious liberties of observant Jews without infringing on the rights of others.

Indeed, the widespread building of *eiruvim* in many Jewish communities, both in Israel and abroad, has enhanced religious life by allowing families – including mothers with young children and the handicapped – to attend synagogue services and celebrate the Sabbath outside their homes. Many twentieth-century rabbis desired to build *eiruvim* lest their congregants violate, accidentally or otherwise, Shabbat regulations that greatly inhibited their activity. This sentiment, in part, was already expressed by medieval scholars, who ostracized rabbis for not constructing halakhically acceptable *eiruvim* within their locales (*Shu"t HaRosh* 21:8–9).

The building of *eiruvim* within modern metropolises, however, generated a second, more fundamental disagreement regarding which areas may be enclosed within an *eiruv*, as recently evidenced in the London *eiruv* controversy. The sages asserted that it is biblically forbidden to carry an object more than four *amot* (roughly six to eight feet) within a public domain (*reshut harabbim*, e.g., a desert) or transport something from there into an enclosed private domain (*reshut hayaḥid*). The rabbis imposed similar restrictions on a *karmelit*, a semi-enclosed area not intended for mass thoroughfare, such as an alleyway or courtyard enclosed on three sides (Shabbat 6a). Because the latter prohibitions were rabbinic stringencies, greater leniencies were afforded to enclose the area into a private domain, including the building of a symbolic doorpost (*tzurat hapetaḥ*) on its fourth side (Eiruvin 11b).

For any area (such as a city street) to be characterized as a public domain (and therefore ineligible for some of these leniencies), it must be uncovered and publicly owned, have a minimum width of twenty-four feet (or thirty-two according to some), and offer twenty-four-hour public access (OḤ 345:7). If the street has walls, like some public markets, it must run uninterrupted throughout the area. Most significantly, many medieval authorities – including Rashi (Eiruvin 6a) – claim that a public domain requires the presence of at least 600,000 people (the number of Jews included in the biblical census in the desert), though this requirement is not listed in the Talmud or by Maimonides (MT *Hilkhot Shabbat* 14:1). Accordingly, most medieval scholars asserted that their towns did not constitute a public domain, since they lacked the requisite street width and population (*Tosafot* Shabbat 64b), or since they were locked at night and did not have unobstructed streets (Raavya).

New problems emerged in the modern era as Jews moved from walled neighborhoods into urban environs. Many scholars, including Rabbi Jacob Brukhim of Lithuania, contended that modern streets were sufficiently wide to constitute public domains, and that one could no longer claim there were fewer than 600,000 people on them (*Mishkenot*

Yaakov OḤ 120–22). Depending on how you calculate, one might further argue that every day, more than 600,000 people traverse certain areas or streets within cities like New York or Paris. As such, one cannot turn large metropolitan thoroughfares into "private domains," even as *eiruvim* might remain possible in smaller, less populated areas.

Besides defending the use of the 600,000 population standard, supporters of metropolitan *eiruvim* rely on one or more of the following arguments: (1) Contemporary avenues that twist and turn do not constitute uninterrupted streets. (2) The buildings that frequently surround major streets ("urban canyons") in fact provide two halakhic walls, which are joined by a third when the street dead-ends, thereby making it a *karmelit*. (3) The population count of 600,000 may include only pedestrians, since motorists are encompassed within their own domains, (i.e., their vehicles). (4) The 600,000 people must be found on a particular street, not just in the area encompassed by the *eiruv*. (5) Some dispensations afforded to a *karmelit* may also be used in a public domain. (6) Substantive material that could theoretically block a street, such as a tarpaulin wrapped around a utility pole, suffices to enclose areas that would not be impacted by more symbolic strings or doorposts.

Taken together, these arguments have facilitated the widespread building of metropolitan *eiruvim* and arguably comprise the most creative yet accepted leniency in contemporary halakhic discourse.

Chapter 113

Two-Day Festivals

Why are there different customs in Israel and the Diaspora?

As an immigrant who previously (and happily) observed two days of the festivals, but now enjoys the Israeli norm of observing only one day, I can assure all prospective *olim*: Switching to one day will be the easiest part of your acclimation!

In all seriousness, the observance of a second day of festivals (*yom tov sheni shel galuyot*) like Sukkot and Passover has greatly divided the Jewish people over the past two centuries, reflecting schisms regarding acculturation, tradition, and the legal process.

The Torah mandates several national festivals, on which we are to abstain from creative work (Lev. 23). These holidays are Rosh HaShana (on the first day of the Hebrew month of Tishrei), Yom Kippur (10 Tishrei), Sukkot (15 Tishrei), Shemini Atzeret (22 Tishrei), the first and last days of Passover (15 and 21 Nisan), and Shavuot (6 Sivan).

Even as these dates were set, the year's schedule fluctuated, since the lunar month could contain twenty-nine or thirty days. Jews in antiquity did not establish a fixed monthly calendar, but instead, following biblical mandate (Ex. 12), declared the new month based on sightings of the new moon. Once the new month was proclaimed by judicial bodies in Jerusalem, torches were lit on the Mount of Olives and subsequent hilltops to announce the date to outlying communities. When the sectarian Cutheans challenged the rabbinic calendar and interfered with the mode of communicating the new month to the Diaspora, the sages instituted an authorized messenger system (Rosh HaShana 22b).

From the outset, this system remained complex for Rosh HaShana, as testimony regarding the new moon – which triggered numerous ritual obligations – could be received on the day itself. While various decrees ensured the proper fulfillment of the Temple ceremonies, it became customary to abstain from work on 30 Elul (the month before Tishrei) and the following day, lest either one be declared Rosh HaShana (Beitza 5a). Because the other festivals occur later in the month, after the messengers had publicized its beginning, communities in Eretz Yisrael observed the singular biblical date. In the Diaspora (primarily Babylonia), however, two festival days were observed, in case the messengers would not reach the Jews there in time.

Following the turmoil of the Temple's destruction, a fixed calendar was established in the mid-fourth century CE by Hillel II and was disseminated throughout the Jewish world, making the second festival day theoretically unnecessary. Nonetheless, scholars in Eretz Yisrael declared to their Diaspora brethren, "Heed the customs of your ancestors" (Beitza 4b, Y. Eiruvin 3:9). This conservatism reflected both messianic hopes for the restoration of the old system as well as fear that evil promulgations against Torah study might lead to mistakes in the fixed calendar. Within the Land of Israel itself, it appears that local inhabitants initially observed only one day of Rosh HaShana (Baal HaMaor, Beitza 4b), but began in the tenth century to celebrate two (*Milḥamot*). (With the exception of rare pious sages, Yom Kippur was never observed anywhere for two days, given the difficulties of extended fasting [OḤ 624:5].)

This stringent ruling regarding the second day of festivals was challenged by the medieval Karaites, who criticized rabbinic scholars for illegitimate augmentations of biblical law. Medieval rabbis retorted that the Torah itself empowered the sages to govern the calendar (*Terumat HaDeshen Pesakim* 116). They further asserted that the second-day observance was a rabbinic decree that could not be nullified (*Otzar HaGeonim* Beitza, pp. 3–10), for only a greater synod could overturn a previous enactment, even if its underlying reason had become irrelevant (Eduyot 1:5).

This last claim became especially common in the nineteenth century, when the nascent Reform movement clamored to abolish this practice. As Prof. Jacob Katz documented, many of these Enlightened Jews found it irrational and contrary to the biblical spirit to observe this outdated custom. Many Reform Jews had begun to abandon the festivals entirely, and those who hadn't were nonetheless unwilling to accept the perceived economic hardships that the additional days of rest imposed. (One compromise proposal reflects this discomfort well: Recite the festival prayers, but drop the work restrictions!) Similar tensions have emerged in recent decades within the Conservative movement, which continues to debate this issue.

As with other reforms, the Orthodox response was firm and uncompromising, ranging from the legal (this custom constitutes an unbreakable law) to the sentimental (your poor ancestors sacrificed under worse conditions, their wealthier descendants can do the same) to the polemical (these neo-Karaites simply want to assimilate). These standpoints have largely defined denominational polemics, turning these joyful days into contentious ones.

Chapter 114

Two-Day Festivals for Diaspora Jews in Israel

Should visitors to Israel observe the festivals as they would abroad?

With the advent of modern transportation, the sight of tourists in Israel observing a second day of a festival has become common, if sometimes comical. Witness, for example, the post-Simḥat Torah festivities (*hakafot sheniyot*) in Jerusalem's Liberty Bell Park, where foreigners dressed in suits dance with Torah scrolls while the natives play musical instruments and snap photographs!

The Talmud ordains that Diaspora Jews must "heed the customs of their ancestors" and observe a second festival day (Beitza 4b). Based on this description of the observance of a second day as a "custom" (MT *Hilkhot Yom Tov* 6:14), many scholars asserted that holiday travelers should follow the rules governing all visitors to places with differing practices.

The sages were wary of tourists quickly dropping their hometown customs, but they were also concerned about creating dissonance by introducing differing practices into well-established communities. The rabbis therefore instructed a visitor to observe the stringencies of both his hometown and the local practice (Pesaḥim 51b). When possible, he should observe his hometown customs privately, avoiding a rift with the locals; but if this is not feasible, he should abandon his personal practice (MB 468:14). However, when tourists travel to a place where there is no established community, they may unabashedly maintain their personal custom.

Based on this logic, Rabbi Joseph Karo (sixteenth century, Safed) contended that foreigners visiting the Land of Israel (*Avkat Rokhel* 26), or those from Eretz Yisrael traveling in the Diaspora (OḤ 496:3), must act stringently in all cases. As such, an Israeli visiting an established Diaspora Jewish community must refrain from publicly performing any forbidden activities (*melakha*) and should dress appropriately for the holiday (MB 496:13). One exception might be a tropical island containing Passover resort hotels, where no communal practice has been established.

Accordingly, an Israeli should be allowed to perform *melakha* in private, and a minority of decisors did indeed rule this way (*Taz* OḤ 496:2). The majority, however, forbid it entirely, either because these activities are impossible to hide, or because the Diaspora's universal acceptance of the second-day festival renders it a "super-custom" from which one may not even slightly divert (AH OḤ 496:4). An Israeli, however, should privately recite the Ḥol HaMoed or weekday prayers and, when appropriate, don *tefillin*.

By the same logic, a foreigner visiting Israel should refrain from donning *tefillin* and performing any forbidden activity on "his" second day, and should recite festival prayers, but only privately (MB 496:13). The earliest sources, however, attest that visitors regularly formed separate public prayer quorums (*Kaf HaḤayim* OḤ 496:38), and this remains a popular practice, especially in hotels that cater to foreigners (*Yalkut Yosef* OḤ 496:23).

Determining the status of long-term travelers has proven difficult throughout the centuries. In earlier generations, Jews moving with their families, even if they intended to shortly return to their native land, lost their old "citizenship," since their current activities established a new domicile for them (*Shu"t HaRadbaz* 4:73). Transportation improvements have made these determinations more complicated, with scholars debating the status of extended stays for diplomatic, professional, and educational purposes.

Be that as it may, the entire model established by Rabbi Karo was challenged by Rabbi Tzvi Ashkenazi (d. 1718), who argued that the paradigm of a custom was inappropriate in this case, since every stringency (e.g., not performing work) came with significant "cost" (e.g., not fulfilling the biblical commandment of *tefillin*), and possibly violated the Torah's prohibition of augmenting or detracting from the established number and form of the mitzvot (*Ḥakham Tzvi* 167). Instead, Rabbi Ashkenazi maintained that one's current location determines his festival observance (*She'elat Yaavetz* 1:68). Jerusalem's Chief Rabbi Shmuel Salant (d. 1909) concurred, noting that before the calendar was fixed, Diaspora pilgrims visiting Jerusalem followed local practice. As such, when the Talmud demands that Jews heed their ancient customs, this actually means that Diaspora residents visiting Israel should observe only one day, and traveling Israelis, two (*Sefer Eretz Yisrael*).

Moreover, particularly regarding visitors to Israel, Rabbi Shneur Zalman of Liadi and Rabbi Chaim Soloveitchik of Brisk both claimed (the former for mystical reasons, the latter based on talmudic analysis) that only one day could be sanctified in Eretz Yisrael, precluding any second-day observances (*Shulḥan Arukh HaRav* OḤ 496:11).

Relying on these cogent arguments, some decisors have adopted Rabbi Karo's paradigm, but used Rabbi Ashkenazi's position to justify leniency in determining who constitutes an Israeli, including those who (1) own property in Israel (*BeMareh HaBazak* 4:57); (2) spend every festival in the country (*Minḥat Shlomo* 1:19, para. 7); (3) are visiting their Israeli children or parents (*Peninei Halakha*); or (4) are unmarried students who might find a spouse and settle in Israel (*Yeḥaveh Daat* 1:26). Others, like Rabbi Joseph B. Soloveitchik (and possibly Rabbi Salant himself), argued that Diaspora visitors should maintain the stringencies of both positions, colloquially known as "keeping a day and a half." This increasingly popular approach, according to which one refrains from *melakha* but prays and dons *tefillin* like an Israeli, has added new dimensions to the various ways Diaspora Jews observe holidays in the Holy Land.

Chapter 115

Tashlikh on Rosh HaShana

Can one really "wash away" his sins?

As with many customs, the origins of *Tashlikh* (lit. "casting off") remain unknown. Most likely rooted in folklore, the ritual developed a rich and fascinating history as scholars offered various interpretations of its mysterious symbolism.

The earliest recording of *Tashlikh,* performed on the first afternoon of Rosh HaShana, was by the German scholar Rabbi Yaakov Moelin in the early fifteenth century (*Minhagei Maharil* Rosh HaShana 9). He describes how the masses would walk to rivers and "cast away their sins" by reciting the last verses in the Book of Micah, which include, "He will take us back in love; He will cover up our iniquities; You will hurl all our sins into the depths of the sea" (7:19). Yet the ritual is undoubtedly older, with much speculation about its origin and meaning.

God reveals Himself near water in several biblical passages, including the vision of the divine chariot (Ezek. 1:3) and Daniel's end-of-days prophecies (Dan. 10:4). One midrash even claims that *all* prophecies took place near water (*Mekhilta Rashbi Shemot* 12:1). As in the story of Creation (Gen. 1:2), God's presence is said to hover over water, making it an appropriate place for prayer (Baal HaTurim, Gen. 16:7). Indeed, many medieval European synagogues were built close to waterfronts.

Great bodies of water connote majesty and glory. As such, riverfronts are appropriate sites for coronations, since this backdrop symbolizes the new reign's perpetuity (Horayot 12a). Later writers speculated that *Tashlikh* similarly celebrates God's Kingship over the world, a central theme of the Rosh HaShana prayers (*Yabia Omer* OḤ 4:47). Other commentators contend that the ceremony recalls Ezra's Rosh HaShana assembly, which rededicated the Torah by the water gate (Neh. 8:1–2). Rabbi Moelin suggests that the waters recall Abraham's eagerness to bind Isaac despite being (according to one midrash) neck-deep in a river created by Satan to stymie him.

These theories, however, rid the rite of the vivid symbolism captured in its rich details. While the earliest depictions of *Tashlikh* vary, most require using water that contains fish. Rabbi Mordekhai Jaffe (sixteenth century, Poland) explained that fish, constantly in danger of being caught by fishermen, warn us of the snares of death and therefore inspire repentance (*Levush* OḤ 596). Others believe that because fish are always alert with their roving eyes, they remind us of the ever-watchful gaze of God (*Shlah* Rosh HaShana 23). Alternatively, fish might ward off the "evil eye," and represent the blessing of fecundity (MB 583:8).

Early sources also allude to throwing bread or other food into the water, possibly signifying the casting away of our sins. Many sages, however, deem this practice a violation of the holiday restrictions, especially if Rosh HaShana falls on the Sabbath, when carrying food and prayer books in unenclosed public domains is prohibited. (For this reason, many communities perform *Tashlikh* in those years on Sunday, the second day of Rosh HaShana.) When codifying this custom in the *Shulḥan Arukh*, Rabbi Moshe Isserles (sixteenth century, Poland) omits any reference to throwing food (OḤ 583). In his lesser-known philosophical work, he describes how the mighty waters make us contemplate the grandeur of God's creation and His dominance over nature, leading us to repentance and the casting away of sins (*Torat HaOla* 3:56).

These diverse and conflicting practices and interpretations most likely reflect emendations of a potentially problematic folk custom. In a detailed study of this custom's history, Prof. Jacob Lauterbach speculated that *Tashlikh* stemmed from an attempt to pacify satanic forces and protect children from harm. Historians have further pointed to a similar medieval ritual documented in Rashi's eleventh-century talmudic commentary (Shabbat 81b). Suspicious of *Tashlikh*'s origins, the Vilna Gaon (d. 1797) abstained from the entire practice (*Maaseh Rav* 202), as do my family and many others who follow Lithuanian practices (AH OḤ 583:4).

Be that as it may, the ritual remains widespread. In Jerusalem, the lack of bodies of water has not deterred people from flocking to empty ancient wells, artificial ponds, the City of David's wellspring, and even kiddie pools in synagogue courtyards! Nonetheless, no interpretation of the practice has been universally embraced. While the famed sixteenth-century mystic Rabbi Isaac Luria ordained shaking out one's clothing to aid the extraction of harmful forces, more rationalist scholars shunned this embellishment, instead framing *Tashlikh* as a mere springboard to repentance. Indeed, many thinkers have stressed that this and other symbolic ceremonies have no "hocus-pocus" power to attain atonement, which comes only from genuine introspection and change.

Chapter 116

Kapparot on Erev Yom Kippur

Must this ritual be performed with a chicken?

In recent years, animal rights groups have launched worldwide campaigns against the pre-Yom Kippur *Kapparot* ritual. Beyond the catchy newspaper headlines, such as "Groups Cry Fowl Over Mass Chicken Slaughter," this latest controversy adds another chapter to the history of this disputed custom.

In its contemporary version, *Kapparot* entails a person waiving a chicken over his head while confessing how he deserves death for his sins. He then offers the chicken as a substitute, slaughters it in accordance with kashrut, and oftentimes donates the food to the poor.

As with many customs, *Kapparot* emerged in the early medieval period as a folk custom that scholars later attempted to understand. Authorities questioned the origin and meaning of the ritual, along with other seasonal customs, such as the consumption of sweet foods on Rosh HaShana, which appeared as an attempt to magically manipulate one's fate or judgment (*Otzar HaGeonim* Yoma, pp. 62–64).

Historically, *Kapparot* had several variations. In some locales, a bean sprout was planted in a palm wreathe two to three weeks before Rosh HaShana. On the eve of the holiday, the plant was waived seven times over the head of each child in the home, and then thrown into a river (Rashi, Shabbat 81b). Elsewhere, the custom was performed by everyone and before Yom Kippur, yet with different types of animals for different people (Rosh, Yoma 8:23). The rich preferred horned animals, alluding to the ram that replaced Isaac on the sacrificial altar (*Pesikta Rabbati* 47).

Ultimately, the chicken became the animal of choice, in part because it was cheaper. Equally significant, one Aramaic term for rooster is *gever,* which also means "man" in Hebrew (Yoma 20b). As such, the chicken was seen as an appropriate substitute for the condemned penitent, with male and female specimens used for each gender, and additional birds taken for pregnant women. In some places the entrails were thrown on top of a person's house to feed the birds, which was seen as an act of kindness to those creatures (*Baḥ* OḤ 605).

Kapparot enjoyed widespread popularity among scholars and laity alike, especially in Ashkenazic lands (*Orḥot Ḥayim, Erev Yom HaKippurim*). Yet some harshly criticized this custom, calling it a foreign ritual akin to many idolatrous practices (*darkhei Emori*). Rabbi Shlomo ibn Aderet, for example, successfully protested the version of the ritual in his native Barcelona, which included killing one chicken for each child in the house and then hanging the chicken heads on the doorpost along with garlic (*Shu"t HaRashba* 1:395).

Following Rashba's lead, Rabbi Joseph Karo banned *Kapparot* (OḤ 605:1). Rabbi Moshe Isserles, however, contended that its antiquity proved its legitimacy. Furthermore, the Arizal and other mystics ascribed redemptive value to the practice (*Shaar HaKavanot, Derushei Yom Kippur*), with some later Sephardic decisors legitimizing it if one donates the chicken to charity (*Shu"t HaRadbaz* 2:640). While a few authorities still had reservations (*Pri Ḥadash* OḤ 605), the dominant position was to endorse the custom provided that its practitioners engage in introspection and repentance (*Yeḥaveh Daat* 2:71).

The climax of the ritual is the confessional, in which the penitent lays his hands on the chicken, proclaims his guilt, and declares that the bird is to be killed in his stead. While some demurred due to the confessional's semblance to the Temple rite, others believed that there was no fear of people confusing *Kapparot* with a formal sacrifice (MB 605:8). Indeed, a few sources (*Maḥzor Vitry* 1:339) highlight the parallels to the biblical Yom Kippur ceremony (Lev. 16) in which the High Priest laid his hands in confession on a goat that was then thrown off a desert cliff.

According to Maimonides, this procedure was not a formal sacrifice, but rather a symbolic gesture to distance ourselves from sin (Guide 3:46).

In the fifteenth century, Rabbi Yaakov Moelin suggested that one could "redeem" the chicken with money to be given as charity, since monetary donations would be less embarrassing to the poor (*Darkhei Moshe* OḤ 605:4). Others noticed that the killing of so many chickens at once caused errors in ritual slaughter, rendering the food non-kosher. As such, some decisors suggested using fish (*Shalmei Moed*, p. 55) or money (*Ḥayei Adam* 2:144, para. 4) instead. The latter alternative appears in many High Holy Day prayer books. Rabbi Ḥayim David HaLevi further noted that the mass killing of animals contradicts the historical notion of refraining from slaughter before the New Year as an act of increased mercy on God's creatures (*Aseh Lekha Rav* 3:20). In this spirit, and given increased accusations of mishandling the chickens, Rabbi Shlomo Aviner recently argued that we should err on the side of treating animals kindly and use money set aside for charity as an alternative, thereby preventing this request for mercy from becoming an act of cruelty.

Chapter 117

Yom Kippur Prohibitions

May one wear Crocs?

The permissibility of wearing comfortable, non-leather shoes on Yom Kippur has been much talked about over the last several years, following proclamations by Rabbis Yosef Shalom Elyashiv and Yaakov Ariel, among others, which strongly discouraged the wearing of Crocs brand shoes on Yom Kippur. Despite the brouhaha, this debate is actually a continuation of a millennia-old discussion regarding the prohibitions of Yom Kippur.

The Torah never specifies which actions are forbidden on Yom Kippur. Rather, five times the Bible states that a person should afflict (*innui*) himself, in addition to refraining from the work that is forbidden on Shabbat (Lev. 16, 23; Num. 29). Unlike the medieval Karaites, for whom affliction included wearing sackcloth and ashes, abstaining from sleep, and other deprivations, the sages limited this term to five areas of self-denial: bathing, anointment, sexual relations, donning shoes, and nourishment (eating and drinking), with the latter seen as the most severe prohibition, whose violation was punishable by spiritual banishment, *karet* (Yoma 73–74).

Some scholars believed that despite this affliction, an element of festive joy is also mandated, as on other holidays (*mikra'ei kodesh*) mentioned in the Torah (Lev. 23:27). In addition to dressing nicely (Shabbat 119a), we recite the *sheheḥeyanu* blessing, which commemorates special occasions. Mourners even halt their seven-day (*shiva*) bereavement practices so as to accord some measure of festivity to the day (Rabbi

Yonatan of Lunel, Eiruvin 40a). Indeed, some understood the requirement to eat before Yom Kippur as fulfilling the obligation to feast on festivals (BY OḤ 604). The Talmud further states that Yom Kippur was deemed a happy occasion because of the atonement afforded by the day (Taanit 30b).

Nonetheless, most scholars understood the day to be uniquely lacking in holiday festivities (*Ḥizkuni*, Rabbi Ovadia Seforno, Lev. 23:27). We refrain from reciting the joyful Hallel prayer or engaging in excessive happiness (MT *Hilkhot Megilla VeḤanukka* 3:6), both deemed inappropriate for a day of judgment (Arakhin 10b). Ultimately, the Torah aims to achieve a day of respite (*shabbaton*) from physical pleasure along with a feeling of affliction (Maimonides, *Sefer HaMitzvot, Aseh* 164).

This goal, however, might afford certain leniencies with respect to activities that are clearly not intended for pleasure. The Talmud, for example, allows people to rinse dirt from their bodies and wash their hands after using the bathroom or before performing ritual activities (OḤ 613). These dispensations led some to assert that the activities prohibited on Yom Kippur for the sake of affliction – with the exception of nutrition – originated as rabbinic edicts (Rosh, Yoma 8:1). Others, however, believed that the Torah prohibited only acts of pleasure, leaving room for leniency in other circumstances (*Yere'im* 420). By nature, however, anointment and nutrition entail enjoyment; therefore they remain prohibited, except in cases of medical necessity (OḤ 614:1, 618).

An interesting debate exists regarding actions that alleviate discomfort. Many decisors permitted the use of snuff (AH OḤ 612:6), for example, which some considered an appropriate way to mark the festivity of the day (*Gan HaMelekh* 145). Other scholars allowed people to swallow slow-release pills before the fast to prevent headaches (*Tzitz Eliezer* 7:32).

Contrary to popular belief, the Talmud never explicitly limits the ban on footwear to leather shoes. The Mishna states a blanket prohibition (Yoma 73b), with a parallel tannaitic text further forbidding socks (Tosefta Yoma 4:1). The only explicit exceptions are for cases of illness, inclement weather, or walking in hazardous areas. However, some sages covered their feet in reeds or rags (Yoma 78b). Some understood that these rabbis limited the prohibition to formal "shoes," rendering all other protective devices permissible. Others, however, allowed such footwear only if one's foot still felt discomfort from the ground; anything providing greater protection was disqualified (Nahmanides, Shabbat 66a).

This dispute continued into the medieval era, with Maimonides (MT *Hilkhot Shevitat Asor* 3:7) and others requiring one's foot to feel the ground, while others, followed by Rabbi Joseph Karo, forbade only footwear made of leather or wood (OḤ 614:2). Despite the latter, normative ruling, many prominent figures, including Rabbis Yisrael Meir Kagan (MB 614:5) and Yeḥiel Michel Epstein (AH OḤ 614:4), deemed it meritorious to wear slippers or soft-soled shoes in which one feels the ground. While Rabbi Joseph B. Soloveitchik also discouraged padded sneakers (*Nefesh HaRav*, p. 210), Rabbi Moshe Sternbuch further suggested that any regularly worn, comfortable shoes should not be donned on Yom Kippur (*Moadim U'Zemanim* 6:28). Despite these sentiments, the widespread practice – as noted by Israel's chief rabbi during the recent Crocs controversy – is to wear any type of non-leather shoe.

Chapter 118

Hoshanot on Sukkot

What is the meaning behind this custom?

The *Hoshanot* ritual, which entails circling the *bima* with the four botanical species taken on Sukkot while reciting supplications, regularly confounds worshippers. I vividly recall how one Hoshana Rabba during my college years, after whacking the willow branches on the ground to conclude the service, I gave a perplexed look to two young rabbis in the room, who simply responded, "We're not sure either!"

To better understand this ritual, it is important to first note the unique role Sukkot plays in the calendar. On the one hand, Sukkot is the third and final pilgrimage holiday that, alongside other historical events, marks the agricultural year. While Passover and Shavuot commemorate the reaping of various crops, Sukkot celebrates the completion of the harvest (Ex. 23:16, Lev. 23:39). The Torah emphasizes the joy of this holiday, for after a season of labor, we celebrate our prosperity. Yet, as Maimonides emphasizes, to remind ourselves that God is the source of our sustenance, we dedicate our celebrations to Him and sing Hallel praises for the provisions He gives us (Guide 3:43).

On the other hand, Sukkot completes the cycle of Tishrei holidays, including the Days of Awe. Some texts indicate that the books of judgment, sealed on Yom Kippur, get "put away" only on Hoshana Rabba, the seventh day of Sukkot (*Sefer HaManhig* 38). The Talmud adds that while God judges all creatures on Rosh HaShana, the amount of rain to fall in the upcoming winter is determined during Sukkot (Rosh HaShana 16a).

Consequently, a number of rituals developed to beseech God for rain. The Temple hosted a *Simḥat Beit HaShoeva,* in which thousands of people witnessed the joyful bringing of water from the City of David to the Temple, where it was used for libations. The Talmud asserts, "One who has not seen the rejoicing of the *Simḥat Beit HaShoeva* has never seen joy in his life" (Sukka 50a). Today, commemorative celebrations take place in different venues to recreate this joyous spectacle (although usually without the water!).

Similarly, willow branches (*aravot*) ringed the altar on each day of Sukkot. The talmudic sages dispute how this ritual was performed. While the Mishna states that the branches were placed upright alongside the altar, others claimed the willows were held by *kohanim,* while a third group asserted that the branches were beaten on the ground (Sukka 43b). An alternative opinion states that, in actuality, it was the *lulav* that was used to circle the altar.

Despite this ambiguity, it remains clear that members of the four species were used, since as the Talmud states, they represent different plants which require rain to grow (Taanit 2b). Throughout the ceremony, the worshippers pray for merciful rains by reciting, "We beseech You (*hosha na* in Hebrew), God, save us!" from which the ritual derived its name. The last day of Sukkot included seven circles around the altar and special prayers, and was subsequently dubbed Hoshana Rabba, "The Great Supplication." After the Temple's destruction, we commemorate these events by circling the synagogue *bima* and reciting the same ancient prayers. On Hoshana Rabba, we pay homage to the different opinions regarding the *Hoshanot* ritual by first circling with the *lulav,* and then picking up and thrashing the *aravot* (OḤ 660, 664).

Though the Torah mentions none of these rituals, the sages traced them to ancient oral traditions or prophetic decrees. As with other practices not written in the Torah, sectarian groups opposed them. In one spirited incident, the public pelted a Sadducee high priest with *etrogim* after he failed to perform the water libations (Sukka 48b). Another year, when Hoshana Rabba fell on Shabbat, the Boethusians crushed the *aravot* placed by the Pharisees in the Temple before the Sabbath began. These rites, however, were ultimately enshrined in Jewish law, with the rabbis even setting up the calendar so that Hoshana Rabba would never fall on Shabbat.

Over the centuries, different customs have embellished Hoshana Rabba, such as the recitation of festival prayers and the *ḥazan*'s donning a white *kittel*, as on Yom Kippur. In the early Middle Ages, Jerusalem rabbis performed elaborate *Hoshanot* services on the Mount of Olives, overlooking the Temple Mount. Another popular practice is special Torah study. The idea is first mentioned in the thirteenth century (*Avudraham*, Laws of Sukkot), as a prelude to Simḥat Torah. In the sixteenth century, however, Safed kabbalists attributed mystical powers to this learning, giving rise to all-night *tikkun leil Hoshana Rabba* study sessions, thereby adding new meaning to this day.

Chapter 119

Simḥat Torah

Why does the Torah never mention this important holiday?

Although I find it annoying when people respond to me this way, allow me to answer this question with a more basic one: Where are we told to read the Torah publicly in the first place? To understand the development of this holiday, which celebrates the completion and restarting of the Torah reading cycle, we must first appreciate the history of public Torah recitation.

While the Torah never mentions it, the sages asserted that Moses established the public reading of the Torah on Shabbat mornings and on the festivals. Ezra subsequently ordained that the Torah be read on Mondays, Thursdays, and Shabbat afternoons (Y. Megilla 4:1). Based on passages in Philo and in the Talmud, Prof. Yitzḥak Gilat has conjectured that these ancient readings followed no set order; rather, they were chosen based on timely topics and on the local rabbi's inclinations. (Public prayer always came with a sermon!)

By late antiquity, an order was established for the weekly public readings, yet the two major centers of Judaism differed on how to apportion them. Communities in Eretz Yisrael divided the Torah into over 150 sections. As such, the idea of an annual holiday to celebrate the Torah's completion was unfathomable, since it took three (Megilla 29b) to three and a half years (*HaḤillukim SheBein Anshei Mizraḥ U'Vnei Eretz Yisrael* 48) to complete the reading. Instead, each community, reading at a different pace, would hold its own celebration upon completing its local cycle.

Seeking to complete the Torah each year, Babylonian communities uniformly divided the Torah into fifty-four portions (*sedrot* or *parashot* in Hebrew), the maximum number of non-festival Shabbatot that can occur in a Jewish leap year. Non-leap years include the reading of "double *parashot*," with two portions read in one week. By completing the cycle after Sukkot, as opposed to before Rosh HaShana, these communities were able to place Deuteronomy's major speeches of admonition before major holidays (Megilla 31b). Additionally, Moses' concluding blessing to the people was read on Shemini Atzeret, embellishing its joy (*Maḥzor Vitry* 385) and providing a fitting conclusion to the Tishrei holiday season. While the custom in the Land of Israel survived until the early Middle Ages, the Babylonian practice, as with many matters, ultimately won the day.

The completion of the Torah cycle on Shemini Atzeret, a one-day festival immediately after Sukkot, was potentially problematic, since each holiday demands its own thematically appropriate reading. Like all Diaspora communities, Babylonian congregations observed two days of each festival, providing an easy solution. On the first day of Shemini Atzeret, the holiday portion is read, while on the second day (colloquially known today as Simḥat Torah), the congregation reads *Parashat VeZot HaBerakha*, concluding Deuteronomy. With only one day in Israel, however, only *VeZot HaBerakha* could be read, giving priority to Simḥat Torah and relegating recognition of Shemini Atzeret to the *maftir* reading.

Another distinctive element of Simḥat Torah is that in addition to reading the day's portion and its *maftir*, we take out a third Torah scroll to begin Genesis. As Avraham Yaari's chronicle of Simḥat Torah documents, this was not the practice in Babylonia. Rather, twelfth-century European communities began reciting the first verses of Genesis (frequently orally or from a Bible, not a Torah scroll) to display their love of the Torah and eagerness to study it anew.

Another important change that stemmed from Simḥat Torah was the reading of the *haftara*. According to the Talmud (Megilla 31a), the *haftara* for Shemini Atzeret draws from 1 Kings 8, where King Solomon blesses the people on this very day after completing the building of the

Temple. (This passage remains the Diaspora's *haftara* on the first day of Shemini Atzeret.) In the early medieval period, however, congregations began chanting the beginning of Joshua to continue the Torah's narrative as well as to highlight the importance of the rest of Scripture.

Simḥat Torah's unique reading arrangement and the joyousness of the occasion gave rise to the practice of honoring communal figures by having them chant the major readings. Ashkenazic communities also repeat *VeZot HaBerakha* continually until every man has received an *aliya* (OḤ 669). While joyful dancing has been a feature from the beginning, other modes of celebration have varied, including special poems and meals, games for children, and – on a few controversial occasions – the use of musical instruments.

Unfortunately, this joy has sometimes turned into frivolity, and today select communities face problems of drinking and licentiousness. Such behavior reflects a digression in the evolution of this holiday, which has sought to instill a love for Torah and its values. One hopes that a greater understanding of the day's history will help people appreciate the genuine joy of Torah.

Chapter 120

Ḥanukka Meals

Must one celebrate with a feast?

While we all enjoy the potato latkes and *sufganiyot* (jelly donuts) that pervade our cafés and homes on Ḥanukka, it remains striking that the holiday uniquely lacks an official festive meal. The three major pilgrimage holidays – Passover, Sukkot, and Shavuot – all include festive meals based on the requirement of rejoicing (*simḥa*) on these occasions (*Sefer HaMitzvot* 54). Many early medieval scholars believed that the trepidation of Rosh HaShana, a time of judgment, precludes such feasting, and some even encouraged fasting. Others, however, maintained that one must rejoice on Rosh HaShana with festive meals, as on all holidays (OḤ 597), even if it remains appropriate to temper the luxuriousness of the menu (*Magen Avraham*). While one obviously may not eat on Yom Kippur, many scholars considered the pre-fast meal to be a festive one in celebration of the holiday and the atonement it promises (*Shaarei Teshuva* 4:8–9).

Given the association between festive meals and holidays, it is not surprising that the sages instituted a Purim feast. Yet the Talmud mentions no such requirement for Ḥanukka, which is, like Purim, a holiday created by the sages. (The custom of commemorating the miracle of the oil by consuming oily foods, like latkes or donuts, emerged later and remains optional.)

In truth, according to Maimonides and other scholars, Ḥanukka does contain an element of *simḥa* that must be fulfilled through a festive meal (MT *Hilkhot Megilla VeḤanukka* 3:3). Rabbi Shlomo Luria forcefully endorsed this position, arguing that this banquet should publicize the miracle (*Yam shel Shlomo* Bava Kamma 7:37). However, many authorities, including Rabbi Joseph Karo, contend that there is no mitzva of festive eating on Ḥanukka (OḤ 670:2). They note that in the talmudic passage describing the essence of the holiday, the sages assert only that this is a day of praise and thanks (Shabbat 21b).

In support of this view, Rabbi Mordekhai Jaffe (*Levush* OḤ 670:2) explained that Purim reminds us of how our enemies tried to annihilate us physically. To celebrate our physical salvation, the sages decreed that a physical, festive celebration accompany the spiritual actions we perform to give thanks and praise to God. The Greeks, on the other hand, attacked our *spiritual* heritage with Hellenization. As such, Ḥanukka celebrates spiritual salvation; therefore, no festive meal – a mark of physical redemption – is required. Others deem a festive celebration inappropriate for Ḥanukka, since in contrast to Purim, the Jews suffered heavy casualties during this period (*Yosef Lekaḥ*).

A middle-ground position adopted by some Ashkenazic decisors, including Rabbi Moshe Isserles, asserts that there is a "small mitzva" to have a festive meal, because the holiday marks the rededication of the Temple altar. Moreover, Rabbi Isserles writes, "We are accustomed to singing songs of happiness and praise at these meals, and thereby they become *seudot mitzva* (celebratory meals)." In other words, the possibility of *seudot mitzva* exists on this holiday, yet they can take place only through human initiative. When these meals include praises of God, highlighting the religious significance of the day, they become mitzvot. Without these spiritual ingredients, they are just regular repasts.

As Prof. Meir Rafeld has noted, many hasidic masters emphasized this chance to sanctify the mundane (*Minhagei Yisrael* 5). The Munkácser Rebbe, for example, held special dinners on Ḥanukka, while others emphasized the unique opportunity to initiate a spiritual experience.

This position highlights an important message of the holiday. According to Maharal of Prague, God performed (and the sages emphasized) the miracle of the oil to underscore that the Maccabees' military victory ultimately came from Him. As such, one theme of this festival is the sanctification of the mundane via the recognition of God's

Omnipresence and control of the world, whether on the battlefield or in the Temple.

Ḥanukka feasts allow us to appreciate this lesson. Every time we eat, we can transform a normal meal into a *seudat mitzva* through songs of praise and thanks. Just as the Jews of old understood their physical accomplishments as divine intervention, we can turn our "holiday parties" into religious events. Festive meals might not be obligatory, but the ability to create a *seudat mitzva* reflects the opportunity of internalizing this central theme of Ḥanukka.

Chapter 121

Drinking on Purim

Is there any justification for getting drunk?

While Judaism certainly allows for alcohol consumption, and sometimes even mandates it in rituals like Kiddush, it condemns drunkenness as irresponsible and dangerous. In fact, much of the Book of Esther revolves around frivolous and licentious feasts, highlighting the debauchery to which this behavior leads. At the same time, the Bible recalls the banquets held to celebrate the Jews' salvation, and we are subsequently commanded to commemorate those festivities through our own Purim feasts.

The Talmud seemingly contradicts itself regarding the role of wine at our Purim meal (Megilla 7b). At first, the Talmud states, "One is obligated to become intoxicated on Purim until he does not know the difference between 'cursed is Haman' and 'blessed is Mordekhai.'" Immediately afterward, however, it relates how the sage Rabba became so drunk that he violently slew his colleague R. Zeira. The latter was ultimately revived, but the following year, he turned down Rabba's invitation to feast with him again, exclaiming, "Miracles don't always happen!"

Talmudic commentators debated how to resolve this contradiction. Many medieval scholars, such as Rabbi Isaac Alfasi and Rabbenu Asher, affirmed the obligation to become intoxicated. They either ignored the story about R. Zeira, or saw Rabba's drunkenness as proof of this requirement. Rabbi Joseph Karo codified this opinion in his *Shulḥan Arukh* (OḤ 695:2).

According to others, the Talmud uses the word "obligated" loosely here, meaning that inebriation on Purim is a *mitzva be'alma* – permissible but not mandatory. Rabbi Eliezer HaLevi (Raavya), for example, allowed a person to abstain from getting drunk. Similarly, Rabbi Yosef ben Moshe contended that the obligation falls only on someone who enjoys drinking, but not on one who feels it will harm him (*Leket Yosher*).

Rabbi Zeraḥia HaLevi, however, prohibited getting drunk on Purim. He approvingly quotes Rav Ephraim, who contended that the Talmud's account of Rabba's nearly fatal feast proves that the sages ultimately ruled that people should not become intoxicated (Baal HaMaor, Megilla 7b). A particularly harsh condemnation of Purim drunkenness was issued by Rabbi Aharon HaKohen of Lunel. This fourteenth-century Provençal scholar banned intoxication, asserting that it leads only to cardinal sins such as murder and illicit relations (*Orḥot Ḥayim*, Purim 38). True happiness, he contended, stems not from frivolity, but rather from rejoicing with one's friends and sharing with the less fortunate.

Several commentators limited the required level of intoxication. Many argued that one should drink only until confusing Mordekhai and Haman, but not beyond. Rabbi Moshe Isserles novelly ruled that one must imbibe only a little more than usual. He should then take a nap, rendering himself unable to distinguish between Haman and Mordekhai (OḤ 695:2)!

Many modern authorities adopted this moderate position, including the two most prominent Ashkenazic decisors of the early twentieth century, Rabbis Yeḥiel Michel Epstein (AH OḤ 695:5) and Yisrael Meir Kagan (MB 695:5). Rabbi Kagan further notes that intoxication does not justify boorish behavior or neglecting other mitzvot. Therefore, one must be sober enough by the end of the meal to recite *Birkat HaMazon* and the evening prayers.

Rabbi Isserles concludes with the talmudic dictum that "One can do more or less, as long as he intends to serve God." These remarks echo the sentiments of many authorities, including Rabbi Menaḥem HaMeiri, who wrote, "We are not obligated to become inebriated and degrade ourselves ... [or] to celebrate frivolity and foolishness, but rather to engage in a joyful celebration that should lead to love of God and thankfulness for the miracles He has performed for us."

I strongly urge people not to get drunk on Purim. From my perspective, many don't maintain proper intentions. Even well-intentioned revelers end up in drunken stupors, vomiting, or acting boorishly. In recent years, moreover, there have been growing reports of people endangering themselves and others, especially with drinking outside the context of the meal. Let us instead celebrate the continued vitality of the Jewish people by sharing our happiness with our friends and those less fortunate, and through the other mitzvot of the day, such as *matanot la'evyonim* (gifts to the poor).

Chapter 122

Purim Revelry

Are all costumes allowed?

For many children and adults alike, Purim costumes are the highlight of the festive customs that have developed around the holiday. While sometimes entertaining and usually innocuous, this practice remains a contentious matter in Jewish law and lore.

The Book of Esther never discusses Purim costumes, nor does the Talmud. The custom seems to have originated in early medieval Germany. One early halakhic discussion appears in a responsum of Rabbi Yehuda Mintz (Padua, d. 1508), who permitted people to wear masks, despite the opposition of earlier figures (*Shu"t Mahari Mintz* 15). He further allowed men and women to wear clothing of the opposite gender, even as this violates the biblical prohibition of cross-dressing (Deut. 22:5).

The responsum provides no rationale for wearing Purim costumes. Some scholars have speculated that the practice commemorates how Mordekhai was dressed in regal clothing and escorted by Haman (Est. 6:11), a clear turning point in the Megilla (*Eliya Rabba* OḤ 696). Others believe that concealing one's identity symbolizes God's hidden hand in the miraculous salvation. Noting that Esther similarly hid her own identity (Est. 2:20), Dr. Zohar Hanegbi contends that perhaps we dress up to mimic the many costume parties in the story (*Minhagei Yisrael* 6). Whatever its message, the custom has been linked to medieval European Christian carnivals (*fastnacht*) that coincided with Purim. If true, this evolution would be akin to the development of the contemporary American custom of Ḥanukka presents during the "holiday season."

Yet costumes represent just one of many festive customs that have sprung up around Purim, albeit not without controversy and dissent. The Talmud, for example, obligates people to become intoxicated on Purim, yet immediately warns of the dangers (Megilla 7b). As noted in the previous essay, the fear of such wayward behavior has led many prominent decisors, such as Rabbis Yisrael Meir Kagan (MB 695:5) and Yeḥiel Michel Epstein (AH OḤ 695:5), to discourage inebriation.

The custom of making noise during the recitation of Haman's name has taken many forms. Children used to bang together stones bearing his name, thereby rubbing it out and symbolically fulfilling the commandment to wipe out Amalek, Haman's ancestor (BY OḤ 690). Others would stamp their feet (MB 690:59). Today people use rattlers (*groggers*) or other instruments. Yet some decisors opposed this practice, because it prevents listeners from properly hearing the Megilla and makes it difficult for people to endure the lengthy reading (*Sdei Ḥemed*, Purim 10). Most authorities allow these interruptions, but insist that congregants restore sufficient decorum to fulfill the central commandment of Megilla reading (MB 690:60). (I favor readings in which rattlers are limited to the first and last references to Haman.)

Another controversial custom is the performance of *Purim Spiels*, plays that regularly include clown performances or parodies. The frequency of personal insult caused by these productions, even when well-intentioned, led many to object to them (*Moadim U'Zemanim* 2:191), particularly when students mock their teachers. Many decisors contend that such denigration of Torah scholars is never permitted, even with their consent (*Yeḥaveh Daat* 5:50).

Some recite "Purim Torah," using the style and content of talmudic or halakhic discourse to make jokes. Yet the line between humor and irreverence is easily crossed. One fourteenth-century literary parody, known as *Masekhet Purim*, drew the ire of many scholars, who deemed it utter depravity (*Be'er Hetev* 696:13).

Similar reservations existed about costumes and masks. While he discouraged the pious from donning them (*Darkhei Moshe* OḤ 696), Rabbi Moshe Isserles defended the practice. Even when costumes violated the prohibitions of *shatnez* (combining wool and linen) or cross-dressing, he maintained that the intent was to celebrate Purim, not to benefit inappropriately from forbidden actions (OḤ 696:8). Indeed, as Prof. Yaakov Spiegel has shown, cross-dressing enlivened many medieval holiday and life-cycle celebrations, despite occasional rabbinic condemnation (*Baḥ* YD 182).

Yet scholars such as Rabbi Shmuel Abuhab (seventeenth century, Italy) criticized the wearing of Purim costumes as debauchery that detracted from the genuine, religious joy one should feel on this holy day (*Dvar Shmuel* 247). Other decisors concurred, especially with regard to cross-dressing (*Be'er Hetev* 696:13), leading Rabbis Yeḥiel Michel Epstein (AH OḤ 696:12) and Ovadia Yosef (*Yeḥaveh Daat* 5:50) to ban such garb, even for children. Costumes in good taste, however, remain within the letter of the law and the spirit of historical practice.

Chapter 123

Preparing for Passover

Are cosmetics considered ḥametz?

The Torah commands that we eradicate (*tashbitu*) all *ḥametz* (leaven) from our homes (Ex. 12:15), thereby ensuring that we not violate the prohibition of possessing or consuming *ḥametz* on Passover (12:19, 13:7). Some commentators, like Maimonides, believe this commandment requires the renunciation of one's *ḥametz* (*bittul*), severing any connection to it (MT *Hilkhot Ḥametz U'Matza* 2:2). Others contend that the Torah envisaged a search (*bedika*) and destroy (*biur*) operation that removes the *ḥametz* from one's possession (Ritva, Pesaḥim 2a). In any case, all agree that the sages demanded both procedures, for perhaps one's renunciation was halfhearted, or one might find and accidentally eat *ḥametz* over the holiday (Ran, Pesaḥim 1a).

The sages declared that the search for *ḥametz* should take place on the night of the fourteenth of Nisan, allowing for proper attention before the prohibition of owning *ḥametz* kicks in midday on the fourteenth (Pesaḥim 4a). Although this search was traditionally conducted by candlelight, many decisors today believe it is safer and more effective to use a flashlight (*Yabia Omer* OḤ 4:40). While one must search all property where he regularly brings food, including cars and offices, he need not inspect areas that never contain *ḥametz*. While some sources deem it meritorious to go beyond the letter of the law in searching for *ḥametz* (OḤ 442:6), Rabbi Chaim P. Scheinberg and others have warned that unwarranted overexertion (including spring cleaning) leaves well-intentioned people too tired to enjoy the Seder.

To ensure quality cleaning, many people thoroughly cleanse their homes before the night of the search. A few medieval authorities asserted that in such a case, one need not even search that night (Baal HaMaor, Pesaḥim 4a). Yet many disagree (*Tur* OḤ 433). Some believe that a previously cleaned home requires only a quick look on the fourteenth (*Teshuvot HaGeonim Shaarei Teshuva* 433:11); others require a proper inspection, including double-checking for missed areas (MB 433:45).

Because of this dispute, many questioned whether one who has already fulfilled his cleaning obligation should recite a blessing over the search on the fourteenth (MB 433:1). To resolve this dilemma, some proposed that one room be left uncleaned until that night (*Magen Avraham* 433:20), while others encouraged people to place small pieces of bread around the house (and remember where!) to ensure that the search turns up something (OḤ 432:2).

The Talmud asserts that one may ignore tiny crumbs (Pesaḥim 6b), unless they can plausibly combine into an edible object (*Bei'ur HaGra* OḤ 442:11). Some, however, believe that one should search for anything he might eat (*Ḥayei Adam* 2:119, para. 6). Similarly, one may possess and benefit from *ḥametz* products that are unfit for canine consumption (Pesaḥim 45b), since they are comparable to mere dust, but he may not consume them, because doing so upgrades their status into a significant object (MB 442:43).

These factors play a major role in the debates over the use of many cosmetics and toiletries containing active *ḥametz* ingredients, such as ethanol (grain alcohol). Most ointments and certain cosmetics (like mascara) may clearly be used during Passover, since they can never be consumed. Some believe that bad-tasting or unflavored pills and liquid medications are upgraded to *ḥametz* when consumed by a patient (*Shaagat Aryeh* 75). They therefore should be avoided if an equally effective substitute is available, but only after consultation with one's doctor and rabbi. Others counter that such medications – especially in pill form – never become reclassified as food, even when ingested (*Nishmat Avraham* OḤ 466:1). More pleasant-tasting cough syrups are generally considered fit for consumption and may require Passover supervision (SSK 40:74).

Scholars have further debated the use of products containing denatured alcohol derived from ethanol, such as deodorants and colognes. While inedible at the time of purchase, their *ḥametz* ingredients can *become* edible through distillation or adding certain ingredients. (Some products with completely denatured alcohol – as well as alcohol in paints and shampoos – are reportedly not restorable and remain definitively permissible.) While Rabbis Tzvi Pesaḥ Frank (*Mikra'ei Kodesh, Pesaḥ* 1:54) and Moshe Feinstein (IM OḤ 3:62) ruled stringently, Rabbis Joseph B. Soloveitchik and Ovadia Yosef (*Yalkut Yosef, Kitzur Shulḥan Arukh* 2, 447:2) contended that these ingredients are deemed inedible based on their current composition. Others note that today ethanol is regularly synthesized from chemicals, not derived from grain. Since many kashrut agencies adopt varying standards, one should consult his or her halakhic authority for proper guidance.

Chapter 124

Selling *Ḥametz*

Is this practice really legitimate?

Every year, Israel's Chief Rabbinate sells an average of 150 billion dollars' worth of *ḥametz* (leavened products) to a non-Jewish Israeli. The sheer vastness of this number, as well as the scattered locations of the *ḥametz,* leads many to wonder about the legality of the sale. This mass transaction, however, is only the latest stage in the history of *mekhirat ḥametz,* the selling of Jewish leaven to non-Jews before Passover.

Beyond forbidding the consumption of bread and the like, the Torah twice forbids owning *ḥametz* (Ex. 12:19, 13:7). According to most scholars, the biblical prohibition applies to all *ḥametz* that a person owns, even if currently in someone else's physical possession (*Ḥatam Sofer* OḤ 1:113). To uphold these commandments, one must relinquish all claims to the *ḥametz* (*bittul*) and remove it from one's possession (*biur*). To accomplish the latter goal, one may either consume or burn the *ḥametz,* or he may permanently give it to a non-Jew (Pesaḥim 21a, 13a).

One talmudic-era source, however, discusses a case in which a Jew may give his *ḥametz* to a non-Jew and then receive it back after Passover. If a person is stuck on a boat, and will require bread after the holiday, he may unconditionally sell his *ḥametz* to a non-Jew – or ask the non-Jew to purchase additional rations during Passover – with the implicit understanding that the non-Jew will sell him the *ḥametz* after the festival (Tosefta Pesaḥim 2:12–13). While the rabbis deemed this sale legitimate, it was clearly a case of dire need.

Indeed, a number of medieval decisors prohibited sales of *ḥametz* carried out in an attempt to avoid fulfilling the law (*haarama*). Rabbi Yom Tov ibn Asevilli (d. 1330, Spain), for example, banned yearly sales to prevent Jews from regularly circumventing these biblical prohibitions (Ritva, Pesaḥim 21a). He further forbade the consumption of sold *ḥametz* after Passover, applying the same prohibition imposed on leaven illegally owned over the holiday.

Two major decisors, however, defended the yearly selling of *ḥametz* to non-Jews. Rabbis Israel Isserlein (fifteenth century, Germany) and Joseph Karo (sixteenth century, Safed) both ruled that as long as one fulfills the technical requirements of a proper transaction, the sale remains valid, even though the gentile sells the *ḥametz* back after the holiday (OḤ 448:3). Yet both rabbis demanded that one remove the sold *ḥametz* from his house. Some Jews still follow this directive, bringing their *ḥametz* to a location owned by the non-Jew.

This stipulation remained practical in eras without refrigeration and food preservatives, when Jews possessed little *ḥametz* that would still be edible after Passover. However, as Rabbi Shlomo Zevin has noted, in the late sixteenth century, Polish Jews entered the liquor industry, and could not rid their large warehouses of *ḥametz*. Meeting this challenge, Rabbi Yoel Sirkes (1561–1640) employed several legal mechanisms that would allow the sale to take place without requiring company owners to remove the *ḥametz* from their premises (*Baḥ* OḤ 448).

While this method was intended for businesses, homeowners soon adopted it, with Passover Haggadot sometimes providing forms and instructions. Some scholars objected to this use of a legal loophole to avoid the relatively minimal financial losses incurred by removing *ḥametz* from one's possession. Furthermore, individuals made mistakes in the intricacies of the transaction. As such, for over a century, most people have appointed a rabbi to sell their *ḥametz*, informing him of its location and approximate value. Today, one can even complete this process via numerous Internet sites.

These developments made such transactions more common yet also more indirect, and have therefore generated opposition. Many decisors, ranging from the eighteenth-century Lithuanian authority, the Vilna Gaon (*Maaseh Rav* 180), to such recent figures as Rabbi Joseph

B. Soloveitchik (*Nefesh HaRav*, p. 177), have discouraged the use of this mechanism, especially to sell full-fledged bread (*ḥametz gamur*). Yet major rabbinic authorities like Rabbis Moshe Sofer (*Ḥatam Sofer* OḤ 1:62) and Moshe Feinstein (IM OḤ 4:95) have defended these sales as both valid and authentic. All agree, however, that sellers must take the sale seriously (*Kitzur Shulḥan Arukh* 114:1).

Parenthetically, in recent years, many communities have launched "food drives" before Passover to donate unwanted *ḥametz* products to the needy (in Israel, these goods are sold before the holiday and distributed afterward). This is a most worthwhile cause in the holiday spirit.

Chapter 125

Kitniyot

What is the status of quinoa?

While it looks like a grain, quinoa is actually a chenopod, a species related to beets and spinach. Grown primarily for its seeds, quinoa has skyrocketed in popularity in recent years, becoming one of Bolivia's primary exports. Because of its nutritious content and grain-like flavor, many have suggested it as a great alternative during Passover, engendering much controversy relating to a centuries-old debate regarding the permissibility of eating *kitniyot* (legumes) on Passover.

The sages asserted that matza (permissible unleavened bread) must be made of a grain flour that, when combined with water, becomes *ḥametz* unless it is prevented from fermenting. Only five grains are prohibited as *ḥametz* and may therefore be consumed as matza: rye, oats, barley, spelt, and wheat (Pesaḥim 35a). Although one sage also wanted to include rice in this prohibition, the Talmud ultimately excluded this grain, as well as millet (114b). Maimonides categorized these foods (and legumes) as *kitniyot,* which are permissible to eat even if ground and baked as bread (MT *Hilkhot Ḥametz U'Matza* 6:4).

Yet starting in the thirteenth century, numerous Ashkenazic authorities mention a custom of not consuming *kitniyot.* Some feared that people would mistake *ḥametz* products for *kitniyot* ones and come to eat forbidden grains (*Smak* 222). Others claimed that stunted wheat looks like *kitniyot,* or that wheat and *kitniyot* easily mix in fields and will ultimately be cooked together (Rabbenu Manoaḥ MT *Hilkhot Ḥametz U'Matza* 5:1).

Sephardic decisors rejected this custom as an excessive stringency (BY OḤ 453). Nonetheless, some advised sifting through rice to ensure that grains of *ḥametz* did not get mixed in (Ritva, Pesaḥim 35a), or even abstaining from rice consumption altogether (*Kaf HaḤayim* 453:10). While a few medieval Ashkenazic decisors also balked at this stricture, it ultimately gained widespread acceptance and was codified into Ashkenazic law (OḤ 453). In the eighteenth century, Rabbi Yaakov Emden wanted to nullify the custom, since he felt it led to such excessive demand for matza products that people made mistakes with bona fide *ḥametz* prohibitions (*She'elat Yaavetz* 2:147). Yet Orthodox leaders like Rabbi Tzvi Hirsch Chajes defended the practice, especially against the criticisms of the Reform movement.

All agree, however, that unlike *ḥametz*, there is no prohibition of owning or benefiting from *kitniyot*, such as by feeding it to animals (MB 453:12). Many further argue that there is no problem of feeding *kitniyot* (including many baby formulas) to young children (*Yeḥaveh Daat* 1:9). During famines, several Eastern European rabbis waived this stringency (*Ḥayei Adam* 2:127, para. 6), and while there were a few dissenters (*Teshuva MeAhava* 2:259), most agreed to suspend it in times of need, including illness (MB 453:7). In addition, Ashkenazim may eat non-*kitniyot* foods served in Sephardic homes, even if cooked in pots previously used to cook *kitniyot* (*Az Nidberu* 8:20, para. 4).

Some sources indicate that liquid derivatives of *kitniyot*, such as oils and syrups, were included in the medieval prohibition (*Nishmat Adam* 119:20). Rabbi Yitzḥak E. Spektor and others, however, contended that the process of making oil before Passover – including sifting the seeds and preserving their dryness – precludes the concerns that led to this custom, thereby rendering all such derivatives permissible (*Be'er Yitzḥak* OḤ 11). This position led Rabbi Abraham Isaac Kook in 1909 to permit sesame oil, for which he was severely condemned by one of Jerusalem's prominent rabbinic courts (*Oraḥ Mishpat* OḤ 108–111).

A certain amount of ambiguity and dispute relates to defining which foods are *kitniyot*. Some grain-like products were prohibited, others were not, while mustard seeds were included in the ban because they grow in pods like beans (*Taz* OḤ 453:1). Rabbi Moshe Feinstein asserted that we follow only the traditional custom and do not add new items, like peanuts (IM OḤ 3:63). Accordingly, many authorities allow safflower oil, even as the recently invented canola oil remains disputed, since it is modeled on rapeseed oil, which was historically assumed by some to be problematic (Maharsham 1:183). Regarding quinoa, some decisors – such as Rabbi Yaakov Ariel – discourage its consumption because these seeds look very similar to grains. Yet Rabbis Gedalia Dov Schwartz, Moshe Heinemann, and Dov Lior, along with a growing number of scholars, permit quinoa as long as it is not mixed with other grains in the production plant.

Chapter 126

Seder Night

May we start the ritual before nightfall for the sake of the children?

While children are not obligated in mitzvot, they play an influential role in the Seder. In four places, the Torah speaks of the necessity of retelling and recreating the Exodus story for the next generation. These verses inspired the "four children of the Haggada," for whom the story must come alive over this holiday. Their inquisitiveness creates the edifying environment that makes the Seder so enriching.

While no similar obligation exists on Shabbat, many people start the day early, so their children can gain spiritual nourishment from the meal. Shabbat technically begins on Friday at sunset but ends Saturday night only after three stars emerge. The reason for this discrepancy is that the rabbis were not sure when exactly nighttime begins. They therefore erred on the side of caution, declaring the entire twilight period (*bein hashemashot*) Shabbat (Shabbat 34b). While there are limited leniencies during this period, virtually all Shabbat restrictions and requirements apply (OḤ 261:1).

Around the world, most communities light Shabbat candles eighteen to twenty minutes before sunset (MB 261:23), with Jerusalem lighting forty minutes before sunset. This practice stems from a talmudic mandate to extend Yom Kippur (Yoma 81b). Unlike Maimonides, most medieval scholars applied this rule to Shabbat as well, and this became the normative practice, known as *tosefet Shabbat* (OḤ 261:2).

Rashi (1040–1105, France) believes this "cushion" protects us from accidentally working on Shabbat due to miscalculations in time (Rashi, Gen. 2:2). Rabbenu Nissim (fourteenth century, Spain), however, sees *tosefet Shabbat* as a pious attempt to draw sanctity into the week. Thus, one is not allowed to end Shabbat early, even to begin the Seder (when Passover immediately follows the Sabbath), since we are not to diminish this most sanctified time. One may not even prepare for the Seder before the Sabbath concludes, since doing so constitutes inappropriate planning on Shabbat.

On the other hand, one may not start Shabbat too early, with 90–110 minutes before sunset being the earliest time. (One should consult a halakhic time calendar to determine the proper time on a given week.) This rule causes difficulties in countries with an extremely late summer sunset, such as Norway, and a rich literature addresses this issue (*BeMareh HaBazak* 5:32).

In theory, the virtue of *tosefet Shabbat* should apply to Passover as well, thereby allowing the Seder to commence (when it does not follow Shabbat) at an earlier hour. The mitzva of retelling the Exodus, however, is intrinsically connected to the other central mitzva of the night, eating matza. Historically, matza was consumed with the Paschal sacrifice, which cannot be eaten before nightfall. Since the Seder can last a few hours, one could theoretically begin it earlier and eat matza only after nightfall. However, Rabbi Israel Isserlein (fifteenth century, Germany) ruled that Kiddush, which begins the Seder, must also take place after nightfall (BY OḤ 472). This became the normative practice, precluding an early Seder. Some recently suggested beginning evening prayers a little earlier, so the Seder can begin immediately at nightfall, although this idea has not yet taken root.

The contemporary author Rabbi Moshe Harari discusses whether certain dispensations might be made for hospital personnel and soldiers who might not have time to perform the Seder after nightfall. While a few decisors rule leniently, especially for soldiers who do not know when their mission will end, no such dispensation applies for children, who are not obligated in mitzvot. After all, the obligation to conduct the Seder – and even ask the four questions – exists even when no children are present, and even if one eats alone.

Recognizing the difficulties of the late hour, the talmudic sages kept children awake by distributing snacks, while urging people to start the Seder on time (Pesaḥim 109a). Scholars debate whether the Talmud also ordained speeding up the Seder to ensure that children eat matza and the meal (*Shaar HaTziyun* 472:2). Most parents keep children awake – especially until the four questions and the beginning of the Haggada – with games like stealing the *afikoman* (though such activities should not be at the expense of a thoughtful Seder). My father's distribution of candy for every question or song worked wonders in my family!

Chapter 127

The Four Cups

Is it better to drink wine or grape juice?

The obligation to drink four cups of wine at the Seder presents definite problems for those who have difficulty imbibing that much alcohol at one meal. Particularly since the halakha determines that one must drink at least several ounces per cup (sipping is not sufficient), the question of using non-alcoholic substitutes remains pressing.

Jewish law dictates that all men and women consume four cups of wine at the Seder, each at the appropriate time: Kiddush, *Maggid* (the recitation of the Passover story), Grace After Meals, and Hallel (OḤ 472:8–15). This rabbinic obligation creates an ambience of liberty (*ḥerut*) and regality while marking each stage of the evening and publicizing our praise of God for our miraculous salvation (*pirsumei nisa*). Given the significant impact of this mitzva on the Seder, the sages ruled that even the poor must consume all four cups, with the community providing the wine if necessary (Pesaḥim 99b).

To appreciate the status of grape juice, we must understand the complex laws that regulate the special place of wine in halakha. Wine receives a blessing (*Borei pri hagafen*) distinct from other fruit juices because of its unique role in rituals and because of the pleasure and satisfaction it provides (Berakhot 35a). While it may be diluted with water or combined with other fragrances or liquids, it must contain a certain amount (debated by the sages) of natural juice to retain its status as wine (OḤ 204:5). Nahmanides declared white wine invalid for Kiddush, yet most authorities permitted it, though some preferred red, especially if high-quality (272:4).

In natural wine production, workers crush the grapes, then transfer the juice ("must"), pulp, and skin to fermentation vats that convert the liquid into alcohol. To avoid complex legal restrictions related to wine handled by non-Jews (*stam yeinam*), some producers heat the juice at the beginning of this process and then add wine enzymes to facilitate artificial fermentation, producing wine known as *yayin mevushal* (cooked wine). While a few medieval authorities believed this process rendered the wine tasteless and therefore no longer worthy of its unique blessing, most disagreed (OḤ 202:1).

A different potential problem regarding cooked wine stems from the requirement that Kiddush wine must also be fit for Temple libations (Bava Batra 97b). Accordingly, Maimonides invalidated all cooked wine for ritual use. Other medieval scholars maintained that since the wine's basic character remains unchanged, one may still use it in rituals. This opinion follows the declaration in the Jerusalem Talmud that one may drink cooked wine at the Seder, which includes Kiddush (Pesaḥim 10:1). Although Rabbi Joseph B. Soloveitchik preferred uncooked wines for Kiddush, contemporary practice follows the lenient opinion, especially when the cooked wine tastes better (OḤ 272:8).

(In a controversial ruling, Rabbi Shlomo Zalman Auerbach contended that contemporary pasteurization does not heat the juice enough to render it cooked [*Minḥat Shlomo* 1:25]. However, most decisors, including Rabbis Moshe Feinstein [IM YD 3:31] and Ovadia Yosef [*Yabia Omer* YD 8:15], consider such wine as *yayin mevushal* but acceptable for Kiddush.)

The Talmud states that one may squeeze a cluster of grapes before Shabbat and immediately consume it, which suggests that grape juice may be used for Kiddush (OḤ 272:2). Normative halakha adopts this position, even as many assert that wine is preferable (*Magen Avraham* 272:3). While today we pasteurize grape juice to prevent bacterial growth, most believe that this heating doesn't invalidate it (*Yalkut Yosef* Shabbat 1, 272:9).

During the Prohibition era, in the early twentieth century, American law allowed wine distribution for religious purposes. Embarrassed by the widespread abuse of this exemption, the non-Orthodox movements argued – in a responsum written by Rabbi Louis Ginzberg and released at a press conference (!) – that Jews did not need this dispensation, as grape juice or raisin wine (OḤ 272:6) could serve as acceptable alternatives. Although this pronouncement led one Orthodox polemicist to attempt to invalidate grape juice, the beverage became universally accepted for Kiddush (*Har Tzvi* OḤ 1:158). Rabbi Auerbach has further questioned the use of reconstituted grape juice for Kiddush, since the dilution process may leave an insufficient amount of juice, but most decisors have dismissed this concern.

Nonetheless, Rabbis Moshe Feinstein and Tzvi Pesaḥ Frank deemed grape juice unacceptable for the Seder, as the Talmud requires a fine wine that commemorates our freedom (Pesaḥim 108b) and gives a person joy (*Mikra'ei Kodesh, Pesaḥ* 2:35). Many decisors counter that grape juice is sufficiently distinguished and, more importantly, should be used if one enjoys it more than wine (*Nefesh HaRav*, p. 185). This directive is particularly applicable to those who become easily intoxicated or drowsy from wine, inhibiting their commemoration of the Exodus experience (*Mishneh Halakhot* 10:67).

Chapter 128

Matza I

Is there any difference between handmade and machine-made matzot?

Matza making has undergone major changes over the past two hundred years, amidst great controversy. In many ways, today's matza industry reflects uniquely diverse ways of producing this ancient food.

The Torah juxtaposes the prohibition of consuming *ḥametz* (leaven) on Passover with the commandment to consume matza, the unleavened bread whose meagerness and "incompleteness" recall the impoverished slavery of the Israelites and their hasty exodus from Egypt (Deut. 16:3). The sages derived from this juxtaposition that matza must be made from grain flour that, when combined with water, could become *ḥametz*, but is made in a way that prevents it from doing so. As such, matza flour may be made only from rye, oats, barley, spelt, and wheat (Pesaḥim 35a). While wheat was historically preferred (OḤ 453:1), companies recently started producing spelt and oat matza to accommodate those who are allergic to gluten, because these grains are especially soluble and easier to digest.

Many medieval authorities, followed by Rabbi Joseph Karo, believe that flour mixed exclusively with fruit juice or eggs (and no water added) cannot ferment into *ḥametz* (OḤ 462:1). Many Sephardim follow this opinion and therefore permit the consumption of egg matza (*matza ashira*). Ashkenazim, however, follow Rabbi Moshe Isserles, who bans the use of fruit juice in making matza, either because water may accidentally be added, or because he felt that fruit juice may indeed cause fermentation (MB 462:15). Children and the elderly may eat such matzot, although preferably not at the Seder, since the richness of egg matza does not reflect the "bread of affliction" (*leḥem oni*) depicted in the Torah.

Matza baking is quick and intensive, since the sages ruled that any dough made of the aforementioned grains and left unhandled for eighteen minutes ferments (MB 459:2). The bakery is also kept cool, since the rabbis further required that the flour be mixed only with water that was chilled overnight (*mayim shelanu*).

While *ḥametz* is forbidden all Passover, matza is required (Ex. 12:18) only at the Seder (OḤ 475:7). The Torah dictates that one should "guard" this matza (Ex. 12:17), making extra-sure that it did not become *ḥametz*. While some medieval authorities required this additional supervision only once the flour becomes mixed with water, Rabbi Joseph Karo discouraged reliance upon this lenient opinion, except in times of great need (OḤ 453:4). (Most flour bought in stores today comes in contact with water during its production, rendering it *ḥametz*.)

Some authorities required that the matza eaten at the Seder be made of grain that was "guarded" from the time of its harvest (*shemura matzot*). Others deem it sufficient if this supervision starts when the grain is milled into flour (*matzot peshutot*). Today, the former criterion is used for almost all handmade matzot, while most machine matzot adhere to the latter. Some people follow the strictest standard only at the Seder, while others maintain it throughout the holiday, as they deem matza consumption a mitzva (even if not obligatory) for all seven days (MB 453:25).

The sages further understood that the commandment to "guard" the matza dictates that its bakers perform their job "*lishmah*," conscientiously acknowledging that their actions fulfill a mitzva (Pesaḥim 40a). This requirement renders immature minors ineligible to produce matza (OḤ 460:1). It also became the center of halakhic dispute in the mid-nineteenth century, when questions were raised over whether to use machines to produce matzot. Proponents claimed that automation would produce more matza for less money, while maintaining better kashrut control during the laborious and meticulous process.

Rabbi Shlomo Kluger, along with several prominent hasidic rebbes, vociferously argued against this innovation, contending that machines could not have the requisite intent of performing a mitzva (*Modaa LeVeit Yisrael*). He also warned that automation would destroy the livelihood of many laborers, who also provided better kashrut quality control than machines. Rabbi Yosef Shaul Nathanson and others countered that the "intent" requirement was fulfilled by workers' consciousness of the mitzva, and did not necessitate their physical involvement (*koaḥ gavra*), and that in any case, humans started the process and maintained physical contact with the matza (*Bittul Modaa*).

Many of the Eastern European opponents additionally feared that any departure from tradition – the use of machinery along with the change from round matzot to square (which minimized waste and leftover dough) – might represent or lead to Reform antinomianism. Others dismissed these concerns, and today machine-made matzot are an inexpensive, high-quality Passover staple, and names like Manischewitz and Streit's are household words.

Chapter 129

Matza II

How much matza must one eat at the Seder?

The Torah commands us to perform many actions and prohibits many more, yet it never quantifies them. We are told to eat of the Paschal sacrifice or immerse in a ritual bath (*mikve*); yet we are never told how much to eat, or how much water the bath must contain. Like many other minutia of Jewish law, these details – known as *shiurim* (measurements) – are provided only through the Oral Law, as documented in rabbinic sources. While *shiurim* are relevant year-round, they become particularly pertinent at the Passover Seder, when we consume matza several times, in addition to *maror* (bitter herbs) and four cups of wine.

As Prof. Yitzḥak Gilat has documented, the sages offered various perspectives regarding the necessity of *shiurim*. In a number of realms of law, including the Sabbath (Tosefta Beitza 4:4) and ritual impurity (Kelim 27:5), R. Eliezer argued that even the most minimal amounts are significant in Jewish law. Yet most authorities asserted that various volumes or lengths – measured by foods (like eggs and figs) or body parts (like thumbs and handbreadths) – are required. For example, with regard to many commandments involving food intake, one must eat the equivalent of the size of an olive (*kezayit*) within a brief period (Sukka 6a). While some sages contended that these measurements were determined by the rabbis, others categorized them as *halakhot leMoshe miSinai*, ancient traditions transmitted throughout the generations (Y. Pe'ah 1:1).

A system of measurements based on body parts and foods is of course inexact. This problem is compounded by variations in food size in different periods and regions. Yet such a system has the advantage of being accessible throughout time (*Teshuvot HaGeonim Shaarei Teshuva* [Lick ed.] 95). Based on manuscripts published in the twentieth century, we know that a few Geonim (early medieval authorities) concluded that one simply estimates the volume of various local foods (*Sefer HaEshkol,* Ḥalla 126a). Yet historically many measurements were based on a ratio to the size of a specific food, with the gold standard being the readily available egg.

Unfortunately, various talmudic passages offer contradictory indications regarding the ratio of an egg to an olive. Some have asserted that this confusion hinges on whether we include the eggshell (Gra OḤ 486:1), while others contend that the talmudic passages simply conflict (*Yeshuot Yaakov* OḤ 301).

In any case, Maimonides implied that an olive is less than a third of an egg (MT *Hilkhot Eiruvin* 1:9), with other Sephardic scholars depicting it as even smaller (Rashba *Mishmeret HaBayit* 4:1). Many Ashkenazic figures, however, concluded that an olive is roughly equivalent to half an egg (*Tosafot* Yoma 80a). As Rabbi Natan Slifkin has emphasized, this seemingly errant calculation was made by northern European scholars who confessed that they had no exposure to olives (Raavya, Berakhot 1:107). While acknowledging this incongruity, numerous scholars adopted this stringent ratio (*Taz* YD 44:12), perhaps in light of the ambiguous position taken by Rabbi Joseph Karo (OḤ 368:3, 409:7, 486:1).

A second source of confusion stemmed from talmudic ratios of length to volume (Pesaḥim 109a–b). Using a water displacement test, Rabbi Yeḥezkel Landau noted that the talmudic ratio of eggs to thumbs was inaccurate (*Tzelaḥ* Pesaḥim 116b). This discrepancy had already been noted by medieval scholars (*Shu"t Tashbetz* 3:33) but was historically accepted with relative equanimity (*Yehuda Yaaleh* YD 1:205). Yet based on the theological notion of "the decline of the generations," Rabbi Landau concluded that contemporary eggs are half the size of those in early eras, and that in consonance with the Ashkenazic ratio of eggs to olives, the legal measurement of an "olive" is actually equivalent to a contemporary egg! This amount has been estimated at 47.5 cc, or roughly three-fourths of a standard machine-made matza.

Many eminent scholars, including Rabbis Yisrael Meir Kagan (MB 486:1) and Avraham Karelitz (*Kuntres HaShiurim* 39:6) accepted this position, even as they questioned its logic (BH 271:13, s.v. *vehu*) or drew conflicting conclusions in other writings (*Kovetz Iggerot Ḥazon Ish* 1:194). Other figures, including Rabbi Yeḥiel Michel Epstein (AH OḤ 168:13), rejected Rabbi Landau's assessment, with Rabbi Ḥayim Na'eh measuring an olive as 27 cc, or half of a machine-made matza.

For those who find it difficult to consume so much matza, particularly within the requisite time span – roughly four minutes (*kedei akhilat pras*) – other authorities recommend eating the equivalent of the Maimonidean olive: 17–19 cc, or slightly less than a third of a matza (*Shiurei Torah*, pp. 194–95). Rabbi Ḥayim Volozhiner offered the most lenient modern position (*Kehillat Yaakov* Pesaḥim 43). He asserted, in the spirit of the geonic responsa cited above, that fundamentally one need consume only a small piece of matza (5–6 cc), since at the end of the day, an olive is an olive.

Chapter 130

Yom HaShoah

Why are commemorations held in high regard by some but ignored by others?

In 1951, the State of Israel declared 27 Nisan "Holocaust and Ghetto Uprising Day." The day was meant both to memorialize Holocaust victims and to commemorate the ghetto rebellions, with a particular eye to the Warsaw Ghetto uprising. Contrary to popular belief, the uprising began on 15 Nisan, but since that is the first day of Passover, 27 Nisan was chosen as a date comfortably between the end of the holiday and Israel Independence Day (5 Iyar). Commemoration of the day became widespread only in 1959, however, when it was renamed "Holocaust and Heroism Day," or *Yom HaShoah VeHaGevura* in Hebrew.

Yom HaShoah has become deeply enmeshed with the religious and cultural meaning of both the Holocaust and the Jewish state. As many have documented, Israel's founding generation struggled with the idea of commemorating the Holocaust, seeking to leave behind the downtrodden image of the exiled Jew while forging a national identity of strength and independence. Zionist leaders thus required that the day instill the notion that Jews must defend themselves. Others, however, believed that Holocaust-era valor manifested itself in different ways, and therefore the more generic "Heroism" replaced "Ghetto Uprising" in the day's title.

Yom HaShoah also represents a potentially symbolic break with the Jewish memorial tradition, which includes fasting, prayers, and repentance. Sacred texts and rituals, loaded with theological meaning, were abandoned in favor of modern ceremonies, which occasionally contained explicitly secular or even anti-religious messages. Indeed, the date of Yom HaShoah was chosen despite protests that halakha forbids eulogies in Nisan (OḤ 429:2).

As Rabbi Jacob Schacter (*Tradition* 41:2) and Prof. Arye Edrei have documented, the religious community has also grappled with commemorating Yom HaShoah and the Holocaust in general. One emotionally charged question, regarding when to recite Kaddish for loved ones killed on unknown dates, was resolved in 1948 when the Israeli Chief Rabbinate established 10 Tevet, a fast day, as "General Kaddish Day." Additionally, many attempts were made to memorialize the Holocaust on Tisha B'Av, the summertime fast commemorating Jewish tragedies throughout the centuries. This date was proposed in 1977 by Rabbi Joseph B. Soloveitchik and Prime Minister Menachem Begin, but was roundly rejected.

Some Orthodox Jews have rejected the establishment of a Holocaust memorial day, arguing that no dates may be added to the ritual calendar and that in any case, Tisha B'Av memorializes all Jewish tragedies. This position, based on an interpretation of a Tisha B'Av elegy, was first advocated in 1942 by Rabbi Yitzḥak Soloveitchik, and was later endorsed by such rabbis as Moshe Feinstein (IM YD 4:57) and Joseph B. Soloveitchik. The latter further opposed the composition of new Tisha B'Av elegies, although numerous communities have introduced them.

For many, the insistence on a Tisha B'Av memorial date stems from the belief that the Holocaust, while unprecedented in its violence and scope, does not represent a unique theological event. Rather, it continues two millennia of affliction and chastisement that we remember on Tisha B'Av. To that end, Rabbi Yitzchak Hutner (d. 1980) refused to use the distinctive terms "Holocaust" or "Shoah," and instead referred to the *ḥurban* (destruction) of Eastern European Jewry. In stark contrast, for many non-Orthodox thinkers the Holocaust has shattered their understanding of God's goodness, His covenant with His people, and Jewish history.

Other traditional figures, including Rabbis Yeḥiel Yaakov Weinberg (d. 1966) and Pinchas Teitz (d. 1995), favored a Holocaust memorial day, though not necessarily considering 27 Nisan the wisest choice (*Seridei Esh* 1:31). They believed that such a day was essential to remembering the Eastern European communities, and that combining it with the traditional fast day would shortchange either Tisha B'Av or Yom HaShoah. Some have further noted that medieval Jews chose special dates to memorialize tragedies, such as 20 Sivan, which commemorated both the 1171 Edicts of Bloise and later, the 1648 Chmielnicki massacres (*Magen Avraham* 580:9).

Given the different outlooks on the Holocaust, it remains difficult to unite for communal and national commemorations. Nonetheless, it behooves us to find a way to come together to console survivors, remember what was lost, and affirm our common destiny.

Chapter 131

Dwelling in Places of Jewish Tragedy

May one live in Egypt, Spain, and Germany?

When 30 percent of polled Israelis said they were rooting for Germany to win the World Cup in 2010, some wondered how Jews could rally around that country with its disgraceful past. Yet the same could be said about much of the world, including Germany's opponent in the semifinals that year, Spain, which violently expelled its Jews in 1492. Sports aside, larger moral and legal questions surround the propriety of Jews returning to these countries.

The Torah prohibits Jews from living in Egypt. "[The king] shall not send the people back to Egypt…you shall never return by that way again" (Deut. 17:16). This commandment reflects the promise made to the Israelites that they would never see Egypt again (Ex. 14:13, Deut. 28:68). Egyptian Jewish communities certainly existed in antiquity, however, including refugees from the First Temple's destruction. The Talmud explains that the community of Alexandria, including its grandiose synagogue, was ultimately destroyed because the people violated this biblical command (Sukka 51b).

Yet prominent Jewish communities continued to thrive in Egypt during the medieval era, boasting such renowned scholars as Maimonides and Rabbi David ibn Zimra. One medieval writer claimed that Maimonides himself viewed his residence in Egypt as a sin that could be absolved only because he initially fled there and then could not leave because he had become a physician to the Egyptian elite (*Kaftor VaFeraḥ* 5).

Most authorities justified living in Egypt for various reasons. The Talmud allowed temporary residence there, such as for work purposes (MT *Hilkhot Melakhim* 5:8). Rabbi ibn Zimra himself maintained that Jews initially came to Egypt temporarily, for their livelihood, but stayed because they lacked economic opportunities elsewhere (Radbaz MT *Hilkhot Melakhim* 5:7). Elsewhere he argued that as long as these Jews still desired to return to the Land of Israel, they did not violate the prohibition (*Shu"t HaRadbaz* 4:73). Others contended that the prohibition applied only when Jews lived in Eretz Yisrael. Once they were exiled, the ban became dormant (Ritva, Yoma 38a).

A different approach to whether the prohibition remains in force focuses on its rationale. Maimonides, followed by Nahmanides (Deut. 17:16), asserted that the Torah's goal was to prevent the Jews from learning from Egyptian decadence (Lev. 18:3). Indeed, the Talmud permitted Jews to return as conquerors, since they would then control the culture (Y. Sanhedrin 10:8). As such, some claimed that this prohibition itself was only temporary and did not apply to later generations (Rabbenu Baḥya). Alternatively, since other nations have become equally degenerate, Egypt is no worse than anywhere else (*Pirḥei Tziyon* 110). Yet another reason for leniency was that following the dispersal of nations by King Sennacherib of Assyria, the ancient Egyptians no longer resided there (MT *Hilkhot Issurei Biah* 12:25).

As stated, however, the Talmud reports that Alexandrian Jews were punished many centuries later. As such, many interpreters tied the prohibition to the territory itself (*Ḥayim She'ol* 1:91). One popular explanation was offered by Rabbi Eliezer of Metz (*Yere'im* 309). Taking the verse literally, he contended that Jews were forbidden to return via the same route they'd originally traveled from Egypt to Eretz Yisrael, but they were permitted to move to Egypt from other countries.

Despite a widespread belief that a similar ban was issued regarding Spain following the 1492 expulsion, rabbis and historians alike have found no evidence of such (*Yeḥaveh Daat* 3:81). While a few European communities imposed social sanctions on members who visited Spain, this censure stemmed from the inability to live a Jewish life there, not from the Spanish expulsion. Many rabbis have further questioned who was authorized to promulgate such a ban, and noted that similar bans were not imposed on England and France after their expulsions (*Seridei Esh* 2:6).

Nonetheless, given this oral tradition, Rabbi Eliezer Waldenburg advised against settling in Spain (*Tzitz Eliezer* 5:17). Rabbi Abraham Isaac Kook ruled similarly, although he added that any prohibition could not be stricter than the ban regarding Egypt, which allowed for temporary residency (*Iggerot HaRaaya* 2:632). He himself believed that returning to Egypt was forbidden only to individuals, not to communities (*Mishpat Kohen* 145). Many asserted that any such ban on living in Spain would have ceased with the historical Spanish monarchy in 1873, and they therefore supported the 1968 construction of a Madrid synagogue following the formal repeal of the expulsion.

Agreeing with the majority of scholars that no ban existed, Rabbi Meshulam Roth argued that a similar prohibition could not be imposed on post-Holocaust Germany (*Kol Mevasser* 1:13). First, no authority possessed the power to impose one, and more fundamentally, such a ban was unfeasible for those who needed to dwell or visit there. Indeed, history has shown that for pragmatic reasons, Jews will return to lands in which they were previously persecuted.

Chapter 132

Hallel and the State of Israel

Should one recite Hallel on Yom HaAtzma'ut and Yom Yerushalayim?

Since 1948, religious Zionists have debated how to celebrate our national sovereignty. Among rabbis and laypeople alike, there remains a strong sense that beyond outdoor hikes and barbecues, we must express our joy and gratefulness religiously. This sentiment only grew stronger after the grand victory of the Six-Day War, when new questions arose regarding the celebration of Jerusalem's reunification. The Talmud buttresses this intuition by noting that King Hezekiah was not anointed as the Messiah because he did not properly express his gratitude for the miracles God performed for him (Sanhedrin 94a).

One might have expected these debates to have been settled in 1949, when Israel celebrated its first Independence Day. Yet as Rabbi Shmuel Katz has documented, a combination of factors, including late planning by the Israeli government and the influence of non-Zionist religious scholars, prevented the Chief Rabbinate from issuing clear-cut instructions to Zionist synagogues. Most significantly, rabbis passionately debated whether to create a ritual for this occasion. While somewhat frustrating, one should remember, as pointed out by Nahmanides (Megilla 2a), that it took several years before the sages determined how to celebrate the Purim miracle. We should also note that it takes many societies years or even decades to determine the proper way to establish national commemorations.

As Prof. Nahum Rakover has shown, a few scholars objected that the creation of a national holiday would violate the biblical prohibition (Deut. 4:2) of adding mitzvot to the Torah (*bal tosif*). Most authorities dismissed this concern, arguing that one violates that proscription only by declaring such celebrations mandatory and originating in the Torah (MB 31:5). Furthermore, Jewish communities historically established "Purim Katan" or "Purim Sheni" festivals to commemorate local miracles, and these enactments remained binding for generations (Maharam Alshakar 49). While a few scholars protested these initiatives (*Pri Ḥadash* OḤ 496), most decisors – including Rabbis Moshe Sofer (*Ḥatam Sofer* OḤ 1:191) and Avraham Danziger (*Ḥayei Adam* 2:155, para. 41) – argued that many communities, including their own, had established such days, marking them with festive meals and candle lighting, and by giving charity and reciting Psalms.

While the vast majority of religious Zionist authorities supported the establishment of a national holiday, they disagreed about how to celebrate it. One central question related to the recital of Hallel, the set of psalms traditionally chanted on most festivals. Hallel was instituted to express either holiday joy, as on Sukkot, or thanksgiving for salvation from danger, as with Ḥanukka (Rashi, Pesaḥim 117a). The commentators debated what level of salvation mandates Hallel. Some argued that the miracle had to be blatant and undisputed (*nes nigleh*), as with the parting of the Red Sea (*Ḥiddushei Maharatz Chajes* Shabbat 21b), while others contended that it had to occur to the entire Jewish people (*Tosafot* Sukka 44b). Rabbi Menaḥem HaMeiri further ruled that even in such circumstances, Hallel should not be recited with a blessing (*Beit HaBeḥira* Pesaḥim 117a). Beyond these legalistic considerations, Rabbis Ovadia Hedaya (*Yaskil Avdi* OḤ 6:10), Ovadia Yosef (*Yabia Omer* OḤ 6:41), and Moshe Tzvi Neria noted that Israel's precarious security and spiritual shortcomings must temper our celebrations. As such, these authorities contended that Hallel was not mandated, and therefore one could not recite it with its traditional opening and closing benedictions. A similar position was held by Rabbi Joseph B. Soloveitchik, who opposed liturgical innovation in general, even if he reluctantly allowed Hallel to be recited without a blessing at the end of services on Israel Independence Day (*Nefesh HaRav*, p. 97). Based on these arguments, and under pressure from non-Zionist rabbinic leaders, in 1949 the Israeli Chief Rabbinate – led by Rabbis Isaac Herzog and Ben-Zion Uziel – declared that Hallel should be recited without a blessing.

Other scholars – including Rabbis Meshulam Roth (*Kol Mevasser* 1:21), Yehuda Gershuni, and Ḥayim David HaLevi (*Dat U'Medina*, p. 82) – forcefully argued for the full-fledged recital of Hallel. They contended that Hallel may be recited even over non-blatant, naturalistic miracles, and that in any case, Israel's victory over the powerful surrounding Arab armies was a bona fide miracle worthy of thanksgiving. Moreover, this miracle clearly affected the entire Jewish people, since the State of Israel served as a place of refuge after the Holocaust as well as a source of deep Jewish pride throughout the world. This position was later adopted by the Chief Rabbinate under the leadership of Rabbi Shlomo Goren, and is followed today in most religious Zionist congregations and yeshivas.

Rabbis Uziel, Roth, and Goren added that one may recite the *sheheḥeyanu* blessing traditionally said on other holidays, although this view has garnered only limited support. Rabbi Goren further contended that just as we say Hallel on the first night of Passover, we should celebrate our contemporary redemption by reciting Hallel at night, but this opinion was widely rejected.

After the amazing victory in the Six-Day War, Chief Rabbis Isser Unterman and Yitzḥak Nissim – supported by Rabbis Shaul Yisraeli and Shlomo Zevin – ruled that one should recite Hallel with a blessing on Jerusalem Day. Based on considerations similar to those of Independence Day, other scholars objected, and different communities continue to follow divergent practices in celebrating this momentous occasion.

Chapter 133

Mourning on Tisha B'Av

Why continue commemorating the Destruction if Jewish sovereignty has been restored to Jerusalem?

The ninth of Av (Tisha B'Av) fast day concludes a three-week mourning period that begins with a fast on 17 Tammuz. Among other tragedies, the primary events attributed to these dates relate to the loss of political sovereignty and the destruction of the Temples (Taanit 4:6). The mourning rites include refraining from festive celebrations, haircuts and shaving, and consuming meat.

With the restoration of political autonomy in 1948, and particularly after the reunification of Jerusalem in 1967, some began to question whether such mourning remained appropriate. Based on Zechariah's prophecy (8:19), the sages believed that when peace returned to the Land of Israel, the minor fast days – including 17 Tammuz, 10 Tevet, and the Fast of Gedaliah – would become holidays (Rosh HaShana 18b). Some commentators defined "peace" in this context as the cessation of gentile rule over the Jewish people (Rashi). Others asserted that these days will become festivals only with the rebuilding of the Temple (Ritva). The Talmud further asserted that under non-violent gentile rule, these fast days would be optional, even as Tisha B'Av would remain obligatory because of the gravity of the day's tragedies.

Following the reunification of Jerusalem, Israel's Masorti (Conservative) movement indeed declared these fasts optional, while a group of Orthodox academics shared a *leḥayim* together at the Western

Wall on 17 Tammuz! The Orthodox rabbinate, however, has universally affirmed the continuation of these fasts (*Maḥatzit HaShekel* 550:1), contending that centuries of observance have made them binding until the rebuilding of the Temple (*Teshuvot HaGeonim Shaarei Teshuva* 77). Nonetheless, recent decades have seen greater dispensations for pregnant and nursing women and for those suffering even from minor illness.

As Dr. Yael Levine has documented, some questioned whether the new political reality mandated a change in the recitation of *Naḥem* ("Comfort Us"), the Tisha B'Av insertion in the *Amida*, which speaks of our mourning over the destruction of Jerusalem (*Tchumin* 21). Mentioned in the Jerusalem Talmud (Berakhot 4:3), this passage has evolved over the centuries, including the substitution of its original opening word, *Raḥem* ("Have Mercy"). Today, Ashkenazim recite it in the afternoon *Amida* on Tisha B'Av, while many Sephardim insert it in the evening and morning prayers as well.

The prayer describes Jerusalem as a "city in sorrow, laid waste, scorned and desolate," conquered and destroyed by foreign armies and idolaters. In August 1967, Rabbi Shlomo Goren, then chief rabbi of the Israel Defense Forces, emended the IDF prayer book to reflect the new reality. Basing himself on historical textual variants, he removed the depictions of a Jerusalem "scorned and desolate… sitting in mourning like a barren, childless woman."

The non-Orthodox movements adopted the more comprehensive changes suggested by Prof. Ephraim Urbach, whose text pleads for compassion for a Jerusalem that is being "rebuilt upon its ruins, restored upon its ravages, and resettled upon its desolation." Prof. Urbach also included a reference to those who died in the Holocaust and in Israel's wars, as did an alternate version penned by Rabbi Abraham Rosenfeld, who further included a plea for vengeance and the ingathering of Jews back to Zion. Netanya's Chief Rabbi David Shloush changed the bulk of the text to refer exclusively to the lack of religious worship on the Temple Mount (*Ḥemda Genuza* 22).

For various reasons, most Orthodox scholars rejected these changes. While refusing to condemn those who recited alternative texts, Rabbis Tzvi Yehuda Kook and Shaul Yisraeli deemed such modifications inappropriate as long as the Temple remained destroyed. Similar sentiments were expressed by Chief Rabbis Isser Unterman and Ovadia Yosef (*Yeḥaveh Daat* 1:43), who further noted the continued non-Jewish worship on the Temple Mount and Israel's general spiritual deficiency. Rabbi Joseph B. Soloveitchik added his general opposition to ritual emendations, particularly with regard to prayers (*Masora* 7). Indicative of this trend, Soncino Press removed Rabbi Rosenfeld's alternative version after purchasing the rights to his Tisha B'Av prayer book, used in many Diaspora synagogues.

Proponents of the emendations retorted that this prayer's text was always fluid and allowed for alterations, especially if the crucial concluding blessing remained intact. They also contended that failure to change the text made our prayers dishonest, while further insinuating that the opposition stemmed from polemical concerns about appearing like Reform innovators.

The most modest proposal was offered by Tel Aviv Chief Rabbi Ḥayim David HaLevi (*Aseh Lekha Rav* 2:36), who suggested merely emending the depiction of Jerusalem to past tense (e.g., the city "*was* in sorrow"). While seconded by Rabbi She'ar Yashuv HaKohen of Haifa, this change has not received popular acceptance.

Chapter 134

Sacrifices in a Future Temple

May we pray for the rebuilding of the Temple without the restoration of animal sacrifices?

When I was an active member of Harvard Hillel, I always found it interesting to compare the various prayer books of the groups that prayed there. Flipping through those siddurim, one could see how contemporary Jewish denominations sharply disagree over the legacy of animal sacrifices and their potential abrogation in the Messianic era.

Already in the nineteenth century, Reform siddurim excised all references to the Temple and sacrifices, deeming them primitive and uncouth in their progressive temples. Recent Conservative siddurim have also omitted prayers to restore sacrifices, but allude to these offerings (in the past tense) within prayers for the rebuilding of the Temple. Orthodox Jews, on the other hand, continue to pray in numerous contexts for the complete restoration of the Temple service, especially in the festival *Amida*.

This issue relates to a larger question regarding the abrogation of biblical mitzvot in the Messianic era. In his Thirteen Principles of Faith, Maimonides interprets the Torah's prohibition of adding or subtracting commandments (Deut. 4:2) to mean that even a prophet may not do so. In the Messianic era, therefore, Jews will reinstate all dormant mitzvot, including Temple sacrifices (MT *Hilkhot Melakhim* 11:1–3). Maimonides seemingly bases himself on a rabbinic assertion that prophets cannot institute new commandments (*Sifra Beḥukkotai* 8:7).

Nonetheless, as Prof. Marc Shapiro has shown, a few scholars challenged this dogma. Maimonides' most important detractor was the esteemed medieval philosopher Rabbi Yosef Albo (Spain, d. 1444). Albo asserted that the Bible prohibits tampering only with the details of the commandments, lest these alterations stem from foreign influences (*Sefer HaIkkarim* 3:14). More fundamentally, he contended that God Almighty always retains the power to change the mitzvot, and that a bona fide prophet in the Messianic era might one day receive such a directive (3:19). Rabbi Albo further suggested that this fluidity is particularly reasonable with regard to prohibitions, such as the proscription of consuming certain animal fats, whose historical rationales have expired (3:16). This notion, shared by Rabbi Yaakov Emden, echoes earlier rabbinic texts that speak of the nullification of the commandments in the Messianic era (Nidda 61b, *Midrash Tehillim* 146).

Interestingly, in the *Guide for the Perplexed,* Maimonides states that God permitted animal sacrifices only because the Israelites could not easily abandon the idolatrous culture of Egypt (3:32). Rather than banning these offerings, God therefore regulated them, ordaining that they be directed exclusively toward Him and performed under specific circumstances. Maimonides implies that the Jewish people will ultimately be weaned from sacrifices and adopt a different form of worship.

This position seems to contradict the above-cited Maimonidean vision of an unchanged halakha in the Messianic era, and scholars have spilled much ink trying to resolve this tension. In any case, this passage in the *Guide* was severely criticized by the prominent legalist and exegete Nahmanides (thirteenth century, Spain), who contended that animal sacrifices contain intrinsic value (and mystical significance), as seen from the fact that Abel, Noah, and Abraham all offered sacrifices long before the Israelites descended to Egypt (Lev. 1:9).

Zionism renewed interest in this topic, even as it remained entirely theoretical. Though most Orthodox rabbis continue to believe in the restoration of sacrifices in a rebuilt Temple, two prominent religious Zionists – Rabbis Abraham Isaac Kook and Ḥayim David HaLevi – both asserted that at some point in the Messianic era, Jews will offer only grain sacrifices, not animals. This view resonates with a rabbinic dictum that, with the exception of the Thanksgiving offering, sacrifices will be nullified in the time of the Messiah (Leviticus Rabba 9:7). This passage, however, has been differently interpreted by others.

One less renowned yet fascinating Orthodox American rabbi, Rabbi Ḥayim Hirschensohn (d. 1935), went further, contending that modern religious Jews will not be able to adapt to a sacrificial culture and that therefore the future Temple will not restore sacrifices (*Malki BaKodesh* 1:1). Interestingly, Rabbi Kook himself ostracized Rabbi Hirschensohn, claiming that he was overly influenced by Western thought, and that it was preferable to believe the complete sacrificial order would be reinstated (*Iggerot HaRaaya* 4:994). In an essay promoting vegetarianism, Rabbi Kook challenged modern critics of sacrifices for hypocritically failing to abstain from slaughtering animals for their mundane dietary needs.

The intricate array of factors makes this a fascinating topic in Judaism's vision for the future of religious worship.

The fonts used in this book are from the Arno family